John F Olgok

The IDG Books Advantage

We at IDG Books Worldwide created *Danny Goodman's JavaScript Handbook* to meet your growing need for quick access to the most complete and accurate computer information available. Our books work the way you do: They focus on accomplishing specific tasks — not learning random functions. Our books are not long-winded manuals or dry reference tomes. In each book, expert authors tell you exactly what you can do with your computer and how to do it. Easy-to-follow, step-by-step sections; comprehensive coverage; and convenient access in language and design — it's all here.

The authors of IDG books are uniquely qualified to give you expert advice as well as to provide insightful tips and techniques not found anywhere else. Our authors maintain close contact with end users through feedback from articles, training sessions, e-mail exchanges, user group participation, and consulting work. Because our authors know the realities of daily computer use and are directly tied to the reader, our books have a strategic advantage.

Our authors have the experience to approach a topic in the most efficient manner, and we know that you, the reader, will benefit from a "one-on-one" relationship with the author. Our research shows that readers make computer book purchases because they want expert advice. Because readers want to benefit from the author's experience, the author's voice is always present in an IDG book.

In addition, the author is free to include or recommend useful software in an IDG book. The software that accompanies each book is not intended to be casual filler but is linked to the content, theme, or procedures of the book. We know that you will benefit from the included software.

You will find what you need in this book whether you read it from cover to cover, section by section, or simply one topic at a time. As a computer user, you deserve a comprehensive resource of answers. We at IDG Books Worldwide are proud to deliver that resource with *Danny Goodman's JavaScript Handbook*.

Brenda McLaughlin
Senior Vice President and Group Publisher
Internet: YouTellUs@idgbooks.com

D1400667

John Olgak

Danny Goodman's
JavaScript® Handbook

Danny Goodman's JavaScript® Handbook

Danny Goodman

IDG Books Worldwide, Inc.
Foster City, CA • Chicago, IL • Indianapolis, IN • Braintree, MA • Southlake, TX

Danny Goodman's JavaScript® Handbook

Published by
IDG Books Worldwide, Inc.
An International Data Group Company
919 E. Hillsdale Blvd.
Suite 400
Foster City, CA 94404

Text, art, and software compilations copyright © 1996 by IDG Books Worldwide, Inc. All rights reserved. No part of this book, including interior design, cover design, and icons, may be reproduced or transmitted in any form, by any means (electronic, photocopying, recording, or otherwise) without the prior written permission of the publisher.

Library of Congress Catalog Card No.: 96-75747

ISBN: 0-7645-3003-8

Printed in the United States of America

10 9 8 7 6 5 4 3 2 1

1E/SS/QU/ZW/IN

Distributed in the United States by IDG Books Worldwide, Inc.

Distributed by Macmillan Canada for Canada; by Computer and Technical Books for the Caribbean Basin; by Contemporanea de Ediciones for Venezuela; by Distribuidora Cuspide for Argentina; by CITEC for Brazil; by Ediciones ZETA S.C.R. Ltda. for Peru; by Editorial Limusa SA for Mexico; by Transworld Publishers Limited in the United Kingdom and Europe; by Al-Maiman Publishers & Distributors for Saudi Arabia; by Simron Pty. Ltd. for South Africa; by IDG Communications (HK) Ltd. for Hong Kong; by Toppan Company Ltd. for Japan; by Addison Wesley Publishing Company for Korea; by Longman Singapore Publishers Ltd. for Singapore, Malaysia, Thailand, and Indonesia; by Unalis Corporation for Taiwan; by WS Computer Publishing Company, Inc. for the Philippines; by WoodsLane Pty. Ltd. for Australia; by WoodsLane Enterprises Ltd. for New Zealand.

For information on IDG Books Worldwide's books in the U.S., please call our Consumer Customer Service department at 800-762-2974. For reseller information, including discounts and premium sales, please call our Reseller Customer Service department at 800-434-3422.

For information on where to purchase IDG Books Worldwide's books outside the U.S., contact IDG Books Worldwide at 415-655-3021 or fax 415-655-3295.

For information on translations, contact Marc Jeffrey Mikulich, Director, Foreign & Subsidiary Rights, at IDG Books Worldwide, 415-655-3018 or fax 415-655-3295.

For sales inquiries and special prices for bulk quantities, write to the address above or call IDG Books Worldwide at 415-655-3200.

For information on using IDG Books Worldwide's books in the classroom, or ordering examination copies, contact the Education Office at 800-434-2086 or fax 817- 251-8174.

For authorization to photocopy items for corporate, personal, or educational use, please contact Copyright Clearance Center, 222 Rosewood Drive, Danvers, MA 01923, or fax 508-750-4470.

Limit of Liability/Disclaimer of Warranty: Author and Publisher have used their best efforts in preparing this book. IDG Books Worldwide, Inc., and Author make no representation or warranties with respect to the accuracy or completeness of the contents of this book and specifically disclaim any implied warranties of merchantability or fitness for any particular purpose and shall in no event be liable for any loss of profit or any other commercial damage, including but not limited to special, incidental, consequential, or other damages.

Trademarks: All brand names and product names used in this book are trademarks, registered trademarks, or trade names of their respective holders. IDG Books Worldwide is not associated with any product or vendor mentioned in this book.

 is a trademark under exclusive license to IDG Books Worldwide, Inc., from International Data Group, Inc.

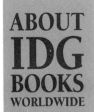

ABOUT IDG BOOKS WORLDWIDE

Welcome to the world of IDG Books Worldwide.

IDG Books Worldwide, Inc., is a subsidiary of International Data Group, the world's largest publisher of computer-related information and the leading global provider of information services on information technology. IDG was founded more than 25 years ago and now employs more than 7,700 people worldwide. IDG publishes more than 250 computer publications in 67 countries (see listing below). More than 70 million people read one or more IDG publications each month.

Launched in 1990, IDG Books Worldwide is today the #1 publisher of best-selling computer books in the United States. We are proud to have received 8 awards from the Computer Press Association in recognition of editorial excellence and three from Computer Currents' First Annual Readers' Choice Awards, and our best-selling ...For Dummies® series has more than 19 million copies in print with translations in 28 languages. IDG Books Worldwide, through a joint venture with IDG's Hi-Tech Beijing, became the first U.S. publisher to publish a computer book in the People's Republic of China. In record time, IDG Books Worldwide has become the first choice for millions of readers around the world who want to learn how to better manage their businesses.

Our mission is simple: Every one of our books is designed to bring extra value and skill-building instructions to the reader. Our books are written by experts who understand and care about our readers. The knowledge base of our editorial staff comes from years of experience in publishing, education, and journalism — experience which we use to produce books for the '90s. In short, we care about books, so we attract the best people. We devote special attention to details such as audience, interior design, use of icons, and illustrations. And because we use an efficient process of authoring, editing, and desktop publishing our books electronically, we can spend more time ensuring superior content and spend less time on the technicalities of making books.

You can count on our commitment to deliver high-quality books at competitive prices on topics you want to read about. At IDG Books Worldwide, we continue in the IDG tradition of delivering quality for more than 25 years. You'll find no better book on a subject than one from IDG Books Worldwide.

John J. Kilcullen

John Kilcullen
President and CEO
IDG Books Worldwide, Inc.

WINNER
Eighth Annual
Computer Press
Awards ≥ 1992

WINNER
Ninth Annual
Computer Press
Awards ≥ 1993

IDG BOOKS WORLDWIDE

IDG Books Worldwide, Inc., is a subsidiary of International Data Group, the world's largest publisher of computer-related information and the leading global provider of information services on information technology. International Data Group publishes over 250 computer publications in 67 countries. Seventy million people read one or more International Data Group publications each month. International Data Group's publications include: **ARGENTINA:** Computerworld Argentina, GamePro, Infoworld, PC World Argentina; **AUSTRALIA:** Australian Macworld, Client/Server Journal, Computer Living, Computerworld, Digital News, Network World, PC World, Publishing Essentials, Reseller; **AUSTRIA:** Computerwelt, PC TEST; **BELARUS:** PC World Belarus; **BELGIUM:** Data News; **BRAZIL:** Annuário de Informática, Computerworld Brazil, Connections, Super Game Power, Macworld, PC World Brazil, Publish Brazil, SUPERGAME; **BULGARIA:** Computerworld Bulgaria, Networkworld/Bulgaria, PC & MacWorld Bulgaria; **CANADA:** CIO Canada, ComputerWorld Canada, InfoCanada, Network World Canada, Reseller World; **CHILE:** Computerworld Chile, GamePro, PC World Chile; **COLUMBIA:** Computerworld Colombia, GamePro, PC World Colombia; **COSTA RICA:** PC World Costa Rica/Nicaragua; **THE CZECH AND SLOVAK REPUBLICS:** Computerworld Czechoslovakia, Elektronika Czechoslovakia, PC World Czechoslovakia; **DENMARK:** Communications World, Computerworld Danmark, Macworld Danmark, PC World Danmark, PC World Danmark Supplements, TECH World; **DOMINICAN REPUBLIC:** PC World Republica Dominicana; **ECUADOR:** PC World Ecuador, GamePro; **EGYPT:** Computerworld Middle East, PC World Middle East; **EL SALVADOR:** PC World Centro America; **FINLAND:** MikroPC, Tietoverkko, Tietoviikko; **FRANCE:** Distributique, Golden, Info PC, Le Guide du Monde Informatique, Le Monde Informatique, Reseaux & Telecoms; **GERMANY:** Computer Business, Computerwoche, Computerwoche Extra, Computerwoche Focus, Electronic Entertainment, GamePro, I/M Information Management, Macwelt, PC Welt; **GREECE:** GamePro, Macworld & Publish; **GUATEMALA:** PC World Centro America; **HONDURAS:** PC World Centro America; **HONG KONG:** Computerworld Hong Kong, PCWorld Hong Kong, Publish in Asia; **HUNGARY:** ABCD CD-ROM, Computerworld Szamitastechnika, PC & Mac World Hungary, PC-X Magazine; **INDIA:** Computerworld India, PC World India, Publish in Asia; **INDONESIA:** InfoKomputer PC World, Komputek Computerworld, Publish in Asia; **IRELAND:** ComputerScope, PC Live!; **ISRAEL:** PC World 32 BIT, People & Computers; **ITALY:** Computerworld Italia, Computerworld Italia Special Editions, Lotus Italia, Macworld Italia, Networking Italia, PC Shopping, PC World Italia, PC World/Walt Disney; **JAPAN:** Macworld Japan, Nikkei Personal Computing, SunWorld Japan, Windows World Japan; **KENYA:** East African Computer News; **KOREA:** Hi-Tech Information/Computerworld, Macworld Korea, PC World Korea; **MACEDONIA:** PC World Macedonia; **MALAYSIA:** Computerworld Malaysia, PC World Malaysia, Publish in Asia; **MEXICO:** Computerworld Mexico, GamePro, Macworld, PC World Mexico; **MYANMAR:** PC World Myanmar; **NETHERLANDS:** Computable, Computer! Totaal, LAN Magazine, Macworld, Net Magazine; **NEW ZEALAND:** Computer Buyer, Computerworld New Zealand, MTB, Network World, PC World New Zealand; **NICARAGUA:** PC World Costa Rica/Nicaragua; **NIGERIA:** PC World Africa; **NORWAY:** Computerworld Norge, Computerworld Privat, CW Rapport Klient/Tjener, CW Rapport Nettverk & Telecom, CW Rapport Offentlig Sektor, IDG's KURSGUIDE, Macworld Norge, Multimedia World, PC World Ekspress, PC World Nettverk, PC World Norge, PC World's Produktguide, Windows Spesial; **PAKISTAN:** Computerworld Pakistan, PC World Pakistan; **PANAMA:** GamePro, PC World Panama; **PARAGUAY:** PC World Paraguay; **P. R. OF CHINA:** China Computerworld, China Infoworld, Computer & Communication, Electronic Product World, Electronics Today, Game Camp, PC World China, Popular Computer Week, Software World, Telecom Product World; **PERU:** Computerworld Peru, GamePro, PC World Profesional Peru, PC World Peru; **POLAND:** Computerworld Poland, Computerworld Special Report, Macworld, Networld, PC World Komputer; **PHILIPPINES:** Computerworld Philippines, PC Digest, Publish in Asia; **PORTUGAL:** Cerebro/PC World, Correio Informático/Computerworld, Mac•In/PC•In Portugal; **PUERTO RICO:** PC World Puerto Rico; **ROMANIA:** Computerworld Romania, PC World Romania, Telecom Romania; **RUSSIA:** Computerworld Rossiya, Network World Russia, PC World Russia; **SINGAPORE:** Computerworld Singapore, PC World Singapore, Publish in Asia; **SLOVENIA:** MONITOR; **SOUTH AFRICA:** Computing S.A., Network World S.A., Software World; **SPAIN:** Computerworld España, COMUNICACIONES WORLD, Dealer World, Macworld España, PC World España; **SWEDEN:** CAP&Design, Computer Sweden, Corporate Computing, MacWorld, Maxi Data, MikroDatorn, Nätverk & Kommunikation, PC/Aktiv, PC World, Windows World; **SWITZERLAND:** Computerworld Schweiz, Macworld Schweiz, PCtip; **TAIWAN:** Computerworld Taiwan, Macworld Taiwan, PC World Taiwan, Publish Taiwan, Windows World; **THAILAND:** Thai Computerworld, Publish in Asia; **TURKEY:** Computerworld Monitör, MACWORLD Turkiye, PC WORLD Turkiye; **UKRAINE:** Computerworld Kiev, Computers & Software Magazine, PC World Ukraine; **UNITED KINGDOM:** Acorn User, Amiga Action, Amiga Computing, Amiga, Appletalk, CD Powerplay, CD-ROM Now, Computing, Connexion, GamePro, Lotus Magazine, Macaction, Macworld, Open Computing, Parents and Computers, PC Home, PC Works, The WEB; **UNITED STATES:** Cable in the Classroom, CD Review, CIO Magazine, Computerworld, Computerworld Client/Server Journal, Digital Video Magazine, DOS World, Electronic, InfoWorld, I-Way, Macworld, Maximize, MULTIMEDIA WORLD, Network World, PC World, PUBLISH, SWATPro Magazine, Video Event, WebMaster; **URUGUAY:** PC World Uruguay; **VENEZUELA:** Computerworld Venezuela, GamePro, PC World Venezuela; and **VIETNAM:** PC World Vietnam   10/17/95a

Credits

Senior Vice President & Group Publisher
Brenda McLaughlin

Software Acquisitions Editor
Tracy Lehman Cramer

Managing Editor
Andy Cummings

Editorial Assistant
Timothy J. Borek

Production Director
Beth Jenkins

Production Assistant
Jacalyn L. Pennywell

**Supervisor of
Project Coordination**
Cindy L. Phipps

Supervisor of Page Layout
Kathie S. Schnorr

Supervisor of Graphics and Design
Shelley Lea

Reprint Coordination
Tony Augsburger
Todd Klemme
Theresa Sánchez-Baker

Blueline Coordinator
Patricia R. Reynolds

Media/Archive Coordination
Leslie Popplewell
Melissa Stauffer
Jason Marcuson

**Acquisitions Editor &
Development Editor**
Michael Roney

Editor
Kerrie Klein

Copy Editor
Jayne Jacobsen

Technical Reviewer
Bill Dortch

Associate Project Coordinator
Debbie Sharpe

Project Coordination Assistant
Regina Snyder

Graphics Coordination
Gina Scott
Angela F. Hunckler

Production Page Layout
E. Shawn Aylesworth
Brett Black
Anna Rohrer
Michael Sullivan
Todd Klemme

Proofreaders
Joel Draper
Jenny Kaufield
Dwight Ramsey
Carl Saff
Robert Springer

Indexer
Sharon Hilgenberg

About the Author

Danny Goodman is the author of numerous critically acclaimed and best-selling books, including *Danny Goodman's AppleScript Handbook, Danny Goodman's Windows 95 Handbook, Living At Light Speed*, and *The Complete HyperCard Handbook*, one of the all-time, best-selling Macintosh titles, with nearly one-half million copies in print. He is renowned as an authority and expert teacher of scripting and non-technical application building and has been described as a voice that has compassion for the reader's sometimes difficult path, with a pedagogy that earns praise from teachers around the world. He is also a respected observer of technology's impact on society: his *Living at Light Speed* garnered rave reviews from the *New York Times,* the *New Yorker,* the *Chicago Tribune, PC Magazine, Los Angeles Magazine*, and other publications.

(The publisher would like to give special thanks to Patrick J. McGovern, without whom this book would not have been possible.)

Contents

Part II: The JavaScript Language 37

Chapter 4: JavaScript and Your HTML Documents 39

Chapter 5: A Crash Course in Programming Fundamentals 49

Chapter 6: A Crash Course in Object Orientation 67

$\mathcal{I}$ntroduction

The release of any new programming environment that is accessible to everyday folks is a cause for celebration. Through my work in the Macintosh community over the years — teaching hundreds of thousands of non-programmers to program with HyperCard and AppleScript — I have seen people uncover creative juices they never knew they had. Ideas about what they'd like to have happen on the screen had been flying around their minds for years. All those ideas needed was a medium. For vast numbers of people, user programming and scripting is that medium.

JavaScript is a liberating technology. It lifts many severe restraints imposed by HTML without requiring users to have a degree in computer science. Millions of ideas in HTML authors' minds now have a medium in which they can be expressed. The original framers of the language at Netscape Communications Corporation (who worked with input from Sun Microsystems) have placed a powerful tool into the hands of the world's Web page builders. Soon these Web authors will take over the language, directing its future enhancements by citing the features most often needed for their implementation. The language could likely evolve into an environment never envisioned by its founders. That's a good sign because it means that users are stretching the language's boundaries. This is an exciting time to get started in JavaScript and help mold its future by pushing and pulling it in the directions you need.

Whenever I approach the task of writing a book such as this one, I think about what I wanted while I was learning the technology and using it on a daily basis. My book must not only provide an entry path into the language for newcomers, but must also serve as a meaningful reference once you learn the basics and are working on JavaScript-enabled pages. As I wrote the later chapters of this book, I found myself going back to earlier chapters to look up language syntax details and examples. Like the guy on television who is not only the president of his company but a client, I am not only the author of this book but a daily user as well.

Part I of the book begins with a chapter that shows how JavaScript compares to Java and discusses its role within the rest of the World Wide Web. Chapter 2 offers suggestions on the best way to learn JavaScript, depending on your programming background — or lack of it. Chapter 3 provides our first foray into JavaScript. Here's where you get to write your first practical script.

Part II, the largest section of the book, provides in-depth coverage of the language. In case you're not a code jockey, separate chapters offer crash courses on programming fundamentals and object-oriented programming. Chapters 7 through 12 divide the JavaScript syntax up into logical sections. Descriptions of JavaScript objects in Chapters 7 and 8 — two lengthy chapters — are designed to facilitate learning now and to serve as reference material later. The essential concepts and terminology for getting started with the language are clearly marked, so you can focus only on those sections your first time through the chapters. Discussions about more advanced subjects are identified as such, and details that even advanced users will appreciate are presented clearly and with plenty of examples. Chapters 7 through 9 also feature "phone-book style" footers on key pages to help you locate information on JavaScript terminology with ease.

The accompanying CD-ROM contains complete HTML documents that serve as examples of most of the JavaScript vocabulary words in Part II. You can run them with your JavaScript-enabled browser. I could have provided you with humorous little fragments out of context, but I think it's important to see full-fledged HTML documents (simple though they may be) employing these concepts.

In Part III, I get down to the business of applying JavaScript. Chapter 13 discusses methods of implementing JavaScript into your site, whereas Chapter 14 presents lots of debugging tips. Examples of ways you can use JavaScript for data entry validation occupy Chapter 15. Lengthy annotated examples surrounding tables, frames, and multiple windows fill Chapter 16.

The final four chapters are devoted to full-fledged JavaScript-enhanced applications. All four examples also run on my Web site (http://www.dannyg.com), so you can use them from the CD-ROM or see how well they work on-line from a server. Each application demonstrates important concepts that you will likely want to include in your applications. You'll read about each segment of JavaScript code and learn about the implementation decisions I made in designing these pages — the same kinds of decisions you will have to make for your site.

The script listings in this book are presented in a monospace font to set them apart from the rest of the text. Due to restrictions in page width, these lines of script may, from time to time, break unnaturally. In such cases, the remainder of the script appears in the following line, flush with the left margin of the listing's box. If you encounter this problem in one of the numbered script listings, you can access the corresponding listing on the CD-ROM to see how it should look when you type it.

I developed these applications and the book using Netscape Navigator 2.0, initially in beta form and eventually in the final release. A number of bugs in the JavaScript implementation exist in Navigator 2.0. Some bugs afflict only one or two platform versions of the browser, whereas others impact all versions. If you are using Navigator 2.0 in conjunction with this book, download the latest release notes from the Netscape Web site. It explains the reported bugs for your browser platform. Not every 2.0 bug is listed in this book — just the most lethal ones.

By the time this book is available, I anticipate that Netscape will have released beta versions of the next generation of browser. The Navigator 2.0 bugs highlighted throughout this book may be gone in this beta. If so, all the better.

Before closing, I would like to acknowledge the contributions of many folks who helped make this book possible: Len Feldman, Frank Hecker, and the ever-patient, all-knowing Brendan Eich (Netscape); Brenda McLaughlin, Michael Roney, and David Ushijima (IDG Books); copy editor Jayne Jacobson; tech reviewer and "cookie man" Bill Dortch; fellow scripters and newsgroup kibbitzers Lourdes Yero, Paul Colton, and Gordon McComb (to name but a few), who sent my JavaScripting imagination off in various directions; and the first-class designers (Lynne Stiles, Maria Giudice, and Ben Seibel) at YO in San Francisco (info@yodesign.com) who brought the art spots of my JavaScript Web site pages to life.

Now it's time to get down to the fun of learning JavaScript. Enjoy!

Danny Goodman

Part One

GETTING STARTED WITH

JAVASCRIPT

*C*hapter One

JavaScript's Role in the World Wide Web

For the many individuals responsible today for content on the World Wide Web, it wasn't that long ago that terms such as *HTML* (Hypertext Markup Language) and *URL* (Universal Resource Locator) would have seemed like words from a foreign language. Growth in activity on the Web — producing content and surfing it — has been nothing short of phenomenal. Some might even call the hyperactivity "scary." The number of Web sites I could quote here would be woefully outdated before these words ever reached a printing press.

Developers of software technologies on the Web are now in a desperate race to catch up with the enthusiasm that people have for the Internet — and for the World Wide Web in particular. Web site authors are constantly on the lookout for tools that will make their sites engaging (if not "cool") with the least amount of effort. This is particularly true when the task is in the hands of people more comfortable with writing, graphic design, and page layout than with hard-core programming. Not every Webmaster has legions of experienced programmers on hand to whip up some special custom enhancement for the site. Nor does every Web author have control over the Web server that physically houses the collection of HTML and graphics files.

Competition on the Web

Web page publishers revel in logging as many visits to their sites as possible. Regardless of the questionable accuracy of Web page "hit" counts, a site consistently logging 10,000 dubious hits per week is far more popular than one with 1,000 dubious hits per week. Even if the precise number is unknown, relative popularity is a valuable measure.

Encouraging people to visit a site frequently is the Holy Grail of Web publishing. Competition for viewers is enormous. Not only is the Web like a 500,000-channel television (complete with the equivalent of *TV Guides,* requiring a proactive search to find something interesting to browse — no easy-chair, remote-control channel flipping here), but the Web competes for viewers' attention with all kinds of computer-generated information. That includes anything that appears on-screen as interactive multimedia.

Users of entertainment programs, multimedia encyclopedias, and other colorful, engaging, and mouse-finger-numbing actions are accustomed to high-quality presentations. Frequently, these programs have first-rate graphics, animation, live-action video, and synchronized sounds. In contrast, the lowest-common-denominator Web page has little in the way of razzle-dazzle. Even the layout of pictures and text is highly constrained compared to the kinds of desktop publishing documents we see all the time. Regardless of the quality of its content, a vanilla HTML document is flat. At best, interaction is limited to whatever navigation the author offers in the way of hypertext links or filling out forms whose content magically disappears into the Web site's server.

Stretching the Standards

As an outgrowth of SGML (Standard Generalized Markup Language), HTML is generally viewed as nothing more than a document formatting, or *tagging*, language. The tags (inside <> delimiter characters) instruct a viewer program (the *browser*) how to display a chunk of text or an image from a file.

Relegating HTML to the category of tagging language does disservice not only to the effort that goes into fashioning a first-rate Web page, but also to the way users interact with the pages. To my way of thinking, any collection of commands and other syntax that directs the way users interact with digital information is *programming*. Using HTML, a Web page author controls the user experience with the content, just as the engineers who crafted Excel programmed the way users interact with spreadsheet content and functions.

Unfortunately, the HTML standards agreed to by industry groups leave much to be desired in the way HTML programmers can customize the level of interactivity between document and user. Software companies that develop browsers feel the urgency to move the facilities of HTML forward to meet the demands of Web authors who desire more control over the display of various kinds of information. It's a constant game of leapfrog as browser companies race ahead of still-emerging standards. For example, although developers were still debating the details of HTML 3.0, Netscape published a document of its extensions to HTML 3.0. Microsoft also developed its own extensions for its Internet Explorer browser software.

CGI Scripting

One way to extend the interaction between user and content is to have the page communicate with the Web server that houses the Web pages. Popular World Wide Web search sites, such as Yahoo, WebCrawler, and Lycos, let users type search criteria and click on a button or two to specify the way the search engine should treat the query. When you click on the Submit or Search buttons, your browser sends your entries from the form to the server. On the server, a program known as a CGI (Common Gateway Interface) script formats the data you've entered and sends it to a database or other program running on the server. The CGI script then sends the results to your browser, sometimes in the form of a new page or information occupying other fields in the form.

Writing customized CGI scripts typically requires considerable programming skill. It definitely requires the Web page author to be in control of the server, including whatever *back-end* programs, such as databases, are needed to supply results or to message the information coming from the user. Even with the new server-based Web site design tools available, CGI scripting often is not a task that a content-oriented HTML author can do without handing it off to a more experienced programmer.

As interesting and useful as CGI scripting is, it burdens the server with the job of processing queries. A busy server may be processing hundreds of CGI scripts at a time, while the client computers — the personal computers running the browsers — are sitting idle as the browser's logo icon dances its little animation. It's quite a waste of Pentium and PowerPC horsepower. That's why some people regard browsing a basic Web page as little more than using a dumb terminal to access some content.

Of Helpers, Plug-ins, and Applets

Browsers have long (a relative term, because browsers haven't existed that long) relied on helper applications to make up for their internal deficiencies. For example, browsers typically don't know how to deal with audio that comes in from a Web site. Instead, your browser knows that when it encounters a file of an audio type, it must launch a separate helper program (if available on your hard disk) to do the job of making your particular flavor of computer (Windows 3.x, Windows 95, UNIX, MacOS) convert the digitized sound to audio you can hear through speakers.

A current trend in browsers is to bring as much functionality as possible into the browser itself, so that you don't have to run another program to play a movie or audio clip. This integration also helps in making the overall presentation appear cleaner to the user. Instead of having to play in a separate window atop the browser's document window, a movie can appear in the page, perhaps accompanied by label text or a caption.

Plug-ins

Netscape, with its concept of plug-in architecture, is among the leaders in this integration. The technology, which is available in Navigator 2.0, allows other developers to incorporate a variety of capabilities into the browser. One such plug-in is a player for vector-based animations created with SmartSketch Animator (FutureWare Software, Inc., San Diego, CA).

The SmartSketch player plug-in allows a highly efficient animation file to appear in a page as if it were a .gif image. The art can be designed so that a region of the graphic appears highlighted when a user clicks on it — just like a real multimedia program. This action and the temporary handoff to the player is transparent to the user.

Java applets

When the interaction required between user and Web page exceeds the capabilities of HTML, programmers would rather "roll their own" programs to handle the special needs not available in existing plug-ins. To fill this need, Sun Microsystems developed a new programming language (Java) to let serious programmers build small applications (*applets*) that download to the browser (as separate files, like image files), run as the user needs them, and then automatically be discarded (from memory) when the user moves elsewhere in the Web.

The popular scrolling banner was one of the first techniques that used a Java applet to increase the impact of a Web page. Like the horizontal scrolling sign in New York City's Times Square, the banner applet displays rolling text of the author's choice on the Web page. A good application for this device is in a frequently changing Web site, where the banner can be changed to bring the user's attention to new items. That little bit of animation brings an otherwise-static page to life far better than some scattered "new" icon images.

To play a Java applet, a browser company must have licensed the technology from Sun and built it into its browser. Sun's own Java-capable browser is called Hot Java. The next major browser producer to include the technology was Netscape, which incorporated it in its Navigator 2.0 (although not for all operating system platforms). Other browser makers have also adopted Java as an essential part of their products — primarily to allow their customers to take advantage of the Java applets cropping up all around the Net.

A Language for All

The Java language is derived from C and C++, but it is a distinct language. Its main audience is the experienced programmer. That leaves out many Web page authors. I was dismayed at this situation when I first read about the language's specifications. I would have preferred a language that casual programmers and scripters who use authoring tools such as ToolBook, HyperCard, and even Visual Basic could adopt quickly. As these accessible development platforms have shown, non-professional authors can come up with many creative applications, often for very specific tasks that no programmer would have the inclination to work on. Personal needs often drive development in the classroom, office, den, or garage.

A common misconception about JavaScript is that it is a more human-friendly version of Java — putting the power of Java applet development into the hands of mere mortals. Nothing could be further from the truth. Yet there are definitely links between Java and JavaScript. Before we get to that, however, it's important to understand JavaScript's brief heritage.

JavaScript was born at Netscape under the name LiveScript. Developed in parallel with Netscape's LiveWire server software, LiveScript was designed for essentially two purposes with the same syntax. One was as a scripting language that LiveWire server administrators could use to manage LiveWire and connect its pages to other services, such as back-end databases, to act as search engines for users looking up information. Thus the server side of LiveScript would be a LiveWire-specific use of the language.

On the client side — in HTML documents — these scripts could be used to enhance the page in a number of ways. For example, an author could use LiveScript to make sure that the information a user entered into a form would be of the proper type. Instead of forcing the server or database to do the data validation (requiring data exchanges between the client browser and the server), the user's computer handles all the calculation work — putting some of that otherwise wasted horsepower to work. In essence, LiveScript could provide some HTML-level interaction for the user.

The second major goal was to use LiveScript as a way for HTML documents (and their users) to communicate with Java applets. For example, a user might make some preferences selections from checkboxes and pop-up selection lists at the top of a Web page. Scrolling down to the next screenful, the user sees items in the Java applet scrolling banner that are customized to the settings made above. In this case, the LiveScript script sends the text that is to appear in the scrolling banner to the applet. While this is happening, the server doesn't have to worry a bit about it, and the user hasn't had to wait for communication between the browser and the server.

Sun Joins In

In early December 1995, Netscape and Sun jointly announced that the scripting language would thereafter be known as JavaScript. Moreover, Sun Microsystems would become part of the development team to take the language into the future.

Before the announcement, the language was related to Java in many ways. Many of the basic syntax elements of the language were reminiscent of the C and C++ style of Java, but the language designers reduced the vocabulary to a digestible amount. As a stand-alone scripting language (that is, one used to make Web pages more interactive), JavaScript is relatively simple to learn (as programming languages go); as the glue for Java applets in the future, the JavaScript language will allow users to customize solutions around pre-written applets.

Client-Side JavaScript at Work

One hazard of new authoring technology is that some early adopters will do things with it because the technology is there — not because there is a need to fill. It reminds me of the ransom-note syndrome that early Macintosh users experienced because it was so easy to set every character in a different font. Thus, as scripters teach themselves from examples provided by Netscape and in this book, you may see all kinds of JavaScript-enabled HTML documents with functions that are probably better carried out in other venues.

One of the most common applications is an on-screen calculator of some kind. I'm not sure how many mortgage or metric conversion calculators the world needs on the Web, but I do see the value of special-purpose calculators for any number of technical professions and hobbies.

Web page frames — another Netscape innovation — and JavaScript are a potent combination. A JavaScript-enabled document can be viewed in one frame of the browser window while the results of users' actions control what appears in other frames. An application of interest to Web page authors is shown in Figure 1-1. Designed by Bill Dortch of hIdaho Design, the JavaScript-enhanced page of his ColorCenter lets you enter color values for various screen objects (background color, link color, and so on) and preview the results in another frame. This simplifies the method of experimenting so that you can come up with the exact color combination that you want in your Web page attributes.

Small databases of information can be assembled into JavaScript scripts (embedded in an HTML document) to provide a semblance of database access without a database back-end running on the server. This is an example of the serverless CGI scripting that should have a large potential for JavaScript.

We'll have to wait for the next version of JavaScript to take advantage of its powers to communicate with Java applets. But much of what JavaScript will be able to do for you then depends on the functions available in Java applets and what parts of the applets are open to manipulation by a script. The more powerful these applets become over time, the more exciting the opportunities will be to use JavaScript to assemble existing building blocks into valuable, customized solutions.

The child's building block metaphor is a good one for Java applets. On their own, applets have intrinsic functions. But just as wood blocks may be strung together to spell out a word, arranged to build a doll house, or stacked to support a sagging shelf, so will Java applets be glued together to perform customized jobs. JavaScript will supply the glue; you'll supply the imagination to turn the glue and blocks into castles.

Figure 1-1: Bill Dortch's ColorCenter Web page combines frames and JavaScript.

JavaScript: The Right Tool for the Right Job

Knowing how to match an authoring tool to a solution-building task is an important part of being a well-rounded Web page author. A Web page designer who ignores JavaScript is akin to a plumber who bruises his knuckles by using pliers instead of the wrench at the bottom of the toolbox. By the same token, JavaScript won't fulfill every dream.

The more you understand about JavaScript's intentions and limitations, the more likely you will be to turn to it immediately when it is the proper tool. In particular, look to JavaScript for the following kinds of solutions:

- You want your Web page to respond or react directly to user interaction with form elements (input fields, text areas, buttons, radio buttons, checkboxes, selection lists) and hypertext links.

- You want to distribute small collections of database-like information and provide a friendly interface to that data.

- You want data preprocessed on the client before submission to a server.

Should you turn to JavaScript and find that it doesn't have the capabilities you need, speak up! Let the JavaScript development team know what you'd like it to do in the future. JavaScript will certainly evolve and grow as scripters stretch its powers.

*C*hapter Two

If you have little programming experience, or if object-oriented programming is new to you, you may feel that you need to know everything about JavaScript before you can digest your first lesson. This happens when learning a programming language because writing even the simplest program often requires several features or capabilities of the language. So much material appears to depend on other material that it all seems like a fast-spinning merry-go-round. One of the goals of this book is to slow down that merry-go-round enough so that you can hop on. You should find here a gradual pathway to learning every facet of JavaScript that you'll need to implement it successfully in your HTML documents.

Understanding when to call upon JavaScript, as we discussed in the preceding chapter, is a big help in learning the language. Over the years I've found that you learn fastest when you have a specific goal in mind: a problem that begs for a solution. Without such a goal, you end up trying to learn a language in the abstract — a difficult task at best. Throughout this book, I'll describe many scenarios as a way to put concepts into context. In most cases, the scenarios will be solutions to problems that crop up in the design of a Web page or site.

Programming or Scripting?

You may be wondering why there seems to be a distinction between hard-core programming and scripting. To my mind, the distinction is purely artificial, promulgated largely by those programmers who slaved over learning one or more serious programming languages in school. Differences certainly exist between programming and scripting, but doing a good job in either one entails many of the same tasks.

A scripting language implies that the code writer doesn't have to create as much code as a programmer. This is true in most environments, including JavaScript. In typical software production environments, a programmer (or team of programmers) fashions every tiny piece of a program: determining every screen element, managing memory usage, and tackling dozens of other technical aspects of the program. A scripter, according to popular perception, merely writes little snippets of code to produce a working product or solution. The scripting environment or the language itself takes care of much of the dirty work for the scripter. Therefore, although programmers such as the ones at Netscape must write thousands of lines of code to get a browser to display forms and elements in an HTML document, a JavaScripter can make those existing elements come alive by writing a few lines of code.

That's not to say that an HTML document can't contain tons of JavaScript code. It could easily do so if the scripter feels it necessary, and the amount of code doesn't take long to load into the browser. But the amount of script you typically create for a document is minuscule compared to a full-fledged program that does the same task.

If quantity of code is a distinction between programming and scripting, quality should be on par, if not a tad better, in a script than in a program. As you'll see later, there are plenty of opportunities in JavaScript to write elegant (or ugly) code that performs the same calculations or other functions as a C++ program. One advantage that a programmer usually has over a scripter is that the program is compiled into machine language. Users of the program cannot judge the quality of the code except through external measurements, such as performance and ease of use. A JavaScript author, on the other hand, can't hide behind compiled code: the scripts will be visible to anyone who wants to view or save the source version of the document. Although any script that works as it's supposed to is a good script, there may be ways to do the same work with less code or with more clever use of math or logic. Other scripters will certainly be watching — not so much to criticize as to learn new techniques or alternative ways of accomplishing a task.

Scripting and programming, for all their differences, are both programming. The same care should go into planning, implementing, and testing a program and a script. The user is still in your hands.

Where You Write JavaScript

As mentioned earlier, JavaScript scripts are written as part of HTML documents. If you write HTML documents in a standard text editor, then you will use the same editor to add lines of JavaScript code to the plain text documents that you upload to your Web server (or service). With the proliferation of HTML editing tools available, many page authors are creating pages in WYSIWYG (What You See Is What You Get) or semi-WYSIWYG environments on their PCs and Macs. These graphical editors eventually generate a plain text file — an HTML file—for each page of your Web site. It may take a while for these editors to include facilities for writing and debugging JavaScript scripts in their fancy environments. Until then, you'll have to rely on standard text editors to add the JavaScript code to whatever HTML files these Web authoring tools create.

The scripts don't run in the text files. Rather, the browser software interprets the JavaScript commands and statements from the text files, just as it interprets HTML tags in those files to turn something like `<H1>WhizCorp Home Page</H1>` into a large font title. The browser contains all the mechanisms to convert your code into actions. The browser essentially "reads" your script(s), and follows the lines as an actor might — but without any room for artistic interpretation. Only browsers that are equipped to interpret JavaScript can take advantage of whatever scripts you build into your pages. Because of the shared corporate connection between Java and JavaScript, you can be reasonably assured that any Java-compatible browser will also be able to interpret JavaScript scripts. Fortunately, this includes the vast majority of modern graphical browsers.

To learn JavaScript, therefore, the only software you will need are a JavaScript-compatible browser and a text editor program. If a graphical authoring tool makes it easier to arrange the other content of your pages, you'll have even more time to experiment with JavaScript enhancements to your pages.

Prerequisites to Learning JavaScript

Although this book doesn't demand that you have a geat deal of programming experience behind you, the more Web pages you've created at the HTML level, the easier you will understand how JavaScript interacts with the familiar elements you normally place in your pages. Occasionally, you'll need to modify HTML tags to take advantage of scripting. If you are familiar with those tags already, the JavaScript enhancements will be simple to digest.

Forms and their elements (text fields, buttons, and selection lists) play an especially important role in much of typical JavaScript work. You should be familiar with these elements and their HTML attributes. Fortunately, you won't need to know about CGI scripting or passing information from a form to a server. Our focus here is client-side scripting, which operates independently of the server once the JavaScript-enhanced HTML page is fully loaded into the browser.

Any current Netscape extensions to the HTML standard should be part of your working knowledge. As you'll see later, tables and frames are handy user-interface elements for Web pages that use JavaScript. When we get to using frames, for instance, we'll provide only rudimentary guidance about how to design multi-frame windows. Netscape and other sources on-line provide more detailed explanations of frames.

Gradus Ad Scriptum

If you have a working knowledge of HTML, you don't need a great deal of programming experience to find your way to JavaScript success with the help of these pages. Although extensive instruction of basic programming concepts are below the level of this book, you will, nonetheless, find crash course chapters on programming concepts and object-oriented programming — perfect if you've had programming experience in the past (self-taught or otherwise) and you need a refresher.

The chapters in Part II are carefully organized to present JavaScript in a sequence that will help you grasp the key elements quickly. Many chapters contain complete descriptions of terms and concepts of the JavaScript language syntax. But to help you separate the essential from the nice-to-know, I have rated sections (especially

JavaScript vocabulary elements) according to their difficulty. The symbol I've chosen to represent each level is the pocket protector (remember what I said about scripting being programming). A topic's difficulty may range from one to three pocket protectors according to the following scale:

beginner

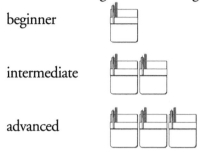

intermediate

advanced

As you first read each chapter, you can skim over items marked with two or three pocket protectors — just be aware of their existence. Later, you can reread these chapters and begin to fill out your knowledge with the more advanced items.

Once you learn the basics, you can refer to this book for detailed or advanced information. It is all here in a form that makes finding a reference extremely easy. The pocket protector codes, however, will speed your learning because you won't be bogged down with mind-numbing details in the early stages.

As a preview of the stages of learning JavaScript, here is an outline of the sequence I recommend:

1. Write a simple script that runs as a Web page loads (Chapter 3).

    This is the simplest kind of script to write because it doesn't rely on any user intervention. When the page loads, some portion of content is defined by a script that the browser interprets along with any other text formatting.

2. Acquaint yourself with JavaScript objects (Chapters 7 and 8).

    Part of the ease of learning JavaScript (compared to full languages, such as Java) is that your scripts work almost exclusively with a well-defined set of objects that correspond to the "things" you already work with in HTML. It's not difficult to visualize in one mental model all the JavaScript objects you'll have at your disposal.

3. Understand the way JavaScript likes to work with data (Chapter 9).

    If a programming language were an economic system, then values and expressions would be the currency. Most programming is about moving information (data) around: How that data is represented in the language is of critical importance.

4. Start programming via custom functions (Chapters 10 through 12).

   Extracting the data-crunching actions of your scripts as distinct functions will start you on your way to creating reusable snippets of code that will make future JavaScripting tasks go much faster. Your HTML documents will also be easier to read and debug.

5. Design user interfaces in HTML documents to communicate between user and script (Chapters 15 and 16).

   Writing a cool script is one thing; integrating the script into an intuitive page design is quite another task.

These may seem like many arduous step but, as you move through the sequence, you'll be trying out things for yourself. Seeing even the simplest script work as you planned is a rewarding experience. You should have plenty of those experiences in the following chapters. I tried to anticipate where you'll be scratching your head in bewilderment and backed up that discussion with a solid example.

If You've Never Programmed Before

To someone who learned HTML from a slim guidebook, the size of this book and the preceding learning sequence must appear daunting. JavaScript may not be the easiest language in the world to learn, but believe me, it is a far cry from having to learn a full programming language such as Java or C. Unlike developing a full-fledged monolithic application (such as the productivity programs you buy in the stores), JavaScript lets you experiment by writing small snippets of program code to accomplish big things. The JavaScript interpreter built into every compatible browser does a great deal of the technical work for you.

Programming at its most basic level is nothing more than writing a series of instructions for the computer to follow. We humans follow instructions all the time, even if we don't realize it. Traveling to a friend's house is a sequence of small instructions: Go three blocks that way; turn left here; turn right there. Amid the instructions we follow are some decisions: If the stoplight is red, then stop; if the light is green, then go; if the light is yellow, then floor it. Occasionally, we must repeat some operations many times (kind of like going around the block until a parking space opens up). A computer program not only contains the main sequence of steps but it anticipates what decisions or repetitions may be needed to accomplish the goal of the program (such as how to handle the various states of a stoplight or what to do if there is no immediate parking).

The initial hurdle of learning to program is becoming comfortable with the way a programming language wants its words and numbers organized in these instructions. Such rules are called *syntax*, just as they are in a living language.

Because computers are generally dumb electronic hulks, they aren't very forgiving if we don't communicate with them in the specific language they understand. When speaking to another human, we can flub a sentence's syntax, and there's a good chance the other person will understand fully. Not so with computer programming languages. If the syntax isn't perfect (or at least within the language's range of knowledge that it can correct), the computer has the brazenness to tell us that *we* have made a syntax error.

It's best to just chalk up the syntax errors you receive as learning experiences. Even experienced programmers get them. Every syntax error you get — and the resolution of that error by rewriting the statement — adds to your knowledge of the language.

If You've Done a Little Programming Before

Programming experience in a procedural language such as BASIC or Pascal may almost be a hindrance rather than a help to learning JavaScript. Although you may have an appreciation for precision in syntax, the overall concept of how a program fits into the world is probably radically different from JavaScript. Part of this has to do with the typical tasks a script performs (carrying out a very specific task in response to user action within a Web page), but a large part also has to do with the nature of object-oriented programming.

I'll have more to say about this in Chapter 6, but a brief introduction here can't hurt. In a typical procedural program, the programmer is responsible for everything that appears on the screen and everything that happens under the hood. When the program first runs, a great deal of code is dedicated to setting up the visual environment. Perhaps there are text entry fields or clickable buttons on the screen. To determine which button a user clicked, the program examines the coordinates of the click and compares those coordinates against a list of all button coordinates on the screen. Program execution then branches out to carry out the instructions reserved for clicking in that space.

Object-oriented programming is almost the inverse. A button is considered an object — something tangible. An object has properties, such as its label, size, alignment, and so on. An object may also contain a script. At the same time, the system software and browser, working together, can send a message to an object — depending on what the user does — to trigger the script. For example, if a user clicks in a text entry field, the system/browser tells the field that somebody has clicked there (that is, has set the focus to that field), leaving it up to the field to decide what to do about it. That's where the script comes in. The script is part of the field, and it contains the instructions the field carries out when the user activates it. A separate set of instructions may be listed if the user types an entry and tabs or clicks out of the field, thereby changing the content of the field.

Some of the scripts you'll write may seem to be procedural in construction: They contain a simple list of instructions that are carried out in order. But when dealing with data from forms elements, these instructions will be working with the object-oriented nature of JavaScript. The form is an object; each radio button or text field is an object as well. The script then acts on the properties of those objects to get some work done.

Making the transition from procedural to object-oriented programming may be the most difficult challenge for you. When I first introduced to object-oriented programming a number of years ago, I didn't get it at first. But when the concept clicked — a long pensive walk helped — so many light bulbs went on inside my head that I thought I might be glowing in the dark. From then on, object orientation seemed to be the only sensible way to program.

If You Have Programmed in C Before

By borrowing Java syntax, JavaScript (which is in turn derived from C and C++) shares many syntactical elements of C. Programmers familiar with C will feel right at home. Operator symbols, conditional structures, and repeat loops are very much in the C tradition. You will be less concerned about data typing in JavaScript than in C. In JavaScript, data is either a number (an integer or floating point value), a string, a Boolean, an object, or null. Sometimes you need to convert one type to the other, and JavaScript is pretty straightforward (from a C perspective) in that regard.

With so much of JavaScript's syntax familiar to you, you'll be able to concentrate on the unique aspects of JavaScript, notably the object hierarchy. You'll still need a good grounding in HTML (especially form elements) to put your expertise to work in JavaScript.

If You Have Scripted (or Macro'd) Before

Experience in writing scripts in other authoring tools or macros in productivity programs is helpful in grasping a number of aspects of JavaScript. Perhaps the most important is the concept of combining a handful of statements to perform a specific task on some data. For example, you can write a macro in Microsoft Excel that performs a data transformation on daily figures that come in from a corporate financial report on another computer. The macro is built into the Macro menu, and you run it by choosing that menu item whenever a new set of figures arrives.

More sophisticated scripting, such as that found in Toolbook or HyperCard, prepares you for the object orientation aspect of JavaScript. In those environments, screen objects contain scripts, which are executed when a user interacts with those objects. A great deal of the scripting you'll do in JavaScript matches that pattern exactly. In fact, those environments resemble JavaScript in another way: They provide a finite set of pre-defined objects that have fixed sets of properties and behaviors. This predictability makes it easier to learn the entire environment and to plan an application.

Enough Talk: Let's Script!

If I haven't frightened you away by now, we're ready to get underway. Be sure you have Netscape Navigator 2.0 (or later) or another JavaScript-compatible browser installed on your computer, as well as a text editor in which to enter and edit HTML content. In the next chapter, you'll create a simple HTML document that contains a JavaScript script.

Chapter Three

YOUR FIRST JAVASCRIPT

SCRIPT

In this chapter, we'll set up a productive script writing and previewing environment on your computer — and then write a simple script whose results you'll see in your JavaScript-compatible browser.

25

Because of differences in the way various personal computing operating systems behave, I present details of environments for two popular variants: Windows 95 and the MacOS. For the most part, your JavaScripting experience will be the same regardless of the operating system platform you're using — including UNIX. Although there may be slight differences in font designs depending on your browser and operating system, the information will be the same. All illustrations of browser output in this book are made from the Windows 95 version of Netscape Navigator 2.0. If you're running another version of Navigator 2.0 or another JavaScript-enabled browser, don't fret if every pixel doesn't match with the illustrations in this book.

The Software Tools

You write scripts or add scripts to existing HTML documents in a text editor. Your choice of editor is up to you. HTML files are raw ASCII text files, and any scripting has to be done in those files. While learning JavaScript, you may be better off using a simple text editor rather than a high-power word processor with HTML extensions.

Choosing a text editor

For purposes of learning JavaScript in this book, avoid WYSIWYG (What You See Is What You Get) Web-page authoring tools for now. They'll certainly come in handy afterward, when you can productively utilize those facilities for molding the bulk of your content and layout. But examples in this book focus more on script content (which you must type anyway), so there won't be much HTML that you have to type. You can even find templates for basic scripted HTML pages on the disc accompanying this book. The templates take care of general tags while you can focus on entering just the JavaScripted parts. Files for all complete Web page listings are also included on the disc.

An important factor to consider in your choice of editor is how easy it is to save standard text files. In the case of Windows 95, any program that not only saves the file by default as text but also lets you set the extension to .htm or .html will prevent a lot of problems. If you were to use Microsoft Word, for example, the program tries to save files as binary Word files — something that no Web browser can load. To save the file initially as a text or HTML extension file requires mucking around in the Save As dialog box. This is truly a nuisance.

There is nothing wrong with using bare essentials text editors. In Windows 95, that includes the WordPad program. For the MacOS, SimpleText will also do, although the lack of a search-and-replace function may get in the way when you start managing your Web site pages.

Choosing a browser

The other component required for learning JavaScript is the browser. You don't have to be connected to the Internet to test your scripts in the browser. It can all be done off-line. This means that you can learn JavaScript and create cool-scripted Web pages with a laptop computer even on a boat in the middle of an ocean.

The only requirement for the browser is that it be compatible with the first release of JavaScript. Netscape's Navigator 2.0 is the first to include JavaScript support. Most other modern browser versions to be released later in 1996 will likely include JavaScript support as well. Custom browsers developed for commercial on-line services, such as America Online, may not immediately offer that support. In some early versions, such as American Online's first Macintosh browser, it was nearly impossible to open the browser without being connected to AOL. The more independent your browser is of the service to which you connect, the more likely you'll have the requisite features built in.

Setting up your authoring environment

To make the job of testing your scripts easier, make sure that you have enough free memory in your computer to let both your text editor and browser run at the same time. You need to be able to switch quickly between editor and browser as you experiment and repair any errors that may creep into your code.

The typical workflow entails the following steps:

1. Enter HTML and script code into the source document.

2. Save the latest version to disk.

3. Switch to the browser.

4a. If this is a new document, open the file via the browser's Open menu.

   or

4b. If the document is already loaded, reload the file into the browser.

Steps 2 through 4 (a or b) are the key ones you'll be following frequently. I call this three-step sequence the save-switch-reload sequence. You will do this so often as you script that the physical act will quickly become second nature to you. How you arrange your application windows and effect the save-switch-reload sequence will vary according to your operating system.

Windows

You don't have to have either the editor or browser window maximized (at full screen) to take advantage of them. In fact, it may be easier if you adjust the size and location of each window so that both windows are as large as they can be while allowing you to click on a sliver of the other's window; or, in Windows 95, leave the Taskbar visible so that you can click on the desired program's button to switch (Figure 3-1). A monitor that displays more than 640 × 480 pixels certainly helps in offering more screen real estate for these windows and Taskbar.

In practice, however, Windows' Alt+Tab task-switching keyboard shortcut makes the job of the save-switch-reload steps outlined earlier a snap. If you are running Windows 95 and use a Windows 95-compatible text editor (which will more than likely have a Ctrl+S file-saving keyboard shortcut) and the Netscape Navigator 2.0 browser (which has a Ctrl+R reload keyboard shortcut), you can effect the save-switch-reload from the keyboard, all with the left hand:

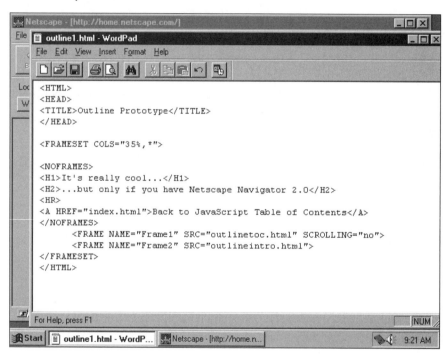

Figure 3-1: Editor and browser window arrangement in Windows 95.

Ctrl+S   (save the source file)

Alt+Tab   (switch to the browser)

Ctrl+R   (reload the saved source file)

As long as you keep switching between the browser and text editor via Alt+Tab task switching, either program is always just an Alt+Tab away.

MacOS

If you expand the windows of your text editor and browser to full screen, you have to use the rather inconvenient Application menu (right-hand icon of the menu bar) to switch between the programs. A better method is to adjust the size and location of both programs' windows so that they overlap, while allowing a portion of the inactive window to be visible (Figure 3-2). That way, all you have to do is click anywhere on the inactive window to bring its program to the front.

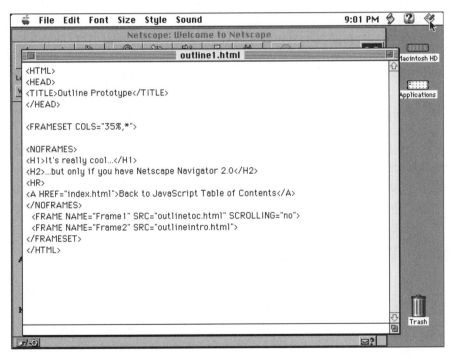

Figure 3-2: Editor and browser window arrangement on the Macintosh screen.

With this arrangement, the save-switch-reload sequence is a two-handed affair. Assuming that you have Netscape Navigator 2.0 (which lets you reload the current URL with a ⌘-R keyboard shortcut), the sequence is as follows:

1. ⌘-S   (save the source file)

2. Click in the browser window

3. ⌘-R   (reload the saved source file)

To return to editing the source file, click on any exposed part of the text editor's window.

What Your First Script Will Do

For the sake of simplicity, the kind of script we'll be looking at is the kind that runs automatically when the browser opens the HTML page. Although all scripting and browsing work here is off-line, the behavior of the page would be identical if you placed the source file on a server and someone were to access it via the Web.

Figure 3-3 shows the page as it will appear in the browser when you're finished. The part of the page that is defined in regular HTML contains nothing more than an <H1>-level header with a horizontal rule underneath it. If somebody was not using a JavaScript-equipped browser, all he or she could see would be the header and horizontal rule (unless that person had a truly outmoded browser, in which case some of the script words would appear in the page).

Below the rule, the script displays plain body text that combines static text with information about the last date and time you modified the source document. You may already recognize a practical application of the second line of the script: adding a line of text to your home page that indicates when you last updated your Web site.

Entering Your First Script

Launch your text editor and browser. If your browser offers to dial your Internet Service Provider (ISP) or begins dialing automatically, cancel or quit the dialing operation. If the browser's Stop button is active, click it to halt any network searching it may be trying to do. You may receive a dialog message indicating that the URL for your browser's home page (usually the home page of the browser's publisher — unless you've changed the settings) is unavailable. That's fine. You want the browser open, but you shouldn't be connected to your ISP. If you are automatically connected via a local area

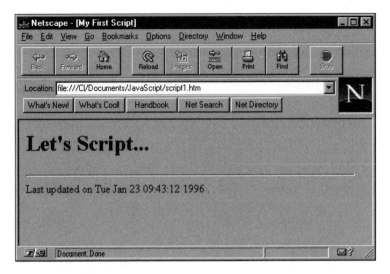

Figure 3-3: The finished page of your first JavaScript script.

network in your office or school, that's also fine, but you won't be needing the network connection for now.

Next, follow these steps to enter and preview your first JavaScript script:

1. Activate your text editor, and create a new blank document.

2. Type the following script into the window, exactly as shown in Listing 3-1.

```
<HTML>
<HEAD>
<TITLE>My First Script</TITLE>
</HEAD>
<H1>Let's Script...</H1>

<BODY>
<HR>
<SCRIPT LANGUAGE="JavaScript">
<!-- hide from old browsers
document.write("Last updated on " + document.lastModified + ".")
// end script hiding -->
</SCRIPT>
</BODY>
</HTML>
```

Listing 3-1: Source code for script1.htm.

3. Save the document with the name script1.htm.

(This is the lowest common denominator file-naming convention for Windows 3.1 — feel free to use a .html extension if your operating system allows it.)

4. Switch to your browser.

5. Choose Open File from the File menu, and select script1.htm.

If you typed all lines as directed, the document in the browser window should look like the one in Figure 3-3. If the browser indicates that there is a mistake somewhere, don't do anything for now. Let's first examine the details of the entire document so you understand some of the finer points of what the script is doing.

Examining the Script

It's not important for you to memorize any of the commands or syntax we'll be discussing in this section. Instead, relax and watch how the lines of the script become what you see in the browser.

All lines up to the <SCRIPT> tag are very standard HTML. Your JavaScript-enhanced HTML documents should contain the same style of opening tags you normally use.

The <SCRIPT> tag

Anytime you include JavaScript verbiage in an HTML document, you must enclose those lines inside a <SCRIPT>...</SCRIPT> tag pair. These tags alert the browser program to begin interpreting all the text between these tags as a script. Because other scripting languages may arrive in the future, you must specify the precise name of the language in which the enclosed code is written. Therefore, when the browser receives this signal that our script uses the JavaScript language, it uses its built-in JavaScript interpreter to handle the code. There are parallels to this in real life: If you have a French interpreter at your side, you need to know that the person with whom you are conversing also knows French. If you encounter someone from Russia, the French interpreter won't be able to help you. Similarly, if your browser has only a JavaScript interpreter inside, it won't be able to understand code written in VBScript.

Now is a good time to instill an aspect of JavaScript that will be important to you throughout all your scripting ventures: JavaScript is case-sensitive. Therefore, any item in your scripts that uses a JavaScript word, such as the name of the JavaScript language in the <SCRIPT> tag, must be entered with the correct upper- and lowercase letters.

Your HTML tags (including the `<SCRIPT>` tag) can be in your choice of upper- or lowercase, but everything in JavaScript is case-sensitive. When a line of JavaScript doesn't work, that's the first thing to look for. Always compare your typed code against the listings printed in this book and against the various vocabulary entries discussed throughout.

A script for all browsers

The next line after the `<SCRIPT>` tag appears to be the beginning of an HTML comment tag. It is, but the JavaScript interpreter treats comment tags in a special way. Although JavaScript dutifully ignores a line that begins with an HTML comment start tag, it treats the next line as a full-fledged script line. In other words, the browser begins interpreting the next line after a comment start tag. If you want to put a comment inside JavaScript code, the comment must start with a double slash (`//`). Such a comment may go at the end of a line (such as after a JavaScript statement that is to be interpreted by the browser) or on its own line. In fact, the latter case appears near the end of the script. The comment line starts with two slashes.

Step back for a moment and notice that the entire script (including comments) is contained inside a standard HTML comment tag (`<!-comment->`). The value of this containment is not clear until you see what happens to your scripted HTML document in a non-JavaScript-compatible browser. Such a browser would blow past the `<SCRIPT>` tag as being an advanced tag it doesn't understand. Although the browser would respect the regular comment start tag (`<!--`), it would treat the one line of script as regular body text. Figure 3-4 shows the results of our first script when viewed in a pre-Java version of Microsoft's Internet Explorer. Remember that many users don't have access to modern browsers or graphical browsers (they use the Lynx text-oriented UNIX Web reader software). By embracing your script lines within these comments, your Web pages won't look completely broken in relatively modern non-JavaScript browsers.

Notice, too, that the comment lines that shield older browsers from your scripts go inside the `<SCRIPT>...</SCRIPT>` tags. Do not put these comment lines above the `<SCRIPT>` tag or below the `</SCRIPT>` tag and expect them to work.

One more issue about the script-hiding comment lines in this book. To save space on the page, most examples do not have comment lines inserted in them. But as you will see in later chapters where full-fledged examples are provided, the comment lines are where they should be. For any pages you produce for public consumption, always encase your script lines inside these comments.

Displaying some text

The script line utilizes one of the possible actions a script can ask a document to perform (`document.write()`, meaning display text in the current document). You'll learn more about the document object in Chapter 8.

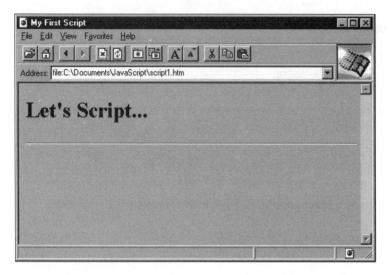

Figure 3-4: Failing to contain script lines in comments causes those lines to be treated as body text in an old browser.

Whenever we ask an object (a document in this case) to perform a task for us, the name of the task is always followed by a set of parentheses. In some cases — the `write()` task, for example — JavaScript needs to know what information it should act on. That information (called a *parameter*) goes inside parentheses after the name of the task. Thus, if we wanted to write the name of the first U.S. President to a document, the commands would be

```
document.write("George Washington")
```

The line of text that our script writes includes some static text (`"Last updated on"`), some evaluated text (the date and time at which the current HTML document was last modified), and one more character of static text for the sentence's period (`". "`). JavaScript uses the plus symbol (+) to join (*concatenate*) text components into a larger, single string of text characters. Neither JavaScript nor the + symbol knows anything about words and spaces, so it is up to the script to make sure that the proper spaces are passed along as part of the parameter. Notice, therefore, that there is an extra space after the word "updated" in the first part of the `document.write()` parameter.

To fetch the last modified date of the document for our parameter, we call upon JavaScript to extract one of the document's properties. We extract a property by appending the property name to the object name (`document` in this case), and separate the two names with a period. If you are searching for some English to assign to this scheme in your head as you read it, start from the right side and call the right side item a property "of" the left side: the `lastModified` property of the document object. This dot syntax looks a lot like the `document.write()` task, but a property name does not have parentheses after it. In any case, the reference to the property in the script tells JavaScript to insert the value of that property in the spot where the call is made. For your first attempt at the script, JavaScript substitutes the last modified date recorded by your computer for that call as part of the text string that gets written to the document.

Have Some Fun

If you encountered an error in your first attempt at loading this document into your browser, go back to the text editor and check the lines of the script section against Listing 3-1, looking carefully at each line in light of our explanations. There may be a single character out of place, a lowercase letter where an uppercase one belongs, or a quote or parenthesis missing. Make the necessary repairs, switch to your browser, and click the Reload button.

To see how dynamic the script is, go back into the text editor and replace the word "updated" with "changed." Save, switch, and reload to see how the script has changed the text in the document and that the time is more recent than your first attempt. Feel free to substitute other text for the quoted text in the `document.write()` statement. Or add more text with additional `document.write()` statements. The parameters to `document.write()` are HTML text, so you can even write a "`<BR>`" to make a line break. Always be sure to save, switch, and reload to see the results of your handiwork.

On We Go

From here we dive into the JavaScript language, beginning with an aerial view of the landscape prior to targeting specific features. Much of what you've experienced in this chapter and in your first script will be explained in greater detail in the chapters ahead.

Part Two

THE JAVASCRIPT

LANGUAGE

Chapter Four

Now that you've seen what a script looks like, we'll take a closer look at how JavaScript impacts the HTML documents you've grown accustomed to creating. Rather than get into syntax specifics just yet, this chapter will focus on structural issues and will preview the kinds of actions your scripts can take.

What Happens When a Document Loads

Documents load into a JavaScript-enabled browser the same way they do in other browsers. The HTML that you've written in the past consists of instructions that the browser uses to lay out elements of the page from left to right and top to bottom. The tags you use to define visual elements and characteristics on the page instruct the browser when to begin laying out text on the next line, display an image, and highlight a link.

A JavaScript-enabled browser behaves precisely the same way as far as the regular HTML goes. Should the browser encounter any JavaScript code (it's set off by tags of its own), the browser works its way through that code in the same top-to-bottom sequence as HTML code. Sometimes JavaScript code directs the browser to lay out text or other elements on the page, just as if the instructions were coming from traditional, hard-wired HTML instructions. Other times, that code prepares the browser (invisibly to the person viewing the page) to respond to user entries and actions that may come along later via scripting. This part reminds me of setting the dinner table in anticipation of expected guests.

When the document finishes loading (the `Document:Done` message appears in the status bar at the bottom of the window), then all HTML and JavaScript has been read by the browser. Except for user-interface elements designed for interaction and dynamic updating (elements of HTML forms), the page remains fixed in the browser's memory and cannot be altered from a script. Anything that happens next will be instigated by the person viewing the page. The next action may involve JavaScript, if you've designed your page that way, or it may involve plain old HTML, such as jumping to another URL when a user clicks on a link.

Where Scripts Belong in Documents

I've mentioned that scripts can run when the document loads and when users interact with form elements in a document. There may be times when you have both of these dynamics working in the same document: One part of the document's scripting helps lay out part of the page; other parts respond to users' actions. Let's examine how each type is embedded into your HTML documents.

For this discussion, imagine an HTML document framework based on the simplified HTML structure shown in Listing 4-1.

```
<HTML>
<HEAD>
</HEAD>

<BODY>
<FORM>
    <INPUT TYPE="text">
    <INPUT TYPE="button">
</FORM>
</BODY>
</HTML>
```

Listing 4-1: Basic HTML document skeleton structure with one form.

Immediate scripts

I use the term *immediate scripts* to indicate lines of JavaScript that not only run when the browser loads the document, but also influence the layout of the page. Such scripts must be placed in the HTML document precisely where the output of the script will render the necessary content on the page. There may be standard HTML all around the script block, but that script block must be located where it is because it contributes content to that portion of the page. That's exactly the structure of script1.htm, your first JavaScript document in the preceding chapter. The document hard-wired the <H1> header and horizontal rule; then it called upon JavaScript to capture the lastModified property of the document and write that into the page below the rule.

Getting back to the sample structure for this chapter: In Listing 4-2, for example, a script block appears in the Body before the form definition. This means that whatever the script does to create content for the page appears on the page above the form elements.

```
<HTML>
<HEAD>
</HEAD>

<BODY>
<SCRIPT>
    // script that produces content for the Body
</SCRIPT>
```

(continued)

```
<FORM>
      <INPUT TYPE="text">
      <INPUT TYPE="button">
</FORM>
</BODY>
</HTML>
```

Listing 4-2: Adding a script block to display content as part of the Body content but before the form elements.

Deferred scripts

A *deferred script* is one that the browser sees when the document loads, but the wording of the script tells the browser not to do anything with the code other than to be aware that it exists. Such script sections usually consist of small groups of script lines that massage information in some fashion. As the document loads, no data massaging takes place. Instead, the browser thinks (as though it were human): "Yes, having read those lines of script, I now know how to perform that action, should any script ask me to do it later on."

The recommended location for deferred script segments is in the document's Head block, as sketched in Listing 4-3. Script-tagged sections can coexist happily with the other Head block definitions you normally put into your HTML documents, such as the document title or BASE FONT specifications.

```
<HTML>
<HEAD>
<SCRIPT>
      //script that initializes items for user-driven actions
</SCRIPT>
</HEAD>

<BODY>
<FORM>
      <INPUT TYPE="text">
      <INPUT TYPE="button">
</FORM>
</BODY>
</HTML>
```

Can also be put outside of the <HTML> tag.

Listing 4-3: Adding a deferred script to the Head block prepares the browser to respond to user interaction later.

The primary reason you are encouraged to put deferred scripts into the Head is that they load into the browser's memory first — even before any visible content appears on the page. Therefore, if the user interrupts the loading of the page after a clickable button appears in the window, the browser knows how to react to the button's action because its deferred script is already loaded. If the deferred script had been written at the end of the Body block of the document, a premature click of the button by the user would ask the browser to run a deferred script it knows nothing about or has only partially loaded. The user might get no response from the click or could encounter a scripting error.

Hybrid scripts

It won't be long before you will be designing pages that require both immediate and deferred scripts. The immediate script lines help create the content of the page; deferred script lines react to user's actions once the page has fully loaded. In fact, you will see many examples in this book in which an immediate script in the Body block calls a script deferred in the Head — but not deferred for very long. When you need both kinds of script blocks in a document, you simply insert them where needed, as demonstrated in Listing 4-4.

```
<HTML>
<HEAD>
<SCRIPT>
    // script that initializes items for user-driven actions
</SCRIPT>
</HEAD>

<BODY>
<SCRIPT>
    // script that produces content for the Body
</SCRIPT>
<FORM>
    <INPUT TYPE="text">
    <INPUT TYPE="button">
</FORM>
</BODY>
</HTML>
```

Listing 4-4: Combining immediate and deferred script blocks in the same document.

Catching user actions

JavaScript calls user actions *events*. This terminology comes from programming in graphical user interfaces, such as Windows and the Macintosh. In those environments, the system software constantly monitors input devices, such as the keyboard and mouse. Whenever a user types a key or moves the mouse, the system registers the action as an event.

Events in JavaScript-enabled browsers have a great deal in common with this behavior. The browser constantly monitors document elements that have been designated as capable of reacting to user actions. As the scripter, your job is to indicate which user interface element(s) respond to user actions and what the element(s) should do in response to a particular action.

Each type of element responds to a limited range of events. We'll get into more detail about this later in Chapters 7 and 8, but for now, consult Table 4-1 for a summary of typical user interface elements in documents and the types of events they can detect.

Table 4-1
Typical JavaScript User Interface Objects and Events They Respond To

Element	User Action	Event Name
Button	Mouse click	Click
Checkbox	Mouse click	Click
Link	Mouse click	Click
	Mouse pointer atop	MouseOver
Radio button	Mouse click	Click
Select	Tab to/click on	Focus
	Tab/click away from	Blur
	Change selection and click	Change
Text field	Tab to/click on	Focus
	Tab/click away from	Blur
	Change text and click	Change
	Select text	Select

For a user interface element to respond to an event, it must have an extra attribute in its definition: the *event handler*. An event handler contains instructions about what to do when a particular kind of event reaches the on-screen element. An event handler attribute's name is the name of the event preceded by the word "on" (for example, onClick=); the other half of the attribute defines what action takes place whenever the event happens. When non-JavaScript-equipped browsers recognize the element tags, they display the object but ignore the extra event handler attribute of these elements, so no conflict occurs with older browsers.

To demonstrate the impact of an event handler on an object definition, let's look at the Netscape Navigator 2.0 button input type. A button that does nothing (other than display itself in the document) would be defined in a way not unlike standard HTML attributes:

```
<INPUT TYPE="button" NAME="oneButton" VALUE="Press Me!">
```

To give that button the power to respond to a mouse click, you add the `onClick=` event handler attribute. The value of the attribute consists of either the actual JavaScript statements that you want to run in response to the click or the name of a deferred script to run. For example, to make the preceding button display an alert dialog box when someone clicks on it, you would add the `onClick=` attribute plus the command that tells the browser to display an alert dialog box:

```
<INPUT TYPE="button" NAME="oneButton" VALUE="Press Me!"
    onClick="alert('Ouch!')">
```

The schematic of an HTML document following this methodology looks like Listing 4-5.

```
<HTML>
<HEAD>
</HEAD>

<BODY>
<FORM>
    <INPUT TYPE="text">
    <INPUT TYPE="button"… onClick="script code">
</FORM>
</BODY>
</HTML>
```

Listing 4-5: The event catcher is an extra attribute to the <INPUT> definition.

Handing off action to a deferred script

It is more efficient from the standpoint of programming style, code maintenance, and other factors to not write extensive script code (that is, more than a few words) as part of the event handler attribute. Instead, call upon a deferred script that has already been defined in the HTML document. Such a deferred script is a JavaScript mechanism called a *function,* based on the JavaScript word that tells the browser to load, but defer, the next group of statements. Part of the task of writing a function is assigning it a name; this name is what goes on the right side of the attribute's equal sign. Let's look at a simple example derived from the single button routine listed earlier.

Instead of including the `alert` command in the button definition, it's better to define a function that does that task:

```
function alertUser() {
    alert("Ouch!")
}
```

Don't worry about the curly brackets or other punctuation yet. It was included merely to demonstrate where scripting components go in your HTML documents. This `alertUser()` function, whose name I arbitrarily devised to describe what it does, belongs within the `<SCRIPT>...</SCRIPT>` tags of the document's Head. Once that part of the document loads into the browser, the browser knows what to do when another entity in the document asks to run the `alertUser()` function.

Down in the button definition, the `onClick` event handler attribute requires either actual script lines or the name of a function in the browser's memory. Here we specify the `alertUser()` function name:

```
<INPUT TYPE="button" NAME="oneButton" VALUE="Press Me!"
    onClick="alertUser()">
```

By specifying a function name for the `onClick=` attribute, we're telling the browser to run that particular function whenever the user clicks on the button. Adding these details to the schematic document we've been using in this chapter, the complete page is shown in Listing 4-6. I urge you to enter this listing into your text editor and to open the file in your browser to see the results.

```
<HTML>
<HEAD>
<SCRIPT LANGUAGE="JavaScript">
function alertUser() {
    alert("Ouch!")
}
</SCRIPT>
</HEAD>

<BODY>
<FORM>
    <INPUT TYPE="text">
```

```
    <INPUT TYPE="button" NAME="oneButton" VALUE="Press Me!"
    onClick="alertUser()">
</FORM>
</BODY>
</HTML>
```

Listing 4-6: When the user clicks the button, the browser runs the associated function (already in memory).

You may be wondering why you'd use what appears to be a longer and more roundabout way of building and calling a function to handle the user's click. In real life (that is, not in simple demonstrations such as the preceding one), functions are usually multiple lines of code that make your HTML form element definitions long and more difficult to debug. You'll learn later to design functions so that they may be called by more than one object in a document (if appropriate). Having all deferred JavaScript code conveniently located in the Head part of the document also makes it easier to locate any portion that needs repair or changes. A heavily scripted HTML document may have more than a dozen function definitions in the document's Head section, each one performing a specific task for one or more document objects in the Body. If these functions were scattered around your document, you might have a tough time finding the one you need to adjust.

Mixed Syntaxes in HTML Documents

For anyone who has spent a great deal of time writing HTML documents, the sight of the C-like syntax of JavaScript scripts in your documents may be upsetting at first. By and large, however, the JavaScript segments of your documents are fully segregated from the HTML parts. Scripts are delimited by the <SCRIPT>...</SCRIPT> tags, so they should be readily identifiable as you read the HTML.

In theory, the issue can get a bit more complicated if browsers are capable of interpreting multiple scripting languages. Script segments (which are always labeled with the name of the language) from more than one language may grace your HTML documents in the future. This would likely happen only if no language had all the facilities your document design requires and you must summon the powers of more than one language. The point is, if you are viewing the source for a scripted HTML document, be sure you observe the LANGUAGE= attribute of the <SCRIPT> tag so that you know which language the statements are in.

In the next two chapters, I'll take non-programmers (and those who need a refresher) on a quick tour of basic programming concepts as they apply to JavaScript. Experienced programmers should also take a look because they'll be able to see how much of what they already know automatically applies to their future work in JavaScript.

$\mathcal{C}$hapter Five

A CRASH COURSE IN

PROGRAMMING

FUNDAMENTALS

Though I deem writing HTML tags to be a form of programming, HTML experience offers precious little in the way of preparation for the kind of scripting you must do in JavaScript (and other scripting environments). Virtually everything you write in HTML has some immediate visual impact on the content of a page. That's not always the case with JavaScript. Many times — as shown in some of the schematic examples in the preceding chapter — not all JavaScript code you write runs the instant the document is loaded into the browser. Moreover, many lines of JavaScript code help the script manipulate information either entered by the user or stored in the script. Only when the information is properly calculated, checked, and compared does the script do something with the results — perhaps displaying them in a field or showing a new Web page in a separate frame of the window.

Cooking Up Some Fine Information

Writing a JavaScript-enhanced Web page is like writing and publishing a cookbook recipe for a sumptuous dish. The browser software is the cook, following your steps without question. Your first task as an author is knowing what dish you will be instructing the cook to prepare. The better you can visualize the result, the easier it will be to write down the steps.

Once you know what the dish will be, consider the list of ingredients — the items that the cook will be cutting, chopping, blending, heating, and otherwise transforming in the process. At various points, you write down an instruction about doing something with (or to) one or more ingredients. Occasionally, you might anticipate that the cook won't be able to purchase a hard-to-find ingredient and recommend a substitute to cover that situation. If the recipe calls for a sliced vegetable, your instructions imply that the cook will repeat the slicing step until the necessary quantity is ready. During another part of the process, your recipe instructs the cook to prepare a sauce in a separate pan by blending a few ingredients. Once the sauce is ready, the cook pours the results atop the main ingredients cooking in the first pan.

At long last, the cooking is finished, and the final product is delivered to the table for all to enjoy. Even though you're not there to hear it, the cook who followed your instructions will be rewarded with compliments for a job well done. The guests will either request a copy of the recipe or ask to be invited back sometime for another evening.

As far fetched as this extended metaphor may sound, it applies to programming with one important exception. Although you may be able to get by with specifying a pinch of salt or "about" one-and-a-half tablespoons of olive oil, programming requires far more precision. A recipe designed by a computer programmer would indicate how many salt crystals of a specific size and how many molecules of olive oil the cook needs. This level of accuracy is not forced into the program by the programmer, but rather by the computer, which does only what it's told. It's like having a robot for a cook. Fortunately, the ingredients for a JavaScript program aren't so small that you have to get down to the atomic level. But accuracy is extremely important because today's computers can't infer what you mean so you must type exactly what you mean. Be that as it may, in the rest of the chapter, I make occasional references to the cooking metaphor as we look at basic programming concepts and terminology.

Step This Way . . .

A script consists of one or more lines of JavaScript words — collectively called *code*. Like the steps in a recipe, each line is a command of sorts. Instead of commands such as "slice" or "heat to 350 degrees," JavaScript commands instruct the browser/computer duo to do such things as add some numbers together or move information from one location to another.

Unlike many other languages, however, JavaScript does not have a vocabulary of commands per se. Still, every line of code performs an action of some kind, even if the command verb is not explicitly visible. For example, when you learn about variables later in this chapter, you will discover that it's common to put a number or string of text into a variable to make it easier for the program to move it around in subsequent lines of code. Such a line in JavaScript would like look this:

```
myName = "Barney Rubble"
```

The action going on here is that the text "Barney Rubble" is being given to a variable called `myName`. After this line of code runs, the variable `myName` can be used in a script line instead of "Barney Rubble." How you decide to read this line in your mind may help you understand the action taking place here. On face value, you could say "myName equals Barney Rubble" and be perfectly correct, as long as you comprehend the power of the "equal" verb meaning "is now exactly the same as 'Barney Rubble'."

Although it may be convenient to think of the equal sign (=) as a command verb, that isn't precisely the case in JavaScript. That symbol belongs to another category of word (operators) that I'll introduce shortly.

To make matters more confusing for newcomers, words or constructions that look like commands don't go by that name. For instance, you've already written a script (Chapter 3) that displayed some text within a Web page. Recall the code line

```
document.write("Last updated on " + document.lastModified + ".")
```

In JavaScript, this kind of construction, which indicates an action directed at a physical Web page object, goes by yet another name: a *method*. Full discussion about this will wait until the next chapter.

Making a Statement

It is common practice in programming languages to consider each self-contained line of code that performs an action as a *statement*. The official JavaScript documentation is more restrictive in its definition — limiting a statement to those lines of code that use JavaScript keywords.

A *keyword* is any word that a programming language has built into its core. In other words, if you look at the keyword list of any language, you will see the language's most basic vocabulary (excluding such things as math symbols). You will get to know JavaScript's keywords over time, so it's not vital to memorize them now. The distinction of a keyword recedes into the background, except for the fact that you cannot use those words as names of things you create in your scripts (for example, variables, as described later in this chapter). Keywords are reserved for use only by the programming language.

It is perhaps a fine point of terminology, but I prefer not to limit statements to those lines of code that include keywords. For my money, any line of code, including those that assign values to variables with a simple math symbol (for example, `myName = "Barney Rubble"`) is a statement. Therefore, hereafter, I will refer to any line of JavaScript code as a statement, keyword or not. As I show you more advanced constructions later on, you will sometimes see listings such as this:

```
function name() {
    [statements]
}
```

Don't worry about the curly brackets just yet. This demonstration simply means that one or more lines of code go where the `[statements]` placeholder lies.

In the preceding example, multiple statement constructions are in play. The entire example is, itself, a multiple-line statement (from `function` down to `}`). That it can contain additional statements is part of the way the function statement (and some others) works. Whatever statements go "inside" the main statement are said to be *nested* statements.

It is also legal in JavaScript for one physical line of code to include multiple self-contained statements, provided that you insert a semicolon between statements. Schematically, such a code line would look like this:

```
[statement1]; [statement2]; [statement3]
```

JavaScript interprets this series of statements as if they were typed

```
[statement1]
[statement2]
[statement3]
```

and runs each one in the sequence before proceeding to the next. I discourage placing multiple statements in the same physical line unless JavaScript requires it (as it does in a few limited instances). Stringing together statements on one line makes it more difficult later to find statements or follow the flow of execution while trying to debug a program. Others who will read the code will also have an easier time of it if each statement is on its own line.

The semicolon is used in other languages to end a statement of any kind, including when it has its own line. Recognizing that habits of long-time C programmers are hard to break, JavaScript lets you end a code line with a semicolon — but promptly ignores it. You'll see many examples of JavaScript code in other places that have semicolons at the end of nearly every line. They are not needed, so don't bother adding them to your code if they don't feel natural to you. Because I'm lazy, I don't end my lines with semi-colons. But if I coded C/C++ all day and dabbled in JavaScript, then I'd use the semi-colons — just so that I could stay in shape for my main programming work.

Working with Information

With rare exception, every JavaScript statement you write does something with a hunk of information — you can also call it *data*. It may be the information displayed on the screen by a JavaScript statement or the setting of a radio button in a form. Each single piece of information in programming is also called a *value*. Outside of programming, the term *value* usually connotes a number of some kind; in the programming world, however, the term is not as restrictive. A text name is a value. A number is a value. The setting of a checkbox (whether it is checked or not) is a value.

In JavaScript, a value can be one of several types. Table 5-1 lists JavaScript's data types, with examples of values you will see displayed from time to time.

A language of these few data types simplifies a number of programming tasks, especially those involving what other languages consider incompatible types of numbers (integers versus real or floating-point values). In some definitions of syntax and parts of objects, I have made specific reference to the type of value accepted in placeholders. When the requirement is for a string, any text inside a set of quotes will suffice.

Table 5-1
JavaScript Value (Data) Types

Type	Example	Description
String	`"Howdy"`	A series of characters inside quote marks
Number	4.5	Any number not inside quote marks
Boolean	`true`	A logical true or false
Null	`null`	Completely devoid of any value
Object	-	All properties and methods belonging to the object
Function	-	A function definition

You will see, however, situations in which the value type may get in the way of a smooth step. For example, if a user enters a number into a form's input field, JavaScript receives that number as a string value type. If the script is to perform some arithmetic on that number, then the string must be converted to a number before the value can be applied to any math operations. As you'll learn in Chapter 9, JavaScript sometimes does the conversions automatically; you can (and sometimes must) do them manually in code as well.

Variables

Cooking up a dish according to a recipe in the kitchen has one advantage over cooking up some data in a program. In the kitchen, you work with real things: carrots, milk, or a salmon fillet. A computer, on the other hand, follows a list of instructions to work with data. Even if the data represents something that looks real, such as the text entered into a form's input field, once the value gets into the program, you can no longer reach out and touch it.

In truth, the data that a program works with is merely a collection of bits (on and off states) in your computer's memory. More specifically, data in a JavaScript-enhanced Web page occupies parts of the computer's memory that is set aside for exclusive use by the browser software. In the olden days, programmers had to know the numeric address in memory (RAM) where a value was stored to retrieve a copy of it for, say, some addition. Fortunately, if the innards of a program have that level of complexity, programming languages such as JavaScript hide it.

To work with data, you must assign it to what is called a *variable*. It is usually easier to think of a variable as a basket that holds information. How long the variable holds the information depends on a number of factors that we discuss in Chapter 12. But the instant a Web page clears the window (or frame), any variables it knows about are immediately discarded.

Creating a variable

There are a couple of ways to create a variable in JavaScript, but you can use one that will cover you properly in all cases. It uses the `var` keyword, followed by the name you want to give that variable. Therefore, to *declare* a new variable called `myAge`, the JavaScript statement would be

```
var myAge
```

That lets the program know that we can use that variable later to store information or modify any of the data it may hold.

To assign a value to a variable, use one of the *assignment operators*. The most common one by far is the equal sign. If I want to assign a value to the `myAge` variable at the same time I declare it (a process known as *initializing* the variable) I would use that operator at the end:

```
var myAge = 45
```

On the other hand, if I declare a variable in one statement, and later want to assign a value to it, the assignment statement would be

```
myAge = 45
```

Use the `var` keyword *only for declaration* — once per document for any variable name.

A JavaScript variable can hold any value type. Unlike many other languages, you don't have to tell JavaScript during variable declaration what type of value the variable will hold. In fact, it is possible that the value type of a variable could change during the execution of a program. Still, it is good practice to both declare and initialize a variable in one statement, even if the initial value is zero or an empty string, because it reminds you later about how you originally intended to use that variable in your script.

WEAK DATA TYPING

Variable names

Choose the names you assign to variables with care. You often find scripts that use vague variable names, such as single letters. Other than a few specific times where letters are common practice (for example, using "i" as a counting variable in repeat loops in Chapter 10), I recommend using names that truly describe their contents. This practice can help you follow the state of your data through a long series of statements or jumps, especially for complex scripts.

A number of restrictions help instill good practice in assigning names. First, you cannot use any reserved keyword as a variable name. That includes all keywords currently used by the language and all others held in reserve for future versions of

JavaScript. The designers of JavaScript, however, cannot foresee every keyword that the language might need in the future. By using the kind of single words currently in the list of reserved keywords (see Appendix A) you always run a risk of conflict in the future.

To complicate matters, a variable name cannot contain space characters. Therefore, one-word variable names are fine. Should your description really benefit from more than one word, you can use one of two conventions to join multiple words together as one. One convention is to place an underscore character between the words; the other is to start the combination word with a lowercase letter and capitalize the first letter of each subsequent word within the name. Both of the following are valid variable names:

```
my_age
myAge
```

My personal preference is for the second version. I find it easier to type as I write JavaScript code and easier to read later on. In fact, because of the potential conflict with future keywords, it is a good idea to think up multi-word combinations for variable names. They're unlikely to ever be part of the reserved word list.

Expressions and Evaluation

Another concept closely related to the value and variable is *expression evaluation* — perhaps the most important concept of learning how to program a computer.

We use expressions in our everyday language. Remember the theme song of *The Beverly Hillbillies?*

Then one day he was shootin' at some food
And up through the ground came a-bubblin' crude
Oil that is. Black gold. Texas tea.

At the end, we have four quite different references ("crude," "oil," "black gold," and "Texas tea"). They all mean oil. They're all *expressions* for oil. Say any one of them and we know what you mean. In our minds, we *evaluate* those expressions to one thing: Oil.

In programming, a variable always evaluates to its contents, or value. For example, after assigning a value to a variable,

```
myAge = 45
```

anytime the variable is used in a statement, its value, 45, is automatically extracted from that variable and applied to whatever operation is being called in that statement.

Therefore, if you are 15 years younger than, I could assign a value to a variable representing your age based on the evaluated value of myAge:

```
yourAge = myAge - 15
```

The variable, yourAge, evaluates to 30 the next time it is used in the script. Even if the myAge value should change later in the script, there is no link to the yourAge variable because myAge evaluated to 45 when it was used to assign a value to yourAge.

Expressions in script1.htm

You probably didn't recognize it at the time, but you saw how expression evaluation can come in handy in your first script of Chapter 3. Recall the document.write() statement:

```
document.write("Last updated on " + document.lastModified + ".")
```

The document.write() method (remember, JavaScript uses the term *method* to mean *command*) requires a parameter in parentheses: the text string to be displayed on the Web page. The parameter here consists of one expression that joins together three distinct strings:

```
"Last updated on "
document.lastModified
"."
```

The plus symbol is JavaScript's way of joining strings. Before JavaScript can display this line, it must perform some quick evaluations. The first evaluation is the value of the document.lastModified property. We'll get into the form of the syntax later, but the key point is that this property evaluates to a string of the date and time the document was last saved. With that expression safely evaluated to a string, JavaScript can finish the job of joining the three strings together in the final evaluation. That evaluated string expression is what ultimately appears on the Web page.

Expressions and variables

As one more demonstration of the flexibility that expression evaluation offers, let's go a slightly different route to the document.write() statement. Rather than joining those strings together as the direct parameter to the document.write() method, we could have gathered the strings together earlier in a variable and then applied the variable to the `document.write()` method. Here's how that might have looked, as we simultaneously declare a new variable and assign it a value:

```
var textToWrite = "Last updated on " + document.lastModified + "."
document.write(textToWrite)
```

This works because the variable, `textToWrite`, evaluates to the combined string. The `document.write()` method accepts that string value, and does its display job. As you read a script or try to work through a bug, pay special attention to how each expression (variable, statement, object property) evaluates. I guarantee that while you learn JavaScript (or any language), more head scratching will occur because you haven't stopped to examine how expressions evaluate when a particular kind of value is required in a script. If you have one of those color sticky notes, attach it right here as a reminder.

Testing evaluation in Navigator

You can begin experimenting with the way JavaScript evaluates expressions with the help of a hidden feature of Netscape Navigator. Choose Open Location from the File menu, and enter `javascript:`.

Navigator displays a special two-frame window. The bottom frame contains a field where you can type one-line expressions. Press Enter/Return to view the results in the upper frame.

You can assign values to variables, test comparison operators, and even do math here. Be aware, however, that not all statements containing methods yield results to display in the upper frame. Following the variable examples earlier in this chapter, type each of the following statements into the type-in field and observe how each expression evaluates. Be sure to observe case sensitivity in your entries.

```
var myAge = 45

myAge

var yourAge = myAge - 15

myAge - yourAge

myAge > yourAge
```

To close this display, use the Navigator to open any HTML file or URL.

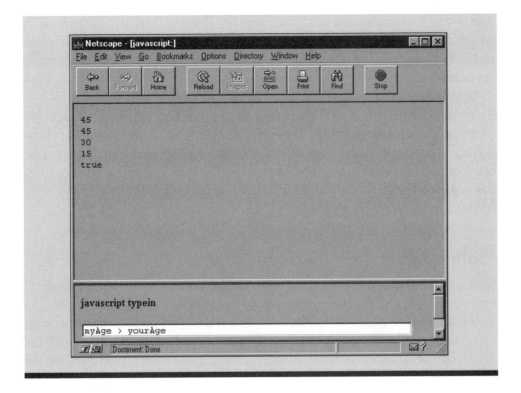

Operators

You will use lots of *operators* in expressions. Earlier, we used the equal sign (=) as an assignment operator to assign a value to a variable. In the previous example with strings, we used the plus symbol (+) to join together (*concatenate*) two strings. An operator generally performs some kind of calculation (operation) or comparison with two values to reach a third value.

The string concatenation operator doesn't know about words and spaces, so the programmer must make sure that any two strings to be joined have the proper word spacing as part of the strings, even if it means having to add a space character:

```
firstName = "John"
lastName = "Doe"
fullName = firstName + " " + lastName
```

JavaScript uses the same plus symbol for arithmetic addition, as you saw in assigning a value to the `yourAge` variable earlier. When both values on either side of the plus sign are numbers, JavaScript knows to treat the expression as an arithmetic addition rather than a string concatenation (but see Chapter 11 about mixing data types with operators). The standard math operators for addition, subtraction, multiplication, and division are built into JavaScript. JavaScript also features a number of special operators that facilitate writing condensed code for such constructions as repeat loops (Chapter 10).

Another category of operator helps you compare values in scripts — whether two values are the same, for example. These kinds of comparisons return a value of the Boolean type — `true` or `false`. Where comparison operators come into greatest play is in the construction of scripts that make decisions as they run. A cook does this in the kitchen all the time: If the sauce is too watery, add a bit of flour. We cover this in all its glory in Chapter 10.

Functions

Back in the kitchen, a recipe may contain instructions such as "add 1 cup boiling water" or "preheat oven to 350 degrees." Recipes assume that the cook has some smarts, so they don't include specific steps for those two tasks. But the cook must perform tasks in a certain order: fill the kettle, put it on the burner, leave it there until the whistle starts singing, and measure a cup of the boiling water before pouring it into the other ingredients.

Had these recipe instructions been written as a JavaScript script, you'd see a statement looking something like this:

```
mixingBowl = previousIngredients + boilWater(1 cup)
```

To get the boiling water into the bowl, the program must make a side trip to a separate series of steps called `boilWater()`, with the instructions to do so with one cup. There has to be a definition for that separate subroutine, part of which includes carrying the cup of boiling water to the mixing bowl when the water is ready. In JavaScript, such a subroutine is called a *function*.

In the preceding chapter, you were introduced to the concept of the function. It's an important one for JavaScript, so we'll dig a little deeper here. You will see many more examples of the function construction when we start working with JavaScript objects in Chapters 7 and 8, and an in-depth discussion comes in Chapter 12.

The function handoff

As we mentioned earlier, a function is one of those multiple-line statements whose execution is deferred until called. It is largely a framework within which many other statements work. When you define a function, it is best to limit the scope of its operations to something that can be named clearly and succinctly: You assign names to functions just as you do to variables. Because a function usually performs some action (whereas a variable is usually just data — a thing), it is helpful to make a verb part of the function name.

If you have experience in any other programming language, you may recognize that a JavaScript function operates like a subroutine or procedure. In JavaScript, all such routines are called functions, even though other languages distinguish between functions (which produce a value at the end) and procedures (which carry out an action without returning any values). A JavaScript function returns a value if your script requires it; otherwise, the function simply performs whatever action it is designed to carry out and hands control back to the script statement that called it in the first place.

Defining a function

A function definition begins with the keyword `function`, followed by the name you assign to the function and a pair of parentheses. To call the function from elsewhere in the script, you enter the name of the function and parentheses.

Quite often, you need to pass along some information with the call to the function. Just as we saw in the call to the hypothetical `boilWater()`, the function has to know how much to boil. That amount was passed as a *parameter* from the function call to the function. Parameters are listed in the parentheses of both a function call and the function definition. Let's look at a couple examples.

Listing 5-1 shows a complete HTML page for a one-button Web page that presents an alert dialog box when the user clicks on the button.

```
<HTML>
<HEAD>
<SCRIPT LANGUAGE="JavaScript">
function alertUser() {
      alert("Ouch!")
}
</SCRIPT>
</HEAD>

<BODY>
<FORM>
      <INPUT TYPE="button" VALUE="Click Me" onClick="alertUser()">
</FORM>
</BODY>
</HTML>
```

Listing 5-1: A one-button function.

When the user clicks the button, the browser executes whatever script is indicated as the argument to the onClick= attribute of the button. In this case, it is the name of a function defined in the Head portion of the document. Recall that such script segments are loaded into memory when the page loads and stand ready for a call, if necessary. In this case, the function returns no value and receives no value from the function call.

A variation on the same functionality is shown in Listing 5-2.

```
<HTML>
<HEAD>
<SCRIPT LANGUAGE="JavaScript">
function alertUser(alertMsg) {
      alert(alertMsg)
}
</SCRIPT>
</HEAD>

<BODY>
<FORM>
      <INPUT TYPE="button" VALUE="Click Me"
onClick="alertUser('Ouch!')">
</FORM>
</BODY>
</HTML>
```

Listing 5-2: Passing a parameter to a function.

The difference here is that we've generalized the function definition to accept any value as a parameter and display that value in the alert dialog box. In the button definition, the call to the function passes the text to be displayed in the alert dialog box. If there were buttons with different messages on this page, they'd all call the same alertUser(alertMsg) function but pass a different parameter for each button.

Functions calling other functions

A function may contain statements that call other functions. We'll see examples of this in Chapter 15 and elsewhere. By keeping functions small and narrowly focused in their tasks, it will be easier to track down any problems you may have while constructing a script. For instance, if you are designing a form that asks a user to enter a number that must be within a specific range, your data validation function must perform checks to make sure that no non-numeric characters were entered (or the math to be performed on the input value later will fail) and that the number is within the proper range. To accomplish this task, you might create one master validation function that calls up specialized functions that check individually for a numbers-only entry and for the range. As a preview of things to come, Listing 5-3 shows an example of such a three-function construction.

```
// general purpose function to see
// if a suspected numeric input is a number
function isNumber(inputStr) {
    for (var i = 0; i < inputStr.length; i++) {
        var oneChar = inputStr.substring(i, i + 1)
        if (oneChar < "0" || oneChar > "9") {
            alert("Please make sure entries are numbers only.")
            return false
        }
    }
    return true
}

// function to determine if value is
// in an acceptable range for this application
function inRange(inputStr) {
    num = eval(inputStr)
    if (num < 1 || num > 586 && num < 596 || num > 599 && num <
700 || num > 728) {
        alert("Sorry, the number you entered is not part of our
database.  Try another three-digit number.")
        return false
    }
    return true
}

// Master value validator routine
function isValid(inputStr) {
    if (!isNumber(inputStr)) {
        return false
    } else {
        if (!inRange(inputStr)) {
            return false
        }
```

(continued)

```
        }
    return true
}
```

Listing 5-3: Three functions that work together to validate a numeric entry.

The process here starts within another function (not shown) that is the first to grab the content of the field entered by the user. That function calls the `isValid()` function (the bottom of the three), which is the main framework for checking validation. It, in turn, calls the `isNumber()` and `inRange()` functions so each can do its specialized task. They return true or false values, depending on how well the user's entry passes the various tests. Just scan Listing 5-3 for the overall construction. Leave the meaning of the if-then constructions and ! symbols for later (Chapters 10 and 11).

The Braces {}

Experienced C programmers may wonder why I make such a big deal about JavaScript's curly brackets — *braces* are the formal term. To C programmers, they're second nature, but because they're not part of most newcomers' keyboard vocabulary, they may seem a little intimidating at first, especially in the way they appear to stand out in the code samples scattered throughout this book.

Fortunately, there is not as much mystery to braces as you might think. They are used in very specific situations — function definitions, if-then constructions, and repeat loops — merely as a way of letting the browser (and human readers) know which lines of script should be grouped together. Because we've been dealing in detail only with function definitions until now, we'll examine how braces are used there (we'll pick up the rest in Chapter 10).

A schematic for a function definition is as follows:

```
function functionName([parameters]) {
        [statement1]
        [statement2]
}
```

Square brackets ([ ]) as shown there indicate that an item is optional. For instance, not all functions need a parameter value passed to them. But all function definitions have a pair of parentheses after the function's name. The opening brace (at the end of the first line) marks the start of the statements that define the action the function performs; the closing brace (on its own line at the end) marks the end of those statements. In truth, the braces don't have to be exactly where they are shown. For instance, JavaScript would know what to do with the following two arrangements:

```
function functionName([parameters]) {[statement1];[statement2]}

function functionName([parameters])
        {[statement1]
        [statement2]}
```

There is a gap, however, between what is acceptable and what is recommended. The recommended format (shown above) becomes more helpful to you over time, even though it may look silly at first to have some of these braces hanging out by themselves. As your functions become more complex, especially when they include nested if...else or repeat-loop constructions (as shown in Listing 5-3), the balance of braces is critical for the script to run properly. By placing the closing brace at the same indentation level as the opening statement that requires a pair of braces, it is easy to spot where the grouping truly ends. Using the format suggested here makes it easier to know you've entered the proper pairs. In Chapter 12, I'll give you some further tips on defining functions and entering them with the right balance of braces.

Comments

The last item I cover in this chapter is another feature of JavaScript you've already seen in some scripts. *Comments* are pieces of script verbiage that you write for your own benefit and perhaps for the benefit of others who read your scripts. You may already use comments in your HTML documents for the same purpose. In JavaScript, however, comments are handled a little differently.

The comments I'm talking about here aren't the ones that you use to hide JavaScript statements from non-JavaScript-enabled browsers. What I want to focus on here are JavaScript comments. To distinguish a JavaScript comment from an HTML/SGML comment, JavaScript has its own comment symbols that depend on whether the comment is on a single line or extends across multiple lines.

For the single-line comment, start the comment with two slashes (//). They do not have to be at the beginning of a line. If you want to place a comment to the right of a line of executable code, type a space after the last character of executable code, type two slashes, and enter your comment on the same line.

JavaScript has a second comment symbology, useful at times when your comment extends across two or more lines. A comment can begin with a slash-asterisk (/*). No more of the script executes until after the comment closing symbol: asterisk-slash (*/). Listing 5-4 shows examples of both styles of JavaScript comments in four different scenarios.

```
// define a function to change decimal values to hexadecimal

document.writeln(document.lastModified) // display update date

/* define a function that converts the current date
to the number of days before Christmas */

// define a function that converts the current date
// to the number of days before Christmas
```

Listing 5-4: Examples of JavaScript comments.

I personally find the /*-*/ pairing for long comments hard to spot while reading scripts. For multiple-line comments, I prefer writing a series of single-line comments preceded by the double slashes (the last grouping in Listing 5-4). They stand out better while scanning a script and looking for guidance from the author about what's going on in the script.

We've Covered a Lot

For the complete newcomer to programming, this chapter is crammed full of new information and terminology — if not new ways of thinking. If your head is spinning, take a break and give the chapter a second read later. The next chapter is equally intensive, but it is essential to understanding the fundamental operation of JavaScript.

*C*hapter Six

Even if you have been on the sidelines of computer programming, you have probably heard the term *object-oriented programming*, sometimes abbreviated *OOP*. The history of OOP is beyond the scope of this book, but suffice it to say that object-oriented programming is one of the hot trends in production programming today. In particular, the object-oriented version of the C language, called C++, may be gaining more new adherents every day than any other language. Sun's Java language for creating network-centric applets is patterned after C++. JavaScript, although not necessarily a direct descendant of Java, is nonetheless object-oriented.

Object-oriented programming may sound as if it is the most complex of all environments to learn. Oddly enough, the less experience you have programming in traditional programming languages (Basic, Pascal, C), the easier time you may have grasping the inner workings and benefits of object orientation. Too much experience in typical procedural languages can be hard to overcome in rethinking the way you work with data and actions in an object-oriented world.

The good news for all JavaScript newcomers is that JavaScript simplifies what you need to know about object orientation. Some advanced object-oriented concepts don't even surface in JavaScript. Therefore, I'll limit discussions in this chapter to only those elements that apply to JavaScript.

What is an Object?

You may recall from our discussion about variables and values in Chapter 5 that a variable can hold a value. In truth, that variable name is merely a convenience for human code writers to use in referring to a slot in memory where the values are stored. Statements in scripts may yank that value from its memory location, perform a calculation on it, and put the new value back in that same slot. If the value needs more space after the calculation (such as adding characters to an existing string), it is up to the programming language interpreter (inside the browser) to deal invisibly and quickly with moving stuff around memory so values don't interfere with each other.

An object is like a variable in some respects. When your script defines an object, the browser creates a slot for it in memory. But an object is far more complex internally than a single value. The purpose of an object is to represent some "thing." Because in JavaScript we're dealing with items that appear in a browser window, an object may be an input text field, a button, or the whole HTML document. Outside of the pared-down world of a JavaScript browser, an object can also represent abstract entities, such as a calendar program's appointment entry or a paragraph in an object-oriented word processor.

To the user of a program that is built with an object-oriented language or development environment, there is no real way of knowing that the program was constructed in such an environment. Word processing programs for decades have been built with procedural languages. To the user, a new one written in an object-oriented language doesn't necessarily look any different or behave in any other way.

Object orientation has become fashionable in this age of the graphical user interface (GUI) because unlike the old text-only screens, the bitmapped graphic screens of today's

Windows, Macintosh, and X-Windows operating systems encourage developers to replicate real-world objects on-screen. For example, in a painting program, a click on an icon in a tool palette turns the screen pointer into that tool—perhaps to draw a circle or erase some marks. To the programmer, having chunks of code represent those on-screen objects often makes it easier to visualize how a complex program works.

Properties

Any physical object you hold in your hand has a collection of characteristics that define it. A coin, for example, has a shape, diameter, thickness, color, weight, embossed images on each side, and any number of other attributes that distinguish a coin from, say, a feather. Each of those features in an object-oriented world is called a *property*. Each property has a value of some kind attached to it (even if the value is empty or null). For example, the shape value of a coin might be "circle," in this case a text value. All coins have the same set of properties, but the values may vary: The diameter of a U.S. quarter is a larger numeric value than that of a U.S. penny. That all coins have the same set of properties is not a coincidence; in a sense, they are all derived from the pure definition of a coin.

Completely different objects may share the same properties as coins, but that is merely a coincidence. Although both a feather and a coin have a weight property, you'll find that a feather has properties that are completely different from those of a coin (or has properties that are of no significance to a coin). For instance, a feather may also have the ability to be wafted by air currents or the ability to tickle. Certainly a coin could also have those properties, but their values would be so far off the scale as to be absurd, as would a feather's ability to be used as vending machine currency.

As you may have gathered, the properties of any object are the values associated with it. They are similar to the values assigned to a variable. But unlike a variable, which usually has a single value of a single type assigned to it, an object may have any number of properties, each of which can be a different data type. Any object created in a program has all of its properties defined at the same time. Even if your script needs to access the value of only one of those properties, the others are there just the same.

The value of an object's property can always be retrieved in a script. But not all properties can be modified by a script. You saw an example of a read-only property in Chapter 3, when your first script retrieved and then displayed the property of the HTML document that contained the date and time the file was last modified. This date is imposed on the file by the computer's operating system. For the sake of security, JavaScript does not grant you direct writing privileges for any file on the server. Therefore, your script cannot modify the value of the lastModified property of a document. A script can, however, modify the value property of a text field in a document. Later chapters will show you this way of displaying output results to the person viewing a JavaScripted HTML document. After the script gathers information entered in fields and button selections in one part of the document, it performs whatever actions you have designed it to do with that information and displays the results in one of the fields. The act of putting the text into that field sets the property of the text field object responsible for what is displayed (the value property).

Most objects you will be working with in JavaScript are pre-defined by JavaScript. For the most part, they represent the on-screen objects you see in documents. All properties are clearly defined (and detailed for you in Chapters 7 and 8). Part of the job of your scripts will be to manipulate the values of those properties — sometimes just retrieving them, other times changing them.

JavaScript also allows scripters to create their own objects to represent whatever kinds of real or abstract items are necessary to carry out the job of a script. We'll discuss these user-defined objects in Chapter 12.

Method actors

An even more powerful attribute of an object is that it knows how to do things. That is, an object has as part of its constitution the steps it needs to follow to carry out specific tasks. All we as scripters have to know about an object is the names of things it can do and what, if any, parameters need to be sent along with the names. The object does the rest for us.

Each of these tasks is called a *method*. A method comes closest to what in other languages would be a command, in so far as they both make something happen. But the underlying mechanisms of methods and commands are quite different.

Perhaps the easiest way to think about a method is to regard it as a function that is attached to an object. Like a JavaScript function (Chapter 5), a method has a name that we use to call it to action; some lines of code that run when called; and, if so designed, a returned value that is the result of whatever went on inside the function.

The inner workings of the methods automatically built into JavaScript's pre-defined objects are hidden from our view because they work with the complex operation of the browser or the inner, low-level structure of an HTML document, as interpreted by the browser. In Chapter 3, you used one such method that belongs to JavaScript's document object. The line of code was

```
document.write("Last updated on " + document.lastModified + ".")
```

The write() method requires a parameter: the string to write to the document.

Notice that a method call includes a pair of parentheses after the name of the method. This should remind you of the way you call a function. That's because a method and a function are very similar in the way they work in JavaScript.

Methods help define the behavior of an object. If an object's properties define what an object *looks like*, then its methods define what it can *do*. As you begin to learn about JavaScript's built-in objects, you will want to become familiar with the range of methods each one is capable of. The more you know about an object's capabilities, the more you will be able to plan to use its properties and methods in your scripts.

Creating JavaScript Objects

Although JavaScript includes a number of pre-defined objects, that doesn't mean that all of the work is done for you. As a page's designer, you are in complete control over what kinds of objects and how many of them are created for that particular page.

Fortunately, there is little more that you need to do over and above the standard HTML tags and attributes that make those objects appear on the screen. In fact, the mere act of loading a document with an HTML tag for a form or radio button creates that object for the current document (in a more formal OOP environment, this act would be called *instantiating* an object — creating an *instance* of an object). Therefore, simply go about the business of laying out visual elements on the page. When the page loads, your JavaScript-enabled browser automatically creates the objects in memory that your scripts act on.

Event Handlers

One last characteristic of a JavaScript object is called an *event handler*. Events are actions that take place in a document, usually as the result of user activity, such as clicking on a button or selecting text in a field. Some events, such as the act of loading a document into the browser window, are not so obvious.

Almost every JavaScript object in a document receives events of one kind or another. What determines whether the object will do anything in response to the event is the extra attribute(s) you enter into the object's HTML definition. The attribute consists of the event name and the name of the method or other function you want to execute in response to that method. Let's look again at a script we used in Chapter 4 that displays an *Ouch!* alert when a user clicks on a button.

The code for this document is shown in Listing 6-1.

```
<HTML>
<HEAD>
<SCRIPT LANGUAGE="JavaScript">
function alertUser(alertMsg) {
    alert(alertMsg)
}
</SCRIPT>
</HEAD>

<BODY>
<FORM>
<INPUT TYPE="button" VALUE="Click Me"onClick="alertUser('Ouch!')">
</FORM>
</BODY>
</HTML>
```

Listing 6-1: A simple button with an event handler.

In the Form definition is what, for the most part, looks like a standard input item (although the "button" type is a Navigator 2.0 invention). But notice the last attribute, `onClick="alertUser('Ouch!')"`. Button objects, as you'll see in their complete descriptions in Chapter 8, react to mouse clicks. When a user clicks on the button, the browser sends an `onClick` message to the button. In this button's definition, the attribute says that whenever the button receives that message, it should run the `alertUser()` function, passing the text "Ouch!" as a parameter. Like most arguments to HTML attributes, the name of the function goes inside quotes. If further quotes are necessary, as in the case of the text to be passed along with the event handler, those inner quotes can be single quotes. In actuality, JavaScript doesn't distinguish between single or double quotes but does require that each set be of the same type. Therefore, the attribute could have also been written

```
onClick='alertUser("Ouch!")'
```

The argument to the event handler could also be a direct object method, as in

```
onClick="alert('You pressed the button!')".
```

The only requirement for this mechanism to work is that the function or object mentioned in the `onClick=` attribute be previously loaded into the browser's memory. Defining a function in the Head of a document assures that will be the case.

Similar method and event handler names

What may be confusing at times when you look at the description of an object is that similar words may be used to describe an object's method and event handler. A button is a good example. It has both an `onClick` event handler and a `click()` method. What's the difference? Quite a lot, actually.

The distinction is that the `onClick` event handler comes into play when the user causes the action; the `click()` method is called only by a statement in a script. Because a method is an action-making element, this means that the method is a scriptable way of clicking the button for the user — automatically checking a checkbox, for example, based on a selection in a pop-up menu. The method and event handler are triggered by almost opposite processes: an event handler by something that happens to the browser; a method by a script.

Object Definitions

In Chapters 7 and 8, you will see full descriptions of every pre-defined, window-related JavaScript object. These descriptions include each object's properties, methods, and event handlers. Some items are not used as frequently as others (look at the pocket protector rankings for guidance on which ones are most important).

JavaScript supplies a few other kinds of objects that you'll meet later in Chapter 9. These offer some important facilities for dealing with strings, math, and dates.

About the "Dot" Syntax

If the period-encrusted statements you've seen so far in JavaScript remind you of the way Usenet newsgroups are named on the Internet, this is no coincidence. The methodology for organizing the thousands of newsgroups is to group them in a hierarchy that makes it relatively easy to both find a newsgroup and visualize where in the scheme of things the current newsgroup you're reading is located.

Newsgroup organization model

Let's analyze briefly a typical newsgroup address:

> rec.sport.skating.inline

The first entry (at the left-hand edge) defines the basic group, recreation, among all the newsgroups. Other groups, such as comp and alt, have their own sections and do not overlap with what goes on in the rec section. Within the rec section are dozens of subsections, one of which is sport. That distinguishes all the sport-related groups from, say, the automobile or music groups within recreational newsgroups.

Like most broad newsgroup categories, rec.sport has many subcategories, each one devoted to a particular sport. In this case, it is skating. Other sport newsgroups include rec.sport.rugby and rec.sport.snowboarding. Even within the rec.sport.skating category, there is further subdivision to help narrow the subject matter for participants. Therefore, a separate newsgroup just for inline skaters exists, just as a group for roller skating exists (rec.sport.skating.roller). As a narrower definition is needed for a category, a new level is formed by adding a "dot" and a word to differentiate that subgroup from the thousands of newsgroups on the Net. When you ask your newsgroup software to view messages in the rec.sport.skating.inline group, you are giving it a map to follow in the newsgroup hierarchy to go directly to a single newsgroup.

Another benefit of this syntactical method is that names for subcategories can be reused within other categories if necessary. For example, with this naming scheme, it is possible to have two similarly named subcategories in two separate newsgroup classifications, such as rec.radio.scanners and alt.radio.scanners. When you ask to visit one, the hierarchical address, starting with the rec. or alt. classification, will assure that you get to the desired place. Neither collection of messages is automatically connected with the other (although subscribers frequently cross-post to both newsgroups).

For complete newbies to the Net, this dot syntax can be intimidating. Because the system was designed to run on UNIX servers (the UNIX operating system is written in C), the application of a C-like syntax for newsgroup addressing is hardly surprising.

JavaScript dots

The C-ness of JavaScript shows through in the way components of objects are represented in statements. For instance, to retrieve the `lastModified` property of a document, the syntax is

```
document.lastModified
```

Reading that expression to another programmer would sound like "document dot lastModified." What it means is "the lastModified property of the document." The purpose of this syntax is to help the browser pinpoint precisely what your script is looking for. Remember that once a document is loaded, the browser maintains a hidden list of every object defined in the HTML tags. In a standard HTML document (without frames in the window), only one document can be showing at a time; so the document object is clearly the document in the window. From that document, you want the browser to locate a particular property.

Things get a little more complicated when there are numerous objects of a particular type in the document. For instance, let's say you have one form consisting of five input elements. Some of those elements are radio buttons, one is a text field, and another is a checkbox. If you want to know what text is in the field, you have to tell the browser exactly what property you want and from which object. An expression in the JavaScript "dot" syntax gives the browser a complete map to the object.

The map to a form object is a bit tortuous, and we'll go into more depth about it in Chapter 8. Let's take a first look at it now to demonstrate how this dot syntax works.

To specify a particular element of a document's form, you must use the `forms` property of the document object. Because there can easily be multiple forms in a document, part of the dot syntax map must include a pointer to a specific numbered form (numbered according to the order in which they appear in the document). Most object numbering in JavaScript begins with zero, so the reference to `document.forms[0]` means the first form of the current document.

Now the statement must dig deeper within that first form to get the value of a particular named input element. For these elements, the road map can use the object's name. Because in this case we want to extract the value property of a text field named birthdate, the complete reference would be

```
document.forms[0].birthdate.value
```

Notice how the road map helps the browser narrow its scope: from the entire document to just the first form, to just the birthdate field, to just that field's value property. This process is like looking backward through a collapsible telescope: The farther you look down the tube, the narrower the opening gets, until only a tiny hole reveals an extremely narrow view of the other side. Listing 6-2 shows this construction at work.

```
<HTML>
<HEAD>
</HEAD>
<BODY>
<FORM>
    <INPUT TYPE="radio" NAME="sex">Male<BR>
    <INPUT TYPE="radio" NAME="sex">Female<BR>
    Enter birthdate: <INPUT TYPE="text" NAME="birthdate"
SIZE="10">
</FORM>
```

(continued)

```
<SCRIPT LANGUAGE="JavaScript">
document.writeln(document.forms[0].birthdate.value)
</SCRIPT>
</BODY>
</HTML>
```

Listing 6-2: Using the "dot" syntax to narrow down to a property of a single form element.

The first time you load this document, only the form elements appear on the page. After entering a value into the field and clicking the Reload button, the value from the field is displayed on a line of text below the form. This example may seem an extreme (getting the property [value] of an object [birthdate field] of a property [forms[0]] of an object [document]), but this is a common way of getting at object property values in JavaScript. The more you use the object-oriented world of JavaScript, the more you will see that it is truly an efficient system.

I've limited the focus of this object-oriented programming crash course to the parts of that world that have roles in JavaScript. You'll begin putting this knowledge to work in the next chapter, where you meet the first of JavaScript's built-in objects in depth.

$\mathcal{C}$hapter Seven

The purpose of most JavaScript scripts is to make a World Wide Web page interactive, whether or not a program is running on the server to enhance that interactivity. Making a page interactive means tracking user action and responding with some visible change on the page. The avenues for the communication between user and script include familiar on-screen elements, such as fields and buttons.

To assist the scripter in working with these elements, JavaScript implements them as software objects — the same objects described in the preceding chapter. These objects have *properties* that often define the visual appearance of the object. Objects also have *methods* that are the actions or "commands" that an object can carry out. Finally, these objects have *event handlers* that trigger scripts you write in response to action in the document (usually instigated by the user). Understanding the realm of possibilities for each JavaScript object is the key to knowing how far you can go in using JavaScript to convert an idea into a useful Web page.

The Object Hierarchy

In the preceding chapter about object orientation, I only hinted at the concept of *object hierarchy*. In other object-oriented languages, object hierarchy plays a much greater role than it does in JavaScript (there are also related terms, such as classes, inheritance, and instances, which we don't have to worry about in JavaScript). Therefore, it's better to discuss the ideas within context of JavaScript's limited library of built-in objects. This will come in handy later in this chapter when we start looking at JavaScript code that relies on these objects and their relationships to each other. Knowledge of the hierarchy will help you write *references* to objects in your code.

Calling these objects *JavaScript objects* is not entirely accurate, but it is convenient. In a JavaScript-enabled browser, such as Netscape Navigator, it is the browser software that creates these objects — creating areas in the browser's program memory for each object's property values and method instructions. These are really browser objects: we just happen to use the JavaScript language to bring them to life. Netscape refers to these objects as Navigator objects because that's the name of the company's browser. But these objects exist in any JavaScript-enabled browser. For convenience, therefore, I will continue to refer to these objects as JavaScript objects.

Hierarchy as road map

The primary role of the JavaScript object hierarchy for the programmer is as a means of providing scripts with a way to reference a particular object among all objects that a browser window may contain. The hierarchy acts as a road map for the script to use to know precisely which object use needs to address.

Consider for a moment a scene in which you and your friend Tony are in a high school classroom. It's getting hot and stuffy as the afternoon sun pours in through the wall of windows on the west side of the room. You say to Tony, "Would you please open a window?" and motion your head toward a particular window in the room. In programming terms, you've issued a command to an object (whether or not Tony appreciates the comparison). This brief human interaction has many advantages over anything you can do in a programming language. First, by making eye contact with Tony before you speak, he knows that he is the intended recipient of the command. Second, your body language passed along some parameters with that command, pointing ever so subtly to a particular window on a particular wall.

If, instead, you were in the principal's office using the public address system and you broadcasted the same command, "Would you please open a window?" no one would know what you meant. Issuing a command without directing it to an object is a waste of time because every object would think, "That can't be meant for me." To accomplish the same goal as your one-on-one command, the broadcasted command would have to be something like, "Would Tony Jeffries in room 312 please open the middle window on the west wall?"

Let's convert this last command to JavaScript "dot" syntax form. Recall that the reference to an object starts with the most global point of view and narrows down to most specific. From the point of view of the principal's office, the location hierarchy of the target object would be

```
room312.Jeffries.Tony
```

You could also say that Tony's knowledge about how to open a window is one of Tony's methods. The complete reference to Tony and his method then becomes

```
room312.Jeffries.Tony.openWindow()
```

Our job isn't complete yet. The method requires a parameter detailing which window to open. In this case, it's the middle window of the west wall of room 312. Or, from the hierarchical point of view of the principal's office, it becomes

```
room312.westWall.middleWindow
```

This object road map is the parameter for Tony's `openWindow()` method. Therefore, the entire command coming over the PA system would be

```
room312.Jeffries.Tony.openWindow(room312.westWall.middleWindow)
```

If, instead of barking out orders while sitting in the principal's office, you were doing the same via radio from an orbiting space shuttle to all inhabitants of Earth, imagine how laborious your object hierarchy would be. The complete reference to Tony's `openWindow()` method and the window to be opened would be mighty long to distinguish them from the billions of objects within the space shuttle's view.

The point is that the smaller the scope of the object-oriented world you are programming, the more you can assume about the location of objects. For JavaScript, the scope is no wider than the browser's window. In other words, every object that a JavaScript script can work with is within the browser window. A script does not access anything about your computer hardware, operating system, desktop, or any other stuff beyond the browser program.

The JavaScript object road map

Figure 7-1 shows the complete JavaScript object hierarchy. Notice that the window object is the topmost object in the entire scheme. Everything you script in JavaScript is in the browser's window — whether it be the window itself or a form element.

Of all objects shown in Figure 7-1, the ones whose names are in boldface are the ones you will likely work with most of the time. Objects whose names are in italics are treated as properties of the window object: Although they are present for every window object, you reference them only in some circumstances. In this chapter, I'll cover the window, location, and history objects. The document object — without question the most important object in JavaScript — gets its own chapter (Chapter 8).

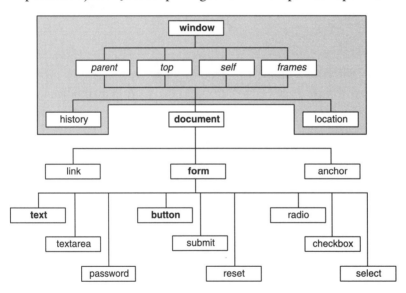

Figure 7-1: The JavaScript object hierarchy.

Study Figure 7-1 for a couple of minutes to establish a mental model for the scriptable elements of a Web page. Once you script these objects a few times, the object hierarchy will become second nature to you — even if you don't necessarily remember every detail (property, method, and event handler) of every object. At least you'll know where to look for information.

A note to experienced object-oriented programmers

Despite the appearance of a class-subclass relationship in the JavaScript hierarchy, many traditional aspects of a true object-oriented environment don't apply to JavaScript. The JavaScript object hierarchy is a containment hierarchy, not an inheritance hierarchy. No object inherits properties or methods of an object higher up the chain. Nor is there any automatic message passing from object to object in any direction. Therefore, you cannot invoke a window's method by sending a message to it by way of a document or form object. Any object reference must be explicit.

JavaScript's predefined objects are generated only when the HTML code containing their definitions loads into the browser. You cannot add to or modify the properties, methods, or event handlers for any of these objects (although you can add a property to a variable that holds an object). At most, you can modify a few built-in property values. In Chapter 12, you'll learn how to create your own objects, but these objects cannot be the type that present new visual elements on the page that go beyond what HTML can portray.

Creating JavaScript Objects

Most of the objects that a browser creates for you are established when an HTML document loads into the browser. The same kind of HTML code you've used in the past to create links, anchors, and input elements tell a Java-enhanced browser to create those objects in memory. They'll be there whether your scripts call them into action or not.

The only differences to the HTML code you'll see for defining those objects are the one or more optional attributes specifically dedicated to JavaScript. By and large, these attributes specify the event you want the user interface element to react to, and what JavaScript should do when the user takes that action. By relying on the document's HTML code to do the object generation for us, we can spend more time figuring out how to do things with those objects or have them do things for us.

Bear in mind that objects are created *in their load order*. This is why you should put most, if not all, deferred function definitions in the document's Head. And if you are creating a multi-frame environment, a script in one frame cannot communicate to another frame's objects until both frames load (and document reloading after a user resizes a window may not occur in frames in the expected order). This trips up a lot of scripters creating multi-frame and multi-window sites (more in Chapter 16).

Some Other Objects

So far, we've been looking only at the objects that are visible inside a browser window. JavaScript includes a few other built-in objects that your scripts will use for performing math calculations, date and time manipulation, text string machinations, and finding out information about the browser that the user has. Our focus in this chapter and the next is on the visible objects. These other scripted objects will be covered fully in Chapter 9.

Object Definitions

In the remaining pages of this chapter and throughout Chapter 8, I present detailed descriptions of each window-related object. Each object definition begins with a summary listing of its properties, methods, and event handlers. This gives you a sense of the scope of everything that a particular object has and does. From there, I go into detailed explanations of when and how to use each term.

Whenever a syntax definition appears, note the few conventions used to designate items, such as optional parameters and placeholders that describe the kind of data that belongs in those slots. All syntax definitions and code examples are in HTML, so expect to see plenty of HTML tags in the familiar angle brackets (<>). Listing 7-1 shows the button object definition.

```
<INPUT
    TYPE="button"
    NAME="objectName"
    VALUE="buttonText"
    [onClick="handlerText"]>
```

Listing 7-1: Sample object definition.

You should recognize most of this as the typical form for an HTML element. The entire definition is surrounded by angle brackets. Some attribute parameters (for NAME=, VALUE=, and onClick=) let you assign names that are meaningful to your script: In this case, how you name the button, what text you want to appear on the button's label, and what you want the button to do when someone clicks it. Those placeholders are in italics to remind you that you need to fill in those blanks with your own names. The placeholders attempt to describe the nature of the parameter. This is nothing more than you'd find in a good HTML guide.

The last attribute of the definition in Listing 7-1 appears inside brackets. This convention means that the attribute is optional. In this case, if you omit the onClick= attribute, then the button is just another HTML button like others you've probably specified before.

In other definitions, especially parameters for methods, the values to be supplied must be a particular data type (string, number, or Boolean). When the value must be of a specific type, the placeholder for that parameter indicates the data type in its name. For example, look at the history object's go() method:

```
go (deltaNumber | "TitleOrURL")
```

In this rare instance of JavaScript accepting either one of two data types (shown on either side of the "|" character), the method can accept either a number or a string (denoted by the quotes) containing a valid Title or URL in the window's history list (described later in this chapter).

Some methods return values after they execute. For example, one window method displays a dialog box that prompts a user to enter text. When the user clicks the OK button, the text entered into the dialog box is passed back as a value that can be assigned to a variable or used directly as a parameter for another method (for a nested configuration, see Chapter 9). Each method listed in the following object definitions indicates what kind of value, if any, is returned by that method.

The last item of note about these definitions is the way we handle property values. Every property has a value that must be one of the valid JavaScript data types. Whether a property returns a Boolean, a string, or a number could be important for your scripting statements. Therefore, we note the kind of value required for each property.

So much for the formalities. Now it's time to dive into JavaScript's objects.

Window Object

Properties	Methods	Event Handlers
frames	alert()	onLoad=
parent	close()	onUnload=
self	confirm()	
top	open()	
status	prompt()	
defaultStatus	setTimeout()	
window	clearTimeout()	

window

Syntax

Creating a window:

```
windowObject = window.open([parameters])
```

Accessing window properties or methods:

```
window. property | method([parameters])
```

```
self. property | method([parameters])
```

```
windowObject. property | method([parameters])
```

About this object

The window object has the unique position of being at the top of the JavaScript object hierarchy. This exalted location gives the object a number of properties and behaviors that are unlike those of any other object.

Chief among its unique characteristics is that because everything takes place in a window, the window object usually can be omitted from all object references. We've seen this behavior in previous chapters when we invoked document methods, such as `document.write()`. The complete reference is `window.document.write()`. But because our activity was taking place in the window that held the document running the script, that window was assumed to be part of the reference. For single-frame windows, this is simple enough concept to grasp.

The situation gets a bit more complex for multiple-frame windows and for times when your scripts create new browser windows. See the following discussions about the `frames`, `parent`, and `top` properties and the `window.open()` method for more details.

Among the list of properties for the window object is one called `self`. This property is synonymous with the window object itself (which is why it shows up in hierarchy diagrams as an object). It may sound confusing that a property of an object is the same object, but it's not that uncommon in object-oriented environments. We discuss the reasons why you may want to use the `self` property as the window's object reference in the `self` property's description that follows.

As indicated in the syntax definition earlier, you don't always have to specifically create a window object in JavaScript code. When you start your browser, it usually opens a window. That is a valid window object, even if it is blank. Therefore, when a user loads your page into the browser, the window object part of that document is automatically created for your script to access as it pleases.

84

window

Why are dialog boxes window methods?

I find it odd that dialog boxes are generated as window methods rather than as methods of a browser or application object. These dialogs don't really belong to any window. In fact, their modality locks out the user from accessing any window. To my way of thinking, these methods (and the ones that create or close windows) belong to an object level one step above the window object in the hierarchy (which would include the properties of the navigator object, described in Chapter 9). I don't lose sleep over this though. If the powers that be insist on making these dialog boxes part of the window object, that's how my code will read.

Your script's control over an existing (already open) window's user interface elements is restricted to the status line at the bottom of the browser window. Only by generating a new window (with the `window.open()` method) can you influence the size, toolbar, or other options of a window.

The window object is also the level at which a script asks the browser to display any of three styles of dialog boxes (a plain alert, an OK/Cancel confirmation dialog box, or a prompt for user text entry).

Although dialog boxes are extremely helpful for cobbling together debugging tools for yourself (Chapter 14), they can be very disruptive to individuals who navigate through Web sites. Because JavaScript's dialog boxes are modal (that is, you cannot do anything on your computer until you dismiss the dialog box), use them sparingly, if at all. Remember that some users may create macros on their computers to visit sites unattended. Should such an automated access of your site encounter a modal dialog box, it would be trapped on your page until a human could intervene.

All dialogs generated by JavaScript identify themselves as being generated by JavaScript. This is primarily a security issue for Netscape (authenticating the source of a dialog box). It should also discourage dialog usage in Web page design. And that's good.

Working with windows in multi-window and multi-frame environments can be tricky business because of loading order behavior and somewhat extended object references. When you're ready to tackle this user interface scheme, be sure to read more details in Chapter 16.

window

Properties

```
status
```

Value: string
Gettable: Yes
Settable: Yes

At the bottom of the browser window is a status bar. Part of that bar includes a text field whose contents normally disclose document loading progress or the URL of a link the mouse points to at any given instant. You can control the temporary content of that text field by assigning a text string to the window object's status property.

You should only adjust the status property in response to events that have a temporary effect, such as a link object's onMouseOver= event handler. When the status property is set in this situation, it overrides any other setting in the status window. If the user then moves the mouse pointer away from the link object that changes the status bar, the bar returns to its default setting (which may be empty on some pages). See Figure 7-2.

Use this window property as a friendlier alternative to displaying the URL of a link as a user rolls the mouse around the page. For example, if you'd rather use the status bar to explain the nature of the destination of a link, put that text into the status bar in response to the onMouseOver= event handler. In multi-frame environments, you can set the window.status property without having to worry about referencing the individual frame.

Netscape Navigator 2.0 Bug: Users may experience less than instantaneous response to status message changes. I have also seen instances in which the status message does not revert to its default setting (usually blank) if there is only one link with a status message change in the document. For Navigator 2.0, do not display mission-critical messages in the status bar.

Example:

```
<HTML>
<HEAD>
<TITLE>window.status Property</TITLE>
</HEAD>
<BODY>
<A HREF="http://home.netscape.com" onMouseOver="window.status='Go
```

window.status

```
to your browser Home page.'; return true">Home</A><P>
<A HREF="http://home.netscape.com"
onMouseOver="window.status='Visit Netscape Home page.'; return
true">Netscape</A>
</BODY>
</HTML>
```

Listing 7-2: Two links featuring custom status bar messages.

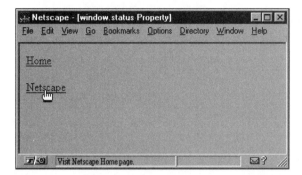

Figure 7-2: The status bar can be set to a custom message when the pointer rolls over a link.

In Listing 7-2, the status property is set in a handler embedded in the `onMouseOver=` attribute of two HTML link tags. Notice that the handler requires a `return true` statement (or any expression that evaluates to `return true`) as the last statement of the handler. This is required or the status message will not display.

If you want to write a generalizable function that handles all window status changes, you can do so, but word the `onMouseOver=` attribute carefully so that JavaScript receives a `return true` statement in the end. Listing 7-3 shows such an alternative.

```
<HTML>
<HEAD>
<TITLE>window.status Property</TITLE>
<SCRIPT LANGUAGE="JavaScript">
function showStatus(msg) {
    window.status = msg
    return true
}
</SCRIPT>
</HEAD>
<BODY>
```

(continued)

87

window.status

```
<A HREF="http://home.netscape.com" onMouseOver="return
showStatus('Go to your browser Home page.')">Home</A><P>
<A HREF="http://home.netscape.com" onMouseOver="return
showStatus('Visit Netscape Home page.')">Netscape</A>
</BODY>
</HTML>
```

Listing 7-3: Writing a generalizable function for handling status message changes.

Notice how the event handler returns the results of the `showStatus()` method to JavaScript. If your status bar message fails to return to its default setting, don't worry. There is instability in both the `status` and `defaultStatus` properties in Navigator 2.0.

One final example of setting the status bar (shown as follows) also demonstrates how to create a scrolling banner in the status bar:

```
<HTML>
<HEAD>
<TITLE>Message Scroller</TITLE>
<SCRIPT LANGUAGE="JavaScript">
<!--
var msg = "Welcome to my world..."
var delay =150
var timerId
function scrollMsg() {
    window.status = msg
    // shift first character of msg to end of msg
    msg = msg.substring (1, msg.length) + msg.substring (0, 1)
    // recursive call to this function
    timerId = setTimeout("scrollMsg()", delay)
}
// -->
</SCRIPT>
</HEAD>
<BODY onLoad="scrollMsg()">
</BODY>
</HTML>
```

window.status

Because the status bar is being set by a stand-alone function (rather than an onMouseOver= event handler, you are not required to append a `return true` statement to set the status property. The `scrollMsg()` function employs more advanced JavaScript concepts, such as the `window.setTimeout()` method (covered later in this chapter) and string methods (covered in Chapter 9). To speed up the pace at which the words scroll across the status bar, reduce the value of `delay`.

Related Items: `window.defaultStatus` property; `onMouseOver=` event handler; `link` object.

`defaultStatus`

Value: string
Gettable: Yes
Settable: Yes

Once a document is loaded into a window or frame, the status bar's message field can display a string that will be visible any time the mouse pointer is not atop an object that takes precedence over the status bar (such as a link or an image map). The `window.defaultStatus` property is normally an empty string, but you can set this property at any time in response to an event handler. Any setting of this property will be temporarily overridden when a user moves the mouse pointer atop a link object (see `window.status` property for information about customizing this temporary status bar message).

Probably the most common time to set the `window.defaultStatus` property is when a document loads into a window. A JavaScript-enhanced browser responds to an `onLoad` event every time a document loads. An `onLoad=` event handler to set the window's default status message should go into the `<BODY>` tag for the document as supplementary attributes (see the window object's `onLoad=` and `onUnload=` event handler descriptions that follow).

Netscape Navigator 2.0 Bug: Setting the `window.defaultStatus` property for an `onLoad=` event handler won't work in most versions of the browser because the browser overwrites the status bar after the `onLoad=` event handler runs. On some browser versions, you can set the property from other event handlers; but even so, the property may not stick. Don't set the default status message to contain mission-critical information (see Listing 7-4).

Example:

```
<HTML>
<HEAD>
<TITLE>window.defaultStatus property</TITLE>
</HEAD>
<BODY onLoad="window.defaultStatus='Welcome to my Web site.'">
<A HREF="http://home.netscape.com" onMouseOver="window.status='Go
to your browser Home page.'; return true">Home</A><P>
<A HREF="http://home.netscape.com"
onMouseOver="window.status='Visit Netscape Home page.'; return
true">Netscape</A>
</BODY>
</HTML>
```

Listing 7-4: Setting the default status message of a window. This listing will not work properly on all versions of Navigator 2.0 due to a bug in the browser.

Unless you plan to change the default status bar text as a user spends time on your Web page, the best place to set the property is when the document loads, as shown in the onLoad= attribute of the <BODY> tag in Listing 7-4.

Related Items: window.onLoad= event handler; window.status property.

---

self

Value: window object
Gettable: Yes
Settable: No

Just as the window object reference is optional, so too is the self property when the object reference points to the same window as the one containing the reference. In what may seem to be an unusual construction, the self property represents the same object as the window. For instance, to obtain the title of the document in a single-frame window, you could use any of the following three constructions:

```
window.document.title
```

```
self.document.title
```

```
document.title
```

window.self

Although self is a property of a window, you should not combine the references within a single-frame window script (for example, don't begin a reference with window.self). Specifying the self property, although optional for single-frame windows, can help in making an object reference crystal clear to someone reading your code (and to you, for that matter). Where you'll need to pay attention to this property is in multiple-frame windows.

When an HTML document defines a frameset for a window, the attributes include references to other HTML documents that will appear in the frames of the windows. The content of the HTML document that specifies the frames (the frame-setting document, I call it) isn't visible to the user, but the browser software keeps that document's information in memory as long as the component frames are visible in the window. Therefore, each frame of a multi-frame window has its own document loaded into it. The user interacts with elements in those documents. Any script that runs in response to a user's action in one of those frames may need to get or set properties or trigger methods for objects in its own document. The trick for the script is to know which object — among ones currently in the browser's memory — is the one being addressed.

To meet that challenge, you can address the object with the proper window property as part of the reference. The self reference indicates that any object tacked onto that address (for example, self.document) will be in the same document (frame) as the statement making the call. References to the master framesetting document and to documents open in other frames can also be referenced via other window properties (see frames, parent, and top properties below).

JavaScript is pretty smart about references to a statement's own window. Therefore, you can generally omit the self part of a reference to a same-window document element. But when a document is intended to be displayed in a multi-frame window, it will be much easier on anyone who reads or debugs your code to track who is doing what to whom by using complete references (including the self prefix) to an object. My personal preference in documents designed to appear in multi-frame windows is to use the entire reference to any object (such as self.document.title).

You are free to retrieve the self property of any window. The value that comes back is an entire window object — a copy of all data that makes up the window (including properties and methods). There are times when a window object is of value to a script (such as when a script creates a new window and must modify the new window's content), but extracting the self property is redundant because you can reference the self object directly anytime you need it (see Listing 7-5).

Example:

```
<HTML>
<HEAD>
<TITLE>self Property</TITLE>
<SCRIPT LANGUAGE="JavaScript">
function showStatus(msg) {
    self.status = msg
    return true
}
</SCRIPT>
</HEAD>
<BODY onLoad="self.defaultStatus='Welcome to my Web site.'">
<A HREF="http://home.netscape.com" onMouseOver="self.status='Go to
your browser Home page.'; return true">Home</A><P>
<A HREF="http://home.netscape.com" onMouseOver="return
showStatus('Visit Netscape Home page.')">Netscape</A>
</BODY>
</HTML>
```

Listing 7-5: Adding the self property to a window property's reference.

In Listing 7-5, we use the same operations as in Listing 7-4, but here we insert the `self` property into all window object references. The application of this added reference is entirely optional but recommended if this HTML document is to appear in one frame of a multi-frame window — especially if other JavaScript code in this document refers to documents in other frames. The `self` property helps anyone reading the code know precisely which frame was being addressed.

Related Items: `window.frames` property; `window.parent` property; `window.top` property; scripting with frames (Chapter 16).

parent

Value: window object
Gettable: Yes
Settable: No

The `parent` property (and the `top` property that follows) comes into play primarily when a document is to be displayed as part of a multi-frame window. HTML documents that users see in the frames of a multi-frame browser window are distinct from the document that specifies the frameset for the entire window. That document, while still in the browser's memory (and appearing as the URL in the location field of the browser), is not otherwise visible to the user (except in source view).

If scripts in your visible documents need to reference objects or properties of the frameset window, you can reference those frameset window items with the `parent` property (do not, however, expand the reference by preceding it with the window object, as in `window.parent.propertyName`). In a way, the `parent` property seems to violate the object hierarchy because, from a single frame's document, the property points to a level seemingly higher in precedence. If you didn't specify the `parent` property or instead specified the `self` property from one of these framed documents, the object reference would be to the frame only rather than to the outermost framesetting window object.

A nontraditional, but perfectly legal, way to use the `parent` object is to store temporary script data in text fields. The elements won't be visible to the user because the parent never displays itself while it builds its children frames. Thus, you can set up a holding area for an array of data (see Chapter 9) to be used as a database for recall by another document that appears in one of the visible frames.

A child window can also call a function defined in the parent window. The reference would be

```
parent.functionName([parameters])
```

At first glance, it may seem as though the parent and top properties point to the same framesetting window object. In an environment consisting of one frameset window and its immediate children, that's true. But if one of the children windows was, itself, another framesetting window, then you wind up with three generations. From the point of view of the "youngest" child (for example, a window defined by the second frameset), the `parent` property points to its immediate parent, whereas the top property points to the very first framesetting window in this chain.

On the other hand, a new window created via the `window.open()` method has no connection to the original window. The new window's `top` and `parent` point to that new window.

Example:

```
<HTML>
<HEAD>
<TITLE>parent Property</TITLE>
</HEAD>
```

(continued)

93

window.parent

```
<FRAMESET ROWS="50%,50%">
    <FRAME NAME="Child1" SRC="1st07-07.htm">
    <FRAME NAME="Child2" SRC="1st07-07.htm">
</FRAMESET>
</HTML>
```

Listing 7-6: Framesetting document for document in Listing 7-7.

```
<HTML>
<HEAD>
<TITLE>Window Revealer</TITLE>
<SCRIPT LANGUAGE="JavaScript">
function gatherWindowData() {
    var msg = ""
    msg = msg + "window object: " + window + "\n"
    msg = msg + "self property: " + self + "\n"
    msg = msg + "self.document.title: " + self.document.title +
"\n\n"
    msg = msg + "parent property: " + parent + "\n"
    msg = msg + "parent.document.title: " + parent.document.title
+ "\n"
    msg = msg + "top property: " + top + "\n"
    alert(msg)
}
</SCRIPT>
</HEAD>
<BODY>
<FORM>
<INPUT TYPE="button" NAME="collector" VALUE="View properties of
this window frame..." onClick="gatherWindowData()">
</FORM>
</BODY>
</HTML>
```

Listing 7-7: HTML document for each frame, revealing various window properties.

To demonstrate how various window object properties refer to window levels in a multi-frame environment, use your browser to load the Listing 7-6 document. It, in turn, sets each of two equal-size frames to the same document: Listing 7-7. A button in each of those frames gathers and displays (in an alert) the values of several window properties plus the document.title properties of two different window references.

window.parent

In the alert dialog boxes (Figure 7-3), the references to the `window` and `self` objects return the window object by the name assigned to the frame in the frameset definition (Child1 for the top frame, Child2 for the bottom). In other words, from the point of view of each frame, the window object is only that frame. Any references to `window.document.x` refer only to the document loaded into that window frame.

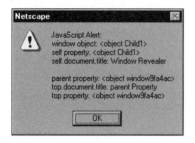

Figure 7-3: Sample alert dialog boxes that appear from clicking each button from Listing 7-7. The left dialog box appears after clicking the top frame's button; the right dialog box appears after clicking the bottom frame's button.

To see the more global view of the browser environment, the references must zoom out to include the `parent` or `top` properties, as shown in the bottom part of the alert dialogs. For the parent (and top) window, the object value is an ID number that the browser uses internally. As scripters, we never have to worry about the specific values of such an object because the references we use (`parent.x`) take care of the job for us.

Related Items: `window.frames` property; `window.self` property; `window.top` property; scripting with frames (Chapter 16).

top

Value: window object
Gettable: Yes
Settable: No

The window object's `top` property refers to the topmost window in the JavaScript hierarchy. For a single-frame window, the reference is to the same object as the window itself (including the `self` and `parent` property), so do not include the window object as part of the reference. In a multi-frame window, the top window is the one that defines the first frameset (in case there are nested framesets). Users don't ever really see the top window in a multi-frame environment, but the browser stores it as an object in its memory. That's because the top window has the road map to other frames (if one frame should need to reference an object in a different frame) and its children frames can call upon it. Such a reference would look like

```
top.functionName([parameters])
```

For more about the distinction between the `top` and `parent` properties, see the preceding discussion about the `parent` property. See also the example for the `parent` property for listings that demonstrate the values of the `top` property.

Related Items: `window.frames` property; `window.self` property; `window.parent` property; scripting with frames (Chapter 16).

frames	

Value: window object
Gettable: Yes
Settable: No

In a multi-frame window, the top or parent window contains any number of separate frames, each of which acts like a full-fledged window object. Although only the top or parent window's properties for the status bar are relevant, the `frames` property (note the plural use of the word as a property name) plays a role when a statement must reference an object located in a different frame. For example, if a button in one frame is scripted to display a document in another frame, the button's event handler must be able to tell JavaScript precisely where to display the new HTML document. The `frames` property assists in that task.

To use the `frames` property effectively, it should be part of a reference that begins with the `parent` or `top` property. This lets JavaScript make the proper journey through the hierarchy of all currently loaded objects to reach the desired object.

To find out how many frames are currently active in a window, use this expression:

```
parent.frames.length
```

This returns a number indicating how many frames are defined for the browser, regardless of their content or whether a document is loaded in the window. This value does not, however, include the invisible window objects containing the frameset specifications. If you fail to specify the `parent` or `top` property in this reference (`window.frames.length` instead of `parent.frames.length`), the number of frames is counted from the point of view of the object making that reference. Often

window.frames[i]

each frame is a single child frame with no child frames of its own, and it properly reports that it has zero frames.

The browser stores information about all visible frames in a numbered (indexed) array, with the first frame (as defined in the framesetting document) as number 0:

```
parent.frames[0]
```

Therefore, if the window shows three frames (whose indexes would be frames[0], frames[1], and frames[2], respectively), the reference for retrieving the title property of the document in the second frame would be

```
parent.frames[1].document.title
```

This reference is a road map that starts at the parent window and extends to the second frame's document and its title property. Other than the number of frames defined in a parent window and each frame's name (top.frames[i].name), no other values from the frame definitions are available from the frame object directly via scripting.

Each frame also has a name attached to it. If you specify a name in the <FRAME> tag of your <FRAMESET> document, that name is available to the JavaScript object. A script can extract a frame's name by referencing a subproperty of the frames property. For example, to extract the name of the second frame in a window, the reference would be

```
parent.frames[1].name
```

You can use a frame's name as an alternative to the indexed reference. For example, in Listing 7-7, two frames are assigned with distinctive names. To access the title of a document in the "Child2" frame, the complete object reference would be

```
parent.Child2.document.title
```

with the frame name (case-sensitive) substituting for the frames[1] array reference. Or, in keeping with JavaScript flexibility, you can use the object name in the array index position:

```
parent.frames["Child2"].document.title
```

Use the form that is most readable to you.

Example:

```
<HTML>
<HEAD>
<TITLE>window.frames property</TITLE>
```

(continued)

```
</HEAD>
<FRAMESET ROWS="50%,50%">
    <FRAME NAME="Child1" SRC="lst07-09.htm">
    <FRAME NAME="Child2" SRC="lst07-09.htm">
</FRAMESET>
</HTML>
```

Listing 7-8: Framesetting document for document in Listing 7-9.

```
<HTML>
<HEAD>
<TITLE>Window Revealer II</TITLE>
<SCRIPT LANGUAGE="JavaScript">
function gatherWindowData() {
    var msg = ""
    msg = msg + "window.frames.length: " + window.frames.length +
"\n"
    msg = msg + "parent.frames.length: " + parent.frames.length +
"\n\n"
    msg = msg + "window.frames: " + window.frames + "\n"
    msg = msg + "parent.frames: " + parent.frames + "\n"
    msg = msg + "parent.frames[0].name: " + parent.frames[0].name
+ "\n"
    alert(msg)
}
</SCRIPT>
</HEAD>
<BODY>
<FORM>
<INPUT TYPE="button" NAME="collector" VALUE="View window
properties for this frame..." onClick="gatherWindowData()">
</FORM>
</BODY>
</HTML>
```

Listing 7-9: HTML document for each frame, showing various window properties.

Listings 7-8 and 7-9 demonstrate how JavaScript treats values of frame references from objects inside a frame. Figure 7-4 shows the results of clicking on both buttons generated after loading the HTML document Listing 7-9. The two buttons are in the same document loaded into the two frames of the window. All statements are located in a script in the framed documents.

window.frames[i]

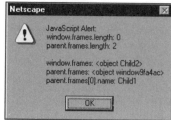

Figure 7-4: The alert dialog boxes that result from clicking on the button in the top frame (left) and the bottom frame (right) of Listing 7-9.

A call to determine the number (length) of frames returns 0 when the current frame is referenced; but add the `parent` property to the reference, and the scope zooms out to take into account all frames generated by the top window's document. The same concern for point of view affects the window objects returned by the frames object. From within a frame, the only frame JavaScript sees is its own frame object (notice that the object name is different for each frame's button that you click). But the parent's frames property points to the topmost frame in the hierarchy — the one that establishes the frameset (and has an otherwise hidden ID number for a name).

The last statement in the example shows how to use the array syntax (brackets) to refer to a specific frame. All array indexes start with 0 for the first entry. In our example, because both buttons ask for the name of the first frame (`parent.frames[0]`), the response is "Child1" for both buttons. This is an example of how one frame's objects can refer to another's without ambiguity.

Related Items: `window.parent` property; `window.top` property; scripting with frames (Chapter 16).

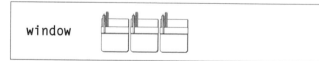

```
window
```

Value: window object
Gettable: Yes
Settable: No

Listing the `window` property as a separate property may be more confusing than helpful. It is the same object as the window object. There is no reason to use a reference that begins with `window.window`. Although the window object is assumed for many references, you can use the `window` as part of a reference, especially if you have defined names for form elements or objects that may conflict with other window properties or methods. This prevents JavaScript from confusing references with each other.

Methods

```
alert(message)
```

Returns: (nothing)

An alert dialog is a modal window that presents a message to the user with a single OK button to dismiss the dialog box. As long as the alert dialog box is showing, no other application or window can be made active. The user must dismiss the dialog box before proceeding with any more work in the browser or on the computer.

The single parameter to the `alert()` method can be a value of any data type, including some unusual data types whose values you don't normally work with in JavaScript (such as complete objects — see Listing 7-9 and Figure 7-4). This makes the alert dialog a handy tool for debugging JavaScript scripts. Anytime you want to monitor the value of an expression, use that expression as the parameter to a temporary `alert()` method. The script proceeds to that point and then stops to show you the value. (See Chapter 14 for more tips on debugging scripts.)

Because the `alert()` method is of a global nature (that is, no particular frame in a multi-frame environment derives any benefit from laying claim to the alert), it is common to omit all window object references from the statement that calls the method. Restrict the use of alert dialog boxes in your HTML documents and site designs. The modality of the windows is disruptive to the flow of a user's navigation around your pages. Communicate with users via forms or by writing to separate document window frames.

Example:

```
<HTML>
<HEAD>
<TITLE>window.alert() Method</TITLE>
</HEAD>
<BODY>
<SCRIPT LANGUAGE="JavaScript">
alert("This document was last saved on " + document.lastModified +
".")
</SCRIPT>
</BODY>
</HTML>
```

Listing 7-10: Displaying an alert dialog box.

window.alert()

The parameter for the example in Listing 7-10 is a concatenated string. It joins together two fixed strings and the value of the current document's `lastModified` property. Loading this document causes the alert dialog box to appear, as shown in Figure 7-5. The `JavaScript Alert:` line cannot be deleted from the dialog box.

Figure 7-5: Results of the alert() method in Listing 7-10 (Windows 95 format).

Related Items: `window.confirm(); window.prompt()`.

`confirm(message)`

Returns: true or false

A confirm dialog box presents a message in a modal dialog box along with OK and Cancel buttons. Such a dialog box can be used to ask a question of the user, usually prior to a script performing actions that will not be undoable. Querying a user about proceeding with typical Web navigation in response to user interaction on a form element is generally a disruptive waste of the user's time and attention. It is possible, however, that you will want this kind of interaction with the user if your script controls Java applets — prior to loading an applet that will take considerable time on a slow Internet connection. Querying a user prior to submitting form data or sending an e-mail message may also be prudent if you want to give the user a chance to reconsider an accidental click of a button.

Because this dialog box returns a Boolean value (OK = `true`; Cancel = `false`), you can use this method as a comparison operation or as an assignment expression. In a comparison operation, you nest the method in any other statement where a Boolean value is required. For example

```
if (confirm("Are you sure?")) {
    alert("OK")
} else {
    alert("Not OK")
}
```

1 0 1

Here, the returned value of the confirm dialog provides the desired Boolean value type for the if ... else construction (Chapter 11).

This method can also appear on the right side of an assignment expression, as in

```
var adult = confirm("You certify that you are over 18 years old?)
if (adult) {
    [statements for adults]
} else {
    [statements for children]
}
```

You cannot specify other alert icons or labels for the two buttons in JavaScript confirm dialog windows.

Example:

```
<HTML>
<HEAD>
<TITLE>window.confirm() Method</TITLE>
<SCRIPT LANGUAGE="JavaScript">
function clearTable() {
    if (confirm("Are you sure you want to empty the table?")) {
        alert("Emptying the table...") // for demo purposes
        //statements that actually empty the fields
    }
}
</SCRIPT>
</HEAD>
<BODY>
<FORM>
<!-- other statements that display and populate a large table -->
<INPUT TYPE="button" NAME="clear" VALUE="Reset Table"
onClick="clearTable()">
</FORM>
</BODY>
</HTML>
```

Listing 7-11: Outline for a document with a large table and a button to reset the values.

The example in Listing 7-11 shows the user interface part of how a *confirm* dialog box might be used to query a user before clearing a table full of user-entered data. The JavaScript Confirm: line cannot be removed from the dialog box.

window.confirm()

Figure 7-6: A JavaScript confirm dialog box (Windows 95 format).

Related Items: `window.alert()`; `window.prompt()`; `document.submit` object.

`prompt(message, defaultReply)`

Returns: String of text entered by user or null.

The third kind of dialog box that JavaScript can display includes a message from the script author, a field for user entry, and two buttons (OK and Cancel). The scriptwriter can supply a prewritten answer so that a user confronted with a prompt dialog box can click OK button (or press Enter) to accept that answer without further typing.

It is important to supply both parameters to the `window.prompt()` method. Even if you don't want to supply a default answer, enter an empty string as the second parameter:

```
prompt("What is your postal code?","")
```

If you omit the second parameter, JavaScript inserts the string <undefined> into the dialog box's field. This will be disconcerting to most Web page readers.

The value returned by this method is a string in the dialog box's field when the user clicks the OK button. If you are asking the user to enter a number, remember that the value returned by this method is a string. You may need to perform data-type conversion with the `parseInt()` or `parseFloat()` functions (see Chapter 9) to use the returned values in math calculations.

When the user clicks the prompt dialog box's OK button without entering any text into a blank field, the returned value is an empty string (""). Clicking the Cancel button, however, makes the method return a null value. Therefore, it is incumbent upon the scripter to test for the type of returned value to make sure that the user entered some data that can be processed later in the script, as in

```
var entry = prompt("Enter a number between 1 and 10:","")
if (entry != null) {
    [statements to execute with the value]
}
```

This script excerpt assigns the results of the prompt dialog box to a variable and executes the nested statements if the returned value of the dialog box is not null (for example, the user clicked the OK button). The rest of the statements would then have to include data validation to make sure that the entry was a number within the desired range (see Chapter 15).

It may be tempting to use the prompt dialog box as a handy user input device. But, like the other JavaScript dialog boxes, the modality of the prompt dialog box is disruptive to the user's flow through a document and can also trap automated macros that some users employ to capture Web sites. Fields in forms are better user interface elements for attracting user text entry. Perhaps the safest way to use a prompt dialog box is to have it appear when a user clicks on a button element on a page — and then only if the information you require of the user can be filled in a single prompt dialog box. Presenting a sequence of prompt dialog boxes is downright annoying to users.

Example:

```
<HTML>
<HEAD>
<TITLE>window.prompt() Method</TITLE>
<SCRIPT LANGUAGE="JavaScript">
function populateTable() {
    var howMany = prompt("Fill in table for how many
factors?","")
    if (howMany != null && howMany != "") {
        alert("Filling the table for " + howMany) // for demo
        //statements that validate the entry and
        //actually populate the fields of the table
    }
}
</SCRIPT>
</HEAD>
<BODY>
<FORM>
<!-- other statements that display and populate a large table -->
<INPUT TYPE="button" NAME="fill" VALUE="Fill Table..."
onClick="populateTable()">
</FORM>
</BODY>
</HTML>
```

Listing 7-12: Outline for a document with a large table and a button to populate the values based on a factor entered by the user in a prompt dialog box.

window.prompt()

The function that receives values from the prompt dialog box in Listing 7-12 (see the dialog box in Figure 7-7) does some data entry validation (but certainly not enough for a commercial site). It checks first to make sure that the returned value is neither null (Cancel) nor an empty string (the user clicked OK without entering any values). See Chapter 15 for more about data entry validation.

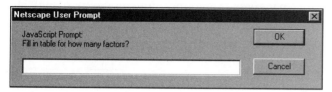

Figure 7-7: The prompt dialog box displayed from Listing 7-12 (Windows 95 version).

Notice one important user interface element in Listing 7-12. Because clicking the button leads to a dialog box requiring more information from the user, the button's label ends in an ellipsis (or, rather, three periods acting as an ellipsis character). This is common courtesy to let users know that a user interface element leads to a dialog box of some sort. As occurs in similar situations in Windows 95 and Macintosh programs, the user should be able to cancel out of that dialog box and return to the same screen state that existed before the button was clicked.

Related Items: `window.alert();` `window.confirm()`.

```
open("URL", "windowName" [, "windowFeatures"])
```

Returns: A window object representing the newly created window; null if method fails.

With the `window.open()` method, a script provides a Web site designer with an immense range of options for the way a Web browser window looks on the user's computer screen. Unlike the default window style that the user has running in the browser (determined in large part by the user's settings in the browser's Options menu), a new window specified by a script can truly customize the set of window elements — this is, perhaps, a preview of the day when Web pages dictate the entire user interface for every document to which a user navigates on the Web. Because the interface elements of a new window are easier to envision, I'll cover those aspects of the `window.open()` method parameters first.

The optional *windowFeatures* parameter is *one string*, consisting of a comma-separated list of assignment expressions (behaving something like HTML tag attributes). If you omit this third parameter, JavaScript creates the same type of new window you'd get from the New Web Browser menu choice in the File menu. But you can control which window elements appear in the new window with the third parameter. If you specify any third parameter value (including an empty string), all features are turned off unless the parameters specify the features to be switched on. Table 7-1 lists the attributes you can control for a newly created window.

Table 7-1
`window.open()` **Method Attributes Controllable via Script**

Attribute	Value	Description
toolbar	Boolean	"Back", "Forward", and other buttons in the row
location	Boolean	Field displaying the current URL
directories	Boolean	"What's New" and other buttons in the row
status	Boolean	Status bar at bottom of window
menubar*	Boolean	Menu bar at top of window
scrollbars	Boolean	Displays scrollbars if document is larger than window
resizable	Boolean	Interface elements allowing resizing by dragging
copyhistory	Boolean	Duplicates Go menu history for new window
width	pixelCount	Window outer width in pixels
height	pixelCount	Window outer height in pixels

*Not on Macintosh because the menu bar is not in the browser window.

Boolean values for true can be either `yes`, `1`, or the feature name by itself; for false, use a value of `no` or `0`. If you omit any Boolean attributes, they are rendered as false. Therefore, if you want to create a new window that shows only the toolbar and status bar and is resizable, the method looks like this:

```
window.open("newURL","New Window", "toolbar,status,resizable")
```

A new window that does not specify the height and width is set to the default size of the browser window that the browser creates from a File menu's New Web Browser command. In other words, a new window does not automatically inherit the size of the window making the `window.open()` method call. Any new window created via a script is positioned at the top left corner of the screen, just as a new Web browser window would be.

The middle parameter is the name for the new window. Don't confuse this with the document's title, which would normally be set by whatever HTML text determines the content of the window.

106

window.open()

A script generally populates a window with one of two kinds of information:

- An existing HTML document whose URL is known beforehand; or

- An HTML page created on the fly

To create a new window that displays an existing HTML document, supply the full URL as the first parameter of the `window.open()` method. If your page is having difficulty loading a URL into a new page (except as noted in the sidebar), try specifying the complete URL of the target document. That means that if the URL is to a document stored in the same server directory as the document whose script creates the new window, the script can either hardwire the URL or algorithmically determine the base reference using other JavaScript objects and properties (see the `document.location` property, Chapter 8).

Leaving the first parameter as an empty string forces the window to open with a blank document, ready to have HTML written to it by your script. Assemble your HTML content as one long string value and then use the `document.write()` method to post that content to the new window. If you plan to append no further writing to the page, also include a `document.close()` method at the end to tell the browser that you are finished with the layout (so that the `Layout:Complete` or `Document:Done` message appears in the status bar if your new window has one).

A call to the `window.open()` method returns a value of the new window's object if the window opens successfully. This value is of vital importance if your script needs to address elements of that new window (such as writing to its document). The minute a script creates a new window, the default window object to which the script normally points is still the one containing the document that holds that script — the new window isn't, even though it may be on top. Therefore, to further manipulate items within the new window you need a reference to that new window object. Once the new window is open, however, no parent-child relationship exists between the windows.

To handle this properly, you should always assign the result of a `window.open()` method to a variable. Test the variable to make sure that it is not a null value — the window may have failed to open because of low memory, for instance. If all is okay, then you can use that variable as the beginning of a reference to any property or object within that new window. For example

```
newWindow = window.open("","")
if (newWindow != null) {
    newWindow.document.write("<HTML><HEAD><TITLE>Hi!</TITLE></
HEAD>")
}
```

window.open()

A Navigator 2.0 bug workaround

Unfortunately, loading a URL into a new window, as specified here, works only on the Windows version of the browser. One workaround requires a second call to a function that invokes the `window.open()` method. Additionally, the second parameter must be an empty string if you add any third-parameter settings. Here is a sample listing you can try:

```
<HTML>
<HEAD>
<TITLE>New Window</TITLE>
<SCRIPT LANGUAGE="JavaScript">
// workaround for window.open() bug on X and Mac platforms
function makeNewWindow() {
  var newWindow =
window.open("http://www.dannyg.com","","status,height=200,width=300")
  newWindow =
window.open("http://www.dannyg.com","","status,height=200,width=300")
}
</SCRIPT>
</HEAD>
<BODY>
<FORM>
<INPUT TYPE="button" NAME="newOne" VALUE="Create New Window"
onClick="makeN ewWindow()">
</FORM>
</BODY>
</HTML>
```

This workaround can also be used without penalty in Windows versions of Navigator 2.0, but be ready to remove it when the bugs are fixed in the next release.

If you initialize the new window's variable as a global variable (see Chapter 9), then any value that the variable receives (even if it gets the value while inside a function) will remain as long as the original document is loaded in the first window. You will be able to come back to that value in another script handler (perhaps some button that closes the subwindow) by making the proper reference to the new window.

In Listing 7-13, we install a button that generates a new window of a specific size and with only the status bar turned on. To build the string that is eventually written to the

window.open()

Example:

```
<HTML>
<HEAD>
<TITLE>New Window</TITLE>
<SCRIPT LANGUAGE="JavaScript">
function makeNewWindow() {
    var newWindow =
    window.open("","","status,height=200,width=300")
    if (newWindow != null) {
        // assemble content for new window
        var newContent = "<HTML><HEAD><TITLE>One Sub Window</
TITLE></HEAD>"
        newContent += "<BODY><H1>This window is brand new.</H1>"
        newContent += "</BODY></HTML>"
        // write HTML to new window document
        newWindow.document.write(newContent)
        newWindow.document.close() // close layout stream
    }
}
</SCRIPT>
</HEAD>
<BODY>
<FORM>
<INPUT TYPE="button" NAME="newOne" VALUE="Create New Window"
 onClick="makeNewWindow()">
</FORM>
</BODY>
</HTML>
```

Listing 7-13: Creating a new window and populating it with scripted HTML content.

document, we use the += operator, which appends the string on the right side of the operator to the string stored in the variable on the left side. In this example, the new window is handed a <H1>-level line of text to display.

Related Items: window.close().

close()

Returns: (Nothing)

The `window.close()` method closes the browser window referenced by the window object. It is most likely that you will use this method to close subwindows created from a main document window. If the call to close the window comes from a window other than the new subwindow, it is vital for the original window object to maintain a record of the subwindow object. This is accomplished by storing the value returned from the `window.open()` method in a global variable that will be available to other objects at a later time (for example, a variable not initialized inside a function). If, on the other hand, the `window.close()` method is called from an object inside the new subwindow, the `window` or `self` object reference is sufficient.

Be sure to include a window as part of the reference to this method. Failure to do so causes JavaScript to regard the statement as a `document.close()` method which has entirely different behavior. Only the `window.close()` method can close the window via script. Closing a window, of course, forces the window to issue an `onUnload` event before the window disappears from view; but once you've initiated the `window.close()` method, you cannot stop it from completing its task.

Example:

```
<HTML>
<HEAD>
<TITLE>Closing a Window</TITLE>
<SCRIPT LANGUAGE="JavaScript">
// declare global variable name
var newWindow = null
function makeNewWindow() {
    // store new window object in global variable
    newWindow = window.open("","","width=200,height=300")
    if (newWindow != null) {
        // assemble content for new window
        var newContent = "<HTML><HEAD><TITLE>Another Sub Window></
TITLE></HEAD>"
        newContent += "<BODY><H1>Many ways to close me.</H1>"
        newContent += "<FORM><INPUT TYPE='button' VALUE='Close Me'
onClick='self.close()'></FORM>"
        newContent += "</BODY></HTML>"
        // write HTML to new window document
        newWindow.document.write(newContent)
    }
}
</SCRIPT>
```

window.close()

```
</HEAD>
<BODY>
<FORM>
<INPUT TYPE="button" NAME="newOne" VALUE="Create New Window"
onClick="makeNewWindow()">
<INPUT TYPE="button" NAME="closeIt" VALUE="Close New Window"
onClick="if (newWindow !=null) newWindow.close()">
</FORM>
</BODY>
</HTML>
```

Listing 7-14: Buttons in both an original and new window are capable of closing the new window.

The main window of Listing 7-14 contains two buttons: One for creating a new window, and one that closes the new window. Because the event handler for the closing button requires a reference to the new window object, we store the result of the window creation in a variable that will be visible to any statement in the entire HTML document (initialized outside of a function — see Chapter 12). Thus, the `newWindow.close()` method does its job from the main window, but only after making sure that the new window is still open (`newWindow` would be null if the window either failed to open initially or the user had closed it).

Included in the definition of the content for the new window is a button whose event handler also closes the new window. But because that event takes place in the new window, the method reference is to the same window as the button: `self.close()`. We could have also used `window.close()`, `self.close()`, `top.close()`, and `parent.close()` because they all refer to this new window from the point of view of the "Close Me" button.

Related Items: `window.open()`; `document.close()`.

`setTimeout("expression", millisecondsDelay)`

Returns: ID value for use with `window.clearTimeout()` method.

The name of this method may be misleading, especially if you have done other kinds of programming involving "timeouts." In JavaScript, a timeout is an amount of time (in milliseconds) *before a stated expression evaluates*. For example, let's say you have a Web page designed to permit users to interact with a variety of buttons or fields within a time limit (this is a Web page running at a free-standing kiosk). You can turn

1 1 1

on the timeout of the window so that if no interaction occurs with specific buttons or fields lower in the document after, say, two minutes (120,000 milliseconds), the window reverts to the top of the document or to a help screen. To let the window know to switch off the timeout when a user does navigate within the allotted time, any button with which the user interacts will need to call the other side of a `setTimeout()` method, the `clearTimeout()` method, to cancel the current timer (see the following).

The expression that comprises the first parameter of the `window.setTimeout()` method can be a call to any function or method. The expression evaluates after the time limit expires.

While the timeout is "holding," the user is not prevented from performing other tasks. And once a timeout timer is ticking, you cannot adjust its time. Instead, clear the timeout and start a new one.

When you try to implement the `setTimeout()` method in your scripts, be aware that any user or script activity that reloads the current document — clicking the Reload button, navigating to an anchor in the same document, navigating to another URL, or resizing the window — cancels any timer that is currently waiting to trigger. You may be able to work around this by using persistent storage in a `document.cookie` (see Chapter 8), but it will require considerable testing and cookie maintenance to ensure that your scheme is working as you intended.

Example:

```
<HTML>
<HEAD>
<TITLE>Status Bar Clock</TITLE>
<SCRIPT LANGUAGE="JavaScript">
<!--
var flasher = false
// calculate current time, determine flasher state,
// and insert time into status bar every second
function updateTime() {
    var now = new Date()
    var theHour = now.getHours()
    var theMin = now.getMinutes()
    var theTime = "" + ((theHour > 12) ? theHour - 12 : theHour)
    theTime += ((theMin < 10) ? ":0" : ":") + theMin
    theTime  += (theHour >= 12) ? " pm" : " am"
    theTime += ((flasher) ? " " : "*")
    flasher = !flasher
```

112

window.setTimeout()

```
        window.status = theTime
        // recursively call this function every second to keep timer
going
        timerID = setTimeout("updateTime()",1000)
}
//-->
</SCRIPT>
</HEAD>

<BODY onLoad="updateTime()">
</BODY>
</HTML>
```

Listing 7-15: Display the current time (with flashing indicator) in the status bar.

When you load the HTML page in Listing 7-15, it triggers the `updateTime()` function, which displays the time (in hh:mm am/pm) format in the status bar (see Figure 7-8). Instead of showing the seconds incrementing one by one, this function alternates the last character of the display between an asterisk and nothing.

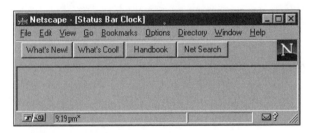

Figure 7-8: A clock ticks in the status bar.

The way the `setTimeout()` method works in this function is that once the current time (including the flasher status) is displayed in the status bar, the function waits one second (1000 milliseconds) before calling the same function again. This circular motion is called *recursion* and is described fully in Chapter 12. We don't have to clear the timerID value in this application because JavaScript does it for us every time the 1000 milliseconds elapse.

One caution about recursive functions that dive into themselves as frequently as this one does: Each nesting eats up a bit more memory for the browser application. If you let this clock run for a while, you could encounter some memory difficulties, depending on the operating system you're using. But considering the amount of time the typical user spends on Web pages (even if 10 or 15 minutes), this shouldn't present a problem.

113

And reloading induced by the user (such as resizing the window) unwinds all of the recursion of this function, freeing up memory once again.

Related Items: window.clearTimeout().

---

clearTimeout(*timeoutIDnumber*)

Returns: Nothing.

Use the window.clearTimeout() method in concert with the window.setTimeout() method, as described earlier, when you want your script to cancel a timer that is waiting to run its expression. The parameter for this method is the ID number that the window.setTimeout() method returns when the timer starts ticking. The clearTimeout() method cancels the specified timeout. It is good practice to check your code for instances in which user action may negate the need for a timer to be running — and to stop that timer before it goes off.

Example:

```
<HTML>
<HEAD>
<TITLE>Count Down Timer</TITLE>
<SCRIPT LANGUAGE="JavaScript">
<!--
var running = false
var endTime = null
var timerID = null

function startTimer() {
    running = true
    now = new Date()
    now = now.getTime()
    endTime = now + (1000 * 60 * 1)
    showCountDown()
}

function showCountDown() {
    var now = new Date()
    now = now.getTime()
    if (endTime - now <= 0) {
        stopTimer()
```

window.clearTimeout()

```
        alert("Time is up.  Put down your pencils.")
    } else {
        var delta = new Date(endTime - now)
        var theMin = delta.getMinutes()
        var theSec = delta.getSeconds()
        var theTime = theMin
        theTime += ((theSec < 10) ? ":0" : ":") + theSec
        document.forms[0].timerDisplay.value = theTime
        if (running) {
            timerID = setTimeout("showCountDown()",1000)
        }
    }
}

function stopTimer() {
    clearTimeout(timerID)
    running = false
    document.forms[0].timerDisplay.value = "0:00"
}
//-->
</SCRIPT>
</HEAD>

<BODY>
<FORM>
<INPUT TYPE="button" NAME="startTime" VALUE="Start 1 min. Timer"
onClick="startTimer()">
<INPUT TYPE="button" NAME="clearTime" VALUE="Clear Timer"
onClick="stopTimer()"><P>
<INPUT TYPE="text" NAME="timerDisplay" VALUE="">
</FORM>
</BODY>
</HTML>
```

Listing 7-16: A count down timer with a button to trigger the clearTimeout() method.

The page in Listing 7-16 features one text field and two buttons (see Figure 7-9). One button starts a count down timer coded to last one minute (easily modifiable); the other button interrupts the timer at any time while it is running. The timer mechanism is a variation of the recursive one in Listing 7-16; but in this case, the script uses a fixed end point in a global variable to compare against the current time. When the minute is up, an alert dialog box lets you know.

115

Notice that the script establishes three variables with global scope: `running`, `endTime`, and `timerID`. These values are needed inside multiple functions, so they are initialized outside of the functions.

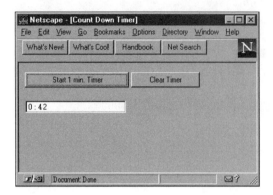

Figure 7-9: The count-down timer page as it displays the time left.

In the `startTimer()` function, we switch the `running` flag on, meaning that the timer should be going. Using some date functions (Chapter 9), we extract the current time in milliseconds and add the number of milliseconds for the next minute (the extra multiplication by one is the place where you can change the amount to the desired number of minutes). With the end time stored in a global variable, the function now calls another function that compares the current and end times and displays the difference in the text field.

Early in the `showCountDown()` function, we check to see if the timer has wound down. If so, we stop the timer and alert the user. Otherwise, the function continues to calculate the difference between the two times and formats the time in mm:ss format. As long as the running flag is set to true, the function sets the one-second timeout timer before repeating itself.

To stop the timer before it has run out (in the `stopTimer()` function), the most important step is to cancel the timeout running inside the browser. The `clearTimeout()` method uses the global `timerID` value to do that. Then the function turns off the `running` switch and zeros out the display.

When you run the timer, you may occasionally notice that the time skips a second. It's not cheating. It's just that it takes slightly more than one second to wait for the timeout and then finish the calculations for the next second's display. What you are seeing is the display catching up with the real time left.

Related Items: `window.setTimeout()`.

window.clearTimeout()

Event handlers

onLoad=

The onLoad event is sent to the current window at the end of the document loading process (after all text and image elements have been transferred from the source file server to the browser). At that point, all objects and script components in the document that the browser can possibly know about are stored in the browser's memory.

The onLoad= handler is an attribute of a <BODY> tag for a single-frame document or of the <FRAMESET> tag for the top window of a multiple-frame document. When the handler is an attribute of a <FRAMESET> tag, the event triggers only after all frames defined by that frameset have completely loaded.

Use either of the following scenarios to insert an onLoad= handler into a document:

```
<HTML>
<HEAD>
</HEAD>
<BODY [other attributes] onLoad="statementOrFunction">
[body content]
</BODY>
</HTML>
```

```
<HTML>
<HEAD>
</HEAD>
<FRAMESET [other attributes] onLoad="statementOrFunction">
    <FRAME>frame specifications</FRAME>
</FRAMESET>
</HTML>
```

The type of operations suited for an onLoad= event handler are those that can run quickly and without user intervention. Users shouldn't be penalized by having to wait for considerable post-loading activity to finish before they can interact with your pages. At no time should a modal dialog box be presented as part of an onLoad= handler. Users who design macros on their machines to visit sites unattended may get hung up on a page that automatically displays an alert, confirm, or prompt dialog box. On the other hand, an operation such as setting the window.defaultStatus property is a perfect candidate for an onLoad= event handler.

Related Items: onUnload= handler; window.defaultStatus property.

117

An unload event reaches the current window just before a document is cleared from view.

Limit the extent of the onUnload= event handler to quick operations that don't inhibit the transition from one document to another. Do not invoke any methods that display dialog boxes.

onUnload= event handlers are specified in the same places in an HTML document as the onLoad= handlers: as a <BODY> tag attribute for a single-frame window or as a <FRAMESET> tag attribute for a multi-frame window. Both onLoad= and onUnload= event handlers can appear in the same <BODY> or <FRAMESET> tag without any difficulty. The onUnload= event handler merely stays safely tucked away in the browser's memory, waiting for the onUnload= event to arrive for processing as the document is about to clear the window.

Frame Object

Properties	Methods	Event Handlers
frames	alert()	onLoad=
parent	close()	onUnload=
self	confirm()	
top	open()	
status	prompt()	
defaultStatus	setTimeout()	
window	clearTimeout()	

Syntax

Creating a frame:

```
<FRAMESET>
ROWS="ValueList"
COLS="ValueList"
[onLoad="handlerTextOrFunction"]
[onUnload="handlerTextOrFunction"]>
```

frame

```
        <FRAME SRC="locationOrURL" NAME="firstFrameName">
    ...
        <FRAME SRC="locationOrURL" NAME="lastFrameName">
</FRAMESET>
```

Accessing properties or methods of another frame:

```
parent.frameName. property | method([parameters])
```

```
parent.frames[i]. property | method([parameters])
```

About this object

A frame object behaves exactly like a window object, except that it has been created as part of a frameset by another document. A frame object always has a `top` and `parent` property different from its `self` property. If you load a document that is normally viewed in a frame into a single browser window, its window is no longer a frame. Consult the earlier discussion about the window object for details on the properties and methods these two objects share.

One other significant difference between a window and frame object occurs in the `onLoad=` and `onUnload=` event handlers. Because each document loading into a frame may have its own `onLoad=` event handler defined in its <BODY> definition, the frame containing that document receives the Load event when the individual document completes loading. But the frameset that governs the frame receives a separate Load event after all frames have finished loading their documents. That event is captured in the `onLoad=` event handler of the <FRAMESET> definition. The same applies to the onUnload= events defined in <BODY> and <FRAMESET> definitions.

Location Object

Properties	Methods	Event Handlers
hash	(None)	(None)
host		
hostname		
href		
pathname		
port		
protocol		
search		

location

Syntax

Assigning a new location to the current window:

```
[window.]location = "URL"
```

Accessing location properties or methods:

```
[window.]location. property | method([parameters])
```

About this object

Because the location object is one level below window-style objects in the JavaScript object hierarchy, it represents information about the URL of any currently open window. For a single-frame window, there is only one URL that applies to the location object: the URL showing in the Location field at the top of the browser window.

A multiple-frame window displays the parent window's URL in the Location field. If you omit the parent or top object in a reference to a location object, however, JavaScript looks to the URL of the frame in which the statement is located. To get URL information about a document located in another frame, the reference to the location object must include the window frame. For example, if you have a window consisting of two frames, Table 7-2 shows the possible references to the location objects for all frames comprising this Web presentation:

Table 7-2
Location Object References in a Two-Frame Browser Window

Reference	Description
location (or window.location)	URL of frame displaying the document that runs the script statement containing this reference
parent.location	URL info for parent window that defined the <FRAMESET>
parent.frames[0].location	URL info for first visible frame
parent.frames[1].location	URL info for second visible frame

Most properties of a location object are concerned with network-oriented information. This includes various data points about the physical location of the document on the network, including the host server, the protocol being used, and other components of the URL. Given a complete URL for a typical WWW page, the window.location object assigns property names to various segments of the URL, as shown here

http://www.giantco.com:80/promos/newproducts.html#giantGizmo

location

Property	Value
protocol	"http:"
hostname	"www.giantco.com"
port	"80"
host	"www.giantco.com:80"

Property	Value
pathname	"/promos/newproducts.html"
hash	"#giantGizmo"
href	"http://www.giantco.com:80/promos newproducts.html#giantGizmo"

The `window.location` object can be handy when a script needs to extract information about the URL, perhaps to obtain a base reference on which to build URLs for other documents to be fetched as the result of user action. This can solve a nuisance problem for Web authors who develop sites on one machine and then upload them to a server (perhaps at an Internet service provider) whose directory structure is entirely different. By building scripts to construct base references from the directory location of the current document, you can construct the complete URLs for loading documents. You won't have to manually change the base reference data in your documents as you shift the files from computer to computer or from directory to directory. For an example, see Chapter 18.

Setting the value of some location properties is the way many script statements control which document gets loaded into a window or frame. Though you may expect to find a method somewhere in JavaScript that contains a plain language "Go" or "Open" word (to replicate what you see in the browser menu bar), the way to "point your browser" to another URL is to set the `window.location` object to that URL, as in

```
window.location = "http://www.dannyg.com/"
```

The equals assignment operator (=) becomes a powerful weapon.

Although there are no methods listed for the location object, a hidden JavaScript method simplifies our lives. Its name is unimportant, but it allows us to assign the location object from a string value when, in truth, it would normally require a location object.

location

Properties

href

Value: string
Gettable: Yes
Settable: Yes

Of all location object properties, the href (hypertext reference) is probably the one most often called upon in scripting. The `location.href` property supplies a string of the entire URL of the specified window object.

Using this property (or just the `window.location` object reference) on the left side of an assignment statement is the JavaScript method of opening a URL for display in a window. Any of the following statements would load my Web site's index page into a single-frame browser window:

```
window.location="http://www.dannyg.com"
```

```
window.location.href="http://www.dannyg.com"
```

```
location="http://www.dannyg.com" // "window" part of reference is
optional
```

It is sometimes necessary to extract the name of the current directory in a script so that another statement can append a known document to the URL before loading it into the window. Although the other location object properties yield an assortment of segments of a URL, none of them provides the full URL to the current URL's directory. But you can use JavaScript's string manipulation techniques to accomplish this task. Listing 7-14 shows such a possibility.

Depending on your browser, the values for the `location.href` property may be encoded with ASCII equivalents of non-alphanumeric characters. Such an ASCII value includes the % symbol and the ASCII numeric value. The most common encoded character in a URL is the space, %20. If you need to extract a URL and display that value as a string in your documents, it is safest to pass all such potentially encoded strings through JavaScript's internal `unescape()` function. For example, if a URL to one of Giantco's pages is http://www.giantco.com/product%20list, you can convert it by passing it through the `unescape()` function, as in the following example:

location.href

```
plainURL = unescape(window.location.href)
    // result = "http://www.giantco.com/product list"
```

The inverse function, `escape()`, is available for sending encoded strings to CGI programs on servers. See Chapter 9 for more details on these functions.

Example:

```
<HTML>
<HEAD>
<TITLE>Extract pathname</TITLE>
<SCRIPT LANGUAGE="JavaScript">

// general purpose function to extract URL of current directory
function getDirPath(URL) {
    var result = unescape(URL.substring(0,(URL.lastIndexOf("/"))
+ 1))
    return result
}
// handle button event, passing work onto general purpose function
function showDirPath(URL) {
    alert(getDirPath(URL))
}
</SCRIPT>
</HEAD>

<BODY>
<FORM>
<INPUT TYPE="button" VALUE="View directory URL"
onClick="showDirPath(window.location.href)">
</FORM>
</BODY>
</HTML>
```

Listing 7-17: A general -purpose function for extracting the URL of the current document's directory.

Listing 7-17 includes the `unescape()` function in front of the part of the script capturing the URL. This is for cosmetic purposes in displaying the pathname in alert dialog boxes of browser versions that normally display the ASCII encoded version.

Related Items: `location.pathname` property; `document.location` property; string objects (Chapter 9).

123

location.href

hash	

Value: string
Gettable: Yes
Settable: Yes

The hash mark (#) is a URL convention that directs the browser to an anchor located in the document. Any name you assign to an anchor (with the <A NAME="..."> ...</A> tag pair) becomes part of the URL after the hash mark. A location object's hash property is the name of the anchor part of the current URL (the hash mark and the name).

If you have written HTML documents with anchors and directed links to navigate to those anchors, you have probably noticed that although the destination location shows the anchor as part of the URL (e.g., in the Location field), the window's anchor value does not change as the user manually scrolls to positions in the document where other anchors are defined. An anchor appears in the URL only when the window has navigated there as part of a link or in response to a script that adjusts the URL.

Just as you can navigate to any URL by setting the window.location property, you can navigate to another hash in the same document by adjusting only the hash property of the location (as shown in the example, below). Such navigation, even within a document, causes Navigator 2.0 to reload the document. Also note that even though a script statement sets the hash property (or any URL-related property, for that matter), the window doesn't truly consider the URL to be the window's location object value until the document loads successfully. Therefore, trying to test for a location.hash value immediately after setting the value will most likely result in a value of the previous location.hash value because the new URL has not yet loaded completely.

Example:

```
<HTML>
<HEAD>
<TITLE>location.hash Property</TITLE>
<SCRIPT LANGUAGE="JavaScript">
function goNextAnchor(where) {
    window.location.hash = where
}
```

location.hash

```
</SCRIPT>
</HEAD>

<BODY>

<A NAME="start"><H1>Top</H1></A>
<FORM>
<INPUT TYPE="button" NAME="next" VALUE="NEXT"
onClick="goNextAnchor('sec1')">
</FORM>
<HR>
<A NAME="sec1"><H1>Section 1</H1></A>
<FORM>
<INPUT TYPE="button" NAME="next" VALUE="NEXT"
onClick="goNextAnchor('sec2')">
</FORM>
<HR>

<A NAME="sec2"><H1>Section 2</H1></A>
<FORM>
<INPUT TYPE="button" NAME="next" VALUE="NEXT"
onClick="goNextAnchor('sec3')">
</FORM>
<HR>

<A NAME="sec3"><H1>Section 3</H1></A>
<FORM>
<INPUT TYPE="button" NAME="next" VALUE="BACK TO TOP"
onClick="goNextAnchor('start')">
</FORM>

</BODY>
</HTML>
```

Listing 7-18: A document that navigates to succeeding anchors by scripting the `location.hash` property.

When you load the script in Listing 7-18, adjust the size of the browser window so that only one section is visible at a time. When you click a button, its script navigates to the next logical section in the progression and eventually takes you back to the top of the document.

Anchor names are passed as parameters with each button's onClick= event handler. Instead of the laborious process of assembling a window.location value in the function by appending a literal hash mark and the value for the anchor, here we simply modify the hash property of the current window's location. This is the preferred, cleaner method. If you attempt to read back the window.location.hash property in an added line of script, however, the window's actual URL will probably not have updated yet and the browser would appear to be giving your script false information. To prevent this problem in subsequent statements in the same function, construct the URLs of those statements from the same variable values as you used to set the window.location.hash property — don't rely on the browser to give you the value you expect.

Related Items: location.href property.

host

Value: string
Gettable: Yes
Settable: Yes

The location.host property describes both the hostname and port of a URL. The port is included in the value only when the port is an explicit part of the URL. If you navigate to a URL that does not display the port number in the Location field of the browser, the location.host property returns the same value as the location.hostname property.

Use the location.host property to extract the hostname:port part of the URL of any document loaded into the browser. This may be helpful in building a URL to a specific document you want your script to access on the fly.

Example:

```
<HTML>
<HEAD>
<TITLE>window.location Properties</TITLE>
</HEAD>
```

location.host

```
<FRAMESET ROWS="50%,50%">
    <FRAME NAME="Frame1" SRC="lst07-21.htm">
    <FRAME NAME="Frame2" SRC="lst07-20.htm">
</FRAMESET>
</HTML>
```

Listing 7-19: Frame-making document for the Property Picker in Listing 7-20.

```
<HTML>
<HEAD>
<TITLE>Property Picker</TITLE>
<SCRIPT LANGUAGE="JavaScript">
function fillTopFrame() {
    newURL = prompt("Enter the URL of a document to show in the
top frame:","")
    if (newURL != null && newURL != "") {
    top.frames[0].location = newURL
    }
}

function showLocationData(form) {
    for (var i = 0; i <3; i++) {
        if (form.whichFrame[i].checked) {
            var windName = form.whichFrame[i].value
            break
        }
    }
    var theWind = "" + windName + ".location"
    theObj = eval(theWind)
    var msg = "", i = ""
    for (i in theObj) {
        msg += theWind + "." + i + ": " + theObj[i] + "\n"
    }
    alert(msg)
}
</SCRIPT>
</HEAD>
<BODY>
```

(continued)

```
Click the "Open URL" button to enter the location of an HTML
document to display in the top frame of this window.
<FORM>
<INPUT TYPE="button" NAME="opener" VALUE="Open URL..."
onClick="fillTopFrame()">
</FORM>

<FORM>
Select a window/frame. Then click the "Show Location Properties"
button to view each window.location property value for the desired
window.<P>
<INPUT TYPE="radio" NAME="whichFrame" VALUE="parent"
CHECKED>Parent window
<INPUT TYPE="radio" NAME="whichFrame" VALUE="top.frames[0]">Upper
frame
<INPUT TYPE="radio" NAME="whichFrame" VALUE="top.frames[1]">This
frame<P>
<INPUT TYPE="button" NAME="getProperties" VALUE="Show
window.location Properties" onClick="showLocationData(this.form)">
</FORM>
</BODY>
</HTML>
```

Listing 7-20: Operative portion of the Property Picker. This document loads into the bottom frame of the window created by the document in Listing 7-21.

```
<HTML>
<HEAD>
<TITLE>Opening Placeholder</TITLE>
</HEAD>
<BODY>
Initial place holder. Experiment with other URLs for this frame
(see below).
</BODY>
</HTML>
```

Listing 7-21: Placeholder for the upper frame that gets loaded initially by the document in Listing 7-19.

Use the documents in Listings 7-19 through 7-21 as tools to help you learn the values that the various window.location properties return. In the browser, open the file for Listing 7-19. This creates a two-frame window. In the upper frame goes a temporary

location.host

placeholder (Listing 7-21) that displays some instructions (if I had wanted a blank frame, I would have specified the SRC= attribute in the <FRAMESET> definition as "about:blank", which is a special empty window URL available in Navigator). In the bottom frame goes a document that lets you load URLs into the upper frame and get readings on three different windows available: the parent window (which creates the multi-frame window), the upper frame, and the bottom frame. Figure 7-10 shows the dual-frame browser window with the top frame loaded with a page from my Web site.

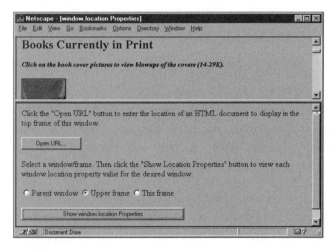

Figure 7-10: Browser window loaded to investigate `window.location` properties.

For the best results, open a URL (for the upper frame) to a Web document on the network, particularly one that includes anchor points to navigate through a long document. Then select the Upper Frame radio button and click on the button that shows all properties. An alert dialog box presents the names and results of seven properties. Figure 7-11 shows the results for a page from my Web site that is set to an anchor point.

Figure 7-11: Readout of all `window.location` properties for the upper frame.

location.host

The script that extracts these properties uses a special form of repeat loop described in detail in Chapter 10. In the alert dialog box are all properties for the location object described in this section. See the following discussion for the meanings of the other properties listed and instructions for viewing their values.

Related Items: `location.port` property; `location.hostname` property.

```
hostname
```

Value: string
Gettable: Yes
Settable: Yes

The hostname of a typical URL is the name of the server on the network that stores the document you are viewing in the browser. For most Web sites, the server name includes not only the domain name, but the "www." prefix as well. The hostname does not, however, include the port number if such a number is specified in the URL.

Example:

See Listing 7-19 through 7-21 for a set of documents to help you view the hostname data for a variety of documents.

Related Items: `location.host` property; `location.port` property.

```
pathname
```

Value: string
Gettable: Yes
Settable: Yes

The pathname component of a URL consists of the directory structure relative to the server's root volume. In other words, the root (server name in an http: connection) is not part of the pathname. If the URL is to a file in the root directory, then the `location.pathname` property is a single slash (/) character. Any other pathname starts with a slash character, indicating a directory nested within the root. The pathname also includes the document name.

Example:

See Listings 7-19 through 7-21 for a multiple frame example you can use to view the `location.pathname` property for a variety of URLs of your choice.

location.hostname | pathname

Related Items: `location.href` property.

`port`	

Value: string
Gettable: Yes
Settable: Yes

Few consumer-friendly Web sites these days need to include the port number as part of their URLs. Port numbers are visible mostly in URLs to sites that have no assigned domain names or in the less-popular protocols. You can retrieve the value with the `location.port` property. If you extract the value from one URL and intend to build another URL with that component, be sure to include the colon delimiter between the server's IP address and port number.

Example:

If you have access to URLs containing port numbers, use the documents in Listings 7-19 through 7-21 to experiment with the output of the `location.port` property.

Related Items: `location.host` property.

`protocol`	

Value: string
Gettable: Yes
Settable: Yes

The first component of any URL is the protocol being used for the particular type of communication. For World Wide Web pages, the HyperText Transfer Protocol (http) is the standard. Other common protocols you'll see in your browser include File Transfer Protocol (ftp), File (file), and Mail (mailto). Values for the `location.protocol` property include not only the name of the protocol, but the trailing colon delimiter, as well. Thus, for a typical Web page URL, the `location.protocol` property is:

```
http:
```

Notice that the usual slashes after the protocol in the URL are not part of the `location.protocol` value. Of all the location object properties, only the full URL (`location.href`) reveals the slash delimiters between the protocol and other components.

131

Example:

See Listings 7-19 through 7-21 for a multiple-frame example you can use to view the `location.protocol` property for a variety of URLs. Also try loading an ftp site to see the `location.protocol` value for that type of URL.

Related Items: `location.href` property.

search

Value: string
Gettable: Yes
Settable: Yes

Perhaps you've noticed the long, cryptic URL that appears in the Location field of your browser whenever you ask one of the WWW search services to look up matches for items you've entered into the keyword field. The URL starts the regular way — with protocol, host, and pathname values. But after the more traditional URL are search commands that are being submitted to the search engine (a CGI program running on the server). That trailing search query can be retrieved or set by using the `location.search` property.

Each search engine has its own formula for query submissions based on the construction of the HTML forms that obtain details from users. These search queries are in an encoded format that appears in anything but plain language. If you plan to script a search query, be sure you fully understand the search engine's format before you start assembling a string to assign to the `location.search` property of a window.

Example:

```
<HTML>
<HEAD>
<TITLE>window.search Property</TITLE>
</HEAD>
<FRAMESET ROWS="50%,50%">
    <FRAME NAME="Frame1" SRC="http://www.yahoo.com/search.html">
    <FRAME NAME="Frame2" SRC="lst07-23.htm">
</FRAMESET>
</HTML>
```

Listing 7-23: A document that creates a two-frame window. The top frame opens the Yahoo search page; the bottom opens the document in Listing 7-24.

location.search

```
<HTML>
<HEAD>
<TITLE>Search Viewer/Changer</TITLE>
</HEAD>
<SCRIPT LANGUAGE="JavaScript">
function scriptedSearch() {
    newSearch=prompt("Enter a new search
string:",top.frames[0].location.search)
    if (newSearch != null && newSearch != "") {
    top.frames[0].location.search = newSearch
    }
}
function showSearchData() {
    var msg = "location.href: " + top.frames[0].location.href + "\n\n"
    msg += "location.search: " + top.frames[0].location.search
    alert(msg)
}
</SCRIPT>
</HEAD>


<BODY>
<FORM>
<B>Perform a search in the Yahoo frame, above.</B> Then click the
 "Show <TT>location.search</TT> Property" button to examine the
<TT>window.location.search</TT> property value for the search.<P>
<INPUT TYPE="button" NAME="getProperties" VALUE="Show
location.search Property" onClick="showSearchData()">
</FORM>
Next, click the "Modify Search..." button to modify the current
search as derived from the upper frame's <TT>location.search</TT>
property. Be sure to follow the codes and conventions for the
 search engine (e.g., a plus sign between terms).
<FORM>
<INPUT TYPE="button" NAME="opener" VALUE="Modify Search..."
onClick="scriptedSearch()">
</FORM>
</BODY>
</HTML>
```

Listing 7-23: The controller document for the bottom frame lets you view and edit the `location.search` **property of the upper frame.**

location.search

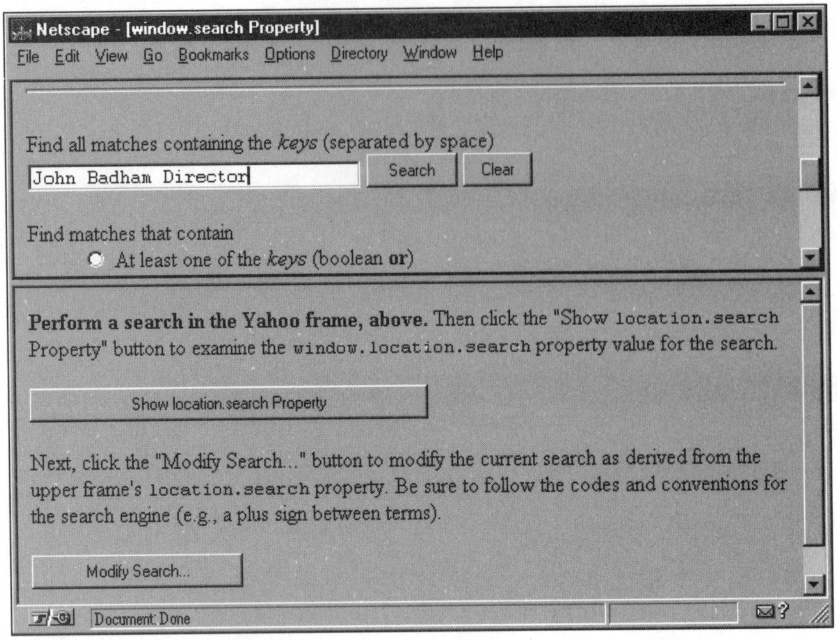

Figure 7-12: The two-frame window used to experiment with the `location.search` property. Yahoo's search page is in the upper frame.

Load Listing 7-22 to view a two-frame window. In the upper frame should appear a Yahoo search engine page that lets you enter search keywords and other specifications (see Figure 7-12). The bottom frame contains two buttons.

After you perform a search in the upper frame, click the bottom button to view both the complete `location.href` value and just the `location.search` portion (shown in Figure 7-13). Click the bottom button to edit the current `location.search` value (Figure 7-14).

Figure 7-13: The alert dialog shows both the full URL and just the search property.

location.search

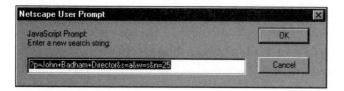

Figure 7-14: Using the existing search property as a model, make small changes to the search property to see how Yahoo responds.

Although this interface is clearly not as friendly as the one presented in either the Yahoo or the other search engine page, this illustration shows that you can control the search activities of a search engine from a script. For example, you may prefer to invent a different user interface to search for specific keywords (or present a limited selection to the user of your page). Your script would gather the user's input in your document's form, construct the appropriate search query (in the search engine's lingo) and then construct a URL that performs the search for the user.

Related Items: `location.href` property.

History Object

Properties	Methods	Event Handlers
length	back()	(None)
	forward()	
	go()	

Syntax

Accessing history properties or methods:

```
[window.]history. property | method([parameters])
```

About this object

As a user surfs the Web, the browser maintains a list of URLs for the most recent stops along the way. This list is represented in JavaScript by the history object. Except for the current URL, actual URLs maintained in that list cannot be surreptitiously extracted by a script. At best, a script can methodically navigate to each URL in the history (by relative number or stepping back one URL at a time), in which case, the user sees the browser navigating on its own, as if possessed by a spirit. Good netiquette dictates that you do not navigate outside of your own Web site without the user's explicit permission.

One application for this object and its `back()` or `go()` methods would be to provide the equivalent of a Back button in your HTML documents. That button would trigger a script that sees if there are any items in the history and then goes back one page. Your document doesn't have to know anything about the URL from which the user landed at your page.

Use the history object and its methods with extreme care. Your design must be smart enough to "watch" what the user is doing (for example, by checking the current URL before navigating with these methods). Otherwise, you run the risk of completely confusing your user by navigating to unexpected places. Your script can also get into trouble because it cannot detect where the current document may be in the Back-Forward sequence in history.

Properties

length

Value: number
Gettable: Yes
Settable: No

Use the `history.length` property to count the items in the history list. Unfortunately, this nugget of information is not particularly helpful in scripting navigation relative to the current location because your script cannot extract from the place in the history queue where the current document is located. If the current document is at the top of the list (the most recently loaded), you can calculate relative to that location. But users can use the Go menu to jump around the history as they like. The position of a listing in the history does not change by virtue of re-navigating to that document. A `history.length` of one, however, indicates that the current document is the first one the user loaded since starting the browser software.

Example:

```
<HTML>
<HEAD>
<TITLE>History Object</TITLE>
<SCRIPT LANGUAGE="JavaScript">
function showCount() {
    var histCount = window.history.length
```

history.length

```
    if (histCount > 5) {
        alert("My, my, you\'ve been busy. You have visited " +
histCount + " pages so far.")
    } else {
        alert("You have been to " + histCount + " Web pages this
session.")
    }
}
</SCRIPT>
</HEAD>

<BODY>
<FORM>
<INPUT TYPE="button" NAME="activity" VALUE="My Activity"
onClick="showCount()">
</FORM>
</BODY>
</HTML>
```

Listing 7-24: A simple button that reveals how many items are in your browser's history list.

The simple function in Listing 7-24 simply displays one of two alert messages based on the number of items in the browser's history.

Related Items: None.

Methods

```
    back()
```

Returns: (Nothing)

This method, which performs via scripting the same action as the user clicking on the Back toolbar button, is one handy navigation facility of JavaScript. If you deliberately lead a user to a dead end in your Web site, you should make sure that the HTML document provides a way to navigate back to a recognizable spot. Because you can easily create a new window that has no tool bar or menu bar (non-Macintosh), your users would have no way to navigate out of a cul-de-sac in such a window. A button in your document should give the user a way back to the last location.

history.back()

Unless you need to perform some additional processing prior to navigating back to the previous location, you can simply place this method as the parameter to the event handler attribute of a button definition.

Example:

```
<HTML>
<HEAD>
<TITLE>Way Back Machine</TITLE>
</HEAD>

<BODY>
<FORM>
<INPUT TYPE="button" VALUE="Take me back"
onClick="history.back()">
</FORM>
</BODY>
</HTML>
```

Listing 7-25: A button that navigates back to the previous item in the browser's history.

If the user clicks the button in Listing 7-25, and there are no other items in the backward direction, no error message is returned to the script or the user.

Related Items: history.forward(); history.go().

forward()

Returns: (Nothing)

Less likely to be scripted than the history.back() action is the method that performs the opposite action: navigating forward one step in the browser's history list. Because it is difficult, if not impossible, for a script to determine the location along the history list at which the current URL is located, your script may not know exactly where it will be going. The only time you can confidently use the history.forward() method is to balance the use of the history.back() method in the same script — where your script closely keeps track of how many steps the script heads in either direction. Use it with extreme caution, and only after extensive user testing on your Web page(s) to make sure that all user possibilities are covered.

history.forward()

Related Items: `history.back();history.go().`

`go(relativeNumber | "URLOrTitleSubstring")`

Returns: (Nothing)

Use the `history.go()` method if you have enough control over your user that you are confident of the destination before jumping there. This "go" command accepts only items that already exist in the history listing, so you cannot use it in place of setting the `window.location` object to a brand new URL.

For navigating *n* steps in either direction along the history list, use the *relativeNumber* parameter to the `history.go()` method. The number is an integer value that indicates which item in the list to use, relative to the current location. For example, if the current URL is at the very top of the list (that is the Forward button in the toolbar is dimmed), then to jump to the URL two items backward in the list requires the following method:

```
history.go(-2)
```

In other words, the current URL is the equivalent of `history.go(0)` (a method that reloads the window). A positive integer indicates a jump so many items forward in the history list. Thus, `history.go(-1)` is the same as `history.back()`, and `history.go(1)` is the same as `history.forward()`.

Alternatively, you can specify one of the URLs or document titles stored in the browser's history list (titles are what appear in the Go menu). The method is a bit lenient with the string you specify as a parameter. It compares the string against all listings. The first item in the history list to contain the parameter string will be regarded as the match. But, again, no navigation takes place if the item you specify is not listed in the history.

Like most other history methods, it is difficult for your script to manage the history list or the current URL's spot in the queue. That makes it even more difficult for your script to intelligently determine how far to navigate in either direction or to which specific URL or title matches it should jump. Use this method only for situations in which your Web pages are in strict control of the user's activity (or for designing scripts for yourself that automatically crawl around sites according to a fixed regimen). Once you give the user control over navigation, there is no guarantee that the history list will be what you expect, and any scripts you write that depend on a history object will likely break.

Example:

```
<HTML>
<HEAD>
<TITLE>Go() Method</TITLE>
<SCRIPT LANGUAGE="JavaScript"> '
// if you've recently run Listing 7-19, then this will find it
function journey() {
    history.go("window")
}
</SCRIPT>
</HEAD>

<BODY>
<FORM>
<INPUT TYPE="button" VALUE="Take me to Way Back"
onClick="journey()">
</FORM>
</BODY>
</HTML>
```

Listing 7-26: A button that navigates to an item in the history containing the words "window" in the URL or title.

When you click on the button in Listing 7-26, JavaScript checks the history list for a match of either the URL or document title for the word "window." If there is no match, the button does not take you to another location.

Related Items: `history.back();history.forward()`.

In the next chapter, we start digging into the more visual objects of a Web page: The document object and all of its elements.

history.go()

*C*hapter Eight

User interaction is a vital aspect of client-side JavaScript scripting, and most of the communication between script and user takes place by way of the document object and its elements. Understanding the scope of the document object is key to knowing how far you can take JavaScript.

Let's review the place of the document object within the JavaScript object hierarchy. Figure 8-1 clearly shows that the bulk of the object model rests within the document. The lower the objects your scripts work with appear in the hierarchy, the longer their object references will be, especially in multi-frame situations. It's not uncommon for a reference to a deeply nested object or property to be six or seven elements long. Don't let that deter you: All references do is provide directions for JavaScript to locate the particular object, property, or method among the objects currently stored in your browser's memory.

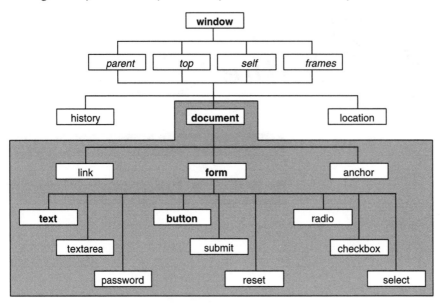

Figure 8-1: The JavaScript object hierarchy.

I cannot stress enough that the content of only two visible elements of an existing document (including one already loaded into a window) can be modified with Navigator 2.0: text and textarea objects. A handful of other invisible properties are modifiable after the fact. More visible items will be added to the list in a future release, but attempts to write to the current document or make other visible changes in Navigator Version 2.0 may result in mysterious behavior or Netscape crashes.

If you are reading this chapter for the first time, remember to focus initially on the items tagged with single pocket protector icons and skim the others. After you've tried some of these items in your own scripts, come back and fill in your repertoire with the next level, and so on. Without further ado, let's dive into the document object.

Document Object

Properties	Methods	Event Handlers
alinkColor	clear()	(None)
anchors	close()	
bgColor	open()	
cookie	write()	
fgColor	writeln()	
forms		
lastModified		
linkColor		
links		
location		
referrer		
title		
vlinkColor		

Syntax

Creating a document:

```
<BODY
    [BACKGROUND="backgroundImageURL"]
    [BGCOLOR="#backgroundColor"]
    [TEXT="#foregroundColor"]
    [LINK="#unfollowedLinkColor"]
    [ALINK="#activatedLinkColor"]
    [VLINK="#followedLinkColor"]
    [onLoad="handlerTextOrFunction"]
    [onUnload="handlerTextOrFunction"]>
</BODY>
```

Accessing document properties or methods:

```
[window.] document. property | method([parameters])
```

About this object

A document object is the totality of what exists inside the content region of a browser window or window frame (excluding toolbars, status lines, etc.). The document is a combination of the content and on-page interface elements that make the Web page worthwhile.

143

document

The officially sanctioned syntax for creating a document object, shown earlier, may mislead you to think that only elements defined within <BODY> tags comprise a document object. In truth, some <HEAD> tag information, such as <TITLE> and, of course, any scripts inside <SCRIPT> tags, are part of the document as well. So are some other values (properties), including the date on which the disk file of the document was last modified and the URL from which the user reached the current document.

Two event handlers defined in the Body, onLoad= and onUnload=, are not document-event handlers but rather window-event handlers. Load and Unload events are sent to the window after the document finishes loading and just prior to the document being cleared from the window, respectively. See Chapter 7's discussion about the window object for more details.

Properties

forms	

Value: array
Gettable: Yes
Settable: No

As shown later in this chapter, an HTML form (anything defined inside a <FORM>...</FORM> tag pair) is a JavaScript object unto itself. You can create a valid reference to a form according to its name (assigned via a form's NAME= attribute). For example, if a document contains the following form definition

```
<FORM NAME="phoneData">
    [input item definitions]
</FORM>
```

your scripts can refer to the form object by name:

```
document.phoneData
```

But a document object also tracks its forms in another way: as a numbered list of forms. This type of list in JavaScript is called an *array*, which means a table consisting of just one column of data. Each row of the table holds a representation of the corresponding form in the document. In the first row of a document.forms array, for instance, is the form that loaded first (it was first from the top of the HTML code). If your document defines one form, the forms property is an array one entry in length; with three separate forms in the document, the array is three entries long.

144

```
document.forms[i]
```

To help JavaScript determine which row of the array your script wants to access, you append a pair of brackets to the `forms` property name and insert the row number between the brackets. This number is formally known as the *index*. JavaScript arrays start their row numbering with zero, so the first entry in the array would be referenced as

```
document.forms[0]
```

At that point, you are referencing the equivalent of the first form object. Any of its properties or methods are available by appending the desired property or method name. For example, to retrieve the value of an input text field named "homePhone" from the second form of a document, the reference would be

```
document.forms[1].homePhone.value
```

One advantage to using the `document.forms` property for addressing a form object or element instead of the actual form name is that you may be able to generate a library of generalizable scripts that know how to cycle through all available forms in a document and hunt for the form that has some special element and property. In the following script fragment (part of a repeat loop described more fully in Chapter 10), we use a loop-counting variable (`i`) to help the script check all forms in a document:

```
for (var i = 0; i < document.forms.length; i++) {
    if (document.forms[i]. ... ) {
        statements
    }
}
```

Each time through the repeat loop, JavaScript substitutes the next higher value for `i` in the `document.forms[i]` object reference. Not only does the array counting simplify a check of all forms in a document, but this fragment is totally independent of whatever names you assign to forms.

As we saw in the preceding script fragment, there is one more aspect of the `document.forms` property that you should be aware of. All JavaScript arrays that represent built-in objects have a length property that returns the number of entries in the array. JavaScript counts the length of arrays starting with 1. Therefore, if the `document.forms.length` property returns a value of 2, the form references for this document would be `document.forms[0]` and `document.forms[1]`. If you haven't programmed these kinds of arrays before, the different numbering systems (indexes starting with zero, length counts starting with one) take some getting used to.

If you are careful in assigning names to objects, then you will likely prefer the `document.formName` style of referencing forms. For documents with one or two forms, I use `document.forms[i]` property references. In this book, you see both styles. **145**

See also the discussion of the `form` object and how using the `form` keyword simplifies even more the verbiage required to pass a form's data to a function.

Example:

```
<HTML>
<HEAD>
<TITLE>document.forms example</TITLE>
<SCRIPT LANGUAGE="JavaScript">
function goMusic() {
    if (document.forms[0].bluish.checked) {
        alert("Now going to the Blues music area...")
    } else {
        alert("Now going to Rock music area...")
    }
}
</SCRIPT>
</HEAD>

<BODY>
<FORM NAME="theBlues">
<INPUT TYPE="checkbox" NAME="bluish">Check here if you've got the
blues.
</FORM>
<HR>
M<BR>
o<BR>
r<BR>
e<BR>
<BR>
C<BR>
o<BR>
p<BR>
y<BR>
<HR>
<FORM NAME="visit">
<INPUT TYPE="button" VALUE="Visit music site" onClick="goMusic()">
</FORM>
</BODY>
</HTML>
```

Listing 8-1: Using the `document.forms` property to access a checkbox setting.

document.forms[i]

The document in Listing 8-1 is set up to display an alert dialog box replicating navigation to a particular music site, based on the checked status of the "bluish" checkbox. The user input is divided here into two forms: One with the checkbox; the other with the button that does the navigation. A block of copy fills the space in between. The function triggered by a click of the bottom button (in the second form) fetches the checked property of the "bluish" checkbox, using the `document.forms[i]` array as part of the address.

Related Items: form object.

`location`

Value: string
Gettable: Yes
Settable: No

The fact that the language frequently reuses the same terms in different contexts may be confusing to JavaScript newcomers. Such is the case with the `document.location` property. You may wonder how it differs from the location object (Chapter 7), especially when a reference to that object, `window.location`, could, to the untrained eye, appear to represent "the location property of the window object." The explanation is no less confusing: The property resembles the object in some ways, but not in others.

To be sure, there are significant structural differences between objects and properties. An object is a large collection of data and functions that define the behavior of a "thing" in the program; a property, on the other hand, is just a value — usually defining one narrow characteristic of an object. Unfortunately, confronted with two references ending in the same word

```
document.location
```

```
window.location
```

there is no way to know explicitly which "location" is the property and which is the object — unless you are completely familiar with the object model and the range of each object's properties. (I didn't repeat the object hierarchy illustration in Chapters 7 and 8 merely to take up space.)

The location object consists of many component pieces of a URL. One component is a text string representing the URL for the document displayed in a particular window or frame. It takes its point of view from the window. If you assign a new value to that object, it changes the content of the window to reflect that new URL.

147

In contrast, the `document.location` property is a read-only value (a string) of the URL for a document. The property doesn't know about windows or frames, but just the document that contains the script statement with the reference. You cannot change (assign another value to) this property value because a document has only one location: the location on the Net (or on your hard disk) where the file exists and what protocol is required to get it.

This may seem like a fine distinction, and it is. The reference you use (location object or `document.location` property) depends on what you are trying to accomplish specifically with the script. If the script is changing the content of a window by loading a new URL, you have no choice but to assign a value to the `window.location` object. Similarly, if the script is concerned with the component parts of a URL, the properties of the location object provide the simplest avenue to that information. For retrieving the URL of a document (whether it be in the current window or in another frame), my preference is the `document.location` property. To access `document.location` properties in other frames of a multi-frame window, simply use the `parent.frames` reference to get there, as in the following example:

```
parent.frames[1].document.location.
```

It's a mouthful, but it's very clear about the value I'm after.

Example:

```
<HTML>
<HEAD>
<TITLE>document.location Reader</TITLE>
</HEAD>
<FRAMESET ROWS="50%,50%">
    <FRAME NAME="Frame1" SRC="1st08-04.htm">
    <FRAME NAME="Frame2" SRC="1st08-03.htm">
</FRAMESET>
</HTML>
```

Listing 8-2: Frame-making document for document.location property reader.

```
<HTML>
<HEAD>
<TITLE>Location Property Reader</TITLE>
<SCRIPT LANGUAGE="JavaScript">
function fillTopFrame() {
    newURL=prompt("Enter the URL of a document to show in the top
frame:","")
```

document.location

```
        if (newURL != null && newURL != "") {
        top.frames[0].location = newURL
        }
    }


function showLocationData(form) {
    for (var i = 0; i <3; i++) {
        if (form.whichFrame[i].checked) {
            var windName = form.whichFrame[i].value
            break
        }
    }
    var theRef = windName + ".document"
    var msg = theRef + ".location: " + eval(theRef + ".location")
+ "\n"
    msg += theRef + ".title: " + eval(theRef + ".title")
    alert(msg)
}
</SCRIPT>
</HEAD>

<BODY>
Click the "Open URL" button to enter the location of an HTML
document to display in the upper frame of this window.
<FORM>
<INPUT TYPE="button" NAME="opener" VALUE="Open URL..."
onClick="fillTopFrame()">
</FORM>


<FORM>
Select a window or frame. Then click the "Show Document Location
Property" button to view each <TT>window.document.location</TT>
property value.<P>
<INPUT TYPE="radio" NAME="whichFrame" VALUE="parent"
CHECKED="true">Parent window
<INPUT TYPE="radio" NAME="whichFrame" VALUE="top.frames[0]">Upper
frame
<INPUT TYPE="radio" NAME="whichFrame" VALUE="top.frames[1]">This
frame<P>
<INPUT TYPE="button" NAME="getProperties" VALUE="Show Document
Location Property" onClick="showLocationData(this.form)">
```

(continued)

149

document.location

```
</FORM>
</BODY>
</HTML>
```

Listing 8-3: Operative portion of document.location property reader. This document loads into the bottom frame of the window created by the document in Listing 8-2.

```
<HTML>
<HEAD>
<TITLE>Opening Placeholder</TITLE>
</HEAD>
<BODY>
Initial place holder. Experiment with other URLs for this frame
(see below).
</BODY>
</HTML>
```

Listing 8-4: Placeholder for the upper frame that gets loaded initially by the document in Listing 8-2.

HTML documents in Listing 8-2 through 8-4 create a test lab that permits you to experiment with viewing the `document.location` property for different windows and frames in a multi-frame environment. The syntax of the reference is provided in the alert as well as the value of the location property for the document currently stored in the window you select. If the alert shows items as `<undefined>`, click the Reload button and try viewing the information again.

Related Items: location object; `location.href` property.

title	

Value: string
Gettable: Yes
Settable: No

A document's title is the text that appears between the <TITLE>...</TITLE> tag pair in an HTML document's Head portion. The title usually appears in the title bar of the browser window in a single-frame presentation. Only the title of the topmost framesetting document appears as the title of a multi-frame window. Even so, the title property for an individual document appearing in a frame is available via scripting. For

document.title

example, if there are two frames (UpperFrame and LowerFrame), a script in the document occupying the LowerFrame frame could reference the title property of the other frame's document like this:

```
parent.UpperFrame.document.title
```

This property cannot be set by a script except when constructing an entire HTML document via script, including the <TITLE> tags.

Example:

See Listings 8-2 through 8-4 for examples of retrieving the document.title property from a multi-frame window.

Related Items: history object.

alinkColor	
vlinkColor	
bgColor	
fgColor	
linkColor	

Values: hexadecimal triplet string
Gettable: Yes
Settable: No

Netscape began using these <BODY> attributes for various color settings with Navigator Version 1.1. Many other browsers now accept these attributes and they are part of HTML Level 3. All five settings can be read via scripting but cannot be adjusted on the fly. To change any color attribute of a document appearing in a window or frame from a script requires that all HTML for the document be composed in a script, in which the normal color attributes of a document would be set in the document's Body (using either hexadecimal triplets or the Netscape color names). If you try to change the color of a document already loaded in a window, you may see some immediate color

151

changes (depending on the operating system); but other strange behavior, such as improper screen refreshing, also results.

JavaScript object property names are case-sensitive. That factor is an important one to remember for these five property names that begin with lowercase letters and have an uppercase C within them.

The value for each of these properties is a hexadecimal triplet quoted as a string. The hexadecimal values are the same as those for the HTML attributes (#rrggbb).

A few JavaScript pioneers created Web pages that provided friendly user interfaces for experimenting with color attributes. Future linkups with color-picking types of Java applets are also intriguing possibilities.

Example:

```
<HTML>
<HEAD>
<TITLE>Color Me</TITLE>
<SCRIPT LANGUAGE="JavaScript">
function defaultColors() {
    return "BGCOLOR='#c0c0c0' VLINK='#551a8b' LINK='#0000ff'"
}


function uglyColors() {
    return "BGCOLOR='yellow' VLINK='pink' LINK='lawngreen'"
}
function showColorValues() {
    var result = ""
    result += "bgColor: " + newWindow.document.bgColor + "\r\n"
    result += "vlinkColor: " + newWindow.document.vlinkColor +
"\r\n"
    result += "linkColor: " + newWindow.document.linkColor +
"\r\n"
    document.forms[0].results.value = result
}
function drawPage(colorStyle) {
    var thePage = ""
    thePage += "<HTML><HEAD><TITLE>Color Sampler</TITLE></
HEAD><BODY "
    if (colorStyle == "default") {
       thePage += defaultColors()
    } else {
       thePage += uglyColors()
```

document.alinkColor

```
        }
        thePage += ">Just so you can see the variety of items and
color, <A "
        thePage += "HREF='http://www.nowhere.com'>here's a link</A>,
and <A HREF='http://home.netscape.com'> here is another link </A>
you can use on-line to visit and see how its color differs from
the standard link."
        thePage += "<FORM>"
        thePage += "<INPUT TYPE='button' NAME='sample' VALUE='Just a
Button'>"
        thePage += "</FORM></BODY></HTML>"
        newWindow.document.open()
        newWindow.document.write(thePage)
        newWindow.document.close()
        showColorValues()
    }
    var newWindow = window.open("","","height=150,width=300")
</SCRIPT>
</HEAD>

<BODY>
Try the two color schemes on the document in the small window.
<FORM>
<INPUT TYPE="button" NAME="default" VALUE='Default Colors'
onClick="drawPage('default')">
<INPUT TYPE="button" NAME="weird" VALUE="Ugly Colors"
onClick="drawPage('ugly')"><P>
<TEXTAREA NAME="results" ROWS=3 COLS=20></TEXTAREA>
</FORM>
<SCRIPT LANGUAGE="JavaScript">
drawPage("default")
</SCRIPT>
</BODY>
</HTML>
```

Listing 8-5: Simple HTML page with two buttons to set colors to default setup and an arbitrary set.

I've selected some color values at random to plug into three settings of the ugly colors group for Listing 8-5. The smaller window displays a dummy button so that you can see how its display contrasts with color settings. Notice that the script sets the colors of the smaller window by rewriting the entire window's HTML code. After changing

153

document.alinkColor

colors, the script displays the values in the original window's text area. Even though some colors are set with the Netscape color constant values, properties come back in the hexadecimal triplet values. You can experiment to your heart's content. Each time you change the values in the script, save the HTML file, and reload it in the browser.

Related Items: document.links property.

---

lastModified

Value: dateString
Gettable: Yes
Settable: No

Every disk file maintains a modified time stamp that the document.lastModified property reads (be sure to observe the uppercase M in the property name). Although few Web sites indicate the time of day a page was last updated, you can use the value of this property to present this information for readers of your Web page. The script would automatically update the value for you, rather than requiring you to hand-code the HTML line every time you modify the home page.

The returned value is not a date object (Chapter 9) but rather a straight string consisting of time and date, as recorded by the document's file system. You can, however, convert the date string to a JavaScript date object and use the date object's methods to extract selected elements for recompilation into readable form. Listing 8-6 shows an example.

Example:

```
<HTML>
<HEAD>
<TITLE>Time Stamper</TITLE>
</HEAD>
<BODY>
<CENTER> <H1>GiantCo Home Page</H1></CENTER>
<SCRIPT LANGUAGE="JavaScript">
update = new Date(document.lastModified)
theMonth = update.getMonth() + 1
theDate = update.getDate()
theYear = update.getYear()
document.writeln("<I>Last updated:" + theMonth + "/" + theDate +
"/" + theYear + "</I>")
```

document.lastModified

```
</SCRIPT>
<HR>
</BODY>
</HTML>
```

Listing 8-6: The month, date, and year are extracted from the document.lastModified property and reassembled into a mm/dd/yy format for the document.

As noted at great length in Chapter 9's discussion about the date object, you should be aware that date formats vary greatly from country to country. Some of these formats use a different order for date elements. When you hard-code a date format, it may take a form that is unfamiliar to other users of your page.

Related Items: date object (Chapter 9).

anchors

Value: array of anchor objects
Gettable: Yes
Settable: No

Anchor objects (described in more detail later in this chapter) are points in an HTML document marked with <A NAME=""> tags and are referenced in URLs by a trailing hash value. Like the `document.forms` property, the `document.anchors` property (notice the plural) delivers an indexed array of anchors in a document. Use the array references to pinpoint a specific anchor for retrieval of any anchor property.

Anchor arrays begin their index counts with zero: The first anchor in a document would have the reference `document.anchors[0]`. And, as is true with any built-in array object, you can find out how many entries are in the array by checking the length property. For example

```
anchorCount = document.anchors.length
```

The `document.anchors` property is read-only. To script navigation to a particular anchor, assign a value to the `window.location` or `window.location.hash` object.

Example:

```
<HTML>
<HEAD>
<TITLE>document.anchors Property</TITLE>
<SCRIPT LANGUAGE="JavaScript">
function goNextAnchor(where) {
     window.location.hash = where
}
</SCRIPT>
</HEAD>

<BODY>

<A NAME="start"><H1>Top</H1></A>
<FORM>
<INPUT TYPE="button" NAME="next" VALUE="NEXT"
onClick="goNextAnchor('sec1')">
</FORM>
<HR>

<A NAME="sec1"><H1>Section 1</H1></A>
<FORM>
<INPUT TYPE="button" NAME="next" VALUE="NEXT"
onClick="goNextAnchor('sec2')">
</FORM>
<HR>

<A NAME="sec2"><H1>Section 2</H1></A>
<FORM>
<INPUT TYPE="button" NAME="next" VALUE="NEXT"
onClick="goNextAnchor('sec3')">
</FORM>
<HR>

<A NAME="sec3"><H1>Section 3</H1></A>
<FORM>
<INPUT TYPE="button" NAME="next" VALUE="BACK TO TOP"
onClick="goNextAnchor('start')">
</FORM>
<HR><P>
```

document.anchors[i]

```
<SCRIPT LANGUAGE="JavaScript">
document.write("<I>There are " + document.anchors.length + "
anchors defined for this document</I>")
</SCRIPT>
</BODY>
</HTML>
```

Listing 8-7: Reading the number of anchors in a document.

In Listing 8-7, I appended an extra script to a listing from Chapter 7 to demonstrate how to extract the number of anchors in the document. It is unlikely that you will ever need to reveal such information to users of your page, and this property is not one you will call frequently. The object model defines it automatically as a document property while defining actual anchor objects.

Related Items: anchor object; `document.links` property.

Value: array of link objects
Gettable: Yes
Settable: No

The `document.links` property is similar to the `document.anchors` property, except that the objects maintained by the array are link objects — items created with `<A HREF="">` tags. Use the array references to pinpoint a specific link for retrieval of any link property, such as the target window specified in the link's HTML definition.

Link arrays begin their index counts with zero: The first link in a document would have the reference `document.links[0]`. And, as with any array object, you can find out how many entries are in the array by checking the length property. For example

```
anchorCount = document.links.length
```

Example:

The `document.links` property is defined automatically as the browser builds the object model for a document that contains link objects. You will rarely access this property, except to determine how many link objects are in the document.

Related Items: link object; `document.anchors` property.

document.links[i]

referrer	

Value: string
Gettable: Yes
Settable: No

When a link from one document leads to another, the second document can, under JavaScript control, reveal the URL of the document containing the link. The `document.referrer` property contains a string of that URL. This can be a useful tool for customizing content of pages based on the previous location the user was visiting within your site.

A referrer has data only when the user reaches the current page via link. Any other navigation (such as through the history) sets this property to an empty string.

Example:

```
<HTML>
<HEAD>
<TITLE>document.referrer Property 1</TITLE>
</HEAD>

<BODY>
<H1><A HREF="1st08-09.htm">Visit my sister document</A>
</BODY>
</HTML>]
```

Listing 8-8: The first of two documents to demonstrate the document.referrer property.

```
<HTML>
<HEAD>
<TITLE>document.referrer Property 2</TITLE>
</HEAD>

<BODY><H1>
<SCRIPT LANGUAGE="JavaScript">
if(document.referrer.length > 0 &&
document.referrer.indexOf("1st08-08.htm") > 0){
    document.write("How is my brother document?")
    } else {
```

document.referrer

```
        document.write("Hello, and thank you for stopping by.")
        }
</SCRIPT>
</H1></BODY>
</HTML>
```

Listing 8-9: Displaying a different message based on the previous location of the user.

For this demonstration, two documents are required. One simply contains one line of text as a link to the second. In the second document, a script verifies the document from which the user came via a link. If it is one that the script knows about, it displays a message relevant to the experience the user had at the first document.

Related Items: link object.

cookie

Value: string
Gettable: Yes
Settable: Yes

JavaScript offers only one possibility for storing information that the user generates in an HTML page. The Netscape Navigator browser was the first to provide this kind of storage, initially for the convenience of server-based CGI programs, whereby intermediate results could be stored on the client's personal computer until the server computer was ready to accept the completed set of input information.

Netscape has dubbed this facility *HTTP Cookies.* A cookie, then, is one piece of string information stored on the client's PC. The browser is in total control over the filename where all cookies are stored. In other words, JavaScript cannot read or write to text files arbitrarily — only to and from the browser's cookie file.

Internally, a cookie contains a number of pieces of information beyond just the string being stored. They include the domain of the Web site that "owns" the information in the cookie and an expiration date. A JavaScript script cannot dig willy-nilly through the cookie file in search of luscious tidbits — the browser mechanism limits its scope to only the entries originally written from a single domain and pathname.

It is strongly recommended that you assign a name to a cookie in a form similar to that of an HTML tag attribute (`cookieName=`). This facilitates managing the cookie data later (retrieving, replacing, and deleting). As you assign new cookies to the file, the browser appends them to the list of cookies for the current domain, separated by a

159

semicolon. A two-cookie entry would have the structure like this:

cookieName1=cookieData1;cookieName2=cookieData2

Notice that there is no trailing semicolon.

It is up to your script to establish the structure of the text for storing complex bits of information (for example, data from several form elements). By the same token, the scripts must parse information retrieved from a cookie to extract useful chunks of data for further scripting. Experience with JavaScript's string manipulation methods (Chapter 9) is essential to exploiting the `document.cookie` property on your own.

The complete specification for the Netscape cookie mechanism is beyond the scope of this book. You can find more information at <http://home.netscape.com/newsref/std/cookie_spec.html>.

To help you start using cookies before you even fully understand the underlying mechanism, Bill Dortch, a JavaScript pioneer, has created a set of functions that let you treat reading, writing, and deleting cookies as relatively easy functions. Listing 8-10 shows the complete listing (reprinted by permission), including example calls whose results display in the window when you load this document. You also have a chance to see another scripter's style. Bill is an experienced C programmer who elects to keep the end-of-statement semicolons in his repertoire.

```html
<html>
<head>
<title>Cookie Functions</title>
</head>
<body>
<script language="javascript">
<!-- begin script
//
// Cookie Functions - Second Helping (21-Jan-96)
// Written by: Bill Dortch, hIdaho Design <bdortch@netw.com>
// The following functions are released to the public domain.
//
//
//
// "Internal" function to return the decoded value of a cookie
//
function getCookieVal (offset) {
 var endstr = document.cookie.indexOf (";", offset);
 if (endstr == -1)
 endstr = document.cookie.length;
 return unescape(document.cookie.substring(offset, endstr));
```

document.cookie

```
}

//
// Function to return the value of the cookie specified by "name".
// name - String object containing the cookie name.
// returns - String object containing the cookie value, or null
// if the cookie does not exist.
//
function GetCookie (name) {
 var arg = name + "=";
 var alen = arg.length;
 var clen = document.cookie.length;
 var i = 0;
 while (i < clen) {
     var j = i + alen;
     if (document.cookie.substring(i, j) == arg)
     return getCookieVal (j);
 i = document.cookie.indexOf(" ", i) + 1;
 if (i == 0) break;
 }
 return null;
}


//
// Function to create or update a cookie.
// name - String object containing the cookie name.
// value - String object containing the cookie value. May
// contain any valid string characters.
// [expires] - Date object containing the expiration data of the
// cookie. If omitted or null, expires the cookie at the end
// of the current session.
// [path] - String object indicating the path for which the
// cookie is valid. If omitted or null, uses the path of the
// calling document.
// [domain] - String object indicating the domain for which the
// valid. If omitted or null, uses the domain of the calling
// document cookie is.
// [secure] - Boolean (true/false) value indicating whether
// cookie transmission requires a secure channel (HTTPS).
//
```

(continued)

161

```
// The first two parameters are required. The others, if supplied,
// must be passed in the order listed above. To omit an unused
// optional field, use null as a place holder. For example, to
// call SetCookie using name, value and path, you would code:
//
// SetCookie ("myCookieName", "myCookieValue", null, "/");
//
// Note that trailing omitted parameters do not require a
// placeholder.
//
// To set a secure cookie for path "/myPath", that expires after
// the current session, you might code:
//
// SetCookie (myCookieVar, cookieValueVar, null, "/myPath",
// null, true);
//
function SetCookie (name, value) {
 var argv = SetCookie.arguments;
 var argc = SetCookie.arguments.length;
 var expires = (argc > 2) ? argv[2] : null;
 var path = (argc > 3) ? argv[3] : null;
 var domain = (argc > 4) ? argv[4] : null;
 var secure = (argc > 5) ? argv[5] : false;
 document.cookie = name + "=" + escape (value) +
 ((expires == null) ? "" : ("; expires=" + expires.toGMTString())) +
 ((path == null) ? "" : ("; path=" + path)) +
 ((domain == null) ? "" : ("; domain=" + domain)) +
 ((secure == true) ? "; secure" : "");
}

// Function to delete a cookie. (Sets expiration date to current
// date/time)
// name - String object containing the cookie name
//
function DeleteCookie (name) {
 var exp = new Date();
 exp.setTime (exp.getTime() - 1); // This cookie is history
 var cval = GetCookie (name);
 if (cval != null)
 document.cookie = name + "=" + cval + "; expires=" +
exp.toGMTString();
```

document.cookie

```
}

//
// Example
//
var expdate = new Date ();
expdate.setTime (expdate.getTime() + (24 * 60 * 60 * 1000)); // 24
hrs from now
SetCookie ("ccpath", "http://www.hidaho.com/colorcenter/",
expdate);
SetCookie ("ccname", "hIdaho Design ColorCenter", expdate);
SetCookie ("tempvar", "This is a temporary cookie.");
SetCookie ("ubiquitous", "This cookie will work anywhere in this
domain",null,"/");
SetCookie ("paranoid", "This cookie requires secure
communications",expdate,"/",null,true);
SetCookie ("goner", "This cookie must die!");
document.write (document.cookie + "<br>");
DeleteCookie ("goner");
document.write ("ccpath = " + GetCookie("ccpath") + "<br>");
document.write ("ccname = " + GetCookie("ccname") + "<br>");
document.write ("tempvar = " + GetCookie("tempvar") + "<br>");
// end script -->
</script>
</body>
</html>
```

Listing 8-10: Bill Dortch's document.cookie functions provide an easy way to put the functionality of the cookie property into your scripts without having to understand all the details.

The essential information you need to provide for a cookie entry is a name you assign to the entry and the data. Bill's functions do the rest. For most applications of the document.cookie, the cookie should be set to delete itself when the browser closes (the default setting).

To see the document.cookie property in action, see the JavaScript applications demonstrated in Chapters 17 and 20.

Example:

Experiment with the last group of statements in Listing 8-10 to create, retrieve, and delete cookies. Also see Chapter 17.

Related Items: string object methods (Chapter 9).

Methods

`write("string")`	

`writeln("string")`	

Returns: Boolean true if successful

Both of these methods send text to a document for display in its window. The only difference between the two methods is that `document.writeln()` appends a carriage return to the end of the string it sends to the document (but you must still write a <BR> to effect a line break).

A common, incorrect conclusion that many JavaScript newcomers make is that these methods allow a script to modify the contents of any document. This is not true. Once a document loads into a window (or frame), only the content of text and textarea objects can be modified by a script. In fact, because of bugs on some versions of Navigator 2.0, attempting to write to an existing document may cause the browser to crash.

The two safest ways to use the `document.write()` and `document.writeln()` methods are to

- Embed a script in an HTML document to write some or all of the page's content

- Send HTML code to either a new window or to a separate frame in a multi-frame window

In the latter case, a script can gather input from the user in one frame and then algorithmically determine the layout and content destined for another frame. The script assembles the HTML code for the other frame as a string variable (including all necessary HTML tags). Before the script can write anything to the frame, it can optionally open the layout stream (to close the current document in that frame) with the `document.open()` method. In the next step, a `document.write()` method pours the entire string into the other frame. Finally, a `document.close()` method assures that the total data stream is written to the window. Such a frame looks just the same as if it were created by a source document on the server rather than on the fly in memory. The document object of that window or frame is a full citizen as a JavaScript document object. You can, therefore, even include scripts as part of the HTML specification for one of these temporary HTML pages.

document.write() | writeln()

Assembling HTML in a script to be written via the `document.write()` method often requires skill in concatenating string values and nesting strings. A number of JavaScript string object shortcuts facilitate the formatting of text with HTML tags (see Chapter 9 for details).

Whether your script should send lots of small strings via multiple `document.write()` methods or assemble a larger string to be sent via one `document.write()` method is a question of style. From a performance standpoint, it is fairly standard procedure to do more in memory and place as few I/O (input-output) calls as possible. On the other hand, it is easier to make a difficult-to-track mistake in string concatenation when you assemble longer strings. My personal preference is to assemble longer strings, but you should use the system that's most comfortable for you.

Using the `document.open()`, `document.write()`, and `document.close()` methods to display .gif images in a document requires some small extra steps. First, any URL assignments you write via `document.write()` must be complete (not relative) URL references. Accomplishing this reliably on your HTML authoring computer and the Web server may require algorithmically establishing the pathname to the current document on the server. The example in Chapter 19 shows how to do this.

The other image trick is to be sure to specify HEIGHT and WIDTH attributes for every image. Some platforms of Navigator 2.0 require it. Performance will be improved on all platforms.

In addition to the `document.write()` example that follows (see Listings 8-11, 8-12, and 8-13), you can find fuller implementations that use this method to assemble images for a custom window frame in Chapter 19 and bar charts in Chapter 20. Because you can assemble any valid HTML into a string to be written to a window or frame, a customized, on-the-fly document can be as elaborate as the most complex HTML document you can imagine.

Example:

```
<HTML>
<HEAD>
<TITLE>Writin' to the doc</TITLE>
</HEAD>
<FRAMESET ROWS="50%,50%">
    <FRAME NAME="Frame1" SRC="lst08-12.htm">
    <FRAME NAME="Frame2" SRC="lst08-13.htm">
</FRAMESET>
</HTML>
```

Listing 8-11: Frame-making document for document.write() method example.

document.write() | writeln()

```
<HTML>
<HEAD>
<TITLE>Document Write Controller</TITLE>
<SCRIPT LANGUAGE="JavaScript">
function takePulse(form) {
    var msg = "<HTML><HEAD><TITLE>On The Fly with " +
form.name.value + "</TITLE></HEAD>"
    msg += "<BODY BGCOLOR='salmon'><H1>Good Day " +
form.name.value + "!</H1><HR>"
    for (var i = 0; i < form.how.length; i++) {
        if (form.how[i].checked) {
            msg += form.how[i].value
            break
        }
    }
    msg += "<P>Make it a great day!</BODY></HTML>"
    top.frames[1].document.close()
    top.frames[1].document.write(msg)
    top.frames[1].document.close()
}
function getTitle() {
    alert("Lower frame document.title is now:" +
top.frames[1].document.title)
}
</SCRIPT>
</HEAD>

<BODY>
Fill in a name, and select how that person feels today. Then click
"Write To Below" to see the results in the bottom frame.
<FORM>
Enter your first name:<INPUT TYPE="text" NAME="name"
VALUE="Dave"><P>
How are you today? <INPUT TYPE="radio" NAME="how" VALUE="I hope
that feeling continues forever." CHECKED>Swell
<INPUT TYPE="radio" NAME="how" VALUE="You may be on your way to
feeling Swell">Pretty Good
<INPUT TYPE="radio" NAME="how" VALUE="Things can only get better
from here.">So-So<P>
<INPUT TYPE="button" NAME="enter" VALUE="Write To Below"
onClick="takePulse(this.form)">
<HR>
```

166

document.write() | writeln()

```
<INPUT TYPE="button" NAME="peek" VALUE="Check Lower Frame Title"
onClick="getTitle()">
</BODY>
</HTML>
```

Listing 8-12: Operative portion of document.write() example. User fills in form elements, and the script assembles HTML text to be written to the second frame.

```
<HTML>
<HEAD>
<TITLE>Placeholder</TITLE>
<BODY>
</BODY>
</HTML>
```

Listing 8-13: Opening placeholder document for lower frame of two-frame window.

The example in Listings 8-11 through 8-13 demonstrates several important aspects of using the `document.write()` or `document.writeln()` methods for writing to another frame. First is the fact that you can write any HTML code to a frame, and the browser accepts it as if the source code came from an HTML file somewhere. In the example, I assemble a complete HTML document, including basic <HTML> tags for completeness. An example of the frame written by the script can be seen in Figure 8-2.

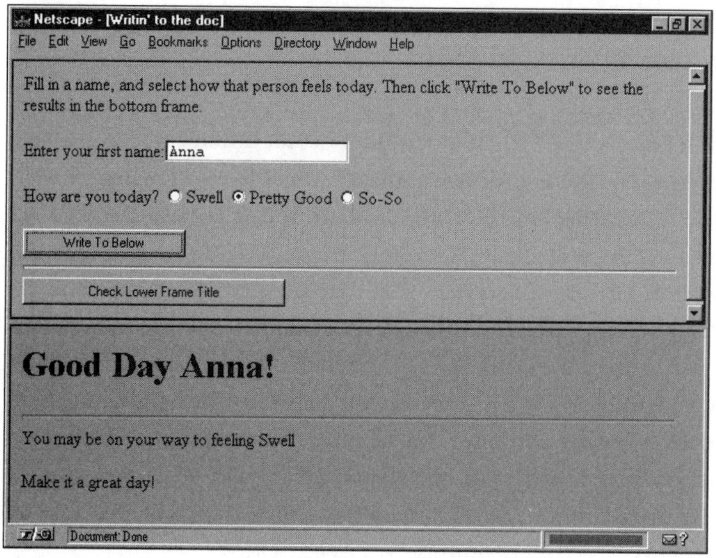

Figure 8-2: Clicking the Write to Below button in the upper frame causes a script to assemble and write HTML for the bottom frame.

document.write() | writeln()

A second point to note is that this example customizes the content of the document based on user input. This makes the experience of working with your Web page feel far more interactive to the user — yet you're doing it without any CGI programs running on the server. While this is a pretty basic computer programming kind of interaction, it is relatively new to Web page authoring.

The third point I want to bring home is that the document created by the `document.write()` method in the separate frame is a real JavaScript document object. In this example, for instance, the <TITLE> tag of the written document changes if you redraw the lower frame after changing the entry of the name field in the upper frame. If you click the lower button after updating the bottom frame, you'll see that the `document.title` property has, indeed, changed to reflect the <TITLE> tag written to the browser in the course of displaying the frame's page (see Figure 8-3). The fact that you can artificially create full-fledged JavaScript document objects on the fly represents one of the most important powers of serverless CGI scripting (for information delivery to the user) with JavaScript. There is much to take advantage of here if your imagination is up to the task.

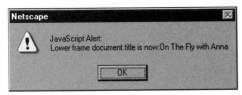

Figure 8-3: Even though the lower frame's document is generated on the fly, it has the same properties as any other document (such as a title).

Unfortunately, ranking it as a full-fledged document object doesn't make the page printable through the browser. Nor is the page's source available for viewing.

The frameset document (Listing 8-11) creates a blank frame by loading a blank document (Listing 8-13). You will likely see many other techniques for creating blank frames, but most of them rely on services that may be specific to the Netscape Navigator or that may not be supported in the future. For example, setting the URL of a frame to the Navigator's internal `about:blank` reference presents a blank frame (except for some extraneous fun on the 2.0 version Navigator for the Mac), but there is no guarantee that other browsers will have this facility. It is much safer to create a genuine blank HTML document on your server and refer to it whenever one of your framesets requires a blank frame.

Related Items: `document.close(); document.clear()`.

document.write() | writeln()

open(["*mimeType*"])

Returns: (Nothing)

Opening a document is different from opening a window. In the case of a window, you are creating a new object, both on the screen and in the browser's memory. Opening a document, on the other hand, tells the browser to get ready to accept some data for display in the window named or implied in the reference to the document.open() method (for example, parent.frames[1].document.open() may refer to a different frame in a frameset, whereas document.open() implies the current window or frame). Therefore, the method name may mislead newcomers because the document.open() method has nothing to do with loading documents from the Web server or hard disk. Rather, it is a prelude to sending data to a window via the document.write() or document.writeln() method. In a sense, the document.open() method merely opens a door; the other methods send the data, and the document.close() method closes that door once the page's data has been sent in full.

An optional parameter to the document.open() method lets you specify the nature of the data being sent to the window. A MIME (Multipurpose Internet Mail Extension) type is a specification for transferring and representing multimedia data on the Internet (originally for mail transmission, but now applicable to all Internet data exchanges). You've seen MIME depictions in the list of helper applications in your browser's preferences settings. A MIME type is represented by a pair of data type names separated by a slash (such as text/html and image/gif). When you specify a MIME type as a parameter to the document.open() method, you instruct the browser about the kind of data it is about to receive, so it knows how to render the data. The values that JavaScript accepts are

```
text/html
text/plain
image/gif
image/jpeg
image/xbm
plugIn
```

If you omit the parameter, JavaScript assumes the most popular type, text/html — the kind of data you typically assembled in a script prior to writing to the window. The text/html type includes any images that the HTML references. Specifying any of the image types means that you have the raw binary representation of the image you want to appear in the new document — possible, but unlikely.

Another possibility is directing the output of a write method to a Netscape plug-in. For the *mimeType* parameter, specify the plug-in's MIME type (for example, `application/x-director` for Shockwave). Again, the data you write to a plug-in must be in a form that it knows how to handle.

The `document.open()` method is optional because a `document.write()` method that attempts to write to a closed document automatically clears the old document and opens a new one. Whether or not you use the `document.open()` method, be sure to use the `document.close()` method after all writing has taken place.

Finally, be aware that you can open a document only in a window or frame *other* than the one containing the script invoking the `document.open()` method. Therefore, it is rare to see a reference to this method that doesn't include a window or frame as part of the complete reference. Attempting to reopen the script's own document with this method will usually lead to a crash of Netscape.

Example:

See Listing 8-2 for an example of using the `document.open()` method for a plain text/html MIME type.

Related Items: `document.close();` `document.clear();` `document.write();` `document.writeln().`

`close()`	

Returns: (Nothing)

Whenever a layout stream is opened to a window via the `document.open()` method or either of the document writing methods (which also open the layout stream), you must close the stream once the document has been written. This causes the `Layout:Complete` and `Document:Done` messages to appear in the status line (although you may experience some bugs in the status message on some platforms). The closing step is very important to prepare the window for the next potential round of replenishment with new script-assembled HTML. If you don't close the window, subsequent writing is appended to the bottom of it.

On certain platforms, especially when images are being drawn as part of the document stream, some or all of the data specified for the window won't display properly until the `document.close()` method is invoked. A common symptom is the momentary appearance and then disappearance of the document parts. If you see

170

document.close()

such behavior, look for a missing `document.close()` method after the last `document.write()` method.

Example:

Make a separate set of the three documents in Listing 8-11 through 8-13 in a different directory or folder. In the `takePulse()` function listing, comment out both the `document.open()` and `document.close()` statements, as shown here:

```
msg += "<P>Make it a great day!</BODY></HTML>"
//top.frames[1].document.open()
top.frames[1].document.write(msg)
//top.frames[1].document.close()
```

Now try the pages on your browser. You will see that each click of the upper button appends text to the bottom frame, without first removing the previous text. That's because the previous layout stream was never closed. The document thinks that you're still writing to it.

Related Items: `document.clear();document.write();document.writeln().`

`clear()`

Returns: (Nothing)

Clearing a document and closing a document are two quite different actions. As described in the preceding `document.close()` section, closing deals with the layout stream previously opened to a document. Frequently, the stream must be closed before all data specified in the HTML of the document appears correctly.

Clearing a document, on the other hand, means that whatever HTML was written to the document is removed from the browser — as is the object model for that document. Though it is unnecessary to clear a document prior to opening or writing to another one (JavaScript clears the old one for you), you are welcome to specify the `document.clear()` method if that helps you feel more in control of the user interface. You can also clear a window or frame with this method if your goal is to leave the area blank temporarily.

Always be sure that you are clearing a document that has been officially closed by the `document.close()` method. Trying to clear an open document results in odd behavior and crashes.

Example:

Create a duplicate set of Listings 8-11 through 8-13 in a different directory or folder. Modify Listing 8-12 so that the second button clears the bottom screen. This can all be accomplished by changing the definition of the bottom button to the following:

```
<INPUT TYPE="button" NAME="peek" VALUE="Clear Lower Frame"
onClick="parent.frames[1].document.clear()">
```

Notice that you can click on this button as often as you like, even when the frame is empty. If you want to tempt fate and crashes, modify the script some more by commenting out the `document.close()` statement in the `takePulse()` function. You'll discover how unstable your PC's browser is by attempting to clear a still-open document.

Related Items: `document.close()`; `document.write()`; `document.writeln()`.

Form Object

Properties	Method	Event Handler
action	submit()	onSubmit=
elements		
encoding		
method		
target		

Syntax

Creating a form:

```
<FORM
    [NAME="formName"]
    [TARGET="windowName"]
    [ACTION="serverURL"]
    [METHOD=GET | POST]
    [ENCTYPE="MIMEType"]
    [onSubmit="handlerTextOrFunction"] >
</FORM>
```

Accessing form properties or methods:

```
[window.] document.formName.property | method([parameters])
```

```
[window.] document.forms[index].property | method([parameters])
```

172

document.form

About this object

Forms and their elements are the primary two-way gateways between users and JavaScript scripts. A form element provides the only way that users can enter textual information or make a selection from a predetermined set of choices, whether those choices are in the form of an on/off checkbox, one of a set of mutually exclusive radio buttons, or a selection from a list.

As you have also seen in many Web sites, the form is the avenue for the user to enter information that gets sent back to the server housing the Web files. Just what the server can do with this information depends on the programs running on the server. If your Web site is on a server directly under your control (that is, it is "in-house"), you have the freedom to set up all kinds of data gathering or database search programs to interact with the user. But if you rely on an Internet Service Provider (ISP) to house your HTML files, you are limited to a usually plain set of programs that are available to all customers of the service. Custom databases or transactional services are rarely provided for this kind of *dial-up* Internet service — popular with individuals and small businesses who cannot justify the cost of maintaining their own servers.

Regardless of your Internet server status, you will find plenty of uses for JavaScript scripts in documents. For instance, rather than using data exchanges (and Internet bandwidth) to gather raw user input and report any errors, a JavaScript-enhanced document can preprocess the information to make sure that it is in the format that will be most easily received by your back-end database or other programs. All corrective interaction takes place in the browser, without one extra bit flowing across the Net.

How you define a form object (independent of the user interface elements, described later in this chapter) depends a great deal on how you plan to use the information from the form's elements. If the form is being used completely for JavaScript purposes (that is, there will be no queries or postings going to the server), the ACTION=, TARGET=, and METHOD= attributes are not necessary. But if your Web page will be feeding information or queries back to a server, you need to specify at least the ACTION= and METHOD= attributes; specify the TARGET= attribute if the resulting data from the server is to be displayed in a window other than the calling window; and specify the ENCTYPE= attribute if your form's scripts fashion the server-bound data in a MIME= type other than a plain ASCII stream.

For most client-side scripting, user interaction comes from the elements within a form; the form object becomes merely a repository for the various elements. If your scripts will be performing any data validation checks on user entries prior to submission or other calculations, many statements will have the form object as part of the reference to the element.

document.form

A complex HTML document can have multiple forms objects. Each <FORM>...</FORM> tag pair defines one form. There is no penalty (except for potential confusion on the part of someone reading your script) if you reuse a name for an element in each of a document's forms. For example, if each of three forms has a grouping of radio buttons with the name "choice," the object reference to each button ensures that JavaScript won't confuse them. The reference to the first button of each of those button groups would be as follows:

```
document.forms[0].choice[0]
```

```
document.forms[1].choice[0]
```

```
document.forms[2].choice[0]
```

Remember, too, that you can create forms (or any HTML object for that matter) on the fly when you assemble HTML strings for writing into other windows or frames. Therefore, you can determine various attributes of a form from settings in an existing document.

When a form or form element contains an event handler that calls a function defined elsewhere in the document, there are a couple shortcuts that you can use to simplify addressing the objects in the function. Failure to grasp this concept will not only make you write more code than you have to, but will hopelessly lose you when you try to trace somebody else's code in their JavaScripted document.

The watchword in event handler parameters is

```
this
```

which represents the current object that contains the event handler attribute. For example, consider the function and form definition in Listing 8-14. The entire user interface for this listing consists of form elements, as shown in Figure 8-4.

```
<HTML>
<HEAD>
<TITLE>Beatle Picker</TITLE>
</HEAD>
<SCRIPT LANGUAGE="JavaScript">
function processData(form) {
    //statements
}
</SCRIPT>

<BODY>
```

document.form

```
<FORM NAME="Abbey Road">
Choose your favorite Beatle:
<INPUT TYPE="radio" NAME="Beatles" VALUE="Lennon"
CHECKED="true">John
<INPUT TYPE="radio" NAME="Beatles" VALUE="McCartney">Paul
<INPUT TYPE="radio" NAME="Beatles" VALUE="Harrison">George
<INPUT TYPE="radio" NAME="Beatles" VALUE="Starr">Ringo<P>

Enter the name of your favorite Beatles song:<BR>
<INPUT TYPE="text" NAME="song"><P>
<INPUT TYPE="button" NAME="process" VALUE="Process Request..."
onClick="processData(this.form)">
</FORM>
```

Listing 8-14: Framework to test passing the form object as parameter.

If you want to summon any properties of the form elements to work on them inside the processData() function, you can go about it in two different ways. One way is to have the onClick= event handler (in the button element at the bottom of the document) simply call the processData() function and not pass any parameters. Inside the function, all references to objects such as the radio buttons or the song field would have to be complete references, such as

```
document.forms[0].song.value
```

to retrieve the value entered into the "song" field.

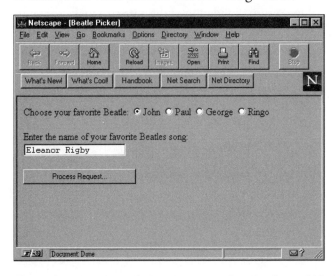

Figure 8-4: A variety of elements comprise the form of Listing 8-14.

A more efficient way is to send the form object as a parameter with the call to the function (as shown in Listing 8-14). By specifying `this.form` as the parameter, we're telling JavaScript to send along everything it knows about the form from which this function is being called. At the function, that form object is assigned to a variable name (`form`) that appears in parentheses after the function name. I've used the parameter variable name `form` here because it represents an entire form. But you can use any valid variable name you like.

One part of the knowledge that comes along with that form is its address among all JavaScript objects loaded with the document. That means that as long as statements refer to that form object (by its variable name), the full address is automatically part of that reference. Thus, here I can use `form` to take the place of `document.forms[0]` in any address. To get the value of the song field, the reference is

```
form.song.value
```

Had I assigned the form object to a parameter variable called `sylvester`, the reference would be

```
sylvester.song.value
```

This referencing methodology works for retrieving or setting properties and calling an object's methods.

Another version of the `this` parameter passing is simply the word `this` as the parameter. Unlike `this.form`, which passes the entire form connected to a particular element, `this` passes only that one element as an object. In Listing 8-14, we could add an event handler to the song field to do some validation of the entry (to make sure it is in a database array of Beatles' songs created elsewhere in the document). Therefore, we want to send only the field object to the function for its analysis. We'd modify the <INPUT> statement from

```
<INPUT TYPE="text" NAME="song"><P>
```

to read

```
<INPUT TYPE="text" NAME="song" onChange="verifySong(this)"><P>
```

We then have to create a function to catch this call. Its structure would look something like this:

```
function verifySong(entryField) {
    if (entryField.value != "") {
        [statements]
    }
}
```

document.form

Inside this function, we can go straight to the heart — the value property of the field element without a long address. The entire field object came along for the ride with its complete address.

My bottom-line recommendation is to pass objects with the `this` or `this.form` keywords as parameters to event handlers whenever an object's event handler needs to access that object (or elements within its scope) in the called function. In the process, be careful with parameter variable names you assign to the objects in function definitions: make sure that they will be meaningful to someone (like you) reading your code a month from now.

Properties

elements

Value: array of sub-objects
Gettable: Yes
Settable: No

Elements encompass all user interface elements defined for a form: text fields, buttons, radio buttons, checkboxes, selection lists, and more. Like some other JavaScript object properties, the elements property is an array of all items defined within the current HTML document. For example, if a form defines three <INPUT> items, the elements property for that form is an array consisting of three entries, one for each item. Each entry is the full object specification for that element; so to extract properties or call methods for those elements, your script must dig deeper in the reference. Therefore, if the first element of a form is a text field, and you want to extract the string entered into it (a text element's value property), the reference would be this:

```
document.forms[0].elements[0].value
```

Notice that this reference summons two array-oriented properties along the way: one for the document's forms property and, subsequently, one for the form's elements property.

You can access an element in other ways, too (see discussions of individual element objects later in this chapter). An advantage to using the elements property occurs when you have a form with lots of elements, each with a related or potentially confusing name. In such circumstances, references that point directly to an element's name may be more difficult to trace or read. On the other hand, the order of entries in an elements array is entirely dependent upon their order in the HTML document — the first <INPUT>

document.forms[i].elements[i]

item in a form is elements[0], the second is elements[1], and so on. If you redesign the physical layout of your form elements after writing scripts for them, the index values you originally had for referencing a specific form may no longer be valid. Referencing an element by name, however, will work no matter how you move the form elements around in your HTML document.

My personal preference is to generate meaningful names for each element and use those names in references throughout my scripts. Just the same, if I have a script that must poll every element or contiguous range of elements for a particular property value, the indexed array of elements facilitates using a repeat loop to examine each one efficiently.

Example:

```
<HTML>
<HEAD>
<TITLE>Elements Array</TITLE>
<SCRIPT LANGUAGE="JavaScript">
function doIt() {
    for (i = 0; i <= 3; i++) {
        if (document.forms[0].elements[i].value == "") {
            alert("Please fill out all fields.")
            document.forms[0].elements[i].focus()
            break
        }
        // more tests
    }
    // more statements
}
</SCRIPT>
</HEAD>
<BODY>
<FORM>
Enter your first name:<INPUT TYPE="text" NAME="firstName"><P>
Enter your last name:<INPUT TYPE="text" NAME="lastName"><P>
Enter your address:<INPUT TYPE="text" NAME="address"><P>
Enter your city:<INPUT TYPE="text" NAME="city"><P>
<INPUT TYPE="radio" NAME="gender">Male
<INPUT TYPE="radio" NAME="gender">Female <P>
<INPUT TYPE="checkbox" NAME="retired">I am retired
</FORM>
```

document.forms[i].elements[i]

```
<FORM>
<INPUT TYPE="button" NAME="act" VALUE="Verify" onClick="doIt()">
</FORM>
</BODY>
</HTML>
```

Listing 8-15: Document with function fragment that uses the forms.elements array in a repeat loop.

The document in Listing 8-15 demonstrates a practical use of the elements property. A form contains four fields and some other elements (Figure 8-5). The first part of the function that acts on these items repeats through all four fields to make sure that they're all filled out. By using the array notation, we can cycle through all four fields by their index. If one field has nothing in it, we alert the user and employ that same index value to place the insertion pointer at that field with the field's focus() method.

Related Items: text, textarea, button, radio, checkbox, and select objects.

Value: URL
Gettable: Yes
Settable: Yes

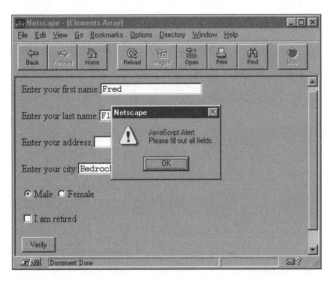

Figure 8-5: A document with many elements and an alert dialog box.

document.forms[i].action

The action property (along with the method and target properties) is primarily for HTML authors whose pages communicate with server-based CGI scripts. This property is the same as the value you assign to the `ACTION=` attribute of a <FORM> definition. The value is typically a URL on the server where queries or postings are sent for submission. Only the URL is contained in this property — not any of the form's element data typically sent to the server for processing.

User input may affect how you want your page to access a server. For example, a checked box in your document may set a form's action property so that that all input is to be handled by a CGI script on one server, whereas an unchecked box means that the form data is sent to a CGI script on an entirely different server. Or one setting might direct the action to be one mailto: address, whereas another setting sets the action property to a different mailto: address.

If you want to incorporate the interplay with an existing public CGI facility (such as a Web search site), you can build your own front-end to the CGI. The trick is in capturing the URL of the CGI program at that site so you'll know how to script the query. You can do this by first using the site's own HTML pages, fashioning a query, and watching the Location field in your browser when the results come back. Typically, you will see the entire URL and query data (loaded with ? and + symbols) in the Location field. Look just for the URL part (usually before the first ? symbol), which generally ends with a .cgi or .cgi-bin extension (the latter standing for CGI binary). Place that URL as the `ACTION=` attribute in your own <FORM> definition and direct the output from the server to any frame or window via the `TARGET=` attribute (below).

Example:

```
formAction = document.forms[0].action
```

Related Items: `form.method` property; `form.target` property.

`method`

Value: "get" or "post"
Gettable: Yes
Settable: Yes

A form's method property is either the GET or POST values assigned to the `METHOD=` attribute in a <FORM> definition. Terminology overlaps here a bit, so be careful to distinguish a form's method of transferring its data to a server from the object-oriented method (action or function) that all JavaScript forms have.

180

document.forms[i].method

Of primary importance to HTML documents that submit a form's data to a server-based CGI script is the method property, which determines the format used to convey this information. Details for this progress are beyond the scope of this book. Consult HTML or CGI documentation to determine which is the appropriate setting for this attribute in your Web server environment.

If no METHOD= attribute is explicitly defined for a form, the default value is GET.

Example:

```
formMethod = document.forms[0].method
```

Related Items: form.action property; form.target property.

---

target

Value: windowNameString
Gettable: Yes
Settable: Yes

Whenever an HTML document submits a query to a server for processing, it is common for that server to send back an HTML page — whether it be a canned response or, more likely, a customized page based on the input provided by the user. You see this all the time when you perform a search at Web search sites, such as Yahoo, Lycos, and WebCrawler. In a multi-frame or multi-window environment, you may want to keep the form part of this transaction in view for the user, while the responding page is viewed in a separate frame or window. The purpose of the TARGET= attribute of a <FORM> definition is to let you specify where the output from the server's query should be displayed.

The value of the target property is the name of the window or frame. For instance, if you define a FRAMESET with three frames and assign the names Frame1, Frame2, and Frame3 to them, you will need to supply one of these names (as a quoted string) as the parameter of the TARGET= attribute of the <FORM> definition. Netscape Navigator 2.0 and compatible browsers also observe four special window names that you can use in the <FORM> definition: _top, _parent, _self, and _blank.

Example:

```
formTarget = document.forms[0].target
```

Related Items: form.action method; form.method method.

181

encoding

Value: MIMETypeString
Gettable: Yes
Settable: Yes

A form can be defined to alert a server that the data being submitted is in a MIME type. This property reflects the setting of the ENCTYPE= attribute in the form definition. If no ENCTYPE= attribute is in the definition, this property is an empty string.

Example:

```
formMIME = document.forms[0].encoding
```

Related Items: form.action method; form.method method

Method

submit()

Returns: (Nothing)

The most common way for a form's data to be sent to a server's CGI program for processing is for a user to click a Submit button whose behavior is designed to send data from all elements of a form according to the specifications listed in the <FORM> definition's attributes. But if you want to submit a form's data to a server automatically for a user or want to use a graphical button for submission, you can accomplish the submission with the form.submit() method.

Invoking this method is the same as a user clicking on a form's Submit button. Therefore, you may have an image on your page that is a graphical type of submission button. If that image is associated with a link object, you can capture a mouse click on that image and trigger a function whose content includes a call to a form's submit() method (see Listing 8-16 that follows).

In a multiple-form HTML document, however, you must be sure to reference the proper form, either by name or according to its position in a document.forms[] array. Always be sure that the reference you specify in your script points to the desired form before submitting any data to a server.

document.forms[i].encoding

Example:

```
<HTML>
<HEAD>
<TITLE>Registration Form</TITLE>
<SCRIPT LANGUAGE="JavaScript">
function doIt() {
    document.forms[0].submit()
}
</SCRIPT>
</HEAD>
<BODY>
<FORM METHOD=POST ACTION="http://www.u.edu/pub/cgi-bin/register">
Enter your first name:<INPUT TYPE="text" NAME="firstName"><P>
Enter your last name:<INPUT TYPE="text" NAME="lastName"><P>
Enter your address:<INPUT TYPE="text" NAME="address"><P>
Enter your city:<INPUT TYPE="text" NAME="city"><P>
<INPUT TYPE="radio" NAME="gender">Male
<INPUT TYPE="radio" NAME="gender">Female <P>
<INPUT TYPE="checkbox" NAME="retired">I am retired
</FORM>

<A HREF="registration.html" onClick="doIt()">
<IMG SRC="niftySubmit.gif" BORDER=0></A>
</BODY>
</HTML>
```

Listing 8-16: Calling the form.submit() method from a graphical "button."

In Listing 8-16, the act of submitting the form is left to the function called by the onClick= event handler of the link object. The link object is attached to an art file which, based on the name of the .gif file, appears to be a flamboyant submission button. In the function, the form.submit() method is part of a reference to the first (and only) form of this document. The method automatically follows instructions in the attributes of the <FORM> definition.

Related Items: form.action property; form.method property.

183

Event handler

onSubmit=

No matter how a form's data is actually submitted (by a user clicking a Submit button or by a script involving the `form.submit()` method), you may want your JavaScript-enabled HTML document to perform some data validation on the user input, especially text fields, before the submission heads for the server. You have the option of doing such validation while the user enters data (see Chapter 15) or in batch mode prior to sending the data to the server. The place to trigger this last-ditch data validation is the form's `onSubmit=` event handler.

When you define an `onSubmit=` handler as an attribute of a <FORM> definition, JavaScript sends the Submit event to the form just prior to dashing off the data to the server. Therefore, any script or function that is the parameter of the `onSubmit=` attribute will execute before the data is actually submitted. This can be tricky, however, because unless you craft your function carefully to prevent the user from letting incorrectly entered data remain in a field, it could be easy for bad data to reach the server. Still, there are many reasons why you may want to trigger a script just before submitting data to a server—filling in the status line with a message about what's going on, for instance. It is also one place where you can logically place a `window.confirm()` dialog box, particularly if the form's action is to send data via e-mail. It is common courtesy to first obtain the viewer's permission to send mail automatically.

Any code that is executed for the `onSubmit=` event handler must evaluate to an expression consisting of the word `return` plus a Boolean value. If the Boolean value is true, the submission executes as usual; if the value is false, no submission is made. Therefore, if your script performs some validation prior to submitting data, make sure that the event handler calls that validation function as part of a `return` statement, as shown in Listing 8-17.

Example:

```
<HTML>
<HEAD>
<TITLE>Elements Array</TITLE>
<SCRIPT LANGUAGE="JavaScript">
function getPermission() {
    return window.confirm("Go ahead and mail this info?")
}
```

(form) onSubmit=

```
</SCRIPT>
</HEAD>
<BODY>
<FORM METHOD=POST ACTION="mailto:trash@dannyg.com"
onSubmit="return getPermission()">
Enter your first name:<INPUT TYPE="text" NAME="firstName"><P>
Enter your last name:<INPUT TYPE="text" NAME="lastName"><P>
Enter your address:<INPUT TYPE="text" NAME="address"><P>
Enter your city:<INPUT TYPE="text" NAME="city"><P>
<INPUT TYPE="radio" NAME="gender">Male
<INPUT TYPE="radio" NAME="gender">Female <P>
<INPUT TYPE="checkbox" NAME="retired">I am retired<P>
<INPUT TYPE="submit">
</FORM>

</BODY>
</HTML>
```

Listing 8-17: The onSubmit= event handler asks for confirmation before mailing off data to the form.

To get permission before mailing off information from this form, the onSubmit= event handler summons a function that displays a confirm dialog box. Because the values returned by this type of dialog box are either true or false (corresponding to the OK and Cancel buttons), the returned value is fed back to the return statement in the event handler to let the form know whether it should proceed with the submission.

Text Object

Properties	Methods	Event Handlers
defaultValue	blur()	onBlur=
name	focus()	onFocus=
value	select()	onChange=
		onSelect=

document.forms[i].*textObject*

Syntax

Creating a text object:

```
<FORM>
<INPUT
    TYPE="text"
    NAME="fieldName"
    [VALUE="contents"]
    [SIZE="characterCount"]
    [onBlur="handlerTextOrFunction"]
    [onChange="handlerTextOrFunction"]
    [onFocus="handlerTextOrFunction"]
    [onSelect="handlerTextOrFunction"]>
</FORM>
```

Accessing text object properties or methods:

```
[window.] document.formName.fieldName.property |
    method([parameters])
```

```
[window.] document.formName.elements[index].property |
    method([parameters])
```

```
[window.] document.forms[index].fieldName.property |
    method([parameters])
```

```
[window.]document.forms[index].elements[index].property |
    method([parameters])
```

About this object

The text object is the primary medium for capturing user-entered text. Browsers tend to display entered text in a monospaced font (usually Courier or a derivative), so it is easy to specify the width (SIZE) of a field based on the anticipated number of characters that a user will put into the field. If your design requires multiple lines of text, use the `textarea` object that follows.

Due to the limitations scripts have in updating information on an existing HTML page (without assembling and rewriting an entire page in JavaScript), it is common to use text objects to display results of script calculation or other processing. Such fields may stand alone on a page or be part of a table.

Unfortunately, these fields are not write-protected, so it's easy to understand how a novice user may be confused when tabbing through a page causes the text pointer or

186

document.forms[i].textObject

selection to activate a field used exclusively for output. Of course, if there is no event handler attached to such a script, there is no harm in manually changing the contents of a results field—but the user may get mighty confused. A better choice for the scripter may be to attach an `onChange=` event handler to output fields so that if a user attempts to change the contents of a field, the calculation is run again, or the previous result (if stored in the script as a global variable) is automatically re-inserted when the user tabs or clicks out of that changed field.

Text object definitions, methods, and event handlers use terminology that may be known to Windows users but not to Macintosh users. A field is said to have *focus* when the user clicks or tabs into the field. When a field has focus, either the text insertion pointer flashes or any text in the field may be selected. Only one text object can have focus at a time. The inverse user action — clicking or tabbing away from a text object — is called a *blur*. Clicking on another object, whether it be another field or a button of any kind, causes a field that currently has focus to blur.

These two terms, *focus* and *blur*, also interact with other possible user actions to a text object: selecting and changing. *Selecting* means clicking and dragging across any text in the field; *changing* means making any alteration to the content of the field and then either tabbing or clicking away from that field.

When you design event handlers for fields, be aware that a user's interaction with a field may trigger more than one event with a single action. For instance, clicking on a field to select text may trigger both a focus and select event. If you have conflicting actions in the `onFocus=` and `onSelect=` event handlers, your scripts can do some weird things to the user's experience with your page. Displaying alert dialog boxes, for instance, also triggers blur events; so a field that has both an `onSelect=` handler (which displays the alert) and an `onBlur=` handler will get a nasty interaction from the two.

As a result, you should be very judicious with the number of event handlers you specify in any text object definition. If possible, pick one user action that you want to initiate some JavaScript code execution. Not all fields require event handlers — only those you want to perform some action as the result of user activity in that field.

The behavior of the Change event is also confused by newcomers. To prevent this event from being sent to the field for every character that the user types, any change to a field is determined only after the field loses focus by the user's clicking or tabbing away from it. At that point, instead of a blur event being sent to the field, only a Change event is sent, triggering an `onChange=` event handler if one is defined for the field. This extra burden of having to click or tab away from a field may entice you to shift any `onChange=` event handler tasks to a separate button that the user must click to initiate action on the field contents.

document.forms[i].*textObject*

Text objects (including the related textarea object) have one unique behavior that can be very important to some document and script designs. Even if a default value is specified for the content of a field (in the VALUE= attribute), any text entered into a field by a user or script persists in that field as long as the document is cached in the browser's disk cache. Therefore, if users of your page enter values into some fields, or your scripts display results in a field, all that data will be there later, even if the user reloads the page or navigates to dozens of other Web pages or sites. Navigating back via the Go or Bookmarks menu entries causes the browser to retrieve the cached version (with its field entries). To force the page to appear with its default text object values, use the Open Location or Open File selections in the File menu. This causes the browser to load the desired page from scratch, regardless of the content of the cache. When you quit and relaunch the browser, the first time it goes to the desired page, the page is loaded from scratch — with its default values.

This level of persistence is not as reliable as the document.cookie property because a user can reopen a URL at any time, thus erasing whatever was temporarily stored in a text or textarea object. Still, this method may suffice for some designs. Unfortunately, you cannot completely hide a text object in case the data you want to store is for use only by your scripts. The TYPE="hidden" form element is not an alternative here because script-induced changes to its value do not persist across page reloads.

If you prefer to use a text or textarea object as a storage medium but don't want users to see it, design the page to appear in a frame whose SCROLLING= attribute is set to "no." Then embed the <FORM> definition that contains the text object within a <PRE> ...</PRE> tag pair. Pad the beginning of the line containing the <INPUT> text element with enough spaces that the field appears too far to the right of the frame to appear in anyone's browser. That's a lot of work. The document.cookie may not seem so complicated after all that.

To extract the current data in a text object, summon the document.formName. fieldName.value property. Once you have the string value, you can use JavaScript's string object methods (Chapter 9) to parse or otherwise massage that text as needed for your script.

Properties

value

Value: string
Gettable: Yes
Settable: Yes

188

document.forms[i].*textObject*.value

A text object's value property is the two-way gateway to the content of the field. A reference to an object's value property returns the string currently showing in the field. Note that all values coming from a text object are string values. If your field prompts a user to enter a number, your script may have to perform data conversion to the number-as-string value ("42" instead of plain old 42) before any math operations can be performed on it. JavaScript tries to be as automatic about this data conversion as possible and follows some rules about it (Chapter 9). If you see an error message that says a value is not a number (for a math operation), the value is still a string.

Assigning a string to the value property of a text object is how your script places text of its own into a field for display to the user. Use the simple assignment operator. For example

```
document.forms[0].ZIP.value = "90210"
```

JavaScript is more forgiving about data types when assigning values to a text object. JavaScript automatically converts any value, such as parameters to `window.alert()` methods, to a string on its way to a text object display. Even Boolean values get converted to their string equivalents "true" or "false." Scripts can place numeric values into fields without a hitch. But remember that if a script later retrieves these values from the text object, they will come back as strings.

Example:

```
<HTML>
<HEAD>
<TITLE>Text Object Value</TITLE>
<SCRIPT LANGUAGE="JavaScript">
function upperMe(form) {
    inputStr = form.convertor.value
    form.convertor.value = inputStr.toUpperCase()
}
</SCRIPT>
</HEAD>

<BODY>
<FORM>
Enter lowercase letters for conversion to uppercase: <INPUT
TYPE="text" NAME="convertor" VALUE="sample"
onChange="upperMe(this.form)">
</FORM>
```

(continued)

189

document.forms[i].*textObject*.value

```
</BODY>
</HTML>
```

Listing 8-18: The long but easily understandable way of extracting a text object's value and assigning a value to the same text object.

As a demonstration of how to retrieve and assign values to a text object, Listing 8-18 shows how the action in an onChange= event handler is triggered. Enter any lowercase letters into the field and tab or click out of the field. We pass the entire form object as a parameter to the event handler, including a reference to the form. The function extracts the value, converts it to uppercase (using one of JavaScript's string object methods — Chapter 9), and assigns it back to the same field in that form.

I'll also show two other ways to accomplish the same task, each one more efficient than the previous example. Both utilize the shortcut object reference to get at the heart of the text object. Listing 8-19 passes the field object — contained in the this reference — to the function handler. Becasue that field object contains a complete reference to it (out of our sight, but there just the same), we can access the value property of that object and assign a string to that object's value property in a simple assignment statement.

```
<HTML>
<HEAD>
<TITLE>Text Object Value</TITLE>
<SCRIPT LANGUAGE="JavaScript">
function upperMe(field) {
    field.value = field.value.toUpperCase()
}
</SCRIPT>
</HEAD>

<BODY>
<FORM>
Enter lowercase letters for conversion to uppercase: <INPUT
TYPE="text" NAME="convertor" VALUE="sample"
onChange="upperMe(this)">
</FORM>
</BODY>
</HTML>
```

Listing 8-19: This version passes the text object (as this) to the function for processing.

document.forms[i].*textObject*.value

A more efficient way is to deal with the field values directly in an embedded event handler — instead of calling an external function (which might still be useful if other objects need this functionality). With the function removed from the document, the event handler attribute of the <INPUT> definition changes to do all the work:

```
<INPUT TYPE="text" NAME="convertor" VALUE="sample"
  onChange="this.value = this.value.toUpperCase()">
```

The right-hand side of the assignment expression extracts the current contents of the field and (with the help of the toUpperCase() method of the string object) converts the original string to all uppercase letters. The result of that operation is assigned to the value property of the field.

Application of the this keyword in the previous examples may be confusing at first, but these examples represent the range of ways to use such references effectively. Using this by itself as a parameter to an object's event handler refers only to that single object — a text object in Listing 8-19. If you want to pass along a broader scope of objects that contain the current object, use the this keyword along with the outer object layer you want. In Listing 8-18, we sent the entire form along by specifying this.form — meaning the form that contains "this" object, which is being defined in this line of HTML code. We could, in fact, have sent the entire document object along by specifying this.document; but the function was concerned only with objects from the form and narrower ones.

At the other end of the scale, we can use similar-looking syntax to specify a particular property of "this" object. Thus, in our last example, we zeroed in on just the value property of the current object being defined — this.value. Although the formats of this.form and this.value appear the same, they encompass entirely different ends of the range of focus — simply by virtue of the meaning of the keywords to the right of the period. As long as you know that a form is an object of larger scope than the currently defined object, you'll know that this.form includes an entire form object (and all its elements); conversely, if you know that a text object has a property named "value," you'll know that a reference to this.value focuses only on the value property of the currently defined object. This is why it is so valuable for JavaScript authors to be completely familiar with both the object hierarchy and the range of property and method names for those objects.

Related Items: defaultValue property

name

document.forms[i].*textObject*.name

Value: string
Gettable: Yes
Settable: No

Text object names are important for two reasons. First, if your HTML page is being used to submit information to CGI scripts, the name of the text object is passed along with the data to help the server program identify the data being supplied by the form. Second, you can use a text object's name in its reference within JavaScript coding. If you assign distinctive, meaningful names to your fields, these names will help you read and debug your own JavaScript listings (and will make it easier for others to follow your scripting tactics).

Be as descriptive about your text object names as you can. Borrowing text from the field's on-page label will also help you mentally map a scripted reference to a physical field on the page. Like all JavaScript object names, text object names must consist of one contiguous string of numbers, characters, and some punctuation symbols.

Although I urge you to use distinctive names for all objects you define in a document, a case can be made for assigning the same name to a series of interrelated fields — and JavaScript is ready to help. Within a single form, any reused name for the same object type is placed in an indexed array for that name. For example, if you define three fields with the name entry, the value property for each field would be retrieved by these statements:

```
data = document.forms[0].entry[0].value
```

```
data = document.forms[0].entry[1].value
```

```
data = document.forms[0].entry[2].value
```

This construction may be useful if you want to cycle through all of a form's fields to determine which are blank. Elsewhere, your script would probably have to know what kind of information each field is supposed to receive so that it can process the data intelligently. I don't recommend reusing object names; but you should be aware of how JavaScript handles them in case you need this construction.

Example:

Consult Listing 8-18, in which we use the text object's name, convertor, as part of the reference when assigning a value to the field. To extract the name of a text object, you can use the property reference. Therefore, assuming that your script doesn't know the name of the first object in the first form of a document, the statement would be

```
objectName = document.forms[0].elements[0].name
```

document.forms[i].*textObject*.name

Related Items: `form.elements` property; all other form element objects' name property.

`defaultValue`	

Value: string
Gettable: Yes
Settable: No

While your users and your scripts are free to muck with the contents of a text object by assigning strings to the value property, you can always extract (and thus restore, if necessary) the string assigned to the text object in its <INPUT> definition. The `defaultValue` property yields the string parameter of the `VALUE=` attribute.

Example:

```
<HTML>
<HEAD>
<TITLE>Text Object DefaultValue</TITLE>
<SCRIPT LANGUAGE="JavaScript">
function upperMe(field) {
    field.value = field.value.toUpperCase()
}
function resetField(form) {
    form.convertor.value = form.convertor.defaultValue
}
</SCRIPT>
</HEAD>

<BODY>
<FORM>
Enter lowercase letters for conversion to uppercase: <INPUT
TYPE="text" NAME="convertor" VALUE="sample"
onChange="upperMe(this)">
<INPUT TYPE="button" VALUE="Reset Field"
onClick="resetField(this.form)">
</FORM>
</BODY>
</HTML>
```

Listing 8-20: A demonstration of resetting a text object to its default contents.

193

document.forms[i].*textObject*.defaultValue

Modifying Listing 8-19 a bit, we add a button that calls a new function (resetField()) to restore the contents of the page's lone field to the value assigned to it in the <INPUT> definition. For a single-field page such as this, defining a TYPE="reset" button works the same way because such buttons re-establish default values of all elements of a form. But if you want to reset only a subset of fields in a form, you can follow the example button and function in Listing 8-20 to do the job.

Related Items: value property

Methods

`select()`

Returns: (Nothing)

Selecting a field under script control means selecting all text within the text object. A typical application is one in which an entry validation script detects a mistake on the part of the user. After alerting the user to the mistake (via a window.alert() dialog box), the script finishes its task by selecting the text of the field in question. Not only does it draw the user's eye to the field needing attention (especially important if the validation code is checking multiple fields), but it also keeps the old text there for the user to examine for potential problems. With the text selected, the next key that the user presses eradicates the former entry.

Trying to select a text object's contents with a click of a button is problematic. For one thing, a click of the button brings the document's focus to the button, which disrupts the selection process. For more assured selection, the script should invoke both the focus() and the select() methods for the field, in that order. There is no penalty for issuing both methods, and the extra insurance provides a more consistent user experience with the page.

Selecting a text object via script does *not* trigger the same onSelect= event handler for that object as the one that would be triggered if a user had manually selected text in the field. Therefore, no event handler script is executed when the select() method is invoked.

Example:

```
<HTML>
<HEAD>
<TITLE>Text Object Select/Focus</TITLE>
```

```
document.forms[i].textObject.select()
```

```
<SCRIPT LANGUAGE="JavaScript">
// general purpose function to see if a suspected numeric input is
a number
function isNumber(inputStr) {
    for (var i = 0; i < inputStr.length; i++) {
        var oneChar = inputStr.substring(i, i + 1)
        if (oneChar < "0" || oneChar > "9") {
            alert("Please make sure entries are numbers only.")
            return false
        }
    }
    return true
}
function checkIt(form) {
    inputStr = form.numeric.value
    if (isNumber(inputStr)) {
        // statements if true
    } else {
    form.numeric.focus()
    form.numeric.select()
    }
}


</SCRIPT>
</HEAD>

<BODY>
<FORM>
Enter any positive integer: <INPUT TYPE="text" NAME="numeric"><P>
<INPUT TYPE="button" VALUE="Verify" onClick="checkIt(this.form)">
</FORM>
</BODY>
</HTML>
```

Listing 8-21: Selecting a field (with focus() and select() methods) after an entry validation fails.

A click of the Verify button in Listing 8-21 sends the contents of the text object to be validated as all numbers. If the validation comes back false, the script pre-selects the field entry for the user. To make sure that the selection takes place, we first set the document's focus to the field and then select its contents. If the field was the focus immediately before clicking the button, the selection may work without setting the

document.forms[i].*textObject*.select()

focus. But you cannot be sure what the user does between entering text and clicking the button. Try commenting out (//) the form.numeric.focus() statement, then reload the document and see how well the selection works by itself under a variety of circumstances. You'll find that setting the focus is a surefire method.

Related Items: focus() method; onSelect= event handler

focus()

Returns: (Nothing)

Focus for a text object means that the text insertion pointer is flashing in that text object's field (it means something different for buttons in a Windows environment). Giving a field focus is like opening it up for human editing. As noted in the discussion about the select() method for text objects, it is a good idea to set a document's focus to a particular text object before a script selects it. That's what happens when a user clicks in a field and selects some of its text — even though the user doesn't see anything special about a field getting focus as a separate event.

Setting the focus of a field with text in it does not let you place the cursor at any specified location in the field. The cursor usually appears at the beginning of the text.

Example:

See Listing 8-21 for an example of an application of the focus() method in concert with the select() method.

Related Items: select() method; onFocus= event handler.

blur()

Returns: (Nothing)

Just as a camera lens blurs when it goes out of focus, a text object blurs when it loses focus — when someone clicks or tabs out of the field. Under script control, blur() deselects whatever may be selected in the field, and the text insertion pointer leaves the field. The pointer does not proceed to the next field in tabbing order, as it would if you blurred by tabbing out of the field manually.

Example:

```
document.forms[0].vanishText.blur()
```

Related Items: focus() method; onBlur= event handler.

document.forms[i].*textObject*.focus() | blur()

Event handlers

onChange=

Of the four event handlers for a text object, the `onChange=` handler is probably the one you will use most often in your forms. This is a convenient event to trigger validation for whatever entry has just occurred in the field. The potential hazard with trying to do data validation of all entries in batch mode before submitting an entire form is that not only does the validation take longer, but the user's mental focus is away from the entry of any given field as well. When you validate immediately, the user is already thinking about the information category in question. See Chapter 15 for more about data entry validation.

Example:

```
<HTML>
<HEAD>
<TITLE>Text Object Select/Focus</TITLE>
<SCRIPT LANGUAGE="JavaScript">
// general purpose function to see if a suspected numeric input is
a number
function isNumber(inputStr) {
    for (var i = 0; i < inputStr.length; i++) {
        var oneChar = inputStr.substring(i, i + 1)
        if (oneChar < "0" || oneChar > "9") {
            alert("Please make sure entries are numbers only.")
            return false
        }
    }
    return true
}
function checkIt(form) {
    inputStr = form.numeric.value
    if (isNumber(inputStr)) {
        // statements if true
    } else {
        form.numeric.focus()
        form.numeric.select()
    }
}
```

(continued)

```
</SCRIPT>
</HEAD>

<BODY>
<FORM>
Enter any positive integer: <INPUT TYPE="text" NAME="numeric"
onChange="checkIt(this.form)"><P>
</FORM>
</BODY>
</HTML>
```

Listing 8-22: A variation of Listing 8-20. This form triggers the data validation with an onChange= event handler in the text object.

Whenever a user makes a change to the text in a field and then either tabs or clicks out of the field, the Change event is sent to that field, triggering the onChange= event handler.

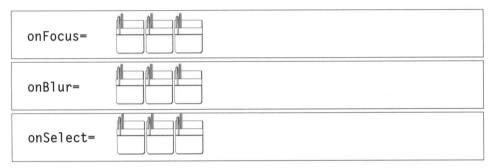

All three of these event handlers should be used only after you have a firm understanding of the interrelatedness of the four events that reach text objects (as discussed earlier in this object's section). You must exercise extreme care and conduct lots of user testing before including more than one event handler in a text object. Because some events cannot occur without triggering others either immediately before or after (for example, an onFocus= occurs immediately before an onSelect= if the field did not have focus before), whatever actions you script for these events should be as distinct as possible to avoid interference or overlap.

Example:

```
<HTML>
<HEAD>
<TITLE>Elements Array</TITLE>
```

(textObject) onFocus= | onBlur= | onSelect=

```
<SCRIPT LANGUAGE="JavaScript">
function prompt(msg) {
    window.status = "Please enter your " + msg + "."
}
</SCRIPT>
</HEAD>

<BODY>
<FORM>
Enter your first name:<INPUT TYPE="text" NAME="firstName"
onFocus="prompt('first name')"><P>
Enter your last name:<INPUT TYPE="text" NAME="lastName"
onFocus="prompt('last name')"><P>
Enter your address:<INPUT TYPE="text" NAME="address"
onFocus="prompt('address')"><P>
Enter your city:<INPUT TYPE="text" NAME="city"
onFocus="prompt('city')"><P>
</FORM>
</BODY>
</HTML>
```

Listing 8-23: Using the `onFocus=` event handler to prompt the user.

To demonstrate one of these event handlers, Listing 8-23 shows how you might use the window's status bar as a prompt message area as a user activates any field of a form. When the user tabs to or clicks on a field, the prompt message associated with that field appears in the status bar.

Password Object

Properties	Methods	Event Handlers
defaultValue	focus()	(None)
name	blur()	
value	select()	

document.forms[i].password

Syntax

Creating a password object:

```
<FORM>
<INPUT
    TYPE="password"
    NAME="fieldName"
    [VALUE="contents"]
    SIZE="characterCount">
</FORM>
```

About this object

Despite the properties and methods defined for the password object, this special-purpose text field offers very little access for JavaScript scripts. A password-style field looks like a text object; but when the user types into the field, only asterisks or bullets (depending on your operating system) appear in the field. For the sake of security, any password exchanges should be handled by a server-side CGI program.

A script cannot extract the contents of the field (the value property) unless the value has been set by the optional VALUE= tag in the object's <INPUT> definition attributes. And while such a value is in plain language internally (and will be returned in that format if queried by the value property), the default value appears in asterisk/bullet form in the field. Future versions of JavaScript may allow for more direct access to the encrypted aspects of passwords, but for Navigator 2.0, the object is rather flat. For that reason, I will skip further discussion of properties and methods for this object.

It is appropriate to use the document.cookie to store a user's password for your site. This must be done with a CGI program on the server, which can send the password back to the cookie. No JavaScript is involved.

Textarea Object

Properties	Methods	Event Handlers
defaultValue	blur()	onBlur=
name	focus()	onFocus=
value	select()	onChange=
		onSelect=

textarea

Syntax

Creating a textarea object:

```
<FORM>
<TEXTAREA
    NAME="fieldName"
    [ROWS="rowCount"]
    [COLS="columnCount"]
    [WRAP="off" | "virtual" | "physical"
    [onBlur="handlerTextOrFunction"]
    [onChange="handlerTextOrFunction"]
    [onFocus="handlerTextOrFunction"]
    [onSelect="handlerTextOrFunction"]>
    defaultText
</TEXTAREA>
</FORM>
```

Accessing textarea object properties or methods:

```
[window.] document.formName.fieldName.property |
    method([parameters])
```

```
[window.] document.formName.elements[index].property |
    method([parameters])
```

```
[window.] document.forms[index].fieldName.property |
    method([parameters])
```

```
[window.] document.forms[index].elements[index].property |
    method([parameters])
```

About this object

Although not in the same syntax family as other <INPUT> elements of a form, a textarea object is indeed a form element. Any definition for a textarea object must be written within the confines of a <FORM>...</FORM> tag pair.

A textarea object closely resembles a text object except for attributes that define its physical appearance on the page. Because a textarea object is intended for multiple-line text input, the attributes include a specification for height (number of rows) and width (number of columns in the monospaced font). No matter what size you specify, the browser displays a textarea with horizontal and vertical scrollbars (Figure 8-6). The

textarea

field is not resizable by the user or by script, nor does text wrap within the visible rectangle of the field unless you specify that the WRAP= attribute should be set to "virtual" or "physical". Instead the user is encouraged to use the Enter key to make manual carriage returns. If the user fails to do so, the text scrolls for significant distance horizontally (the horizontal scrollbar appears when wrapping is in its default off setting). This is, indeed, a primitive text field by GUI computing standards.

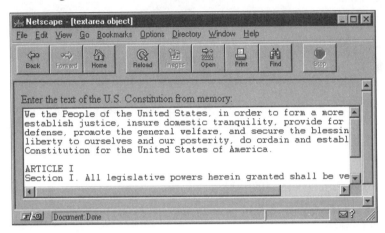

Figure 8-6: A textarea object displays scrollbars.

All properties, methods, and event handlers of text objects apply to the textarea object. They all behave exactly the same way. Therefore, refer to the previous listings for the text object.

The only difference between the properties of the two objects is that the textarea object's value property may likely contain return characters or may need to be assigned text with return characters inside for ease of reading by the user. In Navigator 2.0, many platform-dependent bugs exist that make assigning multiple-lined strings to a textarea object a problem. When assembling text in a variable for eventual assignment to the document.formName.textAreaName.value property, the ideal way to signify a carriage return is to use the \n inline newline character. But some platforms for the browser only obey the \r inline return character. Still other platforms (Windows 95, for example) require the \r\n pair (in that order only). Using the Windows version as the lowest common denominator, however, may leave an odd character in other platforms' textarea fields. Until this feature is repaired in a future version, prepare for odd behavior in the hands of other users (but see the navigator object at the end of this chapter).

textarea

Hidden Object

Properties	Methods	Event Handlers
defaultValue	(None)	(None)
name		
value		

Syntax

Creating a hidden object:

```
<FORM>
<INPUT
    TYPE="hidden"
    NAME="fieldName"
    [VALUE="contents"]>
</FORM>
```

Accessing hidden object properties:

```
[window.] document.formName.fieldName.property
```

```
[window.] document.formName.elements[index].property
```

```
[window.] document.forms[index].fieldName.property
```

```
[window.] document.forms[index].elements[index].property
```

About this object

A hidden object is a simple string holder within a form object whose contents are not visible to the user of your Web page. With no methods or event handlers, the hidden object's value to your scripting is as a delivery vehicle for strings that your scripts need for reference values or other hard-wired data.

I am personally not a fan of the hidden object. I put any data that I want to deliver with my JavaScript-enabled pages into variables and arrays as part of the script. Even so, other scripters might make a case for creating hidden fields corresponding to visible objects. The hidden fields contain related data that a script could access via the same repeat loop counter values as the visible object. I believe it is easier to maintain data in an explicit array. It's all a question of preferred style.

Hidden fields, of course, are useful for CGI applications involving multiple screens. Data from one screen's field can be submitted to a CGI program, which then writes that

203

document.forms[i].hidden

data to a hidden field in the next screen. By the time the user reaches the final screen, all earlier data is in the hidden fields, ready to be submitted as a whole to the CGI program. In the meantime, JavaScript scripts may perform some data validation and comparison between data entered into a regular text field and the hidden data.

Because any scripted changes to the contents of a hidden field are fragile (for example, a reload will erase the changes), the only place you should consider making such changes is in the same script that submits a form to a CGI program. In effect, you're just using the hidden fields as holding pens for scripted data to be submitted. For more persistent storage, use the `document.cookie` property, even if just for the duration of the visit to the page.

For information about the three properties of the hidden object, consult the earlier listing for the text object. But be aware that all properties for hidden objects are read-only.

Button Object, Submit Object, Reset Object

Properties	Method	Event Handler
name	click()	onClick=
value		

Syntax

Creating a button:

```
<FORM>
<INPUT
    TYPE="button" | "submit" | "reset"
    NAME="buttonName"
    VALUE="contents"
    [onClick="handlerTextOrFunction"] >
</FORM>
```

Accessing button object properties or methods:

```
[window.] document.formName.buttonName.property |
    method([parameters])
```

```
[window.] document.formName.elements[index].property |
    method([parameters])
```

document.forms[i].button I submit I reset

```
[window.] document.forms[index].buttonName.property |
    method([parameters])
```

```
[window.] document.forms[index].elements[index].property |
    method([parameters])
```

About these objects

Button objects generate standard pushbutton-style user interface elements on the page, depending on the operating system on which the particular browser runs. Figure 8-7 shows examples of a typical button in both the Windows 95 and Macintosh versions. Because the browsers call upon the operating systems to generate these standard interface elements, the precise look and feel depends entirely on the operating system.

Figure 8-7: Comparison of the button object in the Windows 95 (left) and Macintosh (right) operating systems.

The only visual characteristic of a button under control of the HTML page author is the text that appears on the button. That label text is the parameter to the VALUE= attribute of the button's definition. The width of the button on the screen is calculated for you, based on the width of the button's label text. Always give careful thought to the label you assign to a button. Because a button initiates some action, make sure that the verb in the label clearly defines what will happen. At the same time, take clues from experienced user interface designers who craft operating system and commercial software buttons: be concise. If you find your buttons labels extending past two or three words, reconsider the design of your page so that the purpose of any button can be clearly understood from a shorter label.

Like most user interface elements, buttons are automatically drawn on the page left-aligned. You can surround a button's <INPUT> definition with the new <DIV ALIGN="*where*">...</DIV> tags to align center or right, if you prefer. Or, if fine tuning of placement is necessary, surround the <INPUT> definition with <PRE>...</PRE> tags and pad the beginning of the line (before the start of the <INPUT> tag) with spaces. Because of differences in the way operating systems generate their buttons, precise positioning against other objects or images is difficult or impossible to guarantee.

Buttons in the Windows environment follow their normal behavior in that they indicate the focus with some measure of highlighting around the button label text. You cannot control the focus or blur of a button via JavaScript as you can for a text object. Buttons also highlight according to the conventions of the host operating system and cannot be overridden by any scripting commands.

The lone button object event handler is one that responds to a user's clicking of the pointer atop the mouse: the onClick= event handler. Virtually all action surrounding a button object comes from this event handler. The likelihood of needing to extract property values or invoking the click() method is rare.

Two special variants of the JavaScript button object are the *submit* and *reset* button objects. With their heritages going back to early incarnations of HTML, these two button types perform special operations on their own. The submit-style button automatically sends the data within the same form object to the URL listed in the ACTION= attribute of the <FORM> definition in a format directed by the METHOD= attribute. Therefore, you don't have to script this action if your HTML page is communicating with a CGI program on the server.

The other half of the submit button is the reset style. It, too, has special features. A click of this button type restores all elements within the form to their default values. That goes for text objects, radio button groups, checkboxes, and selection lists. The most common application is to clear entry fields of the last data entered by the user.

All that distinguishes these three types of buttons from each other in the <INPUT> element definition is the parameter of the TYPE= attribute. For buttons not intended for sending data to a server, use the "button" style. Reserve the "submit" and "reset" for their special CGI-related powers.

In the Navigator 2.0 implementation, you cannot assign an image to a button's appearance to turn a piece of art into a client-side map that responds to events. At best, you can fashion such buttons with link objects associated with image files (see "link object" later in the chapter).

Properties

name	

Value: string
Gettable: Yes
Settable: No

document.forms[i].*buttonObject*.name

A button's name is fixed in the <INPUT> definition's NAME= attribute and may not be adjusted via scripting. You may need to retrieve this property in a general-purpose function handler called by multiple buttons in a document: The function can test for a button name and perform the necessary statements for that button.

Example:

```
buttonName = document.forms[0].elements[3].name // 4th element is
a button
```

Related Items: name property of all form elements.

value

Value: string
Gettable: Yes
Settable: No

A button's visible label is determined by the VALUE= attribute of the <INPUT> element's definition. The value property reveals that text. You cannot modify this text on the fly in a script. There is a strong convention that assigns the words "Submit" and "Reset" to their respective button-style labels. As long as the purpose of either button is clear, you can assign whatever label you like to any of the button objects in the <INPUT> definitions. Unlike button (and other object) names, the VALUE= attribute can be more than one word.

It is unlikely that you'll need to extract this property in a script.

Example:

```
buttonLabel = document.forms[0].elements[2].value // 3rd element
is a button
```

Related Items: value property of text object

Method

click()

Returns: (Nothing)

A button's click() method replicates, via scripting, the human action of clicking on that button, except that no click event is sent to the button to trigger its onClick=

event handler. With no change accruing to the interface of the button when it is clicked, there is little need for your scripts to invoke this method.

Example:

```
document.forms[0].sender.click()// sender is the name of a Submit-
style button
```

Related Items: onClick= event handler.

Event handler

onClick=

Virtually all button action takes place in response to the onClick= event handler: the JavaScript code or function that runs when the user clicks on the button. A click is defined as a press and release of the mouse button while the screen pointer is atop the button. The event is sent to the button only after the release of the mouse button, and no events go to the button while the mouse button is held down.

For a submit button object, the event handler can be used to perform last-minute validations or other scripted actions immediately before the form is submitted. For instance, an onClick= event handler function can perform calculations based on user input and selections in a form on the page, and store the results in a hidden field object. When that handler finishes, the form (including the hidden field data) is submitted to the CGI program on the server.

A submit button's onClick= event handler is independent of a form's onSubmit= handler. For example, a function called by an onClick= event handler can set a flag variable to a Boolean value. The form's onSubmit= event handler can then use that flag as part of the required return statement that determines whether the form is actually submitted, or if the submission process should stop short. That flag variable acts as an independent middleman between the two event handlers.

Example:

```
<HTML>
<HEAD>
<TITLE>Button Click</TITLE>
<SCRIPT LANGUAGE="JavaScript">
function displayTeam(btn) {
    if (btn.value == "Abbott") {alert("Abbott & Costello")}
```

(button) onClick=

```
      if (btn.value == "Rowan") {alert("Rowan & Martin")}
      if (btn.value == "Martin") {alert("Martin & Lewis")}
}
</SCRIPT>
</HEAD>

<BODY>
Click on your favorite half of a popular comedy team:<P>
<FORM>
<INPUT TYPE="button" VALUE="Abbott" onClick="displayTeam(this)">
<INPUT TYPE="button" VALUE="Rowan" onClick="displayTeam(this)">
<INPUT TYPE="button" VALUE="Martin" onClick="displayTeam(this)">
</FORM>
</BODY>
</HTML>
```

Listing 8-24: Three buttons, each with an onClick= event handler calling the same function.

Here we demonstrate not only the `onClick=` event handler of a button but how you may need to extract the name or value properties from a button in a general purpose function servicing multiple buttons. In this case, each button passes its own object as a parameter to the `displayTeam()` function. The function then simply displays the results in an alert dialog box. In a production environment, there would probably be a more complex `if...else` decision tree performing more sophisticated actions based on the button clicked.

Related Items: `click()` method.

Checkbox Object

Properties	Method	Event Handlers
checked	click()	onClick=
defaultChecked		
name		
value		

document.forms[i].checkbox

Syntax

Creating a checkbox:

```
<FORM>
<INPUT
    TYPE="checkbox"
    NAME="boxName"
    VALUE="buttonValue"
    [CHECKED]
    [onClick="handlerTextOrFunction"]>
    buttonText
</FORM>
```

Accessing checkbox properties or methods:

```
[window.] document.formName.boxName.property |
    method([parameters])
```

```
[window.] document.formName.elements[index].property |
    method([parameters])
```

```
[window.] document.forms[index].boxName.property |
    method([parameters])
```

```
[window.] document.forms[index].elements[index].property |
    method([parameters])
```

About this object

Checkboxes have a very specific purpose in modern graphical user interfaces: to toggle between "on" and "off" settings. Like a checkbox on a printed form, a mark in the box indicates that the label text is true or should be included for the individual who made that mark. When the box is unchecked or empty, the text is false or should not be included. If two or more checkboxes are physically grouped together, they should have no interaction with each other: Each is an independent setting (see the radio object for interrelated buttons).

I make these user interface points at the outset because to present a user interface in your HTML pages that is consistent with the user's expectations based on exposure to other programs, you must use checkbox objects only for on-off choices that the user makes. Using a checkbox as an action button that, say, navigates to another URL, is not good form. Just as they do in a Windows or Mac dialog box, users make settings with

210

document.forms[i].checkbox

checkboxes and radio buttons and then initiate the action by clicking a standard button.

That's not to say that a checkbox object cannot perform some limited action in response to a user's click. But such actions are typically related to the context of the checkbox button's label text. For example, in some Windows and Macintosh dialog boxes, turning on a checkbox may activate a bunch of otherwise inactive settings elsewhere in the same dialog box. Although we don't have such advanced graphical powers with HTML in Navigator 2.0, there may be other ways to turn a click of a checkbox into a meaningful action. For example, in a two-frame window, a checkbox in one frame may control whether the viewer is an advanced user. If so, the content in the other frame may be more detailed. Toggling the checkbox changes the complexity level of document showing in the other frame (using different URLs for each level).

The bottom line on usage, then, is that checkboxes are for toggling between on-off settings. Regular button objects are for initiating processing.

In the <INPUT> definition for a checkbox, you can preset the checkbox to be checked when the page appears. Add the constant CHECKED attribute to the definition. If you omit this attribute, the default, unchecked appearance rules. As for the checkbox label text, its definition lies outside the <INPUT> tag. If you look at the way checkboxes behave in HTML browsers, this makes sense: The label is not an active part of the checkbox (as it typically is in Windows and Macintosh user interfaces, where clicking on the label is the same as clicking on the box).

Naming a checkbox can be an important part of the object definition, depending on how you plan to use the information in your script or document. For forms whose content is to go to a CGI program on the server, the box name must be chosen for use by the CGI program, so it can parse the form data and extract the setting of the checkbox. For JavaScript client-side use, you can assign not only a name that describes what the button is, but also a value useful for your script for making if...else decisions or for assembling strings that are eventually displayed in a window or frame.

Properties

checked	

Value: Boolean
Gettable: Yes
Settable: Yes

The simplest property of a checkbox reveals (or lets you set) whether or not a checkbox is checked. The value is true for a checked box, false for an unchecked box. To check a box via a script, simply assign *true* to the checkbox's checked property:

```
document.forms[0].boxName.checked = true
```

Setting the checked property from a script does not trigger a click event for the checkbox object.

There may be instances in which one checkbox should automatically check another elsewhere in the same or other form of the document. To accomplish this, create an onClick= event handler for the one checkbox and build a statement similar to the preceding one to set the checkbox setting of the other related box to true. Don't get too carried away by this, however: For a group of interrelated, mutually exclusive choices, use a group of radio buttons instead.

Also, if your page design requires that a checkbox be checked when the page loads, don't bother trying to script this checking action. Simply add the one-word CHECKED attribute to the <INPUT> definition.

Because the checked property is a Boolean value, its results can be used alone as an argument for an if clause, as shown in the following.

Example:

```
<HTML>
<HEAD>
<TITLE>Checkbox Inspector</TITLE>
<SCRIPT LANGUAGE="JavaScript">
function inspectBox(form) {
    if (form.checkThis.checked) {
        alert("The box is checked.")
    } else {
        alert("The box is not checked at the moment.")
    }
}
</SCRIPT>
</HEAD>

<BODY>
<FORM>
<INPUT TYPE="checkbox" NAME="checkThis">Check here<P>
<INPUT TYPE="button" NAME="boxChecker" VALUE="Inspect Box"
onClick="inspectBox(this.form)">
```

document.forms[i].*checkboxObject*.checked

```
</FORM>
</BODY>
</HTML>
```

Listing 8-25: Using the checked property as an argument for an if ... else decision.

The simple example in Listing 8-25 passes the entire form object to the JavaScript function. The function, in turn, extracts the checked value of the form's checkbox object (checkThis.checked) and employs its Boolean value as the test result for the if...else construction.

Related Items: value property; defaultChecked property.

Value: string
Gettable: Yes
Settable: No

Unless a page design submits a form's data to a server for CGI program execution, the primary importance of a checkbox's name is to help you identify it in scripted references to its properties or method. Be as descriptive as you can with the name, so as you read a script reference to an object, the name immediately invokes the vision of the checkbox in your mind.

Example:

Listing 8-25 shows how a checkbox's name is used in a function's reference to the object. Although the name in this particular listing, checkThis, is not exactly a work of fine literature, it is better than generic names such as myBox.

Related Items: name property of all form elements.

Value: string
Gettable: Yes
Settable: No

A checkbox object's value property is a string of any text you want to associate with the box. For instance, the label you attach to a checkbox may not be in wording that

213

document.forms[i].*checkboxObject*.name

is useful to your script. But if you place that useful wording in the VALUE= attribute of the checkbox definition, you can extract that string via the value property.

When a checkbox object's data is submitted to a CGI program, the value property is sent as part of the name=value pair if the box is checked (nothing about the checkbox is sent if the box is unchecked). If you omit the VALUE= attribute in your definition, the property always yields the string "on," which is submitted to a CGI program when the box is checked. From the JavaScript side, don't confuse this with on and off settings of the checkbox: Use the checked property to determine a checkbox's status.

Example:

```
<HTML>
<HEAD>
<TITLE>Checkbox Submission</TITLE>
<SCRIPT LANGUAGE="JavaScript">
function setAction(form) {
    if (form.checkThis.checked) {
        form.action = form.checkThis.value
    } else {
        form.action = "primaryURL"
    }
    return true
}
</SCRIPT>
</HEAD>

<BODY>
<FORM METHOD="GET">
<INPUT TYPE="checkbox" NAME="checkThis" VALUE="alternateURL">Use
alternate<P>
<INPUT TYPE="submit" NAME="boxChecker" onClick="return
setAction(this.form)">

</FORM>
</BODY>
</HTML>
```

Listing 8-26: Adjusting a CGI submission action based on a checkbox's value property.

document.forms[i].*checkboxObject*.value

The scenario for the skeleton HTML page in Listing 8-26 is a form with a checkbox whose selection determines which of two actions to follow for submission to the server. When the user clicks the Submit button, a JavaScript function examines the checkbox's checked property. If it is true (the button is checked), the script sets the action property for the entire form to the content of the value property — thus influencing the recipient of the form on the server side. If you try this listing on your PC, you will receive error messages about being unable to locate a file with the name primaryURL or alternateURL because those files don't exist. The names and the error message come from the submission process for this demonstration.

Related Items: checked property.

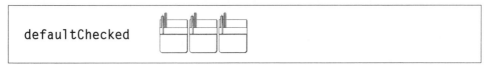

defaultChecked

Value: Boolean
Gettable: Yes
Settable: No

If you add the CHECKED attribute to the <INPUT> definition for a checkbox, the defaultChecked property for that object is true; otherwise, the property is false. Having access to this property lets your scripts examine checkboxes to see if they have been adjusted (presumably by the user, if your script does no automatic clicking).

Example:

```
function compareBrowser(thisBox) {
    if (thisBox.checked != thisBox.defaultChecked) {
        // statements about using a different set of HTML pages
    }
}
```

Listing 8-27: Fragment for examining the defaultChecked property.

The function in Listing 8-27 is designed to compare the current setting of a checkbox against its default value. The if construction compares the current status of the box against its default status. Both are Boolean values, so they can be compared against each other. If the current and default settings don't match, the function goes on to handle the case in which the current setting is other than the default.

Related Items: checked property; value property.

document.forms[i].*checkboxObject*.defaultChecked

Method

`click()`

Returns: (Nothing)

The intention of the `click()` method is to enact, via script, the physical act of checking a checkbox (but without triggering the `onClick=` event handler). Unfortunately, this method does not work in Navigator 2.0 as expected. Even if it worked flawlessly, your scripts are better served by setting the checked property so that you know exactly what the setting of the box is at any time.

Related Items: `onClick=` event handler; checked property.

Event handler

`onClick=`

Because a checkbox is a user-interface element on which users click, it has an event handler for the click event. Use this event handler only when you want your page (or variable values hidden from view) to respond in some way to the action of clicking on a checkbox. Most user actions, as mentioned earlier, are initiated by clicking on standard buttons rather than checkboxes; so be careful not to overuse event handlers in checkboxes.

Example:

```
<HTML>
<HEAD>
<TITLE>Checkbox Event Handler</TITLE>
<SCRIPT LANGUAGE="JavaScript">
function setPort(form) {
    if (form.mouse.checked) {
        form.mousePort.checked = true
    }
}
</SCRIPT>
</HEAD>
```

(checkbox) onClick=

```
<BODY>
<FORM>
<H3>Check all accessories for your computer:</H3>
<INPUT TYPE="checkbox" NAME="colorMonitor" >Color Monitor<P>
<INPUT TYPE="checkbox" NAME="mouse" onClick="setPort(this.form)"
 >Mouse<P>
<INPUT TYPE="checkbox" NAME="mousePort" >Mouse Port<P>
<INPUT TYPE="checkbox" NAME="modem" >Modem<P>
<INPUT TYPE="checkbox" NAME="keyboard" >Keyboard<P>

</FORM>
</BODY>
</HTML>
```

Listing 8-27: The Mouse checkbox handles the click event with an onClick= event handler.

The page in Listing 8-27 shows how you might trap for the click event in one checkbox to influence the setting in another. Here, the assumption is that if your computer has a mouse, there is more than a strong likelihood that it also has a mouse port. Therefore, an onClick= event handler in the Mouse checkbox calls a function to set the Mouse Port's checkbox to true whenever the Mouse checkbox is set to true. But unchecking the Mouse box does not influence the Mouse Port box — perhaps you're using a laptop's touch pad, even though the computer has a mouse port.

Radio Object

Properties	Method	Event Handler
checked	click()	onClick=
defaultChecked		
index		
length		
name		
value		

document.forms[i].radio

Syntax

Creating a radio object:

```
<FORM>
<INPUT
    TYPE="radio"
    NAME="buttonGroupName"
    VALUE="buttonValue"
    [CHECKED]
    [onClick="handlerTextOrFunction"]>
    buttonText
</FORM>
```

Accessing radio object properties or methods:

```
[window.] document.formName.buttonGroupName[index].property |
    method([parameters])
```

```
[window.] document.forms[index].buttonGroupName.property |
    method([parameters])
```

About this object

A radio button object is an unusual one within the body of JavaScript applications. In every other case of form elements, one object equals one visual element on the screen. But a radio object is actually a group of radio buttons. Because of the nature of radio buttons — a mutually exclusive choice among two or more selections — there will always be multiple visual elements within a group. All buttons in the group share the same name — which is how JavaScript knows to group buttons together and let the clicking of a button deselect any other selected button within the group. Beyond that, however, each button can have unique properties, such as its value or checked property.

The way JavaScript lets us access information about an individual button within the button group is to use array syntax. Let's look at an example of defining a button group and see how to reference each button. This button group lets the user select a favorite member of The Three Stooges:

```
<FORM>
<B>Select your favorite Stooge:</B><P>
<INPUT TYPE="radio" NAME="stooges" VALUE="Moe Howard" CHECKED>Moe
<INPUT TYPE="radio" NAME="stooges" VALUE="Larry Fine" >Larry
<INPUT TYPE="radio" NAME="stooges" VALUE="Curly Howard" >Curly
```

document.forms[i].radio

```
<INPUT TYPE="radio" NAME="stooges" VALUE="Shemp Howard" >Shemp
</FORM>
```

When this group displays on the page, the first radio button is preselected for the user (as all radio button groups should have one already selected as a default value). Two of the six properties contained by a radio button object (name and length) apply to the entire group. Thus, the following expressions are valid:

```
groupName = document.forms[0].stooges.name // "stooges"
```

```
groupLength = document.forms[0].stooges.length // how many (4)
```

But the other four properties apply to individual buttons within the group. To access any button, use an array index value as part of the button group name. Thus:

```
firstBtnValue = document.forms[0].stooges[0].value // "Moe Howard"
```

```
secondBtnValue = document.forms[0].stooges[1].value // "Larry
    Fine"
```

Anytime you access the checked, defaultChecked, index, or value property, you must point to a specific button within the group according to its order in the array. The order depends on the sequence in which the individual buttons are defined in the HTML document.

Supplying a VALUE= attribute to a radio button can be very important in your script. Although the text label for a button is defined outside the <INPUT> tag, the VALUE= attribute lets you store any string in the button's hip pocket. In our earlier example, the radio button labels were just first names, whereas the value properties were set in the definition to the full names of the actors. The values could have been anything that our script needed, such as birthdates, shoe sizes, or the first names again (because a script would have no way to retrieve the labels otherwise). The point is that the VALUE= attribute should contain whatever string the script will need to derive from the selection made by the user. The VALUE= attribute contents are also what is sent to a CGI program on a server in a submit action for the form.

How you decide to orient a group of buttons on the screen is entirely up to your design and the real estate available within your document. You can string them in a horizontal row (as shown earlier), place <BR> tags after each one to form a column, or do so after every other one to form a double column. Numeric order within the array is determined only by the order in which they are defined in the document, not by where they appear.

Determining which radio button of a group is checked before processing based on that choice requires constructing a repeat loop to cycle through the buttons in the group (shown in the next example). For each button, your script examines the checked property.

Properties

checked

Value: Boolean
Gettable: Yes
Settable: No

Only one radio button in a group can be highlighted (checked) at a time (the browser takes care of highlighting and unhighlighting buttons in a group for us). That one button's checked property is set to true, while all others in the group are set to false.

For Navigator 2.0, avoid trying to set the checked property of a radio button. It is unreliable at best on some platforms. Leave all radio button settings to the user.

Example:

```
<HTML>
<HEAD>
<TITLE>Extracting Highlighted Radio Button</TITLE>
<SCRIPT LANGUAGE="JavaScript">
function fullName(form) {
    for (var i = 0; i < form.stooges.length; i++) {
        if (form.stooges[i].checked) {
            break
        }
    }
    alert("You chose " + form.stooges[i].value + ".")
}
</SCRIPT>
</HEAD>

<BODY>
<FORM>
<B>Select your favorite Stooge:</B><P>
<INPUT TYPE="radio" NAME="stooges" VALUE="Moe Howard" CHECKED>Moe
```

document.forms[i].*radioObject*[i].checked

```
<INPUT TYPE="radio" NAME="stooges" VALUE="Larry Fine" >Larry
<INPUT TYPE="radio" NAME="stooges" VALUE="Curly Howard" >Curly
<INPUT TYPE="radio" NAME="stooges" VALUE="Shemp Howard" >Shemp<P>
<INPUT TYPE="button" NAME="Viewer" VALUE="View Full Name..."
onClick="fullName(this.form)">
</FORM>
</BODY>
</HTML>
```

Listing 8-28: Finding out which button in a radio group is selected.

For Listing 8-28, we use a repeat loop in the function to cycle through all buttons in the stooges group. For each one, we examine the checked property. When we find the one that is true, we break out of the repeat loop. At that point, the loop counter variable (i) is set to the index value of the button in the selected group. We use that index value to then extract the value property to show it in the alert dialog box.

Related Items: defaultChecked property

name

Value: string
Gettable: Yes
Settable: No

The name property belongs to the entire radio button group. Indeed, if you extract the name of a single button within a group

```
btnName = document.forms[0].groupName[2].name
```

you will receive the same name as for the entire group. In that sense, each radio button element in a group inherits the name of the group. There is probably little need for your scripts to extract the name property of a button or group. More often than not, you will hardwire a button group's name into your script to extract other properties of individual buttons. Getting the name property of an object whose name you know is obviously redundant. But it is important for all scripters to understand the place of radio button group names in the scheme of JavaScript objects.

Related Items: value property

length

221

document.forms[i].*radioObject*[i].name

Value: integer
Gettable: Yes
Settable: No

Only a radio button group has length — the number of individual radio buttons defined for that group. Attempting to retrieve the length of an individual button yields a null value. The length property is valuable for establishing the maximum range of values in a repeat loop that must cycle through every button within that group. If you specify the length property to fill that value (rather than hardwiring the value), the loop construction will be easier to maintain — as you make changes to the number of buttons in the group during page construction, the loop will adjust to the changes automatically.

Example:

See the loop construction within the function of Listing 8-28 for one way to apply the length property.

Related Items: index property.

value

Value: string
Gettable: Yes
Settable: No

As mentioned earlier in this discussion, the value property contains arbitrary information that you assign to it when mapping out the <INPUT> definition for an individual radio button. This is a handy shortcut to correlating a radio button label with detailed or related information that will be of interest to your script or CGI program on a server. If you like, the value property can contain the same text as the label.

Example:

Listing 8-28 demonstrates how a function extracts the value property of a radio button to display otherwise hidden information stored with a button. In this case, it lets the alert dialog box show the full name of the selected stooge.

Related Items: name property.

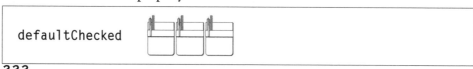

defaultChecked

document.forms[i].*radioObject*[i].defaultChecked

Value: Boolean
Gettable: Yes
Settable: No

If you add the CHECKED attribute to the <INPUT> definition for a radio button, the defaultChecked property for that object is true; otherwise, the property is false. Having access to this property lets your scripts examine individual radio buttons to see if they have been adjusted (presumably by the user, if your script does no automatic clicking).

Example:

```
function groupChanged(form) {
    for (var i = 0; i < form.stooges.length; i++) {
        if (form.stooges[i].defaultChecked) {
            if (!form.stooges[i].checked) {
                alert("This radio group has been changed.")
            }
        }
    }
}
```

Listing 8-29: Function that sees if one of the stooges radio buttons has changed.

In the script fragment of Listing 8-29, a function is passed a form containing the stooges radio buttons. The goal is to see in as general a way as possible (supplying the radio group name where needed) if the user has made a change to the default setting. Looping through each of the radio buttons, we look for the one whose CHECKED attribute was set in the <INPUT> definition. With that index value (i) in hand, we look to see if that entry is still checked. If not (notice the ! negation operator), we display an alert about the change.

Related Items: checked property; value property.

Method

click()	

Returns: (Nothing)

document.forms[i].*radioObject*[i].click()

The intention of the `click()` method is to enact via a script the physical act of clicking on a radio button (without triggering the `onClick=` event handler). Unfortunately, this method does not work in Navigator 2.0 as expected. Even if it worked flawlessly, your scripts are better served by setting the checked properties of all buttons in a group so that you know exactly what the setting of the group is at any time.

Related Items: `onClick=` event handler; `checked` property.

Event handler

`onClick=`

Radio buttons, more than any user interface element available in HTML, are intended for use in making choices that will be acted upon later by other objects, such as submit or standard buttons. You may see in Windows or Macintosh programs cases in which highlighting a radio button — at most — activates or brings into view additional, related settings. Unfortunately, we don't have such dynamic facilities on Web pages with Navigator 2.0.

I strongly advise not using scripting handlers that perform significant actions at the click of any radio button. At best, you may want to use knowledge about a user's clicking of a radio button to adjust a global variable setting that influences subsequent processing. Be aware, however, that if you script such a hidden action for one radio button in a group, you must also script similar actions for others in the same group. That way, if a user changes the setting back to a previous condition, the global variable is reset to the way it was earlier. JavaScript, however, tends to run fast enough so that such adjustments can be made in a batch operation when the user clicks a more action-oriented button.

Example:

```
<HTML>
<HEAD>
<TITLE>Radio Button onClick Handler</TITLE>
<SCRIPT LANGUAGE="JavaScript">
var ShempOPhile = false
function fullName(form) {
    for (var i = 0; i < form.stooges.length; i++) {
        if (form.stooges[i].checked) {
            break
```

(radio) onClick=

```
        }
    }
    alert("You chose " + form.stooges[i].value + ".")
}
function setShemp(setting) {
    ShempOPhile = setting
}
function exitMsg() {
    if (ShempOPhile) {
        alert("You like SHEMP?")
    }
}
</SCRIPT>
</HEAD>

<BODY onUnload="exitMsg()">
<FORM>
<B>Select your favorite Stooge:</B><P>
<INPUT TYPE="radio" NAME="stooges" VALUE="Moe Howard" CHECKED
onClick="setShemp(false)">Moe
<INPUT TYPE="radio" NAME="stooges" VALUE="Larry Fine"
onClick="setShemp(false)">Larry
<INPUT TYPE="radio" NAME="stooges" VALUE="Curly Howard"
onClick="setShemp(false)">Curly
<INPUT TYPE="radio" NAME="stooges" VALUE="Shemp Howard"
onClick="setShemp(true)">Shemp<P>
<INPUT TYPE="button" NAME="Viewer" VALUE="View Full Name..."
onClick="fullName(this.form)">
</FORM>
</BODY>
</HTML>
```

Listing 8-30: An application of the onClick event handler for radio buttons.

Each time a user clicks one of the radio buttons in Listing 8-30, it sets a global variable to true or false, depending on whether the person is a Shemp-lover. This action is independent of the action taking place when the user clicks on the View Full Name button. An onUnload= event handler in the <BODY> definition triggers a function that displays a message to Shemp-lovers just before the page clears (click on the browser's Reload button to leave the current page prior to reloading).

(radio) onClick=

Select Object

Properties	Method	Event Handlers
length	(None)	onChange=
name		
options		
selectedIndex		
options[n].defaultSelected		
options[n].index		
options[n].selected		
options[n].text		
options[n].value		

Syntax

Creating a select object:

```
<FORM>
<SELECT
    NAME="listName"
    [SIZE="number"]
    [MULTIPLE]
    [onBlur="handlerTextOrFunction"]
    [onChange="handlerTextOrFunction"]
    [onFocus="handlerTextOrFunction"]>
    <OPTION [SELECTED] [VALUE="string"]>listItem
    [...<OPTION [VALUE="string"]>listItem]
</SELECT>
</FORM>
```

Accessing select object properties:

```
[window.] document.formName.listName.property
```

```
[window.] document.forms[index].listName.property
```

```
[window.] document.formName.listName.options[index].property
```

```
[window.] document.forms[index].listName.options[index].property
```

document.forms[i].select

About this object

Select objects are perhaps the most visually interesting user interface elements among the standard built-in objects. In one form, they appear on the page as pop-up lists; in another form, they appear as scrolling list boxes. Pop-up lists, in particular, offer efficient use of page real estate for presenting a list of choices for the user. Moreover, only the choice selected by the user shows on the page, limiting the visual clutter of unneeded verbiage.

Compared to other JavaScript objects, select objects are difficult to script — mostly because of the complexity of data that goes into a list of items. Some properties of the object apply to the entire object, whereas other properties pertain only to a single item in the list (each item is called an *option*). For example, you can extract the number (index) of the currently selected option in the list — a property of the entire selection object. To get the text of the selected option, however, you must zero in further, extracting the text property of a single option among all options defined for the object.

When you define a select object within a form, the construction of the <SELECT> ... </SELECT> tag pair is easy to inadvertently mess up. First, most attributes that define the entire object, such as NAME=, SIZE=, and event handlers, are attributes of the opening <SELECT> tag. Between the end of the opening tag and the closing </SELECT> tag are additional tags for each option to be displayed in the list. The following object definition creates a selection pop-up list containing three colors:

```
<FORM>
<SELECT NAME="RGBColors" onChange="changeColor(this)">
    <OPTION SELECTED>Red<OPTION>Green<OPTION>Blue
</SELECT>
</FORM>
```

Formatting the tags in the HTML document is not critical. I indented the line of options merely for the sake of readability.

The SIZE= attribute determines whether a select object appears as a pop-up list or a list box. If you omit the attribute, the browser automatically assigns the default value of 1. This value forces the browser to display the list as a pop-up menu. Assigning any other integer value to the SIZE= attribute directs the browser to display the list as a list box. The number indicates how many options will be visible in the list without scrolling — how tall the box will be, measured in lines. Because scrollbars in GUI environments tend to require a fair amount of space to display a minimum set of clickable areas (including sliding "thumbs"), you should set list box style sizes to no fewer than four. If that makes the list box too tall for your page design, consider using a pop-up menu instead. Figure 8-8 shows two versions of a select object: one with a size of one;

227

document.forms[i].select

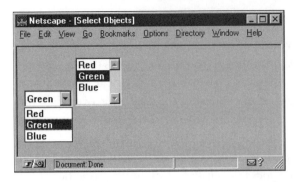

Figure 8-8: Two versions of the select object.

the other with a size of four.

Significant differences exist in the deployment of pop-up menus in each GUI platform. Because each browser relies on the operating system to display its native pop-up menu style, there are considerable differences among the OS platforms in the size of a given pop-up menu. What fits nicely within a standard window width of one OS may not fit in another. In other words, you cannot rely on precision locations of any select object on a page (in case you're trying to align one with an image).

In list box form, a select object can be set to accept multiple, noncontiguous selections. Users typically accomplish such selections by holding down a modifier key (Shift, Control, or Command keys, depending on OS platform) while clicking on additional options. To switch on this capability for a select object, include the MULTIPLE attribute constant in the definition.

For each entry in a list, your <SELECT> definition must include an <OPTION> tag plus the text as you want to appear in the list. If you want a pop-up list to show a default selection when the page loads, you must attach a SELECTED attribute to that item's <OPTION> tag. Without this attribute, the pop-up list appears empty at first — not a friendly way to greet your page's viewers. You can also assign a string value to each option. As with radio buttons, this value can be text other than the wording displayed in the list; so your script can act on that "hidden" value rather than the displayed text. This is also the value sent to a CGI program (as part of the name=value pair) when the select object's form is submitted.

One behavioral aspect of the select object may influence your page design. The onChange= event handler triggers immediately when a user makes a new selection in a pop-up list (except for a Navigator 2.0 bug on Windows versions). If you'd prefer that any action be delayed until other settings are made, omit an onChange= event handler in the select object, but be sure to create a button that lets users initiate whatever action requires those settings.

document.forms[i].select

Properties

options[*index*]

Value: array of options
Gettable: Yes
Settable: No

Despite the one-pocket-protector ranking of the options property, you typically won't summon this one by itself. Rather, it becomes part of a reference to a specific option's properties within the entire select object. In other words, the options property becomes a kind of gateway to more specific properties, such as the value assigned to a single option within the list.

As is true with many JavaScript properties, you can use the options property by itself for debugging purposes. The value it returns is the object definition (complete with tags). If you have more than one select object in your page, you can use this property temporarily to review the definitions as JavaScript sees them. I don't recommend using this data for your working scripts, however, because there are easier ways to extract necessary data.

Example:

```
<HTML>
<HEAD>
<TITLE>Select Inspector</TITLE>
<SCRIPT LANGUAGE="JavaScript">
function inspect(form) {
    alert(form.colorsList.options)
}
</SCRIPT>
</HEAD>

<BODY>
<FORM>
<SELECT NAME="colorsList">
    <OPTION SELECTED>Red
    <OPTION VALUE="Plants"><I>Green</I>
    <OPTION>Blue
</SELECT> <P>
<INPUT TYPE="button" VALUE="Show Stuff"
```

(continued)

document.forms[i].*selectObject*.options[i]

```
onClick="inspect(this.form)">
</FORM>
</BODY>
</HTML>
```

Listing 8-31: Using the options property while authoring to review selection object definition.

To let us inspect how JavaScript sees the selection object defined in the body, the alert dialog box reveals the definition data. Figure 8-9 shows the alert dialog's contents when the first option of Listing 8-31 is selected. This information should be used for debugging purposes only.

Related Items: all `options[index].property` items

Figure 8-9: A typical readout of the options property.

selectedIndex

Value: Integer
Gettable: Yes
Settable: No

When a user clicks on a choice in a selection list, the selectedIndex property changes to a number corresponding to that item in the list. The first item has a value of zero. This is valuable information to a script that needs to extract either the value or text of a selected item for further processing.

You can use this information as a shortcut to getting at a selected option's properties. Rather than cycling through every option in a repeat loop, to examine its selected property, use the selectedIndex property to fill in the index value for the reference to the selected item. The wording gets kind of long; but from an execution standpoint, this methodology is much more efficient.

document.forms[i].*selectObject*.selectedIndex

Example:

```
<HTML>
<HEAD>
<TITLE>Select Inspector</TITLE>
<SCRIPT LANGUAGE="JavaScript">
function inspect(form) {

alert(form.colorsList.options[form.colorsList.selectedIndex].text)
}
</SCRIPT>
</HEAD>

<BODY>
<FORM>
<SELECT NAME="colorsList">
    <OPTION SELECTED>Red
    <OPTION VALUE="Plants"><I>Green</I>
    <OPTION>Blue
</SELECT> <P>
<INPUT TYPE="button" VALUE="Show Stuff"
onClick="inspect(this.form)">
</FORM>
</BODY>
</HTML>
```

Listing 8-32: Using the selectedIndex property to fill the index value of an option's reference.

In the `inspect()` function, notice that the value inside the options[] property index brackets is a reference to the object's selectedIndex property. Because this property always returns an integer value, it fulfills the needs of the index value for the options[] property. Therefore, if Green is selected in the pop-up menu, `form.colorsList.selectedIndex` returns a value of 2; that reduces the rest of the reference to `form.colorsList.options[2].text`, which equals "Green."

Related Items: options[] property.

`options[index].text`	

Value: string
Gettable: Yes
Settable: No

document.forms[i].*selectObject*.options[i].text

The text property of an option is the text of the item as it appears in the list. If that wording can be passed along with your script to perform appropriate tasks, this is the property to extract for further processing. But if your processing requires other strings associated with each option, assign a VALUE= attribute in the definition and extract the options[index].value property (see the following example).

Example:

```
<HTML>
<HEAD>
<TITLE>Color Changer 1</TITLE>
<SCRIPT LANGUAGE="JavaScript">
var newWindow = null
function seeColor(form) {
    newColor =
(form.colorsList.options[form.colorsList.selectedIndex].text)
    if (newWindow == null) {
        var newWindow = window.open("","","HEIGHT=200,WIDTH=150")
    }
    newWindow.document.write("<HTML><BODY BGCOLOR=" + newColor +
">")
    newWindow.document.write("<H1>Color Sampler</H1></BODY></
HTML>")
    newWindow.document.close()
}
</SCRIPT>
</HEAD>

<BODY>
<FORM>
Choose a background color:
<SELECT NAME="colorsList">
    <OPTION SELECTED>Gray
    <OPTION>Lime
    <OPTION>Ivory
    <OPTION>Red
</SELECT> <P>
<INPUT TYPE="button" VALUE="Change It"
onClick="seeColor(this.form)">
</FORM>
```

document.forms[i].*selectObject*.options[i].text

```
</BODY>
</HTML>
```

Listing 8-33: Extracting the options[index].text property for use directly in setting the background color of another window.

To demonstrate the text property of an option, Listing 8-33 applies the text from a selected option to the background color property of a document in a separate window. The color names are part of the collection built into the Navigator browser (see Chapter 7).

Related Items: `options[index].value`.

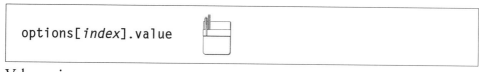

```
options[index].value
```

Value: string
Gettable: Yes
Settable: No

Many instances will certainly crop up when the words in the options list are in a form convenient for the document's users but inconvenient for the scripts behind the page. Rather than set up an elaborate lookup routine to match the `selectedIndex` or `options[index].text` values with the values your script needs, it is easier to store those values in the `VALUE=` attribute of each `<OPTION>` definition of the select object. You can then extract those values as needed and be merrily on your way.

Any string expression can be stored in the `VALUE=` attributes. That includes URLs, object properties, or even entire page descriptions to be sent to a `parent.frames[index].document.write()` method, if you prefer.

Example:

```
<HTML>
<HEAD>
<TITLE>Color Changer 2</TITLE>
<SCRIPT LANGUAGE="JavaScript">
var newWindow = null
function seeColor(form) {
    newColor =
(form.colorsList.options[form.colorsList.selectedIndex].value)
    if (newWindow == null) {
```

(continued)

document.forms[i].*selectObject*.options[i].value

```
            var newWindow = window.open("","","HEIGHT=200,WIDTH=150")
    }
    newWindow.document.write("<HTML><BODY BGCOLOR=" + newColor +
">")
    newWindow.document.write("<H1>Color Sampler</H1></BODY></
HTML>")
    newWindow.document.close()
}
</SCRIPT>
</HEAD>

<BODY>
<FORM>
Choose a background color:
<SELECT NAME="colorsList">
    <OPTION SELECTED VALUE="cornflowerblue">Cornflower Blue
    <OPTION VALUE="darksalmon">Dark Salmon
    <OPTION VALUE="lightgoldenrodyellow">Light Goldenrod Yellow
    <OPTION VALUE="seagreen">Sea Green
</SELECT> <P>
<INPUT TYPE="button" VALUE="Change It"
onClick="seeColor(this.form)">
</FORM>
</BODY>
</HTML>
```

Listing 8-34: Using the options[index].value property to obtain values useful to our scripts.

This variation of Listing 8-33 requires that the option text that the user sees be in familiar multiple-word form. But to set the color using Navigator's built-in color palette, we must use the one-word form. Those one-word values are stored in the VALUE= attributes of each <OPTION> definition. The function then extracts the value property, assigning it to the bgColor of the document in the smaller window. Had we preferred to use the hexadecimal triplet form of color specifications, those values would have been assigned to the VALUE= attributes (<OPTION VALUE="#e9967a">Dark Salmon).

Related Items: options[index].text.

options[*index*].selected	

document.forms[i].*selectObject*.options[i].selected

Value: Boolean
Gettable: Yes
Settable: No

As mentioned earlier in our discussion of this object, there are better ways to determine which option a user has selected from a list than looping through all options and examining the selected property. An exception to that "rule" occurs when a list box is set up to allow multiple selections. In this situation, the selectedIndex property returns an integer of only the topmost item selected. Therefore, your script will need to look at the true or false values of the selected property for each option in the list and determine what to do with the text or value data.

Example:

```
<HTML>
<HEAD>
<TITLE>Accessories List</TITLE>
<SCRIPT LANGUAGE="JavaScript">
function seeList(form) {
    var result = ""
    for (var i = 0; i < form.accList.length; i++) {
        if (form.accList.options[i].selected) {
            result += "\n " + form.accList.options[i].text
        }
    }
    alert("You have selected:" + result)
}
</SCRIPT>
</HEAD>

<BODY>
<FORM>
Control/Command-click on all accessories you use:
<SELECT NAME="accList" SIZE=9 MULTIPLE>
    <OPTION SELECTED>Color Monitor
    <OPTION>Modem
    <OPTION>Scanner
    <OPTION>Laser Printer
    <OPTION>Tape Backup
    <OPTION>MO Drive
```

(continued)

235

document.forms[i].*selectObject*.options[i].selected

```
    <OPTION>Video Camera
</SELECT> <P>
<INPUT TYPE="button" VALUE="View Summary..."
onClick="seeList(this.form)">
</FORM>
</BODY>
</HTML>
```

Listing 8-35: Cycling through a multiple-selection list to extract values of selected options.

To accumulate a list of all items selected by the user, the `seeList()` function systematically examines the `options[index].selected` property of each item in the list. The text of each item whose property is true is appended to a list. We added the `"\n"` inline carriage returns and spaces to make the list in the alert dialog box look nice and indented. Had other values been assigned to the `VALUE=` attributes of each option, the script could have extracted the `options[index].value` property to collect those values instead.

Related Items: `options[index].text` property; `options[index].value` property; `selectedIndex` property.

length

Value: integer
Gettable: Yes
Settable: No

Like all arrays of JavaScript's built-in functions, the options array has a length property of its own. But rather than having to reference the options array to determine its length, the select object has its own length property, which we use to find out how many items are in the list. This value is a count of the options in the object (starting with one). A select object with three choices in it has an length property of 3.

Example:

See Listing 8-35 for an illustration of the way we use the length property to help determine how often to cycle through the repeat loop in search of selected items. Because the loop counter, `i`, must start at zero, the counting continues until the loop counter is one *less* than the actual length value (which starts its count with one).

Related Items: `options` property.

document.forms[i].*selectObject*.options.length

Value: string
Gettable: Yes
Settable: No

A select object's name property is the string you assign to the object by way of its NAME= attribute in the object's <SELECT> definition. This reflects the entire select object rather than any individual options that belong to it. You may want to access this property via the elements[] style of reference to a form's components.

Example:

```
objName = document.forms[0].elements[3].name
```

Related Items: forms[].elements[] property

options[*index*].index

Value: integer
Gettable: Yes
Settable: No

The index value of any single option in a select object will likely be a redundant value in your scripting. Because you cannot access the option without knowing the index anyway (in brackets as part of the options[index] array reference), there is little need to extract the index value. It is a property of the item, just the same.

Example:

```
itemIndex = document.forms[0].listName.options[0].index
```

Related Items: options property

options[*index*].defaultSelected

Value: Boolean
Gettable: Yes
Settable: No

237

document.forms[i].*selectObject*.name

If your select object definition includes one option whose SELECTED attribute is included, that option's defaultSelected property is set to true. The defaultSelected property for all other options is false. However, if you define a select object that allows multiple selections (and whose SIZE= attribute is greater than 1), you can set the SELECTED attribute for more than one option definition. When the page loads, all items with that attribute will be preselected for the user, even in discontiguous groups.

Example:

```
isDefault = document.forms[0].listName.options[0].defaultSelected
```

Related Items: options[index].selected property

Event handlers

```
onChange=
```

As a user clicks on a new choice in a select object, the object receives a change event that can be captured by the onChange= event handler. In examples earlier in this section (Listings 8-33 and 8-34), the action was handed over to a separate button. This design may make sense in some circumstances, especially when you use multiple select lists or any list box (typically, clicking on a list box item does not trigger any action that user sees). But for some pop-up menus, it is desirable to trigger the action when the user makes a choice.

Select objects in Windows

Netscape Navigator 2.0 for Windows (3.1 and 95) contains a bug in the onChange= event handler. It simply doesn't trigger when a user chooses a new item in the pop-up or list box object. Clicking anywhere else on the page triggers the select object's onChange= event handler, but users don't know to do this.

A temporary workaround involves what may be a Navigator-specific object called navigator (discussed more fully at the end of this chapter). One of its properties reveals the platform of the user's browser. In the HTML that creates your select object(s), insert a few lines of JavaScript that adds a button if Windows is the client:

(select) onChange=

```
<SCRIPT LANGUAGE="JavaScript">
<!-- start
if (navigator.userAgent.indexOf("(Win") >= 0) {
    document.write("<INPUT TYPE='button' VALUE='Select'")>
}
// end -->
</SCRIPT>
```

The button has no event handler, because clicking it will force the onChange= event handler of the select object.

Use this workaround only until Netscape fixes the bug in a future release. In the meantime, it may not work with other non-Netscape, JavaScript-enabled browsers that don't implement the navigator object.

To bring a pop-up menu to life, add an onChange= event handler to the <SELECT> definition. If the user makes the same choice as previously selected, the onChange= event handler will not be triggered.

Example:

```
<HTML>
<HEAD>
<TITLE>Color Changer 2</TITLE>
<SCRIPT LANGUAGE="JavaScript">
var newWindow = null
function seeColor(form) {
    newColor =
(form.colorsList.options[form.colorsList.selectedIndex].value)
    if (newWindow == null) {
        var newWindow = window.open("","","HEIGHT=200,WIDTH=150")
    }
    newWindow.document.write("<HTML><BODY BGCOLOR=" + newColor +
">")
    newWindow.document.write("<H1>Color Sampler</H1></BODY></
HTML>")
    newWindow.document.close()
}
</SCRIPT>
</HEAD>
```

(continued)

239

(select) onChange=

```
<BODY>
<FORM>
Choose a background color:
<SELECT NAME="colorsList" onChange="seeColor(this.form)">
    <OPTION SELECTED VALUE="cornflowerblue">Cornflower Blue
    <OPTION VALUE="darksalmon">Dark Salmon
    <OPTION VALUE="lightgoldenrodyellow">Light Goldenrod Yellow
    <OPTION VALUE="seagreen">Sea Green
</SELECT>
</FORM>
</BODY>
</HTML>
```

Listing 8-36: Triggering the color change directly from the pop-up menu.

In Listing 8-36, we converted the document from Listing 8-34 so that all action takes place as the result of a user's selection from the pop-up menu. We removed the action button and placed the onChange= event handler in the <SELECT> object definition. For this application — when direct response to user input is desired — it is appropriate to have the action triggered from the pop-up menu, rather than by a separate action button.

Link Object

Property	Methods	Event Handlers
links[index].target	(None)	onClick=
length		onMouseOver=
[location object properties]		

Syntax

Creating a link object:

```
<A HREF="locationOrURL"
    [NAME="anchorName"]
    [TARGET="windowName"]
    [onClick="handlerTextOrFunction"]
    [onMouseOver="handlerTextOrFunction"]>
    linkDisplayTextOrImage
</A>
```

240

document.link

Accessing link object properties:

```
[window.] document.links[index].property
```

About this object

The lifeblood of the World Wide Web is the link — that clickable magic spot that zips us around a document or the world. JavaScript regards an HTML document link as a distinct object type. When a document loads, the browser creates and maintains an internal list (in an array) of all links defined in the document.

When working with a link object in your scripts, the JavaScript object world begins to wrap around itself in a way. Despite all the attributes that define a link, JavaScript regards a link as the same as a location object (Chapter 7). In other words, if you need to refer to a link, you can access the same properties of that link as you can for any location object (such as href, host, hash, pathname, and so on). This convenience lets your scripts treat all URL-style data the same way.

Defining a link for JavaScript is the same as defining one for straight HTML — with the addition of two possible event handlers. In a multi-frame or multi-window environment, it is important to specify the TARGET= attribute with the name of the frame or window in which the content at the URL is to appear. If you don't specify another frame, the browser replaces the frame that contains the link with the new page. Speaking of the TARGET= attribute, don't forget the shortcut window references: _top, _parent, _self, and _blank.

As you design your links, consider building the onMouseOver= event handler into your link definitions. The most common application for this event handler is adjusting the window.status property. Thus, as a user rolls the mouse pointer atop a link, a descriptive label (perhaps more detailed or friendly than what the link text or image may indicate) appears in the status line at the bottom of the window. Whether a user will notice the change down there is another question, so don't rely on the status line as a medium for mission-critical communication.

For those times when you want a click of the link (whether the link is text or an image) to initiate an action without actually navigating to another URL, you can use a special technique for directing the URL to a JavaScript function. See the outline-style table of contents interface in Chapter 18 for an example of using javascript:functionName() as a valid location parameter for the HREF= attribute. If you don't want the link to do anything other than change the status bar in the onMouseOver= event handler, define an empty function and set the URL to that empty JavaScript function (e.g., HREF="javascript:doNothing()"). Specifying an empty string for the HREF= attribute yields an ftp-like file listing for the client computer — an

241

undesirable artifact. Don't forget, too, that if the URL is to a file of a type that initiates a browser helper application (for example, to play a Real Audio sound file), then the helper app or plug-in will load and play without the page in the browser window changing.

If you don't specify an HREF= attribute in a link tag, the definition becomes an anchor object rather than a link object. The optional NAME= attribute allows the link object to also behave like an anchor object, allowing other links to navigate directly to the link.

Property

```
links[index].target
```

Value: string
Gettable: Yes
Settable: No

The lone property unique to the link object (over and above the properties a link has in common with the location object) is the target. This value reflects the window name supplied to the TARGET= attribute in the link's definition. Because link objects are stored as an array of a document, you can reference the target property of a particular link only via an indexed link reference.

Example:

```
windowName = document.links[3].target
```

Related Items: document.links property; anchor object.

```
length
```

Value: integer
Gettable: Yes
Settable: No

Like any built-in object array, the links array has a length property that you can use to help construct repeat loops through all entries in the array. The length property reveals the number of links in the document. If no links are defined, the value is 0.

document.links[i].target

Example:

```
linkCount = document.links.length
```

Related Items: `anchors.length` property; `selection.options.length` property; `document.links` property.

Event handlers

`onMouseOver=`

You've seen it a million times: As you drag the mouse pointer atop a link in a document, the status line at the bottom of the window shows the URL as defined in the link's `HREF=` attribute. For NetFreaks, URLs are like mother's milk, but for everyday folks, long URLs are more like gibberish. You can override the display of a link's URL with a function triggered by the `onMouseOver=` event handler assigned to a link.

One potentially tricky aspect of this event handler is that no matter what you ask that handler to do — whether it be a statement within the `onMouseOver=` attribute or a call to a JavaScript function — the attribute must end with a `return true` statement. Without this last statement in the `onMouseOver=` attribute, there will be no change to the status bar.

No conventions exist for the kind of text you put in the status line, but it should help the user better understand the impact of clicking on a link. I like to put instructions or a command-like sentence in the status line. For example, for the iconic images of the outline-style table of contents (Chapter 18), the message advises the user to click to expand or collapse the nested items, depending on which icon is in place; for the text links in the outline, the message gives more information about what the user will see as a result of clicking on the link.

Example:

```
<HTML>
<HEAD>
<TITLE>Mousing Over Links</TITLE>
<SCRIPT LANGUAGE="JavaScript">
function setStatus(msg) {
    status = msg
}
// destination of all link HREFs
function emulate() {
```

(continued)

243

```
        alert("Not going there in this demo.")
}
</SCRIPT>
</HEAD>
<BODY>
<H1>Pledge of Allegiance</H1>
<HR>
I pledge <A HREF="javascript:emulate()"
onMouseOver="setStatus('View dictionary definition');return
true">allegiance</A> to the <A HREF="javascript:emulate()"
onMouseOver="setStatus('Learn about the U.S. flag');return
true">flag</A> of the <A HREF="javascript:emulate()"
onMouseOver="setStatus('View info about the U.S.
government');return true">United States of America</A>, and to the
Republic for which it stands, one nation <A
HREF="javascript:emulate()" onMouseOver="setStatus('Read about the
history of this phrase in the Pledge');return true">under God</A>,
indivisible, with liberty and justice for all.
</BODY>
</HTML>
```

Listing 8-38: Using the onMouseOver= event handler to display descriptions of the text links.

Listing 8-38 uses the Pledge of Allegiance with four links to demonstrate how to use the `onMouseOver=` event handler. Notice that for each link, the handler runs a general-purpose function that actually sets the window's status message. But after the call to the function in each `onMouseOver=` attribute is a distinct `return true` statement (a semicolon separates the two statements in each parameter). JavaScript will not allow the `return true` statement to be in the function: It must be in the `onMouseOver=` attribute. The other technique demonstrated here is using an internal location (`javascript:emulate()`) as an HREF attribute value for each of the links. This allows the link to behave like a real link (highlighting the text); but in this case, the link doesn't really navigate anywhere. Instead, it invokes the `emulate()` function, defined in the document. You can use this technique to script client-side image maps, as shown in Chapter 20.

`onClick=`

By and large, the action that a link makes when a user clicks on it is determined by the `HREF=` attribute — generally a navigation action. But if you need to execute a script

(link) onClick=

prior to navigating to a specific link, you can include an `onClick=` event handler in that link's definition. Any statements or functions called by the `onClick=` event handler execute before any navigation takes place.

The `onClick=` event handler can also be used as one way to change the contents of multiple frames from a single link. For example

```
<A HREF="http://URLOfChoice1" target="mainFrame"
onClick="parent.miniFrame.location='http://URLOfChoice2'">Change
display</A>
```

This link uses the `onClick=` event handler to set the location property of a frame named miniFrame, while using the standard link object functionality to load a different document into the frame named mainFrame.

Example:

```
<HTML>
<HEAD>
<TITLE>Link onClick= Handler</TITLE>
<SCRIPT LANGUAGE="JavaScript">
function setStatus(msg) {
    status = msg
}
// destination of link HREFs
function emulate() {
    alert("Not going there in this demo.")
}
function emulate2() {
    alert("Sorry, not going to see any pictures in this demo.")
}
function pickFlagURL(theLink) {
    if (confirm("Do you want to see flag graphics along the
way?")) {
        theLink.href = "javascript:emulate2()"
    } else {
        theLink.href = "javascript:emulate()"
    }
}
</SCRIPT>
</HEAD>
<BODY>
<H1>Pledge of Allegiance</H1>
```
(continued)

(link) onClick=

```
<HR>
I pledge <A HREF="javascript:emulate()"
onMouseOver="setStatus('View dictionary definition');return
true">allegiance</A> to the <A HREF="" onClick="pickFlagURL(this)"
onMouseOver="setStatus('Learn about the U.S. flag');return
true">flag</A> of the <A HREF="javascript:emulate()"
onMouseOver="setStatus('View info about the U.S.
government');return true">United States of America</A>, and to the
Republic for which it stands, one nation <A
HREF="javascript:emulate()" onMouseOver="setStatus('Read about the
history of this phrase in the Pledge');return true">under God</A>,
indivisible, with liberty and justice for all.
</BODY>
</HTML>
```

Listing 8-39: An onClick= event handler in the "flag" link triggers a function that set's that link's URL.

For Listing 8-39, we enhanced Listing 8-38 to include one onClick= event handler. The link surrounding the "flag" word has such a handler that calls a function named pickFlagURL(). We pass the link object as a parameter, because the function will be assigning a value to one of its properties. In the function, a simple confirm dialog box lets the user choose whether the link should go to one with pictures or without pictures (only emulated here). Following the identical behavior as a location object, the function assigns one or the other URL to the href property of the link object. At that point, the link object regains control and applies the new href setting to the action of the link.

Anchor Object

Properties	Methods	Event Handlers
(None)	(None)	(None)

Syntax

Creating an anchor object:

```
<A NAME="anchorName">
     anchorDisplayTextOrImage
</A>
```

document.anchor

About this object

As an HTML document loads into a JavaScript-enabled browser, the browser creates and maintains an internal list (as an array) of all anchors that are defined in the document. Like link objects, anchor objects are referenced according to their indexed value within the `document.anchors[index]` property. Beyond that, an anchor object has little that your script needs to worry about. You can also turn a link object into an anchor by simply adding a `NAME=` attribute to the link's definition (see the preceding example).

Navigator Object

Properties	Methods	Event Handlers
appName	(None)	(None)
appVersion		
appCodeName		
userAgent		

Syntax

Accessing navigator object properties:

```
navigator.property
```

About this object

In Chapter 7, I spoke repeatedly about the window object's being the top banana of the JavaScript object hierarchy. In other programming environments, you would likely find an application level higher than the window. You may think that an object known as the navigator object would be that all-encompassing object. That is not the case, however.

Defined by Netscape for the Netscape Navigator 2.0 browser, the navigator object may appear only in browsers published by Netscape. As of this writing, there is no guarantee that any other JavaScript-compatible browser will have a navigator object. Therefore, I am placing this discussion in an out-of-the-way place amid JavaScript's object definitions. Use the information here at your own risk: Users of other browsers may not be able to take advantage of the knowledge that the navigator object can impart to your scripts.

The properties of the navigator object concern themselves with the browser program that the user is running to view documents. Properties include those for extracting the

navigator

version of the browser and the platform of the client running the browser. Because I don't recommend relying on these values for all browsers, I will group discussions of all four properties together.

Properties

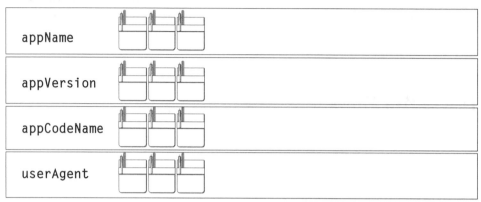

Values: string
Gettable: Yes
Settable: No

The best way to see what these properties hold is to view them from two different versions of Netscape Navigator 2.0: for Windows 95 and Macintosh (Figure 8-10).

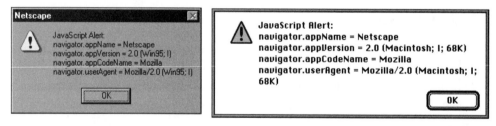

Figure 8-10: Property dumps for the navigator object under Windows 95 (left) and Macintosh (right) versions of Netscape Navigator 2.0.

The `appName` and `appCodeName` properties are simply the official name and internal code name for the browser application. More interesting are the appVersion and `userAgent` properties. They contain not only the version number, but data about the platform of the browser and the country for which the browser is released ("I" is for "international," which has a less rigid encryption facility built into it than the "U" version for the United States). The `userAgent` property is a string similar to the

248

navigator.appName

USER_AGENT header that is sent from the browser to the server at certain points of the connection process between client and server.

Although you can use the navigator object in your scripts as a temporary workaround for Navigator 2.0 platform-specific bugs, be prepared to make changes, should a more universal approach to this information be established for all JavaScript-enabled browsers. You should also check for specific version numbers of browsers that you know have problems. Netscape can release a maintenance upgrade for a problem platform at any time, which could cause your workaround to fail or be obsolete.

Example:

```
<HTML>
<HEAD>
<TITLE>Navigator Object</TITLE>
<SCRIPT LANGUAGE="JavaScript">
<!-- start
function getCRChars() {
    var theAgent = navigator.userAgent
    if (theAgent.indexOf("(Win") >= 0) {
        return "\r\n"
    } else {
        if (theAgent.indexOf("(Mac") >= 0) {
            return "\r"
        }
    }
    return "\n"
}
// end -->
</SCRIPT>
</HEAD>

<BODY>
<FORM>
<SCRIPT LANGUAGE="JavaScript">
<!-- start
var CR = getCRChars()
var msg = "<TEXTAREA NAME='myMsg' ROWS=5 COLS=30 WRAP='SOFT'>"
msg += "Line 1" + CR
msg += "Line 2" + CR
msg += "Line 3"
```

(continued)

249

navigator.appName

```
msg += "</TEXTAREA>"
document.write(msg)
// end -->
</SCRIPT>

</FORM>
</BODY>
</HTML>
```

Listing 8-40: Defining textarea object carriage return characters based on the Navigator 2.0 browser platform.

Listing 8-40 contains an example of how to apply the information in the navigator object's userAgent property to work around platform-specific bugs in the textarea object. As described elsewhere in this chapter, different inline characters are required for various platforms (until the bug is fixed in a future version). The getCRChars() function here looks for the presence of "(Win" or "(Mac" in the userAgent data (see Figure 8-10 for sample data) and supplies the appropriate carriage return characters (assuming, perhaps incorrectly, that all other platforms accept the \n inline character). Again, I stress that you should use this only as a temporary solution.

Related Items: None.

Summary

This was a very long chapter, I know. But without a doubt, the document object and its constituents are at the heart of JavaScript scripting. If this is your first time through the chapter, take a moment to review the one-pocket-protector-level items with which you should be familiar before continuing.

Even if you haven't memorized these items, as long as you have a good mental picture about how the JavaScript object model is organized and the way object properties, methods, and event handlers work, you should not have much difficulty when we next look at the remaining object constructions that are built into JavaScript: strings, math, and dates.

navigator.appName

*C*hapter Nine

In Chapter 5, you were introduced to the concepts of values and the types of values that JavaScript works with — things like strings, numbers, and Boolean values. In this chapter, we'll be looking more closely at JavaScript's data types and other built-in objects that help us massage information that we either define in our documents or that users of our pages enter into fields. Along the way, we'll encounter the many ways JavaScript allows scripters to manipulate strings, perform math operations, and work with information related to date and time.

A lot of the syntax you see in this chapter is identical to that of the Java programming language. Because the scope of JavaScript's activity is much narrower than that of Java, there isn't nearly as much to learn about JavaScript as there is for Java. But if you've had experience with other so-called scripting languages, you may be disappointed to learn that some operations — especially string manipulation — require the same kind of micro-management skills as a C programmer needs. I'll try to soften the blow by providing some general purpose functions that you can plug into your scripts to make those jobs a bit easier.

Strings and Numbers

Although JavaScript is not what is known as a strongly typed language, there are still several data types you need to be aware of because they impact how you work with the information in those forms. In this section, we'll focus on strings and two types of numbers.

Nested strings

A string consists of one or more standard text characters between matching quote marks. JavaScript is forgiving in one regard: You can use single or double quotes, as long as you match two single quotes or two double quotes around a string. Another benefit to this scheme is that there are many times when you need to include a quoted string inside a string. For example, let's say we're assembling a line of HTML code in a variable that we will eventually write to a new window completely under the control of JavaScript. The line of text we want to assign to a variable is this:

```
<INPUT TYPE="checkbox" NAME="candy">Chocolate
```

To assign this entire line of text to a variable, we would have to surround the line in quotes. But because there are quotes placed inside the string, JavaScript (or any language) would have problems deciphering where the string begins or ends. By carefully placing the other kind of quote pairs, however, we can make the assignment work. Here are two ways that are equally valid:

```
result = '<INPUT TYPE="checkbox" NAME="candy">Chocolate'
result = "<INPUT TYPE='checkbox' NAME='candy'>Chocolate"
```

Notice that in both cases the entire string is surrounded by the same unique pair. Inside the string are two quoted strings that will be treated as such by JavaScript. I recommend you settle on one form or the other and employ it consistently throughout your scripts.

Building long string variables

The act of joining strings together – *concatenation* – lets you assemble long strings out of many little pieces. This will be very important in some of your scripting when you need to build an HTML page's specifications entirely in a variable before writing it to another frame.

One tactic I use keeps the length of each statement in this building process short enough to be easily readable in your text editor. It uses a special assignment operator (+=) that appends the right-hand side of the equation to the left-hand side. Here is a simple example, which begins by initializing a variable as an empty string:

```
var newDocument = ""
newDocument += "<HTML><HEAD><TITLE>Life and Times</TITLE></HEAD>"
newDocument += "<BODY><H1>My Life and Welcome to It</H1>"
newDocument += "by Sidney Finortny<HR>"
```

Starting with the second line, each statement adds more to the string being stored in newDocument. We could continue appending string data until the entire page's specification was contained in the newDocument variable.

Joining string literals and variables

There will be in which you need to create a string out of literal strings (characters with quote marks around them) and string variable values. The methodology for concatenating these types of strings is no different from that of multiple string literals. The plus sign operator does the job. Therefore, in the following example, a variable contains a name. That variable value is made a part of a larger string whose other parts are string literals:

```
yourName = prompt("Please enter your name:","")
var msg = "Good afternoon, " + yourName + "."
alert(msg)
```

The common problems encountered while attempting this kind of concatenation include the following:

- Accidentally omitting one of the quotes around a literal string

- Failing to insert blank spaces in the string literals to accommodate word spaces

- Forgetting to concatenate punctuation after a variable value

Don't forget, too, that what we show here as being variable values can be any expression that evaluates to a string, including property references and the results of some methods. For example:

```
var msg = "The name of this document is " + document.title + "."
alert(msg)
```

Special inline characters

The way string literals are created in JavaScript makes it difficult to add certain characters to strings. I'm talking primarily about adding quotes, apostrophes, carriage returns, and tab characters to strings. Fortunately, JavaScript provides a mechanism for entering such characters to string literals. A backslash symbol followed by the character that is to appear inline makes that happen. For the "invisible" characters, a special set of letters following the backslash tell JavaScript what to do.

The most common backslash pairs you'll need are as follows:

\"	double quote
\'	single quote (apostrophe)
\\	backslash
\b	backspace
\t	tab
\n	new line
\r	carriage return
\f	form feed

Use these inside quoted string literals to make JavaScript recognize them. When assembling a block of text that needs a new paragraph, insert the \n character pair. Here are some examples of syntax with these special characters:

```
msg = "You\'re doing fine."
msg = "This is the first line.\nThis is the second line."
msg = document.title + "\n" + document.links.length + " links
present."
```

Technically speaking, a complete carriage return, as we know it from typewriting days, is both a line feed (advance the line by one) and a carriage return (move the carriage all the way to the left margin). Although JavaScript's strings treat a line feed (\n new line) as a full carriage return, you may have to construct \r\n breaks in assembling strings that go back to a CGI script on a server. It all depends on the string parsing abilities of the CGI program. (Also see special requirements for the textarea object in Chapter 8.)

It's easy to confuse assembling strings for display in textarea objects or alert boxes with strings that are to be written as HTML. For HTML strings, be sure you use the standard HTML tags for line breaks (<BR>) and paragraph breaks (<P>) rather than the inline return or line feed symbols.

Integers and floating point numbers

Deep inside our computers, the microprocessor has an easier time of performing math on integer values, whereas any number with a decimal value tacked on must go through extra work to even add two such floating point numbers. We, as scripters, are unfortunately saddled with this historical baggage and must therefore be conscious at times of the type of number we are using in calculations.

Most internal values generated by JavaScript, such as index values and length properties, are all integers. Floating point numbers usually come into play as the result of division of numeric values, special values such as pi, and human-entered values. Fortunately, JavaScript is forgiving if we try to perform math operations on mixed numeric data types. Notice how the following examples resolve to the appropriate data type:

```
3 + 4 = 7 // integer result
3 + 4.1 = 7.0999999999999996 // floating-point result
3.9 + 4.1 = 8 // integer result
```

Of the three examples, perhaps only the last one may be unexpected. When two floating-point numbers yield a whole number, the result is rendered as an integer.

As for the error in the value of the second example, it is unfortunate but not all that uncommon in desktop computers. JavaScript in Navigator 2.0 relies on the operating system's floating-point math for its own math. It's exceedingly rare that any operating system offers accuracy to as many places to the right of the decimal as JavaScript displays. Unfortunately, JavaScript does not now offer any built-in facilities for displaying such numbers with less precision or in other numeric formats. The following pair of functions provide a generic formatting routine for positive values, plus a specific call that turns a value into a dollar value:

```
// generic positive number decimal formatting function
function format (expr, decplaces) {
    // raise incoming value by power of 10 times the
    // number of decimal places; round to an integer; convert to
string
    var str = "" + Math.round (eval(expr) *
```

(continued)

```
Math.pow(10,decplaces))
    // pad small value strings with zeros to the left of rounded
number
    while (str.length <= decplaces) {
        str = "0" + str
    }
    // establish location of decimal point
    var decpoint = str.length - decplaces
    // assemble final result from: (a) the string up to the
position of
    // the decimal point; (b) the decimal point; and (c) the
balance
    // of the string. Return finished product.
    return str.substring(0,decpoint) + "." +
str.substring(decpoint,str.length);
}
// turn incoming expression into a dollar value
function dollarize (expr) {
    return "$" + format(expr,2)
}
```

This may seem like a lot of work, but it is essential if your script relies on floating point values for Navigator 2.0.

Floating-point numbers can also be entered with exponents. An exponent is signified by the letter "e" (upper or lower case), followed by a sign (+ or -) and the exponent value. Here are examples of floating-point values expressed as exponents:

```
1e6 // 1,000,000 (the "+" symbol is optional on positive
exponents)
1e-4 // 0.0001 (plus some error further to the right of the
decimal)
-4e-3 // -0.004
```

For values between 1e-5 and 1e15, JavaScript renders numbers without exponents. All other values outside these bounds come back with exponential notation.

Hexadecimal and octal integers

JavaScript allows you to work with values in decimal (base-10), hexadecimal (base-16), and octal (base-8) formats. There are only a few rules to follow when dealing with any of these values.

Decimal values cannot begin with a leading zero. Therefore, if your page asks users to enter decimal values that may begin with a zero, your script will have to strip those zeroes from the input string before performing any math on the values.

Hexadecimal integer values are expressed with a leading "0x" or "0X". That's a zero, not the letter "o". The A through F values can be in upper- or lower-case as you prefer. Here are some hex values:

```
0X2B
0X1a
0xcc
```

Don't confuse hex values used in arithmetic with the hexadecimal values used in color property specifications for Web documents. Those values are expressed in a special *hexadecimal triplet* format, which begins with a crosshatch symbol followed by the three hex values all bunched together (such as #c0c0c0).

Octal values are represented by a leading zero followed by any digits between zero and seven. Octal values are integers only.

You are free to mix and match base values in arithmetic expressions, but JavaScript renders all results in decimal form. For conversions to other number bases, you have to use a user-defined function in your script. Listing 9-1, for example, is a function that converts any decimal value from 0 to 255 to a JavaScript hexadecimal value.

```
function toHex(dec) {
    hexChars = "0123456789ABCDEF"
    if (dec > 255) {
            return null
    }
    var i = dec % 16
    var j = (dec - i) / 16
    result = "0X"
    result += hexChars.charAt(j)
    result += hexChars.charAt(i)
    return result
}
```

Listing 9-1: Decimal-to-hexadecimal converter function.

The toHex() conversion function assumes that the value passed to the function is a decimal integer.

String and numeric data type conversions

Trying to mix and match strings and numbers in what I call "connubial operations" (joining together by string concatenation or by simple addition) can be tricky. In some cases, it involves one of two built-in JavaScript functions. For the rest of this section, we assume that both sides of a + operator contain numbers. Some may be inside quoted strings; others may be true numeric data types (integer or floating-point values).

For any additive expression (one with a + operator in it), JavaScript begins evaluating that expression from the leftmost value. When it finishes evaluating the first pair, it regards that result as a single, left-side value of the next + operator — the right side being the next single value to the right of the + operator. If any value is a string, the accumulated value thus far converts to a string. Any further addition operators behave as string concatenation operators, regardless of whether the rest of the values on the right side of the operator are strings or numbers.

To better understand this, let's look at a succession of additive operations and examine the intermediate values. Refer to Listing 9-2 and the identifying numbers for each expression.

```
(1)        3 + 3 // result = 6
(2)        3 + "3" // result = "33"
(3)        3 + 3 + "3" // result = "63"
```

Listing 9-2: Mixing numbers and strings in connubial operations.

The first example yields the kind of result everyone would expect: treating both values as numbers and adding them accordingly. For Example 2, however, the second value is a string. That forces JavaScript to regard everything else that comes before it as a string, to which the right-hand value is concatenated. Hence the first value is forced to become a string, and the second value is appended to it. Example 3 follows this methodology for what may seem to be equally illogical results. JavaScript evaluates the first + operation. Because both values are numbers, JavaScript treats the + operator as an arithmetic addition. That yields the numeric value of 6. But the final value is a string. As in Example 2, JavaScript converts the left-side value to a string (6 here) and then concatenates the right-side string to the value, yielding a final result of 63.

Converting strings to numbers

What has been missing so far in our discussion has been a way to convert a number represented as a string to a number that JavaScript's arithmetic operators can work with. Before you get too concerned about this, be aware that most JavaScript operators and math methods gladly accept string representations of numbers and handle them without complaint. You'll run into the data type incompatibilities most frequently when you are trying to accomplish addition with the + operator, but a string representation gets in the way (giving you results like the 63 in Listing 9-2, Example 3).

To make the conversion requires one of two JavaScript functions:

```
parseInt(string)
parseFloat(string)
```

These functions were inspired by the Java language and are used here for compatibility reasons. The term *parsing* has many implied meanings in programming. One is the same as *extracting*. The parseInt() function returns whatever integer value can be extracted from the string passed to it; the parseFloat() function returns the floating point number that can be extracted from the string. Here are some examples and their resulting values:

```
parseInt("42") // result = 42
parseInt("42.33") // result = 42
parseFloat("42.33") // result = 42.3299999999999998
parseFloat("42") // result = 42
parseFloat("fred") // result = 0
```

Because the parseFloat() function can also work with an integer and return an integer value, this may be the preferred function in scripts that may have to deal with either kind of number, depending on the string entered into a text field by a user.

Let's now apply these functions to the problems we faced back in Listing 9-2, but this time we want to get entirely numeric results. In Listing 9-3, we'll use updated versions of Examples 2 and 3 to take care of the strings for us.

```
(2)  3 + parseInt("3") // result = 6
```

```
(3)  3 + 3 + parseFloat("3") // result = 9
```

Listing 9-3: Converting strings to numbers for arithmetic.

Although we show the parameters to the two functions as string literals in Listing 9-3, any expression that evaluates to a string can go in their places. For example, if an input text field asks users to enter numbers that will be added to other values, you can insert a reference to that form element as the parameter, as in the following:

```
parseFloat(document.forms[0].age.value)
```

This assures that the string value of this property is converted to a number (although I'd probably do more data validation—Chapter 15—before trying any math on a user-entered value).

Converting numbers to strings

As you will learn later in this chapter, JavaScript has a set of built-in facilities for massaging strings. But if you attempt to pass a number to these string methods, JavaScript complains. Therefore, you must convert any number to a string before you can, for example, find out how many digits a number is.

To force conversion from any numeric value to a string, precede the number with an empty string and the concatenation operator. For example, assume that a variable named `dollars` contains the integer value of 2500. To use the string object's length property (discussed later in this chapter) to find out how many digits the number is, use this construction:

```
("" + 2500).length // result = 4
```

The parentheses force JavaScript to evaluate the concatenation before attempting to extract the length property.

Evaluating text expressions

So far, we've been looking at how to convert individual string representations of a number to numeric data types for addition or other operations. You may also encounter cases in which your script is faced with a string value that contains an expression that you need to evaluate before proceeding with script execution.

The classic example is a text field into which a user enters an arithmetic expression. When your script extracts the value property of that field, the contents are in the form of a string that JavaScript cannot evaluate. For example, if a user enters the expression 2+2 into a field named entry, the value property contains that entire string:

```
document.forms[0].entry.value // result = "2 + 2"
```

But if you wrap the string inside JavaScript's `eval()` function, JavaScript does everything in its power to evaluate the expression before returning a value. For example

```
eval(document.forms[0].entry.value) // result = 4
```

Therefore, if you find in your debugging that a string expression is sticking when you need the evaluated version of that expression, pass the string as the parameter to the `eval()` function.

Arrays

In programming, an array is defined as *an ordered collection of data*. You can best visualize an array as a table, not much different from a spreadsheet. In JavaScript, arrays are limited to a table one data-column wide, with as many rows as you need to hold your data. As you saw in Chapters 7 and 8, a JavaScript-enabled browser creates a number of internal arrays for the objects in your HTML documents. For example, if your document contains five links, the browser maintains a table of those links. You access them by number (with 0 being the first) in the array syntax: the array name followed by the index number in square brackets, as in `document.links[0]`, which represents the first link in the document.

For many JavaScript applications, you will want to use an array as an organized warehouse for data that users of your page access, depending on their interaction with form elements. In Chapter 17, I'll show you an extended version of this in a page that lets users search a small table of data for a match between the first three digits of their U.S. Social Security numbers and the state in which they were born. Arrays are the way JavaScript-enhanced pages can recreate the behavior of more sophisticated CGI programs on servers. When the collection of data you embed in the script is no larger than a typical .gif image file, the user won't experience significant delays in loading your page; yet he or she will have the full power of your small database collection for instant searching without any calls back to the server. Such database-oriented arrays are an important application of JavaScript for what I call *serverless CGIs*.

Creating an empty array

This first release of JavaScript requires a fairly nonintuitive way of creating an array in the browser's memory. The process entails defining a function that returns itself as an object and calling that function from an assignment statement with the special keyword, `new`. Let's look at these pieces one at a time.

You have a fair amount of leeway in the way you devise the function that actually creates the array in memory. Listing 9-4 shows the canonical version, as prescribed by the official documentation.

```
// initialize array with n entries
function MakeArray(n) {
    this.length = n
    for (var i = 1; i <= n; i++) {
        this[i] = 0
```

(continued)

```
    }
    return this
}
```

Listing 9-4: The canonical array creation function.

The name of the function, MakeArray, is purely arbitrary, but it's descriptive enough to use for your scripts, if you like. To make this function do its array-creation thing requires one more statement elsewhere in the script to set the action in motion:

```
myArray = new MakeArray(n)
```

where myArray is the variable name you want to use for this array and n is the number of data items (rows) you want to use in the table. The new keyword is what tells JavaScript to convert the stuff that goes on inside the MakeArray() function into an array (treated as an actual object that exists only as long as the document is showing in the window).

If you look at the MakeArray() function closely, you'll notice that the first entry (row) of the array is assigned not only a value (the number of rows of the whole array), but also the name (length). This first entry, which has an index value of 0, can now be accessed by your script with what appears to be a familiar array length property reference:

```
arrayLen = myArray.length
```

It's important to note that this is not a special property of the object that is distinct from the data in the table; it just happens to be the name assigned to the first slot in the array. If you dynamically change the number of entries of the array later in your script, the value of myArray.length does not change automatically, as it would in a built-in JavaScript array.

What sometimes disturbs me about this state of affairs is that the syntax for extracting the length of a custom array looks like the truly intelligent and separate length property of JavaScript's built-in arrays. On the custom array side, length is not a true property of the array at all — merely an entry in its data table. The length value is actually the same as this:

```
arrayLen = myArray[0]
```

Unlike JavaScript's own objects and arrays, then, the 0 index of these transient arrays should not contain any real data. Unfortunately, it is easy to accidentally overwrite this length slot by assigning another value to myArray[0]. Therefore, for your own arrays, always begin populating data beginning with index value 1.

In truth, it's not written in stone that you must use the first entry of an array for the length value and assign it that identifier. But I think it is a valuable convention to have the length of any array available for a script to do things such as cycle through every entry. Therefore, I adhere to the convention. Even when a future version of JavaScript offers more intelligent custom arrays (such as ones that dynamically maintain a length property), it shouldn't break the scripts I write the current way.

Getting back to the `MakeArray()` function: Once the length property is assigned and filled, the function builds the array, making an entry for each of the items that will eventually fill the table. In the version shown in Listing 9-4, every entry is initialized with a value of 0. If it makes more sense for your scripts, you can also assign initial values of "" or null.

By the time the repeat loop has finished, the table is built in memory. With all values starting with the second entry (index value 1) set to 0, the function returns the entire array as an object. Now it's time to put data into the array.

Populating an array

Entering data into an array is as simple as a series of assignment statements, one for each element of the array. Listing 9-5 assumes that the document contains the `MakeArray()` function (Listing 9-4), and our goal is to generate an array containing a list of the nine planets of our solar system.

```
solarSys = new MakeArray(9)
solarSys[1] = "Mercury"
solarSys[2] = "Venus"
solarSys[3] = "Earth"
solarSys[4] = "Mars"
solarSys[5] = "Jupiter"
solarSys[6] = "Saturn"
solarSys[7] = "Uranus"
solarSys[8] = "Neptune"
solarSys[9] = "Pluto"
```

Listing 9-5: Script fragment that generates a new array and populates it.

This way of populating a single array is a bit tedious when you're writing the code; but once the array is set, it makes accessing information collections as easy as any array reference:

```
onePlanet = solarSys[4] // result = "Mars"
```

Our example in Listing 9-5 is what you might call a vertical collection of data. Each data point is like the other — the name of a planet — so the indexed array methodology should work well for our scripts. It is not by accident that I designed this array so that the index value also equals the relative order of the planets from the Sun.

But not all data collections are vertical. You may, for instance, just want to create an array that holds various pieces of information about one planet. Earth is handy, so let's use some of its astronomical data to build a completely separate array of earthly info in Listing 9-6.

```
earth = new MakeArray(0)
earth.diameter = "7920 miles"
earth.distance = "93 million miles"
earth.year = "365.25 days"
earth.day = "24 hours"
earth.length = 4 // manually update length "property"
```

Listing 9-6: Creating a "horizontal" array.

What we see in Listing 9-6 is an alternative way to populate an array. In a sense, we saw a preview of this in Listing 9-4 when the `MakeArray()` function grabbed the first array entry and assigned the length property name to it. If you assign a value to a property name that has not yet been assigned for the array, JavaScript is smart enough to append a new property entry for that value. Notice, however, that we initially created the array with a length value of 0. We did this so that the `MakeArray()` function would not create the empty entries for us — just the labeled one for length. Then, when we begin specifying new entry names and assign data to them, the entries are added to the next available indexed entry. Had we initialized the array with a value of 4, the `earth.diameter` entry would have been the fifth in the array. By preserving the sequence, we can now use either the indexed or named references with confidence:

```
earth[1]  holds the same data as  earth.diameter
earth[2]  holds the same data as  earth.distance
earth[3]  holds the same data as  earth.year
earth[4]  holds the same data as  earth.day
```

Most of the single list arrays I've created so far with JavaScript have housed vertically oriented data, so I tend to use the index value reference method for populating and extracting array data in my script. But the named array entry style is useful for creating what appears to be two-dimensional arrays.

Replicating two-dimensional arrays

As you may have detected from my examples in Listings 9-5 and 9-6, what I'm really aiming for in this application is a two-dimensional array. If the data was in a spreadsheet, there would be columns for Name, Diameter, Distance, Year, and Day; each row would contain the data for each planet, filling in a total of 45 cells or data points. Although JavaScript does not have a mechanism for explicit two-dimensional arrays, you can create an array of array objects, which accomplishes the same thing.

The mechanism for the array-array consists of the generic `MakeArray()` function, a separate constructor function that builds the horizontal part of our array, and the main data-stuffing assignment statements we saw for the vertical array style. Listing 9-7 shows the constructor and stuffer parts of our solar system application.

```
function planet(name,diameter, distance, year, day){
    this.name = name
    this.diameter = diameter
    this.distance = distance
    this.year = year
    this.day = day
}
solarSys = new MakeArray(9)
solarSys[1] = new planet("Mercury","3100 miles", "36 million
miles", "88 days", "59 days")
solarSys[2] = new planet("Venus", "7700 miles", "67 million
miles", "225 days", "244 days")
solarSys[3] = new planet("Earth", "7920 miles", "93 million
miles", "365.25 days","24 hours")
solarSys[4] = new planet("Mars", "4200 miles", "141 million
miles", "687 days", "24 hours, 24 minutes")
solarSys[5] = new planet("Jupiter","88,640 miles","483 million
miles", "11.9 years", "9 hours, 50 minutes")
solarSys[6] = new planet("Saturn", "74,500 miles","886 million
miles", "29.5 years", "10 hours, 39 minutes")
solarSys[7] = new planet("Uranus", "32,000 miles","1.782 billion
miles","84 years", "23 hours")
solarSys[8] = new planet("Neptune","31,000 miles","2.793 billion
miles","165 years", "15 hours, 48 minutes")
solarSys[9] = new planet("Pluto", "1500 miles", "3.67 billion
miles", "248 years", "6 days, 7 hours")
```

Listing 9-7: Building the equivalent of a two-dimensional array of planetary data.

After creating the main nine-data-element array, solarSys, the script uses that new keyword again to populate each entry of the solarSys array with an array fashioned in the planet() function. Each call to that function passes five data points, which are, in turn, assigned to named entries in the planet array (the spacing between comma-delimited parameters is for cosmetics in the source code — the spaces have no impact on the data). Thus, each entry of the solarSys array contains a five-element array of its own.

The fact that all of these sub-arrays have the same data structure now makes it easy for our scripts to extract the data from anywhere within this 45-entry, two-dimensional array. For example, to retrieve the name value of the fourth entry of the solarSys array, the syntax would be this:

```
planetName = solarSys[4].name
```

This has the same appearance and behavior as properties of JavaScript's built-in arrays. It is, indeed, the very same model.

To understand why we wanted to create this table, study Listing 9-8. Data extraction from the two-dimensional array is quite simple in the showData() function. The array structure even makes it possible to create a pop-up button listing from the same array data:

```
<HTML>
<HEAD>
<TITLE>Our Solar System</TITLE>
<SCRIPT LANGUAGE="JavaScript">
<!-- start script
// initialize array with n entries
function MakeArray(n) {
    this.length = n
    for (var i = 1; i <= n; i++) {
        this[i] = 0
    }
    return this
}
// stuff "rows" of data for our pseudo-two-dimensional array
function planet(name,diameter, distance, year, day){
    this.name = name
    this.diameter = diameter
    this.distance = distance
    this.year = year
    this.day = day
```

```
}
// create our pseudo-two-dimensional array
solarSys = new MakeArray(9)
solarSys[1] = new planet("Mercury","3100 miles", "36 million
miles", "88 days", "59 days")
solarSys[2] = new planet("Venus", "7700 miles", "67 million
miles", "225 days", "244 days")
solarSys[3] = new planet("Earth", "7920 miles", "93 million
miles", "365.25 days","24 hours")
solarSys[4] = new planet("Mars", "4200 miles", "141 million
miles", "687 days", "24 hours, 24 minutes")
solarSys[5] = new planet("Jupiter","88,640 miles","483 million
miles", "11.9 years", "9 hours, 50 minutes")
solarSys[6] = new planet("Saturn", "74,500 miles","886 million
miles", "29.5 years", "10 hours, 39 minutes")
solarSys[7] = new planet("Uranus", "32,000 miles","1.782 billion
miles","84 years", "23 hours")
solarSys[8] = new planet("Neptune","31,000 miles","2.793 billion
miles","165 years", "15 hours, 48 minutes")
solarSys[9] = new planet("Pluto", "1500 miles", "3.67 billion
miles", "248 years", "6 days, 7 hours")

// fill text area object with data from selected planet
function showData(form) {
    i = form.planets.selectedIndex + 1
    var result = "The planet " + solarSys[i].name
    result += " has a diameter of " + solarSys[i].diameter +
".\r\n"
    result += "At a distance of " + solarSys[i].distance + ", "
    result += "it takes " + solarSys[i].year + " to circle the
Sun.\r\n"
 result += "One day lasts " + solarSys[i].day + " of Earth time."
    form.output.value = result
}
// end script -->
</SCRIPT>
<BODY>
<H1>The Daily Planet</H1>
<HR>
<FORM>
<SCRIPT LANGUAGE = "JavaScript">
```

(continued)

```
<!-- start script again
var page = "" // start assembling next part of page and form
page += "Select a planet to view its planetary data: "
page += "<SELECT NAME='planets'> "
// build popup list from array planet names
for (var i = 1; i <= solarSys.length; i++) {
    page += "<OPTION" // OPTION tags
    if (i == 1) { // pre-select first item in list
        page += " SELECTED"
    }
    page += ">" + solarSys[i].name
}
page += "</SELECT><P>" // close selection item tag
document.write(page) // lay out this part of the page
// really end script -->
</SCRIPT>

<INPUT TYPE="button" NAME="showdata" VALUE="Show the Data"
onClick="showData(this.form)"><P>
<TEXTAREA NAME="output" ROWS=5 COLS=75>
</TEXTAREA>
</FORM>
</BODY>
</HTML>
```

Listing 9-8: An interactive Web page.

The Web page code shown in Listing 9-8 uses two blocks of JavaScript scripts. In the upper block, the scripts create the arrays described earlier and define a function that our page uses to accumulate and display data in response to user action (see Figure 9-1).

The body of the page is constructed partially out of straight HTML, with some JavaScript coding in between. We hard-code the H1 heading, divider, and start of the form definition. From there, we hand off page layout to JavaScript. It begins assembling the next chunk of the page in a string variable, page. A line of instructions is followed by the start of a select object definition. To assign values to the <OPTION> tags of the selection object, we use a repeat loop that cycles through each entry of the solarSys array, extracting only the name property for each and plugging it into our accumulated HTML page for the selection object. Notice how we apply the SELECTED attribute to the first option. We then close out the select object definition in our page variable and write the entire variable's contents out to the browser. The browser sees this rush of

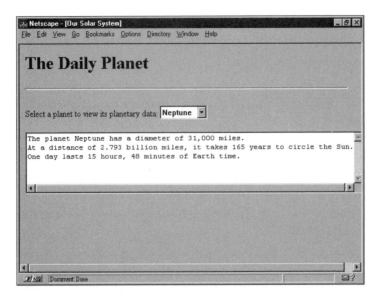

Figure 9-1: The page constructed from Listing 9-8.

HTML as just more HTML to obey as it fills in the page. Once the variable's HTML is loaded, the rest of the hard-wired page is loaded, including a button, an output textarea object, and the close of all opened tag pairs.

Once this document is loaded into the browser, all activity takes place in the browser. If the network connection were to drop, all the planet data would still be intact. In fact, the user could save the source code on the client computer's hard disk and open it as a file at any time, without reconnecting to the server. Without JavaScript, a CGI program on the server would have to reply to a query from the document, fetch the data, and send it back to the PC — involving two extra network transfers. Another serverless CGI has been born.

Working with Strings

With string data often comes the need to massage that text in scripts. In addition to concatenating strings, you will at times need to extract segments of strings, delete parts of strings, and replace one part of a string with some other text. Unlike many plain language scripting languages, JavaScript is fairly low-level in its built-in facilities for string manipulation. This means that you will often have to fashion your own string handling routines out of very elemental powers built into JavaScript. Later in this section I provide several functions you can use in your own scripts for common string handling.

The string object

One way JavaScript helps you visualize string manipulation is to regard every string value as an object. The advantage of this structure is that we are all familiar with the concept of properties and methods in other JavaScript objects. JavaScript defines one property and a slew of methods for any string. The syntax is the same for string methods as it is for any other object method:

```
stringObject.method()
```

What may seem odd at first is that the `stringObject` part of this reference can be any expression that evaluates to a string, including string literals, variables containing strings, or other object properties. Therefore, the following examples of calling the `toUpperCase()` method are all valid:

```
"george burns".toUpperCase()
yourName.toUpperCase() // yourName is a variable containing a
string
document.forms[0].entry.value.toUpperCase() // entry is a text
field object
```

For Navigator 2.0, avoid nesting method calls for the same string object when the methods modify the string. Evaluation does not work as you might expect. Instead, break out each call as a separate JavaScript statement.

It is important to remember that invoking a string method does not change the string object that is part of the reference. Rather, the method returns a value, which can be

- Used as a parameter to another method or function call; or

- Assigned to a variable value

Therefore, to change the contents of a string variable to the results of a method, you must use an assignment operator, as in

```
yourName = yourName.toUpperCase() // variable is now all uppercase
```

The `string.length` property

A string object has only one property (other than its own value, that is): length. To derive the length of a string, extract its property as you would extract the length property of any object:

```
string.length
```

string.length

The length value is an integer count of the number of characters within the string. Spaces and punctuation symbols count as characters. Any backslash special characters embedded in a string count as one character, including such characters as newline and tab. Here are some examples:

```
"Lincoln".length // result = 7
"Four score".length // result = 10
"One\ntwo".length // result = 7
"".length // result = 0
```

The length property is commonly summoned when dealing with detailed string manipulation, as you'll see below.

String methods — part one

There are two basic categories of string methods in JavaScript. One group, which we'll cover first, includes the methods used for string parsing and character-by-character analysis. The second group, covered later, simplifies assembling strings in HTML syntax for those scripts that assemble text to be written into new documents or other frames.

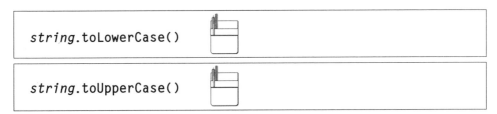

string.toLowerCase()

string.toUpperCase()

Returns: the string in all lower- or uppercase, depending on which method you invoke

A lot of what takes place on the Internet (and in JavaScript) is case-sensitive. URLs on some servers, for instance, are case-sensitive for directory and filenames. These two methods, the simplest of the string methods, convert any string to either all lowercase or all uppercase. Any mixed-case strings get converted to a uniform case. Use these methods with care, however; when the case-sensitive element you're worrying about has mixed cases in it (as often happens in JavaScript), these methods won't help you a bit.

Examples:

```
newString = "HTTP://www.Netscape.COM".toLowerCase()
    // result = "http://www.netscape.com"
```

271

```
newString = "hot".toUpperCase()
    // result = "HOT"
```

Related items: None.

$string$.indexOf($searchString$ [, $startIndex$])

Returns: index value of the character within string where searchString begins

Like some languages' offset string function, JavaScript's indexOf() method lets your script obtain the number of the character in the main string where a search string begins. Optionally, you can specify where in the main string the search should begin — but the returned value is always relative to the very first character of the main string. Like all string object methods, index values start their count with 0. If there is no match within the main string, the returned value is -1. Observing the following examples will tell you more about this method than a lengthy description. In all the examples, we assign the result of the method to a variable named offset.

Examples:

```
offset = "bananas".indexOf("b") // result = 0 (index of first
letter is zero)
```

```
offset = "bananas".indexOf("a") // result = 1
```

```
offset = "bananas".indexOf("a",1) // result = 1 (start from second
letter)
```

```
offset = "bananas".indexOf("a",2) // result = 3 (start from third
letter)
```

```
offset = "bananas".indexOf("a",4) // result = 5 (start from fifth
letter)
```

```
offset = "bananas".indexOf("nan") // result = 2
```

```
offset = "bananas".indexOf("nas") // result = 4
```

```
offset = "bananas".indexOf("s") // result = 6
```

```
offset = "bananas".indexOf("z") // result = -1 (no "z" in string)
```

Related items: string.lastIndexOf(); string.charAt(); string.substring().

string.indexOf()

> *string*.lastIndexOf(*searchString* [, *startIndex*])

Returns: index value of the *last* character within string where *searchString* begins

The `string.lastIndexOf()` method is closely related to the `string.IndexOf()` method. The only difference is that this method starts its search for a match from the end of the string (`string.length - 1`) and works its way backward through the string. All index values are still counted, starting with 0, from the front of the string. In the examples that follow, we use the same values as in the examples for `string.IndexOf` so you can compare the results. In cases where there is only one instance of the search string, the results will be the same; but when there are multiple instances of the search string, the results can vary widely — hence the need for this method.

Examples:

```
offset = "bananas".lastIndexOf("b") // result = 0 (index of first
letter is zero)
```

```
offset = "bananas".lastIndexOf ("a") // result = 5
```

```
offset = "bananas".lastIndexOf ("a",1) // result = -1 (start from
second letter working toward the front: no matches)
```

```
offset = "bananas".lastIndexOf ("a",2) // result = 2 (start from
third letter working toward front)
```

```
offset = "bananas".lastIndexOf ("a",4) // result = 3 (start from
fifth letter)
```

```
offset = "bananas".lastIndexOf ("nan") // result = -1 [Nav 2.0
bug]
```

```
offset = "bananas".lastIndexOf ("nas") // result = 4
```

```
offset = "bananas".lastIndexOf ("s") // result = 6
```

```
offset = "bananas".lastIndexOf ("z") // result = -1 (no "z" in
string)
```

Related Items: `string.lastIndexOf();` `string.charAt();` `string.substring().`

`string.charAt(index)`

Returns: character in string at the *index* count

The inverse of the `string.IndexOf()` and `string.lastIndexOf()` methods is the `string.charAt()` method. For this method, you specify an index value in the string as a parameter to the method. The purpose of the method is to return the one character at the location corresponding to the index value (first character 0). Should your script need to get a range of characters, use the `string.substring()` method.

Examples:

```
char = "banana daquiri".charAt(0) // result = "b"
```

```
char = "banana daquiri".charAt(5) // result = "a" (third "a" in
"banana")
```

```
char = "banana daquiri".charAt(6) // result = " " (a space charac-
ter)
```

```
char = "banana daquiri".charAt(20) // result = "" (empty string)
```

Related Items: `string.lastIndexOf()`; `string.IndexOf()`; `string.substring()`.

`string.substring(indexA, indexB)`

Returns: characters of string between index values *indexA* and *indexB*

The `string.substring()` method allows your scripts to extract a contiguous range of characters from any string. Parameters to this method are the starting and ending index values (first character of the string object is index value zero) of the main string from which the excerpt should be taken. It's important to note that the excerpt goes up to, but does not include, the character pointed to by the higher index value.

It makes no difference which index value in the parameters is larger than the other: The method starts the excerpt from the lowest value and continues to (but does not include) the highest value. If both index values are the same, the method returns an empty string.

string.charAt()

Examples:

```
excerpt = "banana daquiri".substring(0,0) // result = "" (empty
string)
```

```
excerpt = "banana daquiri".substring(0,1) // result = "b"
```

```
excerpt = "banana daquiri".substring(2,10) // result = "nana daq"
```

```
excerpt = "banana daquiri".substring(10,2) // result = "nana daq"
```

```
excerpt = "banana daquiri".substring(10,20) // result = "uiri"
(only to end of string)
```

Related Items: string.lastIndexOf();string.IndexOf();string.charAt().

String utility functions

Figuring out how to apply the various string object methods to a string manipulation challenge is not always an easy task. It is also difficult for me to anticipate every possible way you will need to massage strings in your scripts. But to help you get started, Listing 9-9 contains a library of string functions for inserting, deleting, and replacing chunks of text in a string.

```
// extract front part of string prior to searchString
function getFront(mainStr,searchStr){
    foundOffset = mainStr.indexOf(searchStr)
    if (foundOffset == -1) {
        return null
    }
    return mainStr.substring(0,foundOffset)
}

// extract back end of string after searchString
function getEnd(mainStr,searchStr) {
    foundOffset = mainStr.indexOf(searchStr)
    if (foundOffset == -1) {
        return null
    }
    return
mainStr.substring(foundOffset+searchStr.length,mainStr.length)
}
```

(continued)

275

```
// insert insertString immediately before searchString
function insertString(mainStr,searchStr,insertStr) {
    var front = getFront(mainStr,searchStr)
    var end = getEnd(mainStr,searchStr)
    if (front != null && end != null) {
        return front + insertStr + searchStr + end
    }
    return null
}

// remove deleteString
function deleteString(mainStr,deleteStr) {
    return replaceString(mainStr,deleteStr,"")
}

// replace searchString with replaceString
function replaceString(mainStr,searchStr,replaceStr) {
    var front = getFront(mainStr,searchStr)
    var end = getEnd(mainStr,searchStr)
    if (front != null && end != null) {
        return front + replaceStr + end
    }
    return null
}
```

Listing 9-9: Utility string handlers.

The first two functions extract the front or end components of strings as they are needed for some of the other functions in this suite. The final three functions are the core of these string-handling functions. If you plan to use these in your scripts, be sure to notice the dependence that some functions have on others. Including all five functions as a group ensures that they work as designed.

String methods — part two

We now come to the other group of string object methods, which ease the creation of numerous string display characteristics when you use JavaScript to assemble HTML code. Here is a list of these methods:

string.anchor("*anchorName*")   *string*.big()

string.substring()

```
string.blink()                    string.bold()
string.fixed()                    string.fontcolor(colorValue)
string.fontsize(integer1to7)      string.italics()
string.link(locationOrURL)        string.small()
string.strike()                   string.sub()
string.sup()
```

Let's first examine the methods that don't require any parameters. You'll probably see a pattern: All are font-style attributes that are either on or off. To turn on these attributes in an HTML document, you surround the text in the appropriate tag pairs, such as <B>...</B> for boldface text. These methods take the string object, attach those tags, and return the resulting text, which is ready to be put into any HTML that your scripts are building. Therefore, the expression

```
"Good morning!".bold()
```

evaluates to

```
<B>Good morning!</B>
```

Of course, there is nothing preventing you from building your HTML by embedding real tags instead of calling the string methods. The choice is up to you. One advantage to the string methods is that they never forget the ending tag of a tag pair. Listing 9-10 shows an example of incorporating a few simple string methods in a string variable that is eventually written to the page as it loads.

```
<HTML>
<HEAD>
<TITLE>HTML by JavaScript</TITLE>
</HEAD>

<BODY>
<SCRIPT LANGUAGE="JavaScript">
var page = ""
page += "JavaScript can create HTML on-the fly.<P>Numerous string
object methods facilitate creating text that is " +
"boldfaced".bold() + ", " + "italicized".italics() + ", or even
the terribly annoying " + "blinking text".blink() + "."
document.write(page)
</SCRIPT>
</BODY>
</HTML>
```

Listing 9-10: Using simple string methods to enhance some text.

277

Of the remaining string methods, two more (`string.fontsize()` and `string.fontcolor()`) also affect the font characteristics of strings displayed in the HTML page. The parameters for these items are pretty straightforward: an integer between 1 and 7 corresponding to the seven browser font sizes and a color value (as either a hexadecimal triplet or color constant name) for the designated text. Listing 9-11 adds a line of text to the string of Listing 9-10 that not only adjusts the font size of some parts of the string, but nests multiple attributes inside one another to set the color of one word of a string whose font size is large. Because these string methods do not change the content of the string, it is safe to nest the methods here.

```
<HTML>
<HEAD>
<TITLE>HTML by JavaScript</TITLE>
</HEAD>

<BODY>
<SCRIPT LANGUAGE="JavaScript">
var page = ""
page += "JavaScript can create HTML on-the fly.<P>Numerous string
object methods facilitate creating text that is " +
"boldfaced".bold() + ", " + "italicized".italics() + ", or even
the terribly annoying " + "blinking text".blink() + ".<P>"
page += "We can make " + "some words big".fontsize(5) + " and some
words both " + ("big and " +
"colorful".fontcolor('maroon')).fontsize(5) + " at the same time."
document.write(page)
</SCRIPT>
</BODY>
</HTML>
```

Listing 9-11: Nested string methods for fontcolor and fontsize.

The final two string methods let you create an anchor and a link out of a string. For an anchor, the `string.anchor()` method uses its parameter to create a name for the anchor. Thus, the following expression

```
"Table of Contents".anchor("toc")
```

evaluates to

```
<A NAME="toc">Table of Contents</A>
```

string.anchor()

In a similar fashion, the `string.link()` method expects a valid location or URL as its parameter, creating a genuine HTML link out of the string

```
"Back to Home".link("index.html")
```

which evaluates to the following:

```
<A HREF="index.html">Back to Home</A>
```

Again, whether you choose string methods to build HTML anchors and links over assembling the actual HTML is up to you. The methods may be a bit easier to work with if the values for the string and the parameters are variables whose content may change based on user input elsewhere in your Web site.

ASCII Encoding and Decoding

When browsers and servers communicate, some non-alphanumeric characters that we humans take for granted (like a space) cannot make the journey between them in their native form. Only a narrower set of letters, numbers, and punctuation is allowed. To accommodate the rest, the characters must be encoded with a special symbol (%) and their hexadecimal ASCII values. For example, the space character is hex 20 (ASCII decimal 32). When encoded, it looks like %20. You may have seen this symbol in browser history lists or URLS to files on your hard disk.

JavaScript includes two functions, `escape()` and `unescape()`, that offer instant conversion of whole strings. To convert a plain string to one with these escape codes, use the escape function, as in

```
escape("Howdy Pardner") // result = "Howdy%20Pardner"
```

The `unescape()` function converts the escape codes into human-readable form.

JavaScript Math

In addition to the typical arithmetic operations (covered in detail in Chapter 11), JavaScript includes more advanced mathematical powers that are accessed in a way that may seem odd to you if you have not programmed in true object-oriented environments before. While most arithmetic takes place on the fly (such as `var result = 2 + 2`), the rest require use of JavaScript's internal `Math` object (that's with a capital "M"). The Math object brings with it several properties (which behave like some other languages' constants) and many methods (which behave like some other languages' math functions).

The way you use the Math object in statements is the same way you use any JavaScript object: You create a reference beginning with the Math object's name (`Math`), a period, and the name of the property or method you need.

```
Math.property | method([parameter]...[,parameter])
```

Property references return the built-in values (things like pi); method references require a value be sent as a parameter of the method and return the result of the method performing its operation on the parameter value.

Math properties

JavaScript Math object properties represent a number of valuable constant values in math. Table 9-1 does the best job of showing you what those methods are and their values as displayed to 16 decimal places.

Table 9-1
JavaScript `Math` properties.

Property	Value	Description
`Math.E`	2.718281828459045091	Euler's constant
`Math.LN2`	0.6931471805599452862	Natural log of 2
`Math.LN10`	2.302585092994045901	Natural log of 10
`Math.LOG2E`	1.442695040888963387	Log base-2 of E
`Math.LOG10E`	0.4342944819032518167	Log base-10 of E
`Math.PI`	3.141592653589793116	
`Math.SQRT1_2`	0.7071067811865475727	Square root of 0.5
`Math.SQRT2`	1.414213562373095145	Square root of 2

Because these property expressions return their constant values, you employ them in your regular arithmetic expressions. For example, to obtain the circumference of a circle whose diameter is in variable d, the statement would be

```
circumference = d * Math.PI
```

Perhaps the most common mistakes scripters make with these properties is failing to capitalize the `Math` object name or observe the case-sensitivity of property names.

Math methods

Methods make up the balance of JavaScript's Math object powers. With the exception of the `Math.random()` method, all Math object methods take one or more values as parameters. Typical trigonometric methods operate on the single values passed as

Math

parameters; others determine which of all numbers passed along are the highest or lowest of the group. The `Math.random()` method takes no parameters but returns a randomized floating point value between 0 and 1 — but only on UNIX versions of Netscape Navigator 2.0 (the method does not work on Windows or Macintosh versions of Navigator 2.0). Table 9-2 lists all Math object methods with their syntax and description of the values they return.

Table 9-2
Math object methods

Method Syntax	Returns
`Math.abs(val)`	Absolute value of *val*
`Math.acos(val)`	Arc cosine (in radians) of *val*
`Math.asin(val)`	Arc sine (in radians) of *val*
`Math.atan(val)`	Arc tangent (in radians) of *val*
`Math.ceil(val)`	Next integer greater than or equal to *val*
`Math.cos(val)`	Cosine of *val*
`Math.exp(val)`	Euler's constant to the power of *val*
`Math.floor(val)`	Next integer less than or equal to *val*
`Math.log(val)`	Natural logarithm (base e) of *val*
`Math.max(val1, val2)`	The greater of *val1* or *val2*
`Math.min(val1, val2)`	The lesser of *val1* or *val2*
`Math.pow(val1, val2)`	*Val1* to the *val2* power
`Math.random()`	Random number between zero and one
`Math.round(val)`	N+1 when *val* >= n.5; otherwise N
`Math.sin(val)`	Sine (in radians) of *val*
`Math.sqrt(val)`	Square root of *val*
`Math.tan(val)`	Tangent (in radians) of *val*

HTML is not exactly a graphic artist's dream environment; so using trig functions to obtain a series of values for HTML-generated charting is not a hot JavaScript prospect. But in the future, as we communicate with Java applets that are better at graphical tasks, we may want to use JavaScript for some data generation using these advanced functions — sending the results to the Java applet for charting. For scripters who were not trained in programming, math is often a major stumbling block. But as you've seen so far, you can accomplish a lot with JavaScript with simple arithmetic and a little bit of logic, leaving the heavy-duty math for those who love it.

Scripters who intend to use random numbers in their scripts prior to the availability of Navigator 3.0 (which should have the `Math.random()` method working in all platforms) should look for other solutions in the interim. Some classic random number-generator schemes have been executed in the C language and could be converted to JavaScript with little difficulty. Using JavaScript's Date object functions to assist in creating seed values will also help.

Math object shortcut

In Chapter 10, I show you more details about a JavaScript construction that lets you simplify the way you address Math object properties and methods when you have a bunch of them in statements. The trick is using the `with` statement.

In a nutshell, the `with` statement tells JavaScript that the next group of statements (inside the braces) will be referring to a particular object. In the case of the Math object, the basic construction looks like this:

```
with (Math) {
    [statements]
}
```

For all intervening statements, you can omit the specific references to the Math object. Compare the long reference way of calculating the area of a circle (with a radius of six units)

```
result = Math.pow(6,2) * Math.PI
```

versus the shortcut reference way:

```
with (Math) {
    result = pow(6,2) * PI
}
```

Though the latter occupies more lines of code, the object references are shorter and more natural while you're reading the code. For a longer series of calculations involving Math object properties and methods, the `with` construction saves keystrokes and reduces the likelihood of a case-sensitive mistake with the object name in a reference. You can also include other full object references within the `with` construction; JavaScript attempts to attach the object name only to those references lacking an object name.

The Date Object

Borrowing heavily from the Java world, JavaScript includes a Date object (with a capital "D") and a large collection of methods to help you extract parts of dates and times, as

Date

well as assign dates and times. Understanding the object model for dates is vital to successful scripting of such data.

The fact that JavaScript defines a Date object should clue in experienced scripters that we're dealing with far more than a bunch of functions that dish out data from your desktop computer's clock and let you transform the values into various formats for calculation and display. By referring to a Date object, JavaScript may mislead you into thinking that there is just one such object that you work with. Not at all. Anytime you wish to perform calculations or display dates and/or times, you create a new Date object in the browser's memory. This object is associated only with the current page, just like the array-style objects we created earlier in this chapter.

In the process of creating a Date object, you assign that object to a variable name (behind the scenes, the variable is really just a pointer to the spot in memory where the Date object's data is stored). This, too, operates the same way as creating an array object. In other words, that variable becomes the Date object for further manipulation in your scripts: The variable becomes part of the dot-syntax-style reference to all possible methods for dates (there are no properties or event handlers for date objects).

One important point to remember is that despite its name, every Date object contains information about date and time. Therefore, even if you're concerned only about the date part of an object's data, there will be time data standing by as well. As you'll learn in a bit, the time element can catch you off guard for some operations.

Creating a `date` object

The statement that asks JavaScript to make an object for your script includes that special keyword we learned about in arrays: `new`. The basic syntax for generating a new Date object is as follows:

```
dateObjectName = new Date([parameters])
```

The Date object evaluates to an object, rather than some string or numeric value. Do not attempt to display the Date object variable's value directly in any alert dialog or document field.

With the Date object's reference safely tucked away in the variable name, you access all date-oriented methods in the dot-syntax fashion you're already familiar with:

```
result = dateObjectName.method()
```

It is with variables such as the *result* variable that your scripts perform calculations or displays of the Date object's data (some methods extract pieces of the date and time data from the object). If you then want to put some new value into the Date object (such as adding a year to the Date object), you then assign the new value to the object by way of the method that lets you set the value:

283

Date

```
dateObjectName.method(newValue)
```

This doesn't look like the typical JavaScript assignment statement, which would have an equals sign operator. But this is the way methods that set Date object data work.

Even though I haven't introduced you yet to details of the Date object's methods, let's use two of them to demonstrate adding one year to today's date.

```
oneDate = new Date() // creates object with today's date
theYear = oneDate.getYear() // theYear is now storing the value 95
theYear = theYear + 1 // theYear now is 96
oneDate.setYear(theYear) // new year value now in the object
```

At the end of this sequence, the `oneDate` object automatically adjusts all other settings it knows has today's date for the next year. The day of the week, for example, will be different; and JavaScript takes care of that for us, should we need to extract that data. With next year's data in the `oneDate` object, we may now want to extract that new date as a string value for display in a field on the page or submit it quietly to a CGI program on the server.

The issue of parameters for creating a new Date object is a bit complex, mostly because of the flexibility JavaScript offers the scripter. Recall that the job of the `new Date()` statement is to create a place in memory for all data that a date needs to store. What is missing from that task is the data — what date and time to enter into that memory spot. That's where the parameters come in.

If you leave the parameters empty, JavaScript takes that to mean that you want today's date and the current time to be assigned to that new Date object. JavaScript isn't any smarter, of course, than the setting of the internal clock of your personal computer. If the clock isn't correct, JavaScript won't do any better of a job identifying the date and time.

Remember that when you create a new date object, it contains the current time as well. The fact that the current date may include a time of 16:03:19 (in 24-hour time) may throw off things such as days-between-dates calculations. Be careful.

To create a Date object for a specific date and/or time, you have five ways to send values as a parameter to the `new Date()` constructor function:

```
new Date("Month dd, yyyy hh:mm:ss")
```

```
new Date("Month dd, yyyy")
```

```
new Date(yy,mm,dd,hh,mm,ss)
```

```
new Date(yy,mm,dd)
```

Date

```
new Date(milliseconds)
```

This breaks down into two styles — a long string versus a comma-delimited list of data — each with optional time settings. If you omit time settings, they are set to 0 (midnight) in the Date object for whatever date you entered. You cannot omit date values from the parameters — every Date object must have a real date attached to it, whether you need it or not.

In the long string version, the month is spelled out in full in English. No abbreviations are allowed. The rest of the data is filled with numbers representing the date, year, hours, minutes, and seconds. For single-digit values, you can use either a one- or two-digit version (such as 4:05:00). Hours, minutes, and seconds are separated by colons.

The short version is strictly a non-quoted list of integer values in the order indicated. JavaScript cannot know that a 30 means the date when you accidentally place it in the month slot.

Date methods

The bulk of a Date object's methods are for extracting parts of the date and time information and for changing the date and time stored in the object. These two sets of methods are easily identifiable because they all begin with the word "get" or "set." Table 9-3 lists all of the Date object's methods. Our focus initially will be on the first sixteen methods, which deal with components of the Date object's data.

Table 9-3
Date Object Methods

Method	Value Range	Description
dateObj.getTime()	0-...	milliseconds since 1/1/70 00:00:00
dateObj.getYear()	70-...	Specified year minus 1900
dateObj.getMonth()	0-11	Month within the year (January = 0)
dateObj.getDate()	1-31	Date within the month
dateObj.getDay()	0-6	Day of week (Sunday = 0)
dateObj.getHours()	0-23	Hour of the day in 24-hour time
dateObj.getMinutes()	0-59	Minute of the specified hour
dateObj.getSeconds()	0-59	Second within the specified minute
dateObj.setTime(val)	0-...	milliseconds since 1/1/70 00:00:00
dateObj.setYear(val)	70-...	Specified year minus 1900

(continued)

285

Date

Table 9-3 (continued)
Date Object Methods

Method	Value Range	Description
dateObj.setMonth(*val*)	0-11	Month within the year (January = 0)
dateObj.setDate(*val*)	1-31	Date within the month
dateObj.setDay(*val*)	0-6	Day of week (Sunday = 0)
dateObj.setHours(*val*)	0-23	Hour of the day in 24-hour time
dateObj.setMinutes(*val*)	0-59	Minute of the specified hour
dateObj.setSeconds(*val*)	0-59	Second within the specified minute
dateObj.getTimezoneOffset()	0-...	Minutes offset from GMT/UTC
dateObj.toGMTString()		Date string in universal format
dateObj.toLocaleString()		Date string in your system's format
Date.parse("*dateString*")		Converts string date to milliseconds
Date.UTC(*date values*)		Converts comma-delimited values to milliseconds of GMT date

JavaScript maintains its date information in the form of a count of milliseconds (thousandths of a second) from the beginning of time on January 1, 1970. Regardless of the country you live in or the date and time formats specified for your computer, the millisecond is JavaScript's universal measure of time. Any calculations involving adding or subtracting times and dates should be performed in the millisecond values to assure accuracy. Therefore, though you may never display the milliseconds value in a field or dialog box, your scripts will probably work with them from time to time in variables. To derive the millisecond equivalent for any date and time stored in a date object, use the dateObj.getTime() method, as in

```
startDate = new Date()
started = startDate.getTime()
```

Even though the method has the word "time" in its name, the fact that the value is the total number of milliseconds from January 1, 1970 means that the value also conveys a date, as well.

The other "get" methods extract a specific element of a Date object. You have to exercise some care here, because some values begin counting with 0 when you may not expect it. For example, January is month 0 in JavaScript's scheme; December is month 11. Hours, minutes, and seconds all begin with 0, which, in the end, is logical.

Date

Calendar dates, however, use the actual number that would show up on the wall calendar: The first day of the month is date value 1. The year value is whatever the actual year number is, minus 1900. For 1996, that means the year value is 96; for 2001, the year value will be 101. Through 1999, the numbers will seem normal to us; but in 2000, things will get weird. The bottom line is that a date like July 4, 1996 has the date value of 96,6,4 — not very intuitive.

To adjust any one of the elements of a date value, use the corresponding set method in an assignment statement. If the new value forces the adjustment of other elements, JavaScript takes care of that. For example, consider the following sequence and how some values are changed for us:

```
myBirthday = new Date("September 11, 1996")
result = myBirthday.getDay() // result = 3, a Wednesday
myBirthday.setYear(97) // bump up to next year
result = myBirthday.getDay() // result = 4, a Thursday
```

Because the same date in the following year is on a different day, JavaScript tracks that for us.

Accommodating time zones

Understanding the dateObj.getTimezoneOffset() method involves both your operating system's time control panel setting and an internationally recognized (in computerdom, anyway) format for representing dates and times. If you have ignored the control panel stuff about setting your local time zone, the values you get for this property could be off for most dates and times. In the eastern part of North America, for instance, the Eastern Standard Time zone is five hours earlier than the world standard Greenwich Mean Time (GMT), also known as Coordinated Universal Time (UTC in the French coinage). That means that the time zone offset from GMT is -5 hours. JavaScript tracks this information in minutes, so the time zone offset value for a typical date object would be -300 if your clock is set to the EST zone. But times can also be set to time zones other than the one your machine thinks it is in.

A world standard format for time includes a designation of the offset (in hours and minutes) from GMT. Thus, a date/time in the Eastern Standard Time zone could be represented in a string like this:

```
"Wed, 11 Sep 1996 08:12:00 GMT-0500"
```

If a Date object were created with this data (see the dateObj.parse() method, following) and you and your computer were set to Pacific Standard Time (offset of -480 minutes), the dateObj.getTimezoneOffset() property would still return a value of -300 (-5 hours times 60 minutes per hour). Fortunately, only a few scripters will have to deal with these fine points of the date object.

All of the methods so far yield only numeric values representing specific elements of a date and time. When it comes to showing the time in a document or text field, you can use either of two methods that return the date object in relatively recognizable string form. One, `dateObj.toGMTString()`, converts the date and time to the GMT equivalent on the way to the variable you use to store the extracted data. Here is what such data looks like:

```
Fri, 19 Jan 1996 03:25:28 GMT
```

If you are not familiar with the workings of GMT and how such conversions can present unexpected dates, you should exercise great care in testing your application. Eight o'clock on a Friday evening in California in the winter is four o'clock on Saturday morning GMT.

Navigator 2.0 bug: Macintosh clients miscalculate conversions to GMT with the `dateObj.toGMTString()` method. An extra 24 hours is inserted along the way.

If time-zone conversions make your head hurt, you can use the second-string method, `dateObj.toLocaleString()`. In Netscape Navigator 2.0 for North American computer users, the returned value looks like this:

```
"01/18/96 19:25:28"
```

Friendly date formats

What neither of the two string conversion methods address, however, is allowing the scripter to easily extract string segments to assemble custom date strings. For example, you cannot derive any data directly from a Date object that would let you display the object as

```
Friday, August 9, 1996
```

To accomplish this kind of string generation, you'll have to create your own functions. Listing 9-12 demonstrates one method of creating this kind of string from a Date object.

```
<HTML>
<HEAD>
<TITLE>Date String Maker</TITLE>
<SCRIPT LANGUAGE="JavaScript">
function MakeArray(n) {
    this.length = n
```

Date

```
        return this
}
monthNames = new MakeArray(12)
monthNames[1] = "January"
monthNames[2] = "February"
monthNames[3] = "March"
monthNames[4] = "April"
monthNames[5] = "May"
monthNames[6] = "June"
monthNames[7] = "July"
monthNames[8] = "August"
monthNames[9] = "September"
monthNames[10] = "October"
monthNames[11] = "November"
monthNames[12] = "December"

dayNames = new MakeArray(7)
dayNames[1] = "Sunday"
dayNames[2] = "Monday"
dayNames[3] = "Tuesday"
dayNames[4] = "Wednesday"
dayNames[5] = "Thursday"
dayNames[6] = "Friday"
dayNames[7] = "Saturday"

function customDateString(oneDate) {
    var theDay = dayNames[oneDate.getDay() + 1]
    var theMonth = monthNames[oneDate.getMonth() + 1]
    var theYear = oneDate.getYear() + 1900
    return theDay + ", " + theMonth + " " + oneDate.getDate() +
", " + theYear
}
</SCRIPT>
</HEAD>

<BODY>
<H1> Welcome!</H1>
<SCRIPT LANGUAGE="JavaScript">
document.write(customDateString(new Date()))
</SCRIPT>
```

(continued)

Date

```
<HR>
</BODY>
</HTML>
```

Listing 9-12: Creating a friendly date string from a Date object for display in an HTML page.

Assuming that the user has the PC's clock set correctly (a big assumption), the date appearing just below the opening headline will be the current date — making it appear as though the document had been updated today.

More conversions

The final two methods related to Date objects are in the category known as *static methods*. Unlike all other methods, these two do not act on Date objects. Rather, they convert dates from string or numeric forms into millisecond values of those dates. The primary beneficiary of these actions is the `dateObj.setTime()` method, which requires a millisecond measure of a date as a parameter. This is the method you would use to throw an entirely different date into an existing date object.

`Date.parse()` accepts date strings similar to the ones you've seen in this section, including the internationally approved version. `Date.UTC()`, on the other hand, requires the comma-delimited list of values (in proper order: yy,mm,dd,hh,mm,ss) and then converts that date and time to its GMT/UTC equivalent before calculating the number of milliseconds since January 1, 1970. Here is an example that creates a new date object based on some values for 6 pm one night in California:

```
newObj = new Date(Date.UTC(96,2,4,18,0,0))
result = newObj.toString() // result = "Tue, Mar 05 02:00:00 1996"
```

Again, time zone conversions can bite you if you're not comfortable with them.

Date and time arithmetic

There are any number of reasons why you may need to perform some math with dates. Perhaps you need to calculate a date at some fixed number of days or weeks in the future or figure out the number of days between two dates. When calculations of these types are required, remember the *lingua franca* of JavaScript date values: the milliseconds.

What you may need to do in your date-intensive scripts is establish some variable values representing the number of milliseconds for minute, hours, days, or weeks and then use those variables in your calculations. Here is an example that establishes some practical variable values, building on each other:

Date

```
var oneMinute = 60 * 1000
var oneHour = oneMinute * 60
var oneDay = oneHour * 24
var oneWeek = oneDay * 7
```

With these values established in a script, I can use one of them to calculate the date one week from today:

```
targetDate = new Date()
dateInMs = targetDate.getTime()
dateInMs += oneWeek
targetDate.setTime(dateInMs)
```

In another example, we'll use components of a Date object to assist in deciding what kind of greeting message to place in a document, based on the local time of the user's PC clock. Listing 9-13 adds to the scripting from Listing 9-12, bringing some quasi-intelligence to the proceedings.

```
<HTML>
<HEAD>
<TITLE>Date String Maker</TITLE>
<SCRIPT LANGUAGE="JavaScript">
function MakeArray(n) {
    this.length = n
    return this
}
monthNames = new MakeArray(12)
monthNames[1] = "January"
monthNames[2] = "February"
monthNames[3] = "March"
monthNames[4] = "April"
monthNames[5] = "May"
monthNames[6] = "June"
monthNames[7] = "July"
monthNames[8] = "August"
monthNames[9] = "September"
monthNames[10] = "October"
monthNames[11] = "November"
monthNames[12] = "December"
dayNames = new MakeArray(7)
dayNames[1] = "Sunday"
```

(continued)

```
dayNames[2] = "Monday"
dayNames[3] = "Tuesday"
dayNames[4] = "Wednesday"
dayNames[5] = "Thursday"
dayNames[6] = "Friday"
dayNames[7] = "Saturday"

function customDateString(oneDate) {
    var theDay = dayNames[oneDate.getDay() + 1]
    var theMonth = monthNames[oneDate.getMonth() + 1]
    var theYear = oneDate.getYear() + 1900
    return theDay + ", " + theMonth + " " + oneDate.getDate() +
", " + theYear
}
function dayPart(oneDate) {
    var theHour = oneDate.getHours()
    if (theHour <6 )
        return "wee hours"
    if (theHour < 12)
        return "morning"
    if (theHour < 18)
        return "afternoon"
    return "evening"
}
</SCRIPT>
</HEAD>

<BODY>
<H1> Welcome!</H1>
<SCRIPT LANGUAGE="JavaScript">
today = new Date()
var header = (customDateString(today)).italics()
header += "<BR>We hope you are enjoying the "
header += dayPart(today) + "."
document.write(header)
</SCRIPT>
<HR>
</BODY>
</HTML>
```

Listing 9-13: Changing the welcome message based on the time of day.

Date

I've divided the day into four parts and presented a different greeting for each day part. It is based, simply enough, on the hour element of a Date object representing the time the page is loaded into the browser. Because this greeting is embedded in the page, the greeting does not change no matter how long the user stays logged onto the page.

Summary

By this stage in the book, even if you've been skimming over the more complex subjects, you should have a pretty good grasp of the fundamentals of JavaScript. In the remaining chapters of this part, I'll present the formal definitions of control structures and operators, including those that you won't call upon too often. If I've been doing my job up to now, you should be bursting at the seams with ideas to try on your own. By all means, have at it. But don't yet abandon the details to come, especially debugging tips and examples of sophisticated scripted applications in Part III.

Date

$\mathscr{C}$hapter Ten

You get up in the morning, go about your day's business, and then turn out the lights at night. That's not much different from what a program does from the time it starts to the time it ends. But along the way, both you and a program take lots of tiny steps, not all of which advance the "processing" in a straight line. At times we have to control what's going on by making a decision or repeating tasks until the whole job is finished. Let's look at a trip to the grocery store as an example of the human program and these kinds of controls.

295

To Market

What we'll look at here is what takes place from the moment you enter a grocery store to the moment you clear the checkout aisle. No sooner do you enter the store than you are faced with a decision: Based on the number and size of items you intend to buy, do you pick up a hand-carried basket or attempt to extricate a shopping cart from the metallic conga line near the front of the store? That key decision may have impact later when you see a special offer on an item that is too heavy to put into the hand basket.

Now you head for the aisles. Before entering an aisle, you compare the range of goods stocked in that aisle against items on your shopping list. If an item you need is likely to be found in this aisle, you turn into the aisle and start looking for the item; otherwise, you skip the aisle and move to the head of the next aisle.

At the deli counter, you begin a conversation with the clerk. You say that you'd like one-half pound of sliced turkey breast. You'd also like a pint of the bean salad that you're pointing to. The clerk, who understands all these terms, responds by slicing, scooping, and wrapping up your selections.

Later you reach the produce section, in search of a juicy tomato. Standing in front of the bin of tomatoes, you begin inspecting them, one by one — picking each one up, feeling its firmness, checking the color, looking for blemishes or signs of pests. You discard one, pick up another, and continue this process until one matches the criteria you have set in your mind for an acceptable morsel.

Your last stop in the store is the checkout aisle. "Paper or plastic?" the clerk asks. One more decision to make. What you choose impacts how you get the groceries from the garage to the kitchen as well as your recycling habits.

In your trip to the store, you have gone through the same kinds of decisions, repetitions, and directed statements (to the deli clerk) that your JavaScript programs will also encounter. If you understand these frameworks in real life, we can now look into the JavaScript equivalents and the syntax required to make them work.

If and If...Else Decisions

JavaScript programs frequently have to make decisions based on the current values of variables or object properties. Such decisions can have only two possible outcomes at a time — much like the "Do I go down this aisle?" decision in the store. What determines the path the program takes at these decision points is the truth of some statement.

At the grocery store, the statement under test is something like "this aisle has one or more items on my shopping list." If that statement is true, you go down the aisle; if that statement is false, you skip the aisle.

Simple decisions

JavaScript syntax for this kind of simple decision always begins with the keyword if, followed by the condition to test, and then the statements that execute if the condition yields a true result. There is no "then" keyword (as there is in some other languages); it is implied by the way the various components of this construction are surrounded by parentheses and braces. The formal syntax is

```
if (condition) {
    statementsIfTrue
}
```

This means that if the condition is true, program execution takes a detour to execute statements inside the braces. No matter what happens, the program continues executing statements beyond the closing brace (}). If our grocery store lingo was part of our scripting language, the code would look something like this:

```
if (aisleContents == somethingOnList) {
    turn cart into aisle
    pick up items
}
```

If you're not used to C/C++, the double equals sign may have caught your eye. We'll learn more about this type of operator in the next chapter. This operator compares the equality of items on either side of it. In other words, the condition statement of an if construction must always yield a Boolean (true or false) value. Some object properties, you'll recall, are Booleans, so you can stick a reference to that property into the condition statement by itself. Otherwise, the condition statement will consist of two values separated by a comparison operator, such as == (equals) or != (does not equal).

Looking at some real JavaScript, here is a function that is passed a form object containing a text object called entry.

```
function notTooHigh(form) {
    if (form.entry.value > 100) {
        alert("Sorry, the value you entered is too high. Try
again.")
```

(continued)

```
    return false
  }
  return true
}
```

The `condition` (in parentheses) tests the contents of the field against a hard-wired value of 100. If the entered value is larger than that, the function alerts the user and returns a false value to the calling statement elsewhere in the script. But if the value is less than 100, all intervening code is skipped and the function returns true.

Complex decisions

The type of `if` construction described earlier is fine when the decision is to take a small detour before returning to the main path. But not all decisions — in programming or in life — are like that. Remember the "Paper or plastic" decision? That was a case in which the execution path was distinctly different for each choice — bagging groceries in many smaller bags versus fewer, larger paper bags. Only later, driving home from the store, would both execution paths merge into one.

To present two alternate paths in a JavaScript decision, you can add a component to the construction. The syntax is

```
if (condition) {
    statementsIfTrue
} else {
    statementsIfFalse
}
```

By appending the `else` keyword, you give the `if` construction a path to follow in case the `condition` evaluates to false. The *statementsIfTrue* and *statementsIfFalse* do not have to be balanced in any way: One could be one line of code, the other 100 lines. But when either one of those branches completes, execution continues after the last closing brace. To demonstrate how this can come in handy, here is a script fragment that assigns the number of days in February based on whether the year is a leap year (using modulo arithmetic, explained in the next chapter, to determine if the year is evenly divisible by four):

```
var howMany = 0
var theYear = 1993
if (theYear % 4 == 0) {
```

```
    howMany = 29
} else {
    howMany = 28
}
```

Here was a case where execution had to follow only one of two possible paths to assign the number of days to the howMany variable. Had we not used the else portion, as in

```
var howMany = 0
var theYear = 1993
if (theYear % 4 == 0) {
    howMany = 29
}
howMany = 28
```

then the variable would always be set to 28, occasionally after momentarily being set to 29. The else construction is essential in this case.

Nesting If...Else statements

Designing a complex decision process requires painstaking attention to the logic of the decisions your script must process and the statements that must execute for any given set of conditions. Because JavaScript has no equivalent to the Case statements of other languages, you must fashion the same behavior out of a series of nested if...else constructions. Without a JavaScript-aware text editor to help keep everything indented properly and properly terminated (with closing braces), you'll have to monitor the authoring process very carefully. Moreover, the error messages that JavaScript provides when a mistake occurs (see Chapter 14) may not point directly to the problem line, but only to the region of difficulty.

What's with the formatting?

Indentation of the if construction and the further indentation of the statements executed on a true condition are not required by JavaScript. What you see here, however, is a convention that most JavaScript scripters follow. As you write the code in your text editor, you can use the Tab key to make each indentation level. The browser ignores these tab characters when loading the HTML documents containing your scripts. Until we get HTML editors that automatically format JavaScript listings for us, we will manually make the listings readable and pretty.

Another important point to remember about nesting if...else statements in JavaScript is that the language does not provide a mechanism to break out of a nested part of the construction. For that reason, you have to construct complex assemblies with extreme care to make sure that only the desired statement executes for each set of conditions. Extensive testing, of course, is also required (see Chapter 14).

To demonstrate a deeply nested set of if...else constructions, Listing 10-1 presents a simple user interface to a complex problem. A single text object asks the user to enter one of three letters, A, B, or C. The script behind that field processes a different message for each of the following conditions:

- The user enters no value

- The user enters A

- The user enters B

- The user enters C

- The user enters something entirely different

```
<HTML>
<HEAD>
<SCRIPT LANGUAGE="JavaScript">
function testLetter(form){
    inpVal = form.entry.value  // assign to shorter variable name
    if (inpVal != "") {  // if entry is not empty then dive in…
        if (inpVal == "A") {  // Is it an "A"?
            alert("Thanks for the A.")
        } else {                // No.  Is it a "B"?
            if (inpVal == "B") {
                alert("Thanks for the B.")
            } else {            // No.  Is it a "C"?
                if (inpVal == "C") {
                    alert("Thanks for the C.")
                } else {            // Nope.  None of the above
                    alert("Sorry, wrong letter or case.")
                }
            }
        }
    } else {    // value was empty, so skipped all other stuff
above
        alert("You did not enter anything.")
    }
```

```
    }
</SCRIPT>
</HEAD>
<BODY>
<FORM>
Please enter A, B, or C:
<INPUT TYPE="text" NAME="entry" onChange="testLetter(this.form)">
</FORM>
</BODY>
</HTML>
```

Listing 10-1: A function with deeply nested if...else constructions.

Each condition executes only the statements that apply to that particular condition, even if it takes several queries to find out what the entry is. There is no need to break out of the nested construction because when a true response is found, the relevant statement executes, and there are no other statements in the execution path to run.

Even if you understand how to construct a hair-raising nested construction like the one in Listing 10-1, the trickiest part is making sure that each left brace has a corresponding right brace. My technique for ensuring this is to enter the right brace immediately after I type the left brace. I typically type the left brace; press Enter twice (once to open a free line for the next statement, once for the line that is to receive the right brace); tab, if necessary, to the same indentation as the line containing the left brace; and then type the left brace. Later, if I have to insert something indented, I just push down the right braces entered earlier. If I keep up this methodology throughout the process, then the right side braces will be at the desired indentation when I'm finished, even if they end up being dozens of lines below their original spot.

Conditional Expressions

While we're looking at decision-making constructions in JavaScript, this is a good time to introduce a special type of expression that you can use in place of an if...else control structure for a common type of decision. That's the case in which you want to assign one of two values to a variable depending on the outcome of some condition. The formal definition for the *conditional expression* is as follows:

variable = (condition) ? val1 : val2

What this means is that if the Boolean result of the `condition` statement is true, JavaScript assigns *val1* to the variable; otherwise it assigns *val2* to the variable. Like other instances of `condition` expressions, this one must also be written inside parentheses. The question mark is key here, as is the colon separating the two possible values.

A conditional expression, while not particularly intuitive or easy to read inside code, is very compact. Compare an `if...else` version of an assignment decision

```
var collectorStatus
if (CDCount > 500) {
    collectorStatus = "fanatic"
} else {
    collectorStatus = "normal"
}
```

with the conditional expression version:

```
var collectorStatus = (CDCount > 500) ? "fanatic" : "normal"
```

That's a lot of code lines saved. Of course, if your decision path encompasses more statements than just setting the value of a variable, the `if...else` construction is preferable. Still, this is a handy shortcut to remember when you need to perform very binary actions, such as setting a true-or-false flag in a script.

Repeat (`for`) Loops

As you have seen in numerous examples throughout previous chapters, the ability to cycle through every entry in an array or through every item of a form element is vital to many JavaScript scripts. Perhaps the most typical operation is inspecting a property of many similar items in search of a specific value, such as determining which radio button in a group is selected. One JavaScript structure that allows for these repetitious excursions is the `for` loop, so named after the keyword that begins the structure. Another, called the `while` loop, is covered in the next section.

In real life, often there is a finite number of times you can repeat a task. In searching a bin of tomatoes in the grocery store for one that meets with your approval, you know that you won't have to look through more than the number of tomatoes that are in that bin. In an ideal setup, there would be two bins: one brimming with tomatoes to be inspected, one in which to place the ones you've already seen. In a sense, each tomato has a number attached to it. Perhaps you have a hand counter that you click once for each tomato you inspect and put into the second bin. If the produce manager were to ask you how many you've seen, you could look at your counter digits and safely say "42."

If the forty-second tomato met with your satisfaction (an i f decision), you could stop your repeat loop, with your tomato counter firmly on 42.

JavaScript's for loop works the same way, although the syntax may look mysterious if you're not used to C. Much of the meaning of the elements of this construction is implied. Here's the formal syntax definition:

```
for ( [initial expression]; [condition]; [update expression]) {
    statements
}
```

The three statements inside the parentheses (parameters to the for statement) play a key role in the way a for loop executes. Let's look at each one closely.

An *initial expression* in a for loop is executed one time, the first time the for loop begins to run. The most common application of the initial expression is to assign a name and starting value to a loop counter variable. Thus, it's not uncommon to see a var statement that both declares a variable name and assigns an initial value (generally 0 or 1) to it. An example would be

```
var i = 0
```

Any variable name could be used, but conventional usage calls for the letter i, which is short for *index*. If you prefer the word counter or something else that reminds you of what the variable stands for, that's fine, too. In any case, the important point to remember about this statement is that it executes once at the outset of the for loop.

The second statement is a *condition,* precisely like the condition statement you saw in if constructions earlier in this chapter. When a loop-counting variable is established in the initial expression, the condition statement usually defines how high the loop counter should go before the looping stops. Therefore, the most common statement here is one that compares the loop counter variable against some fixed value — is the loop counter less than the maximum allowed value? If the condition is false to begin with, then the body of the loop is not executed. But if the loop does execute, then every time execution comes back around to the top of the loop, JavaScript evaluates the condition again to determine the current result of the expression. If the loop counter increases with each loop, eventually the counter value will go beyond the value in the condition statement, causing the condition statement to yield a Boolean value of false. The instant that happens, execution drops out of the for loop entirely.

The final statement, the *update expression,* is executed each time through the loop — after all statements nested inside the for construction are executed. Again, the loop counter variable can be a factor here. If you want the counter value to increase by one the next time through the loop (called *incrementing* the value), you can use the

JavaScript operator that makes that happen: the ++ operator appended to the variable name. That's what all those i++ symbols mean in the for loops you've seen already in this book. You're not limited to incrementing by one. You can increment by any multiplier you want or even drive a loop counter backwards by decrementing the value (i--).

Now we'll take this knowledge and beef up the formal syntax definition with one that takes into account a typical loop-counting variable, *i*, and the common ways to use it:

```
//incrementing loop counter
for (var i = minValue; i <= maxValue; i++) {
    statements
}
```

```
//decrementing loop counter
for (var i = maxValue; i >= minValue; i--) {
    statements
}
```

In the top format, the variable, i, is initialized at the outset to a value of whatever *minValue* is. Variable i is immediately compared against *maxValue*. If i is less than or equal to *maxValue*, processing continues into the body of the loop. At the end of the loop, the update expression executes. In the top example, the value of i is incremented by 1. Therefore, if i is initialized as 0, the first time through the loop, the i variable maintains that 0 value during the first execution of statements in the loop. The next time around, the variable has the value of 1.

As you may have noticed in the formal syntax definition, each of the parameters to the for statement is optional. For example, the statements that execute inside the loop may control the value of the loop counter based on data that gets manipulated in the process. Therefore, the update statement would probably interfere with the intended running of the loop. But I suggest that you use all three parameters until such time as you feel absolutely comfortable with their roles in the for loop. Should you omit the condition statement, for instance, and you don't program a way for the loop to exit on its own, your script could end up in an infinite loop — which would do your users no good whatsoever.

Putting the loop counter to work

Despite its diminutive appearance, the i loop counter (or whatever name you want to give to it) can be a powerful tool in working with data inside a repeat loop. For example, let's re-examine the classic JavaScript function that creates a new array object:

```
// initialize array with n entries
function MakeArray(n) {
    this.length = n
    for (var i = 1; i <= n; i++) {
        this[i] = 0
    }
    return this
}
```

The loop counter, i, is initialized to a value of 1, because we want to create an array of empty entries (with value 0) starting with the one whose index value is 1 (the zero-th entry is assigned to the length property) in the previous line. In the condition statement, the loop continues to execute as long as the value of the counter is less than or equal to the number of entries being created (n). After each loop, the counter increments by one. In the nested statement that executes within the loop, we use the value of the i variable to substitute for the index value of the assignment statement:

```
this[i] = 0
```

The first time the loop executes, the value expression evaluates to

```
this[1] = 0
```

The next time, the expression evaluates to

```
this[2] = 0
```

and so on, until all entries are created and stuffed with 0.

Recall the HTML page in Listing 9-8, where JavaScript extracted the names of planets from a previously constructed array (called solarSys). Here is the section of that listing that uses a for loop to extract the names and plug them into HTML specifications for a selection pop-up menu:

```
var page = "" // start assembling next part of page and form
page += "Select a planet to view its planetary data: "
page += "<SELECT NAME='planets'> "
// build popup list from array planet names
for (var i = 1; i <= solarSys.length; i++) {
    page += "<OPTION"          // OPTION tags
    if (i == 1) {              // pre-select first item in list
        page += " SELECTED"
    }
```

(continued)

```
    page += ">" + solarSys[i].name
}
page += "</SELECT><P>"    // close selection item tag
document.write(page)       // lay out this part of the page
```

Notice one important point about the condition statement of the `for` loop: JavaScript extracts the length property from the array to be used as the loop counter boundary. From a code maintenance and stylistic point of view, this is preferable to hard-wiring a value there: If someone should discover a new planet, we would make the addition to the array "database," whereas everything else in the code would adjust automatically to those changes, including creating a longer pop-up menu in this case. More to the point, though, is that we use the loop counter as an index value into the array to extract the `name` property for each entry in the array. We also use the counter to determine which is the first one, so we could take a short detour (via the `if` construction) to add the `SELECTED` tag to the first option's definition.

The utility of the loop counter in `for` loops often influences the way you design data structures, such as two-dimensional arrays (Chapter 9) for use as databases. Always keep the loop-counter mechanism in the back of your mind when you begin writing JavaScript that relies on collections of data you embed in your documents (see Chapter 17 for examples).

Breaking out of a loop

Some loop constructions perform their job when a certain condition is met, at which point there is no further need to continue looping through the rest of the values in the loop counter's range. A common scenario for this is the cycling of a loop through an entire array in search of a single entry that matches some criterion. That criterion test is set up as an `if` construction inside the loop. If that criterion is met, we break out of the loop and let the script continue with more meaningful processing of succeeding statements in the main flow. To accomplish that exit from the loop, use the `break` statement. Here is the schematic of how it may appear in a `for` loop:

```
for (var i = 1; i <= array.length; i++) {
    if (array[i].property == magicValue) {
        statements that act on entry array[i]
        break
    }
}
```

The break statement tells JavaScript to bail out of the nearest for loop (in case you have nested for loops). Script execution then picks up immediately after the closing brace of the for statement. The variable value of i remains whatever it was at the time of the break, so you can use that variable later in the same script to access, say, that same array entry.

We used a construction like this back in Chapter 8's discussion of radio buttons. In Listing 8-23, we showed a set of radio buttons whose VALUE= attributes contained the full names of four members of the Three Stooges. A function used a for loop to find out which button was selected and then used that item's index value — after the for loop had broken out of the loop — to alert the user. Listing 10-2 shows the relevant function:

```
function fullName(form) {
    for (var i = 0; i < form.stooges.length; i++) {
        if (form.stooges[i].checked) {
            break
        }
    }
    alert("You chose " + form.stooges[i].value + ".")
}
```

Listing 10-2: Excerpt showing a for loop from Listing 8-23.

In this case, breaking out of the for loop was for more than mere efficiency: We used the value of the loop counter (frozen at the break point) to summon a different property outside of the for loop.

Directing loop traffic with continue

One other possibility in a for loop is that you may want to skip execution of the nested statements for just one condition. In other words, as the loop goes merrily on its way round and round, executing statements for each value of the loop counter, one value of that loop counter may exist for which you don't want those statements to execute. To accomplish this task, the nested statements need to include an if construction to test for the presence of the value to skip. When that value is reached, the continue command tells JavaScript to immediately skip the rest of the body, execute the update statement, and loop back around to the top of the loop (also skipping the condition statement part of the for loop's parameters).

To illustrate this construction, we'll create an artificial example that skips over execution when the counter variable is the superstitious person's unlucky 13:

```
for (var i = 1; i <= 20; i++) {
    if (i == 13) {
        continue
    }
    statements
}
```

In this example, the statements part of the loop execute for all values of i except 13. The *continue* statement forces execution to jump to the i++ part of the loop structure, incrementing the value of i for the next time through the loop. In the case of nested for loops, a continue statement affects the for loop in whose immediate scope the if construction falls.

Another loop style — While

The for loop is not the only kind of repeat loop you can construct in JavaScript. Another statement, called a while statement, sets up a loop in a slightly different format. Rather than providing a mechanism for modifying a loop counter, a while repeat loop assumes that your script statements will eventually reach a condition that will forcibly exit the repeat loop.

The basic syntax for a while loop is

```
while (condition) {
    statements
}
```

The condition statement is the same kind you saw in if constructions and in the middle parameter of the for loop. You introduce this kind of loop if some condition exists in your code (evaluates to true) before reaching this loop. The loop then performs some action that affects that condition repeatedly until that condition becomes false. At that point, the loop exits, and script execution continues with statements after the closing brace. If the statements inside the while loop do not affect the values being tested in condition, your script never exits and it becomes stuck in an infinite loop.

Many loops can be rendered with either the for or while loops. In fact, Listing 10-3 shows a while loop version of the for loop from Listing 10-2:

```
function fullName(form) {
    var i = 0
```

```
    while (!form.stooges[i].checked) {
        i ++
    }
    alert("You chose " + form.stooges[i].value + ".")
}
```

Listing 10-3: A while loop version of a for loop in Listing 10-2.

One point you'll notice is that if the condition of a while loop depends on the value of a loop counter, it is the scripter's responsibility to initialize the counter prior to the while loop construction and manage its value within the while loop.

Should you need their powers, the break and continue control statements work inside while loops as they do in for loops. But because the two loop styles treat their loop counters and conditions differently, be extra careful (do lots of testing) when applying break and continue statements to both kinds of loops.

There are no hard-and-fast rules about which type of loop construction to use in a script. I generally use while loops only when the data or object I'll be looping through is already a part of my script before the loop. In other words, by virtue of previous statements in the script, the values for any condition or loop counting (if needed) are already initialized. But if I need to cycle through a new object's properties or new array to extract some piece of data for use later in the script, I favor the for loop. But I'll violate my own guidelines from time to time for no apparent reason.

Looping through Properties

JavaScript includes a variation of the for loop, called a for...in loop, which has special powers of extracting the names and values of any object property currently in the browser's memory. The syntax looks like this:

```
for (var in object) {
    statements
}
```

The *object* parameter is not the string name of an object, but the object itself. JavaScript delivers an object if you provide the name of the object as an unquoted string, such as window or document. Using the *var* variable, you can create a script that extracts and displays the range of properties for any given object.

Listing 10-4 is a utility function you can insert into your HTML documents during the authoring and debugging stages of designing a JavaScript-enhanced page.

```
function showProps(obj,objName) {
    var result = ""
    for (var i in obj) {
        result += objName + "." + i + " = " + obj[i] + "\n"
    }
alert(result)
}
```

Listing 10-4: Property inspector function.

You can call this function from anywhere in your script, passing both the object reference and a string to help you identify the object when the results appear in an alert dialog box.

Talking to the Deli Clerk

At the beginning of the chapter, the trip to the grocery store included deli-related conversation with the deli counter clerk. Had you given the same food order to the butcher in the meat department, you would probably be met with a blank stare. The vocabulary you used for sliced turkey and bean salad were within the deli realm, not the butcher realm.

That is where JavaScript's with statement comes in. A with statement lets you preface any number of statements by advising JavaScript precisely which object your scripts will be talking about, so you don't have to use full, formal addresses to access properties or invoke methods of the same object. In our grocery store terms, it's the difference between standing at the front of the store, yelling "deli – sliced turkey; deli – red bean salad," and standing in front of the deli counter and saying "sliced turkey; red bean salad."

Formal syntax definition of the with statement is as follows:

```
with (object) {
    statements
}
```

The *object* reference is any valid object currently in the browser's memory. We saw an example of this in Chapter 9's discussion of the Math object. By embracing several Math encrusted statements inside a with construction, your scripts can call the properties and methods without having to make the object part of every reference to those properties and methods.

An advantage of the `with` structure is that it can make heavily object-dependent statements easier to read and understand. Consider this long version of a function that requires multiple calls to the same object (but different properties):

```
function seeColor(form) {
    newColor =
(form.colorsList.options[form.colorsList.selectedIndex].text)
    return newColor
}
```

Using the `with` structure, we can shorten the long statement:

```
function seeColor(form) {
    with (form.colorsList) {
        newColor = (options[selectedIndex].text)
    }
    return newColor
}
```

When JavaScript encounters an otherwise-unknown identifier inside a `with` statement, it tries to build a reference out of the object specified as its parameter and that unknown identifier. You cannot, however, nest `with` statements that build in each other (in the preceding example, having a `with (colorsList)` nested inside a `with (form)` statement and expecting JavaScript to create a reference to options out of the two object names).

In the next chapter, we cover the last category of JavaScript syntax that you'll encounter every day: operators.

*C*hapter Eleven

JavaScript is rich in *operators:* words and symbols in expressions that perform operations on one or two values to arrive at another value. Any value on which an operator performs some action is called an *operand.* An expression may contain one operand and one operator (called a *unary* operator) or two operands separated by one operator (called a *binary* operator). Many of the same symbols are used in a variety of operators. The combination and order of those symbols is what distinguishes their powers.

313

Operator Categories

To help you grasp the full range of JavaScript operators, I've grouped them into five categories. To one of the groups I have assigned a wholly untraditional name — but a name that I believe better identifies its purpose in the language. Table 11-1 shows the five operator types.

Table 11-1:
JavaScript Operator Categories

Type	What It Does
Comparison	Compares the values of two operands, deriving a result of either true or false (used extensively in condition statements for `if...else` and `for` loop constructions).
Connubial	Joins together two operands to produce a single value that is a result of an arithmetical or other operation on the two.
Assignment	Stuffs the value of the expression of the right-hand operand into a variable name on the left-hand side, sometimes with minor modification, as determined by the operator symbol.
Boolean	Performs Boolean arithmetic on one or two Boolean operands.
Bitwise	Performs arithmetic or column-shifting actions on the binary (base-2) representations of two operands.

Much of what operators are about should resonate with our discussion back in Chapter 5 about expression evaluation. It's pretty hard to find an expression that doesn't have some kind of operator at work, causing one or more values in that expression to change. Even the simple expression

```
5 + 5
```

shows two integer operands joined by the addition operator. This expression evaluates to 10. It's the operator that provides the instruction for JavaScript to follow in its never-ending drive to evaluate every expression in a script.

It is not at all uncommon for two operands that, on the surface, look very different to be compared for their equality. JavaScript doesn't care what they look like — only how they evaluate. Two very dissimilar-looking values can, in fact, be identical when they are evaluated. Thus, an expression that compares the equality of two values

```
fred == 25
```

would, in fact, evaluate to true if the variable `fred` had the integer 25 stored in it from an earlier statement.

Comparison Operators

Any time you compare two values in JavaScript, the result is a Boolean true or false value. You have a wide selection of comparison operators to choose from, depending on the kind of test you want to apply to the two operands. Table 11-2 lists all six comparison operators.

Table 11-2:
JavaScript Comparison Operators

Syntax	Name	Operand Types	Results
==	Equals	All	Boolean
!=	Does not equal	All	Boolean
>	Is greater than	All	Boolean
>=	Is greater than or equal to	All	Boolean
<	Is less than	All	Boolean
<=	Is less than or equal to	All	Boolean

For numeric values, the results are the same you'd expect from your high school algebra class. Some examples follow, including some that may not be obvious:

```
10 == 10   // true
```

```
10 == 10.0 // true
```

```
9 != 10    // true
```

```
9 > 10     // false
```

```
9.99 <= 9.98  // false
```

Strings can also be compared on all of these levels.

```
"Fred" == "Fred" // true
```

```
"Fred" == "fred" // false
```

```
"Fred" > "fred"  // false
```

```
"Fran" < "Fred"  // true
```

To calculate string comparisons, JavaScript converts each character of a string to its ASCII value. Each letter, beginning with the first of the left-hand operator, is compared to the corresponding letter in the right-hand operator. With ASCII values for uppercase letters being less than their lowercase counterparts, an uppercase letter evaluates to being less than its lowercase equivalent. JavaScript takes case-sensitivity very seriously.

Values for comparison can also come from object properties or values passed to functions from event handlers or other functions. A common string comparison used in data entry validation is the one that sees if the string has anything in it:

```
form.entry.value != ""    // true if something is in the field
```

When your script tries to compare string values consisting of numerals and real numbers (e.g., "123" == 123), JavaScript anticipates that you want to compare apples to apples. If you want to make absolutely certain that a number-like string is properly treated as a number, use the parseInt() or parseFloat() functions to convert the strings to number values for comparison:

```
parseInt(aNumberString) == 123
```

Connubial Operators

This is my terminology for those operators that join together two operands to yield a value related to the operands. Table 11-3 lists the connubial operators in JavaScript.

Table 11-3:
JavaScript Connubial Operators

Syntax	Name	Operand Types	Results
+	Plus	Integer, Float, String	Integer, Float, String
−	Minus	Integer, Float	Integer, Float
*	Multiply	Integer, Float	Integer, Float
/	Divide	Integer, Float	Integer, Float
%	Modulo	Integer, Float	Integer, Float
++	Increment	Integer, Float	Integer, Float
− −	Decrement	Integer, Float	Integer, Float
-val	Negation	Integer, Float	Integer, Float

The four basic arithmetic operators for numbers should be straightforward. The plus operator also works on strings to join strings together, as in

```
"Howdy " + "Doody" // result = "Howdy Doody"
```

In object-oriented programming terminology, the plus sign is said to be *overloaded*, meaning that it performs a different action depending on its context. Remember, too, that string concatenation does not do anything on its own to monitor or insert spaces between words. In the preceding example, the space between the names is part of the first string.

Modulo arithmetic is helpful for those times when you want to know if one number divides evenly into another. We used it in an example in the last chapter to figure out if a particular year was a leap year. Although some other leap year considerations exist about the turn of each century, the math in the example simply checked whether the year was evenly divisible by four. The result of the modulo math is the remainder of division of the two values: When the remainder is 0, one divides evenly into the other. Here are some samples of years evenly divisible by four:

```
1994 % 4    // result = 2
```

```
1995 % 4    // result = 3
```

```
1996 % 4    // result = 0 — Bingo! Leap and election year!
```

Thus, we used this operator in a condition statement of an if...else structure:

```
var howMany = 0
today = new Date()
var theYear = today.getYear()
if (theYear % 4 == 0) {
    howMany = 29
} else {
    howMany = 28
}
```

Some other languages offer an operator that results in the integer part of a division problem solution: integral division, or div. Although JavaScript does not have an explicit operator for this behavior, you can recreate it reliably if you know that your operands are always positive numbers. Use the Math.floor() or Math.ceil() methods with the division operator, as in

```
Math.floor(4/3)  // result = 1
```

Math.floor() works only with values greater than or equal to 0; Math.ceil() works for values that are less than 0.

The increment operator (++) is a unary operator (only one operand) and displays two different behaviors, depending on the side of the operand on which the symbols lie. Both the increment and decrement (−−) operators can be used in conjunction with assignment operators, which we'll cover next.

As its name implies, the increment operator increases the value of its operand by one. But in an assignment statement, you have to pay close attention to precisely when that increase takes place. An assignment statement stuffs the value of the right operand into a variable on the left. If the ++ operator is located in front of the right operand (prefix), the right operand is incremented before the value is assigned to the variable; if the ++ operator is located after the right operand (postfix), the previous value of the operand is sent to the variable before the value is incremented. Follow this sequence to get a feel for these two behaviors:

```
var a = 10          // initialize a to 10
var z = 0           // initialize z to zero
z = a               // a = 10, so z = 10
z = ++a             // a becomes 11 before assignment, so a = 11
                       and z becomes 11
z = a++             // a is still 11 before assignment, so z = 11;
                       then a becomes 12
z = a++             // a is still 12 before assignment, so z = 12;
                       then a becomes 13
```

The decrement operator behaves the same way, except that the value of the operand decreases by one.

Increment and decrement operators are used most often with loop counters in for and while loops. The simpler ++ or − symbology is more compact than reassigning a value by adding 1 to it (e.g., z = z + 1 or z += 1). Because these are unary operators, you can use the increment and decrement without an assignment statement to adjust the value of a counting variable within a loop:

```
function doNothing() {
    var i = 1
    while (i < 20) {
        ++i
    }
    alert(i) // breaks out at i = 20
}
```

The last connubial operator is the negation operator. By placing a minus sign in front of any numeric value (no space between the symbol and the value), you instruct JavaScript to evaluate a positive value as its corresponding negative value, and vice versa. The operator does not change the actual value. Here is a sequence of statements to demonstrate:

```
x = 2
y = 8
-x         // expression evaluates to -2, but x still equals 2
-(x + y)   // doesn't change variable values; evaluates to -10
-x + y     // evaluates to 6, but x still equals 2
```

To negate a Boolean value, see the Not (!) operator in the discussion of Boolean operators.

Assignment Operators

Assignment statements are among the most common statements you will write into your JavaScript scripts. This is where you copy a value or results of an expression into a variable for further manipulation of that value.

There are many reasons why you assign values to variables, even though the original values or expressions could probably be used several times throughout a script. Here is a sampling of reasons why you should assign values to variables:

- Variable names are usually shorter

- Variable names can be more descriptive

- You may need to preserve the original value for later in the script

- The original value is a property that cannot be changed

- It is not efficient to invoke the same method several times in a script

The last reason is one that is often overlooked by newcomers to scripting. For instance, if a script is writing HTML to a new document, it is more efficient to assemble the string of large chunks of the page into one variable before invoking the `document.writeln()` method to send that text to the document. This is more efficient than literally sending out one line of HTML at a time with multiple `document.writeln()` method statements. Table 11-4 shows the range of assignment operators in JavaScript.

Table 11-4:
JavaScript Assignment Operators

Syntax	Name	Example	Means
=	Equals	x = y	x = y
+=	Add by value	x += y	x = x + y
-=	Subtract by value	x -= y	x = x - y
*=	Multiply by value	x *= y	x = x * y
/=	Divide by value	x /= y	x = x / y
%=	Modulo by value	x %= y	x = x % y
<<=	Left shift by value	x <<= y	x = x << y
>>=	Right shift by value	x >>= y	x = x >> y
>>>=	Zero fill by value	x >>>= y	x = x >>> y
&=	Bitwise AND by value	x &= y	x = x & y
^=	Bitwise OR by value	x ^= y	x = x ^ y
|=	Bitwise XOR by value	x |= y	x = x | y

As is clearly demonstrated in the top group (see "Bitwise operators" later in the chapter for info on the bottom group), assignment operators beyond the simple equals sign can save some characters in your typing, especially when you have a series of values you are trying to bring together in subsequent statements. You've seen plenty of examples in previous chapters, where we've used the Add by Value operator (+=) to work wonders with strings as we assemble a long string variable to eventually send to a `document.write()` method. Look at this excerpt from Listing 9-8, where we use JavaScript to create the content of an HTML page on the fly:

```
var page = "" // start assembling next part of page and form
page += "Select a planet to view its planetary data: "
page += "<SELECT NAME='planets'> "
// build popup list from array planet names
for (var i = 1; i <= solarSys.length; i++) {
    page += "<OPTION"          // OPTION tags
    if (i == 1) {              // pre-select first item in list
        page += " SELECTED"
    }
    page += ">" + solarSys[i].name
}
page += "</SELECT><P>"  // close selection item tag
document.write(page)    // lay out this part of the page
```

The script segment starts with a plain equals assignment operator to initialize the page variable as an empty string. In many of the succeeding lines, we use the Add by Value operator to tack additional string values onto whatever is in the `page` variable at the time. Without the Add by Value operator, we'd be forced to use the plain equals assignment operator for each line of code to concatenate new string data to the existing string data. In that case, the first few lines of code would have looked like this:

```
var page = "" // start assembling next part of page and form
page = page + "Select a planet to view its planetary data: "
page = page + "<SELECT NAME='planets'> "
```

Within the `for` loop, the repetition of `page +` would make the code very difficult to read, trace, and maintain. These enhanced assignment operators are excellent shortcuts that you should use at every turn.

Boolean Operators

Because a lot of programming involves logic, it's no accident that the arithmetic of the logic world plays an important role. We've already seen dozens of times where programs make all kinds of decisions based on whether a statement or expression is the Boolean value of true or false. What we haven't seen much of yet is how to combine multiple Boolean values and expressions — something that scripts with slightly above average complexity may need to have in them.

In the various condition expressions required throughout JavaScript (such as in an `if` construction), the condition that the program must test for may be more complicated than, say, whether a variable value is greater than a certain fixed value or whether a field is not empty. Look at the case of validating a text field entry for whether the entry contains all numbers that our script might want. Without some magical JavaScript function to tell us whether or not a string consists of all numbers, we have to break apart the entry character by character and examine whether each character falls within the range of 0 through 9. But that actually comprises two tests: We want to reject any character whose ASCII value is less than 0 or greater than 9. Alternatively, we could test whether the character is greater than or equal to 0 and is less than or equal to 9. No matter how we cut it, the test really involves two tests. What we need is the bottom-line evaluation of both tests.

Boolean math

That's where the wonder of Boolean math comes into play. With just two values — true and false — it is possible to assemble a string of expressions that yield Boolean results and then let Boolean arithmetic figure out whether the bottom line is true or false.

But you don't add or subtract Boolean values like numbers. Instead, in JavaScript you use one of three Boolean operators at your disposal. Table 11-5 shows the three operator symbols.

Table 11-5:
JavaScript Boolean Operators

Syntax	Name	Operands	Results
&&	And	Boolean	Boolean
||	Or	Boolean	Boolean
!	Not	One Boolean	Boolean

In case you're unfamiliar with those characters, the symbols for the Or operator are created by typing Shift-backslash.

Using Boolean operators with Boolean operands gets tricky if you're not used to it, so we'll start with the simplest Boolean operator: Not. This operator requires only one operand. The Not operator precedes any Boolean value to switch it back to the opposite value (from true to false or from false to true). For instance

```
!true                                  // result = false
```

```
!(10 > 5)                              // result = false
```

```
!(10 < 5)                              // result = true
```

```
!(document.title == "Flintstones")     // result = true
```

As I've shown here, it's always a good idea to enclose the operand of a Not expression inside parentheses. This forces JavaScript to evaluate the expression inside the parentheses before flipping it around with the Not operator.

The And (&&) operator joins two Boolean values to reach a true or false value based on the results of both. This brings up something called a *truth table,* which helps you visualize all possible outcomes for each value of an operand. Table 11-6 is a truth table for the And operator.

Table 11-6:
Truth Table for the And Operator

Left Operand		Right Operand	Result
true	&&	true	true
true	&&	false	false
false	&&	true	false
false	&&	false	false

Only one condition yields a true result: Both operands must evaluate to true. It doesn't matter which side of the operator a true or false value lives. Here are examples of each possibility:

```
5 > 1 && 50 > 10 // result = true
```

```
5 > 1 && 50 < 10 // result = false
```

```
5 < 1 && 50 > 10 // result = false
```

```
5 < 1 && 50 < 10 // result = false
```

In contrast, the Or (||) operator is more lenient about what it evaluates to true. This is because if one or the other (or both) operands is true, the operation returns true. The Or operator's truth table is shown in Table 11-7.

Table 11-7:
Truth Table for the Or Operator

Left Operand		Right Operand	Result
true	||	true	true
true	||	false	true
false	||	true	true
false	||	false	false

Therefore, if a true value exists on either side of the operator, a true value is the result. We'll take the previous examples and swap the And operators with Or operators so you can see the Or operator's impact on the results:

```
5 > 1 || 50 > 10 // result = true
```

```
5 > 1 || 50 < 10 // result = true
```

```
5 < 1 || 50 > 10 // result = true
```

```
5 < 1 || 50 < 10 // result = false
```

Only when both operands are false does the Or operator return false.

Boolean operators at work

Applying Boolean operators to JavaScript the first time just takes a little time and some sketches on a pad of paper to help you figure out the logic of the expressions. Earlier we talked about using a Boolean operator to see whether a character fell within a range of ASCII values for data entry validation. Listing 11-1 is a function discussed in more depth in Chapter 15. It accepts any string and sees if each character of the string has an ASCII value less than 0 or greater than 9 — meaning that the input string is not a number.

```
function isNumber(inputStr) {
    for (var i = 0; i < inputStr.length; i++) {
        var oneChar = inputStr.substring(i, i + 1)
        if (oneChar < "0" || oneChar > "9") {
            alert("Please make sure entries are numbers only.")
            return false
        }
    }
    return true
}
```

Listing 11-1: Function that examines whether an input string is a number.

Combining a number of JavaScript powers to extract individual characters (substrings) from a string object within a `for` loop, the statement we're interested in here is the condition of the `if` construction:

```
(oneChar < "0" || oneChar > "9")
```

In one condition statement, we use the Or operator to test for both possibilities. If you check the Or truth table (Table 11-7), you will see that this expression returns true if either one or both tests returns true. If that happens, the rest of the function alerts the user about the problem and returns a false value to the calling statement. Only if both tests within this condition prove false for all characters of the string does the function return a true value.

From the simple Or operator, we'll go to the extreme, where the function checking — in one condition statement — whether a number falls within several numeric ranges. The script in Listing 11-2 comes from one of the applications of Chapter 17, in which a user enters the first three digits of a U.S. Social Security card number:

```
// function to determine if value is in acceptable range for this
application
function inRange(inputStr) {
    num = parseInt(inputStr)
    if (num < 1 || (num > 586 && num < 596) || (num > 599 && num
< 700) ||num > 728) {
        alert("Sorry, the number you entered is not part of our
database.  Try another three-digit number.")
        return false
    }
    return true
}
```

Listing 11-2: A function tests whether a number falls within a number of discontiguous ranges.

By the time this function is called, the user's data entry has been validated enough to know that it is a number. Now it's the job of this function to see if the number falls outside of the various ranges for which the application contains matching data. The conditions being tested here are for whether the number

- is less than 1

- is greater than 586 and less than 596 (using the And operator)

- is greater than 599 and less than 700 (using the And operator)

- is greater than 728

Each of these tests is joined by an Or operator. Therefore, if any one of these conditions proves false, the whole if condition is false, and the user is alerted accordingly.

The alternative to combining so many Boolean expressions in one condition statement would be to nest a series of if constructions. But that would require not only a lot more code, but much repetition of the alert message for each condition that could possibly fail. The combined Boolean condition was by far the best way to go.

Bitwise Operators

For scripters, bitwise operations are a four-pocket-protector subject. Unless you are dealing with external processes on CGIs or the forthcoming connection to Java applets, it is unlikely that you will use bitwise operators. Experienced programmers who also concern themselves with more specific data types (such as long integers) are quite comfortable in this arena, so I will simply provide an explanation of JavaScript's capabilities. Table 11-8 lists all JavaScript bitwise operators:

Table 11-8:
JavaScript's Bitwise Operators

Operator	Name	Left Operand	Right Operand
&	Bitwise And	numeric value	numeric value
|	Bitwise Or	numeric value	numeric value
^	Bitwise XOR	numeric value	numeric value
<<	Left Shift	numeric value	shift amount
>>	Right Shift	numeric value	shift amount
>>>	Zero Fill Right Shift	numeric value	shift amount

The numeric value operands can be in any of JavaScript's three numeric literal bases (decimal, octal, or hexadecimal). Once the operator has an operand, the value is converted to binary representation (32 bits long). For the first three bitwise operations, the individual bits of one operand are compared with their counterparts in the other operand. The resulting value for each bit depends on the operator:

- Bitwise And: 1 if both digits are 1
- Bitwise Or: 1 if either digit is 1
- Bitwise Exclusive Or: 1 if only one digit is a 1

The bitwise shift operators operate on a single operand. The second operand is the number of positions to shift the value's binary digits in the direction of the arrows of the operator symbols. For example, the left shift (<<) operator would have the following effect:

```
4 <<2 // result = 16
```

The reason for this is that the binary representation for decimal 4 is 00000100 (to eight digits anyway). Under instruction of the left shift operator to shift all digits two places to the left, the binary result is 00010000, which converts to 16 in decimal.

If you are interested in experimenting with these operators, use the JavaScript: URL to let JavaScript evaluate expressions for you. More advanced books on C and C++ programming will also be of help.

Operator Precedence

When you start working with complex expressions that hold a number of operators (e.g., Listing 11-2), it is vital that you know the order in which JavaScript evaluates those expressions. JavaScript assigns different priorities or weights to types of operators in an effort to achieve uniformity in the way it evaluates complex expressions.

In the following expression

```
10 + 4 * 5 // result = 30
```

JavaScript uses its precedence scheme to perform the multiplication before the addition — regardless of where the operators appear in the statement. In other words, JavaScript first multiplies 4 by 5, and then adds that result to 10 for a result of 30.

That may not be the way you want this expression to evaluate. Perhaps your intention was for the 10 and 4 to be added together first and that sum to be multiplied by 5. To make that happen, you have to override JavaScript's natural operator precedence. To do that, you must enclose an operator with lower precedence in parentheses. Here's how you'd adjust the previous expression to behave differently:

```
(10 + 4) * 5 // result = 70
```

That one set of parentheses had a great impact on the outcome. Parentheses have the highest precedence in JavaScript, and if you nest parentheses in an expression, the innermost set evaluates first.

For help in constructing complex expressions, refer to Table 11-9 for JavaScript's operator precedence. My general practice: When in doubt about complex precedence issues, I build the expression with lots of parentheses according to the way I want the internal expressions to evaluate.

Table 11-9:
JavaScript Operator Precedence

Precedence Level	Operator	Notes
1	()	From innermost to outermost
	[]	array index value
	function()	any remote function call
		(continued)

Table 11-9
JavaScript Operator Precedence (continued)

Precedence Level	Operator	Notes
2	!	Boolean Not
	-	Negation
	++	Increment
	- -	Decrement
3	*	Multiplication, division, modulo
	/	
	%	
4	+	Addition and subtraction
	-	
5	<<	Bitwise shifts
	>>	
	>>>	
6	<	Comparison operators
	<=	
	>	
	>=	
7	==	Equality
	!=	
8	&	Bitwise And
9	^	Bitwise XOR
10	|	Bitwise Or
11	&&	Boolean And
12	||	Boolean Or
13	?	Conditional expression
14	=	Assignment operators
	+=	
	-=	
	*=	
	/=	
	%=	
	<<=	
	>>=	
	>>>=	
	&=	
	^=	
	|=	
15	,	comma (parameter delimiter)

This precedence scheme is devised to help you avoid being faced with two operators from the same precedence level that appear often in the same expression. When it happens (such as with addition and subtraction), JavaScript begins evaluating the expression from left to right.

One related fact involves a string of Boolean expressions strung together for a condition statement (Listing 11-2). JavaScript follows what is called *short-circuit evaluation*. As the nested expressions are evaluated left to right, the fate of the entire condition can sometimes be determined before all expressions have been evaluated. Anytime JavaScript encounters an And operator, if the left operand evaluates to false, the entire expression evaluates to false without JavaScript even bothering to evaluate the right operand. For an Or operator, if the left operand is true, JavaScript short-circuits that expression to true. This can trip you up if you don't perform enough testing on your scripts: Should there be a syntax or other error in a right operand and you fail to test the expression in a way that forces that right operand to evaluate, you may not know a bug exists in your code. Users of your page, of course, will find the bug quickly. Do your testing to head off bugs at the pass.

Notice, too, that all math and string concatenation is performed prior to any comparison operators. This allows all expressions that act as operands for comparisons to evaluate fully before they are compared.

The key to working with complex expressions is to isolate individual expressions and try them out by themselves if you can. See additional debugging tips in Chapter 14.

*C*hapter Twelve

CUSTOM FUNCTIONS AND

OBJECTS

By now, you've seen dozens of JavaScript functions in action and probably have a pretty good feel for the way they work. In this chapter, we cover a few more points about functions and delve into the fun prospect of creating objects in your JavaScript code. That includes objects with properties and methods, just like the big boys.

The Role of the Function

What other languages might call procedures, subroutines, and functions are all accommodated in JavaScript by one type of structure: the *custom function*. I use this term to distinguish the functions scripters write from the built-in functions that JavaScript lets you use at will (such as parseInt()). As we saw in Chapter 4, your scripts may exist in either the head or body of an HTML document. But scripts that run as the document loads are typically not very long sequences of JavaScript statements. Instead, the main running script during a load should operate as a kind of thoroughfare on which script execution flows. To get the bulk of the detailed work done, execution takes detours from the thoroughfare into shopping centers and small towns, only to return after each excursion to continue the journey.

Advantages to dividing a long sequence of scripting into smaller chunks are legion:

- Smaller chunks are easier to write and debug
- Building blocks make it easier to visualize the entire script
- Functions can be made generalizable and reusable for other scripts
- Other parts of the script or other open frames may be able to use the functions

Learning how to write good reusable functions takes time and experience, but the earlier you understand the importance of this concept, the more you will be on the lookout for good examples in other peoples' scripts on the Web.

The function definition

Defining a function in your script means following a simple pattern and then filling in the details. The formal syntax definition for a function is

```
function functionName( [parameter1] … [, parameterN]) {
    statements
}
```

The task of assigning a function name helps you determine the precise scope of activity of the function. If you find that the planned task for the function can't be reduced to a simple one- to three-word name (which would be condensed into one contiguous sequence of characters for the *functionName*), perhaps you're asking the function to do too much. It's probably a good idea to break the job into two or more functions. As you start to design a function, you should also be on the lookout for functions that could be called from the one you're writing. This is especially true if you find yourself copying and pasting lines of code from one part of a function to another because you're performing the same operation in different spots within the function. That's a dead giveaway that you need to write one more function to do the job of the redundant code.

Function parameters

The function definition requires a set of parentheses after the *functionName*. If the function does not rely on any information arriving with it when invoked, the parentheses can be empty. But when some kind of data will be coming with a call to the function, you need to assign names to each parameter. Virtually any kind of value can be a parameter: strings; numbers; Booleans; and even complete object definitions, such as a form or form element. Select names for these variables that help you remember the content of those values; also avoid reusing existing object names because it's easy to get confused when objects and variables with the same name appear in the same statements. You must avoid using JavaScript keywords (including reserved words, in Appendix A) and any global variable defined elsewhere in your script (see more about global variables below).

JavaScript is forgiving about matching the number of parameters in the function definition with the number of parameters passed along from the calling statement. If you define a function with three parameters and the calling statement only specifies two, in the function, that third parameter variable value will be null.

```
function oneFunction(a, b, c) {
    [statements]
}
oneFunction("George","Gracie")
```

In the preceding example, the values of a and b inside the function is "George" and "Gracie," respectively; the value of c is null.

At the opposite end of the spectrum, JavaScript also won't balk if you send more parameters from the calling statement than the number of parameter variables specified in the function definition. In fact, the language even includes a mechanism you can add to your function to gather any extraneous parameters that should read your function.

Any function you define automatically has two "hidden" properties associated with it. They're named functionName.arguments and functionName.caller, and they get stuffed with values every time the function is called. The arguments property is an array containing an entry for each parameter sent to the function — whether or not parameters are defined for it. You can find out how many parameters were sent by extracting functionName.arguments.length. For example, if four parameters were passed, `functionName.arguments.length` returns 4. Then use array notation (`functionName.arguments[index]`) to extract the values of any parameter(s) you want.

The `functionName.caller` property reveals the contents of an entire function definition if the current function was called from another function (including an event handler). If the function is called from a regular JavaScript statement (such as in the Body as the document loads), the `functionName.caller` property is null.

To help you grasp all that these two properties yield, study Listing 12-1.

```
<HTML>
<HEAD>
<SCRIPT LANGUAGE="JavaScript">
function hansel(x,y) {
    var args = hansel.arguments
    document.write("hansel.caller is " + hansel.caller + "<BR>")
    document.write("hansel.arguments.length is " +
hansel.arguments.length + "<BR>")
    document.write("formal x is " + hansel.x + "<BR>")
    for (var i = 0; i < args.length; i++) {
        document.write("argument " + i + " is " + args[i] +
"<BR>")
    }
    document.write("<P>")
}

function gretel(x,y,z) {
    today = new Date()
    thisYear = today.getYear()
    hansel(x,y,z,thisYear)
}
</SCRIPT>
</HEAD>
<BODY>
<SCRIPT LANGUAGE="JavaScript">
hansel(1, "two", 3);
gretel(4, "five", 6, "seven");
</SCRIPT>
</BODY>
</HTML>
```

Listing 12-1: A function's arguments and caller properties at work.

When you load this page, the following results appear in the browser window:

```
hansel.caller is null
hansel.arguments.length is 3
formal x is 1
argument 0 is 1
argument 1 is two
argument 2 is 3

hansel.caller is function gretel(x, y, z) { today = new Date();
thisYear = today.getYear(); hansel(x,
y, z, thisYear); }
hansel.arguments.length is 4
formal x is 4
argument 0 is 4
argument 1 is five
argument 2 is 6
argument 3 is 96
```

As the document loads, the hansel() function is called directly in the Body script. It passes three arguments, even though the hansel() function defines only two. The hansel.arguments property picks up all three, just the same. The main Body script then invokes the gretel() function, which in turn calls hansel() again. But when gretel() makes the call, it passes four parameters. gretel() picks up only three of the four sent by the calling statement. It also inserts another value from its own calculations as an extra parameter to be sent to hansel(). The hansel.caller property reveals the entire content of the gretel(), whereas hansel.arguments picks up all four parameters, including the year value introduced by the gretel() function.

These are powerful and useful properties of functions, but I recommend that you not rely on them for your normal script operations. You should be defining functions that take into account all possible parameters that could be sent by other calling functions. I do, however, use these properties as debugging aids when working on complex scripts that have many calls to the same function (see Chapter 14).

Global and local variables in functions

A variable can have two scopes in JavaScript. As you would expect, any variable initialized in the main flow of a script (not inside a function) is a *global variable* in that any statement in the same document's script can access it by name. You can, however, also initialize variables inside a function so that the variable name applies only to statements inside that function. That makes it possible to reuse the same variable name in multiple functions when they carry very different information.

To demonstrate the various possibilities, we'll use the script in Listing 12-2.

```
<HTML>
<HEAD>
<TITLE>Variable Scope Trials</TITLE>
<SCRIPT LANGUAGE="JavaScript">
var headGlobal = "Gumby"
function doNothing() {
    var headLocal = "Pokey"
    return headLocal
}
</SCRIPT>
</HEAD>

<BODY>
<SCRIPT LANGUAGE="JavaScript">
var aBoy = "Charlie Brown"
var hisDog = "Snoopy"
function testValues() {
    var hisDog = "Gromit"  // initializes local version of
"hisDog"
    var page = ""
    page += "headGlobal is: " + headGlobal + "<BR>"
    // page += "headLocal is: " + headLocal + "<BR>" // won't
run: headLocal not defined
    page += "headLocal value returned from head function is: " +
doNothing() + "<P>"
    page += " aBoy is: " + aBoy + "<BR>" // picks up global
    page += "local version of hisDog is: " + hisDog + "<P>" //
"sees" only local version
    document.write(page)
}
testValues()
document.write("global version of hisDog is intact: " + hisDog)
</SCRIPT>
</BODY>
</HTML>
```

Listing 12-2: Variable scope workbench page.

In this page, we define a number of variables — some global, others local — spread out in the document's Head and Body sections. When you load this page, it runs the testValues() function, which accounts for the current values of all variable names. The script then follows up with one more value extraction that was masked in the function. Here's how the results of this page look:

```
headGlobal is: Gumby
headLocal value returned from head function is: Pokey

aBoy is: Charlie Brown
local version of hisDog is: Gromit

global version of hisDog is intact: Snoopy
```

Let's examine the variable initialization throughout this script.

In the Head, we define the first variable, headGlobal, as a global style — outside of any function definition. We then create a short function, which defines a variable (headLocal) that only statements in the function can use.

In the Body, we define two more global variables, aBoy and hisDog. Inside the Body's function, we intentionally (for purposes of demonstration) reuse the hisDog variable name. By initializing hisDog with the var statement inside the function, we tell JavaScript to create a separate variable whose scope is only within the function. This initialization does not disturb the global variable of the same name. It can, however, make things confusing for you as script author.

Statements in the script attempt to collect values of variables scattered around this script. Even from within this script, JavaScript has no problem extracting global variables directly, including the one defined in the Head. But it cannot get the local variable defined in the other function — that headLocal variable is private to its own function. Trying to run a script that gets that variable value results in an error message saying that the variable name is not defined — in the eyes of everyone else outside of the doNothing() function, that's true. If we really need that value, we can have that function return the value to a calling statement, as we do in the testValues() function.

Near the end of the function, we get the aBoy global value without a hitch. But because we initialized a separate version of hisDog inside that function, only the localized version is available to the function. If you reassign a global variable name inside a function, you cannot access the global version from inside that function.

As proof that the global variable, whose name was re-used inside the testValues() function, is untouched, the script writes that value to the end of the page for all to see. Charlie Brown and his dog are reunited.

A benefit of this variable-scoping scheme is that you can reuse "throw-away" variable names in any function you like. For instance, you are free to use, say, the i loop counting variable in every function that uses loops (in fact, you can reuse it in multiple for loops of the same function because the for loop reinitializes the value at the start of the loop). If you pass parameters to a function, you can assign those parameters the same names to aid in consistency. For example, it is common to pass an entire form object as a parameter to a function (using a this.form parameter in the event handler). For every function that catches one of these objects, you can use the variable name form in the parameter, as in

```
function doSomething(form) {
    statements
}
...
<INPUT TYPE="button" VALUE="Do Something"
    onClick="doSomething(this.form)">
```

If five buttons on your page pass their form object as a parameter to five different functions, each function can assign form (or whatever you want to use) to that parameter value.

I recommend reusing variable names only for these "throw-away" variables. In this case, they are all local to functions; so there is no possible mixup with global variables. But the thought of reusing a global variable name as, say, a special case inside a function sends shivers up my spine. It is a tactic doomed to confusion and error.

Some programmers devise naming conventions for themselves to avoid reusing global variables as locals. A popular one puts a lowercase "g" in front of any global variable name. In the example from Listing 12-2, the global variables would have been named

```
gHeadGlobal
```

```
gABoy
```

```
gHisDog
```

Then, if you define local variables, don't use the leading "g." Any scheme you use to prevent reuse of variable names in different scopes is fine as long as it does the job.

In a multiple-frame or multiple-window environment, your scripts can also access global variables from any other document currently loaded into the browser. For details about this level of access, see Chapter 16. JavaScript also offers more persistent data storage on the client — storage that survives the unloading of a document from the browser. See Chapter 8 for details on the cookie property of a document.

Parameter variables

When a function receives data in the form of parameters, remember that the values may be merely copies of the data (in the case of run-of-the-mill data values) or references to real objects (e.g., a form object). In the latter case, you can change the object's modifiable properties in the function when the function receives the object as a parameter. For example

```
function validateCountry (form) {
    if (form.country.value == "") {
        form.country.value = "USA"
    }
}
```

JavaScript knows all about the form object passed to the `validateCountry()` function. Therefore, whenever you pass an object as a function parameter, be aware that changes you make to that object in its "passed" form affect the real object.

As a matter of style, if my function needs to extract properties or results of methods from passed data (such as object properties or string substrings), I like to do that at the start of the function. I initialize as many variables as needed for each piece of data used later in the function. This allows me to assign meaningful names to the data chunks rather than having to rely on potentially long references within the working part of the function (such as using a variable like `inputStr` instead of `form.entry.value`).

Recursion in functions

Functions can call themselves, a process known as *recursion*. The classic example of programmed recursion is the calculation of the factorial (the factorial for a value of 4 is 4 * 3 * 2 * 1), shown in Listing 12-3.

```
function factorial(n) {
    if (n > 0) {
        return n * (factorial(n-1))
    } else {
        return 1
    }
}
```

Listing 12-3: A JavaScript function utilizing recursion.

In the third line of this function, the statement calls itself, passing along a parameter of the next lower value of n. As this function executes, diving ever deeper into itself, JavaScript watches intermediate values and performs the final evaluations of the nested expressions. Be sure to test any recursive function carefully. In particular, make sure that the recursion is finite: There is a limit to the number of times it will recurse. In the case of Listing 12-3, that is the initial value of n. Failure to watch out for this could overpower the limits of the browser's memory and even lead to a crash.

Turning functions into libraries

As you start writing functions for your scripts, be on the lookout for ways to make functions generalizable (written so that you could reuse the function in other instances, regardless of the object structure of the page). The likeliest candidates for this kind of treatment are those functions that perform specific kinds of validation checks (see examples in Chapter 15), data conversions, or iterative math problems.

To make a function generalizable, don't let it make any references to specific objects by name. Names for objects will probably change from document to document. Instead, write the function so that it accepts a named object as a parameter. For example, if you write a function that accepts a text object as its parameter, the function can extract its data or invoke its methods without knowing anything about its enclosing form or name. Look again, for example, at the factorial() function in Listing 12-4 — but now as part of an entire document.

```
<HTML>
<HEAD>
<TITLE>Variable Scope Trials</TITLE>
<SCRIPT LANGUAGE="JavaScript">
function factorial(n) {
    if (n > 0) {
        return n * (factorial(n - 1))
    } else {
        return 1
    }
}
</SCRIPT>
</HEAD>

<BODY>
<FORM>
Enter an input value: <INPUT TYPE="text" NAME="input" VALUE=0><P>
```

```
<INPUT TYPE="button" VALUE="Calc Factorial"
    onClick="this.form.output.value =
        factorial(this.form.input.value)"><P>
Results: <INPUT TYPE="text" NAME="output">
</FORM>
</BODY>
</HTML>
```

Listing 12-4: Calling a generalizable function.

The function was designed to be generalizable, accepting only the input value (n) as a parameter. In the form, the onClick= event handler of the button extracts the input value from one of the form's fields, sending that value to the factorial() function. The returned value is assigned to the output field of the form. The factorial() function is totally ignorant about forms, fields, or buttons in this document. If I need this function in another script, I can copy and paste it into that script, knowing that it has been pre-tested. Any generalizable function becomes part of my personal library of scripts — from which I can borrow — and saves me time in future scripting tasks.

It's not always possible to generalize a function. Somewhere along the line in your scripts, there must be references to JavaScript or custom objects. But if you find that you are frequently writing functions that perform the same kind of actions, it's time to see how you can generalize the code and put the results in your library of ready-made functions.

Custom Objects

You've seen now how convenient the JavaScript object model is as a way of organizing all the descriptive information about an entire window and document. What may not be obvious from the scripting we've done so far is that JavaScript lets you create your own objects in memory — objects with properties and methods. These objects are not user interface elements per se on the page, but rather the kinds of objects that may contain data and script functions (behaving as methods) whose results the user could see displayed in the browser window, depending on your script.

You actually had a preview of this power in Chapter 9's discussion about arrays. An array, you'll recall, is an ordered collection of data. You can create a JavaScript array in which entries are labeled just like properties that you access via the now-familiar dot syntax (arrayName[index].propertyName). An object is typically a different kind of data. It doesn't have to be an ordered collection of data — although your scripts can use objects in constructions strongly resembling arrays. What is genuinely new, however, is that you can attach any number of custom functions as methods for that object. You are in total control, therefore, of the object's structure, data, and behavior.

Planetary objects

Because of your familiarity with the planetary data array created in Chapter 9, we'll use the same information here to build objects. Our goals here are the same: present a pop-up list of the nine planets of the Solar System and display data about the selected planet. From a user interface perspective (and for more exposure to multi-frame environments), the only difference is that the resulting data displays in a separate frame in a two-frame window rather than in a `textarea` object. This means that our object method will be building HTML on the fly and plugging it into the display frame — something pretty typical in these multi-frame, Web-browsing days.

To recap the array style: We created a two-dimensional array — a nine-row, five column table of data about the planets. Each row was an entry in the `solarSys[]` array. For a function to extract and display data about a given planet, it needed the index value of the `solarSys[]` array passed as a parameter so that it could get whatever property it needed for that entry (such as `solarSys[3].name`).

Instead of building arrays, we'll build objects — one object for each planet. The design of our object has five properties and one method. The properties are the same ones we used in the array version: name, diameter, distance from the sun, year length, and day length. To give these objects more intelligence, we give each of them the capability to display their data in the lower frame of the window. We can conveniently define one function that knows how to behave with any of these planet objects rather than having to define nine separate methods.

Listing 12-5 shows the source code for the document that creates the frameset for our planetary explorations; Listing 12-6 shows the entire HTML page for our object-oriented planet document, which appears in the top frame.

```
<HTML>
<HEAD>
<TITLE>Solar System Viewer</TITLE>
</HEAD>
<FRAMESET ROWS="50%,50%">
    <FRAME NAME="Frame1" SRC="lst12-06.htm">
    <FRAME NAME="Frame2" SRC="blank.htm">
</FRAMESET>
</HTML>
```

Listing 12-5: Framesetting document for a two-frame window.

```
<HTML>
<HEAD>
<TITLE>Our Solar System</TITLE>
<SCRIPT LANGUAGE="JavaScript">
<!-- start script
// method definition
function showPlanet() {
    var result = "The planet " + this.name
    result += " has a diameter of " + this.diameter + ".<BR>"
    result += "At a distance of " + this.distance + ", "
    result += "it takes " + this.year + " to circle the Sun.<BR>"
    result += "One day lasts " + this.day + " of Earth time."
    // display results in a second frame of the window
    parent.Frame2.document.close()
    parent.Frame2.document.write(result)
    parent.Frame2.document.close()
}

// definition of planet object type;
// 'new' will create a new instance and stuff parameter data into
object
function planet(name, diameter, distance, year, day) {
    this.name = name
    this.diameter = diameter
    this.distance = distance
    this.year = year
    this.day = day
    this.showPlanet = showPlanet  // make showPlanet() function a
method of planet
}

// create new planet objects, and store in a series of variables
Mercury = new planet("Mercury","3100 miles", "36 million miles",
"88 days", "59 days")
Venus = new planet("Venus", "7700 miles", "67 million miles",
"225 days", "244 days")
Earth = new planet("Earth", "7920 miles", "93 million miles",
"365.25 days","24 hours")
Mars = new planet("Mars", "4200 miles", "141 million miles",
"687 days", "24 hours, 24 minutes")
```

(continued)

```
Jupiter = new planet("Jupiter","88,640 miles","483 million miles",
"11.9 years", "9 hours, 50 minutes")
Saturn = new planet("Saturn", "74,500 miles","886 million miles",
"29.5 years", "10 hours, 39 minutes")
Uranus = new planet("Uranus", "32,000 miles","1.782 billion
miles","84 years", "23 hours")
Neptune = new planet("Neptune","31,000 miles","2.793 billion
miles","165 years", "15 hours, 48 minutes")
Pluto = new planet("Pluto", "1500 miles", "3.67 billion miles",
"248 years", "6 days, 7 hours")

// end script -->
</SCRIPT>
<BODY>
<H1>The Daily Planet</H1>
<HR>
<FORM>
<SCRIPT LANGUAGE = "JavaScript">
<!-- start script again
var page = "" // start assembling next part of page and form
page += "Select a planet to view its planetary data: "
// build popup list from planet object names
page += "<SELECT NAME='planets'> "
page += "<OPTION SELECTED >Mercury"
page += "<OPTION>Venus"
page += "<OPTION>Earth"
page += "<OPTION>Mars"
page += "<OPTION>Jupiter"
page += "<OPTION>Saturn"
page += "<OPTION>Uranus"
page += "<OPTION>Neptune"
page += "<OPTION>Pluto"
page += "</SELECT><P>"  // close selection item tag

document.write(page)     // lay out this part of the page

// called from push button to invoke planet object method
function doDisplay(popup) {
    i = popup.selectedIndex
    eval(popup.options[i].text + ".showPlanet()")
```

```
}
// really end script -->
</SCRIPT>

<INPUT TYPE="button" NAME="showdata" VALUE="Show the Data"
onClick="doDisplay(this.form.planets)"><P>
</FORM>
</BODY>
</HTML>
```

Listing 12-6: Object-oriented version of the planetary data presentation.

The first task in the Head is to define the function that becomes a method. This must be done before any other code that adopts the function as its method. Failure to define the function ahead of time results in an error — the function name is not defined. If you compare the data extraction methodology to the function in the array version, you will notice that not only is the parameter for the index value gone, but the references to each property begin with this. I'll come back to custom method after we look at the rest of the Head code.

Next comes another function that does several things. For one, everything in this function establishes the structure of our custom object: the properties available for data storage and retrieval and any methods that the object can invoke. The name of the function is the name we'll use later to create new instances of the object. Therefore, it is important to choose a name that truly reflects the nature of the object. And, because we'll probably want to stuff some data into the function's properties to get one or more instances of the object loaded and ready for the page's user, the function definition includes parameters for each of the properties defined in this object definition.

Inside the function, we use the this keyword to assign data that comes in as parameters to labeled properties. I've decided to use the same names for the parameter variables coming in and the properties. That's primarily for convenience, but you can assign any variable and property names you want and connect them any way you like. In the planet() function/object definition, five property slots are reserved for every instance of the object whether or not any data actually gets in every property (if not, its value is null).

The last entry in the planet() function/object definition is a reference to the showPlanet() function defined earlier. Notice that the assignment statement doesn't refer to the function with its parentheses — just to the function name. When JavaScript sees this assignment statement, it looks back through any existing definitions (those defined ahead of the current location in the script) for a match. If it finds a function (as it does here), it knows to assign the function to the identifier on the left side of the assignment statement. In doing this with a function, JavaScript automatically sets up the identifier as a method name. And, as you do in every JavaScript method you've encountered, you must invoke a method by a reference to the object, a period, and the method name followed by a set of parentheses. We'll see that in a minute.

The next long block of statements creates the individual objects according to the definition established in the planet() function. Notice that like the array, an object is created by an assignment statement and the keyword new. I've assigned names that are not only the real names of planets (the Mercury object name is the Mercury planet object) but will also come in handy later when extracting names from the pop-up list in search of a particular object's data.

The act of creating a new object sets aside space in memory (associated with the current document) for this object and its properties. In this script, we're creating nine object spaces, each with a different set of properties. Notice that no parameter is being sent (or expected at the function) corresponding to the showPlanet() method. That's fine, because the specification of that method in the object definition means that the method is automatically attached to every version (instance) of the planet object that the script creates.

In the Body portion of our document, and after the page's headline, we use JavaScript to create the rest of the user interface for the top frame of the browser window. I've replaced the array version's for loop for the pop-up list content with a hard-wired approach. The task could have been accomplished in fewer statements, but I set it up so that if I modify or borrow this code for another purpose, the hard-wired strings will be easier to locate, select, and change.

Once the HTML for the top frame is assembled, it is written for the first time (document.write()) to let the user see what's going on. Another function is included (mostly for demonstration purposes) so you can better understand the dynamics of the final action in the button, which is also part of the same form as the select object.

The button does nothing more than pass a copy of the form's selection object to the doDisplay() function. In that function, the select object is assigned to a variable called popup to help us visualize that the object is the pop-up list. The first statement extracts the index value of the selected item. Using that index value, the script extracts the text. But things get a little tricky because we need to use that text string as a variable name — the name of the planet — and append it to the call to the showPlanet() method. To make the disparate data types come together, we use the eval() function. Inside the parentheses, we extract the string for the planet name and concatenate a string that completes the reference to the object's showPlanet() method. The eval()

function evaluates that string, which turns it into a valid method call. Therefore, if the user selects Jupiter from the pop-up list, the method call becomes `Jupiter.showPlanet()`.

Now it's time to look back to the `showPlanet()` function/method definition at the top of the script. By the time this method starts working, JavaScript has already been to the object whose name is selected in the pop-up list, — say the Jupiter object. That Jupiter object has the `showPlanet()` method as part of its definition. When that method runs, its only scope is of the Jupiter object. Therefore, all references to `this.propertyName` in `showPlanet()` refer to Jupiter only. The only possibility for `this.name` in the Jupiter object is the value assigned to the name property for Jupiter. The same goes for the rest of the properties extracted in the function/method.

One more level

We're getting to quite advanced subject matter at this point, so I will merely mention and briefly demonstrate an additional power of defining and using custom objects. A custom object can have another custom object as a property. Let's extend the planet example to understand the implications.

Let's say that we want to beef up the planet page with an image of each planet. Each image has a URL for the image file plus other info, such as the copyright notice and a reference number, both of which would display on the page for the user. One way to handle this is to create a separate object definition for an image database. Such a definition might look like this:

```
function image(name, URL, copyright, refNum) {
    this.name = name
    this.URL = URL
    this.copyright = copyright
    this.refNum = refNum
}
```

You then need to create individual image objects for each picture. One such definition might look like this:

```
mercuryImage = new image("Planet Mercury", "/images/merc44.gif",
"(c)1990 NASA", 28372)
```

To attach an image object to a planet object requires modifying the planet object definition to accommodate one more property. The new planet object definition would look like this:

```
function planet(name, diameter, distance, year, day, image) {
    this.name = name
    this.diameter = diameter
    this.distance = distance
    this.year = year
    this.day = day
    this.showPlanet = showPlanet
    this.image = image // add image property
}
```

Once the image objects are created, you can then create the planet objects, passing one more parameter — an image object you want associated with that object:

```
// create new planet objects, and store in a series of variables
Mercury = new planet("Mercury","3100 miles",  "36 million miles",
"88 days",    "59 days",  mercuryImage)
```

To access a property of an image object, your scripts then have to assemble a reference that works its way through the connection with the planet object:

```
copyrightData = Mercury.image.copyright
```

If, by now, you think you see a resemblance between this object-within-an-object construction and a relational database, give yourself a gold star. There is nothing preventing multiple objects from having the same subobject as their properties — like multiple business contacts having the same company object property.

Using custom objects

There is no magic to knowing when to use a custom object instead of an array in your application. The more you work with and understand the way custom objects work, the more likely you will be to think about your data-carrying scripts in these terms, especially if an object can benefit from having one or more methods associated with it. This is certainly not an avenue for beginners, but I recommend that you give custom objects more than a casual perusal once you gain some JavaScripting experience.

The end of Part II

It may have seemed like a long journey, but we are now finished with all specifications of the JavaScript language — its objects, syntax, and the like. In Part III, I'll show you some extended applications using JavaScript and share some tips about debugging and implementation.

Part Three

Chapter Thirteen

Until JavaScript-enabled browsers become the norm in the Internet

world, you have difficult decisions to make about how quickly and how

deeply you deploy JavaScript in your World Wide Web site. This chapter

lays out some of these considerations on the table—points to consider

in your drive for the coolest Web site.

Browser Dependence

If you have been creating and serving up Web pages for a year or more, you may have faced some of these issues before. Whenever a new version of a popular browser, such as Netscape Navigator, appears on the scene, a host of HTML extensions usually become available that add design flexibility to your pages. Netscape Navigator 1.1's tables attracted a large following because they allowed orderly and appealing display of a lot of data without having to call upon a graphic designer to figure out column shadings and the like. Any other extensions that let your Web page more closely resemble a printed document were always welcome.

The problem, however, is that not every visitor to your site has a browser capable of displaying the results of the fancy tags. Ignoring, for the moment, those users who must use a text-based browser such as Lynx, anywhere from 20 to 30 percent of users accessing your site may not have the proper browser or browser version. As more generations of each browser find their ways onto PC users' hard disks, the fragmentation of browser capabilities could easily grow over time. Witness the bifurcation of Windows users into pioneering Windows 95 users and the staunchly and justifiably conservative band of Windows 3.1 users. Migration to the latest and greatest software or browser version is never assured in the real world.

In the past, it was not uncommon to see messages displayed on a home page that insisted the site yields a more pleasing experience with a particular browser — usually Netscape Navigator and its extensions. But I now also see this message promoting the extensions of Microsoft's Internet Explorer at various sites. Browser religious wars may soon follow. It is no longer adequate to say "to heck with the other 20 percent," because that 20 percent is growing.

This leaves a JavaScript author in a quandary over how much JavaScript to build into the site and how to accommodate the rest of the world.

The Smart Server Method

One of the worst possible solutions from a Web authoring point of view is to let server-based CGI programs determine the browser being used by each user and feed pages that have been tweaked for that browser. If you control your server, you have this option by reading the USER_AGENT data that comes from the client.

This naturally means a great deal more work for the authors because once a set of pages is completed, they must be examined with specific browsers and adjusted accordingly. With the proliferation of browser types and generations (going back to vanilla HTML 2.0), you can go nuts figuring out which browsers to support directly with special features. Moreover, your CGI will have to be continually updated as newer generations of browsers come out. Eventually you have to ask yourself how many versions you want to support. This makes porting an application program from Windows to the Macintosh look like a simple gig.

If your Web site has the resources to manage this kind of customization, and you're willing to do it, more power to you. It takes the posture that "the browser is always right." I just don't know how long you can justify the cost of adopting pages to multiple browsers when the funds and talent could be better spent creating new material for your overall site.

The High Road/Low Road Method

As we all know, not every Webmaster is in total charge of the server on which the site resides. Nor is CGI scripting within the grasp of every Web site provider. As an alternative to letting the server figure out what type of browser the user has, you can allow users to base their selection of the path through your site on links shown on the home page. In other words, the home page acts like the gateway to the rest of your site. Clicking on one link takes the user to pages in one directory for one type of browser; clicking on the other link sends the user down the path of a different directory whose pages are optimized for a particular browser type. The goal is getting both users "to Scotland" eventually, regardless of the route. Both sets of content are the same: Only the presentation (and underlying HTML) is different.

From the Web author's point of view, this requires reworking existing pages to make sure that they look good with each browser type supported by the site. In my experience, what starts out to be a clever idea turns into a burden when it comes time to update or maintain the site. Any impediment to updating a site becomes an excuse for not doing so over time. Incentives to keep your site fresh dwindle as the months roll on.

The Dictator Model

Gung-ho JavaScript scripters will be eager to create exceedingly clever and snazzy pages that absolutely require JavaScript. If you want to share your expertise in calculating tide tables for the Bay of Fundy, your JavaScript tide calculator will work only with JavaScript-enabled browsers. In a home page that all browsers can read in some fashion, you have to alert users that they must have a JavaScript-enabled browser to continue on your site.

Of course, not everyone who accepts your challenge will have a JavaScript-enabled browser, so be sure you add the proper comment lines to your scripts so that the pages these folks see don't look like a programmer's reference manual. In fact, it is always a good idea to keep a copy of an old browser handy so that you can check your pages to see what they look like in a non-JavaScript browser.

If you want to take this heavy-handed approach to incorporating JavaScript into your Web site, be considerate of JavaScript newcomers and add a link from your home page to Netscape's home page so users can download a trial copy of the latest Navigator. As other JavaScript-enabled browsers become available, you can add links to their providers' sites as well.

Athough I call this method the "Dictator Method," it does contribute to an important effort that we, as Web page providers, should support: raising the lowest common denominator of browser in the real world. Layout capabilities of browsers are painfully antiquated compared to desktop publishing. Only by stretching the necessarily tortoise-like advances of the HTML standard can we graduate to more sophisticated pages without having to resort to other formats that require players and plug-ins. If enough users see that they cannot access parts of Web sites because they don't have a JavaScript-enabled browser, they will feel left behind technologically. With the cost of a trial version of an updated browser no more than the cost of a download (which is no incremental cost for many Internet users), this kind of peer pressure is not like forcing everyone to "keep up with Joneses" by spending more money. But it can help advance the cause of Web browser technology so we can deliver better-looking pages year after year.

The Sneak Attack

If you are patient about displaying your JavaScripting skills to the world, you can begin to blend JavaScript enhancements into your existing pages for the benefit of users of JavaScript-enabled browsers. This is my favorite method, but it also requires a dash of the Dictator Method, as I'll describe in a moment.

The greatest benefit of the Sneak Attack is that you don't have to design a new set of pages for JavaScript-enabled browsers. Instead, embed JavaScript code into the HTML documents that everyone sees. In the Body definition, add scripts that insert material into the page as the browser loads it. For example, an extra greeting that welcomes the user with a "Good Morning," "Good Afternoon," or "Good Evening," based on the client computer's time of day, would appear only in JavaScript-enabled browsers. Entire sections of a page set off by horizontal rules could also be used to display links to pages that absolutely require JavaScript.

Users of JavaScript-challenged browsers won't know what they're missing unless you alert them to the possibilities — perhaps at the bottom of your home page. This is where the Dictator Method comes into play. Unless you let users know that there is more to the site for those with JavaScript-enabled browsers, they won't appreciate the entire depth of your Web site.

The Sneak Attack — Interlaced Code Variety

Unfortunately, JavaScript with Navigator 2.0 doesn't let you overwrite HTML sections with JavaScripted sections. Nor is there any built-in mechanism similar to the <NOFRAMES> tag that lets you alert a non-frame browser to display something different. You can, however, play a trick on browsers with comment lines inside <SCRIPT> tags (thanks to Paul Colton for this inspiration). Fashion comments such that some items show in old browsers but not in JavaScript-enhanced browsers; on the flip side, any content written to a page via normal JavaScript doesn't appear in old browsers. Listing 13-1 shows an example of creating one HTML document that shows two different contents depending on the JavaScript-ability of the user's browser. Lines within the script that begin with JavaScript comment symbols (/ /) are for instructional purposes only: Remove them in an actual Web page because they will appear in non-JavaScript browsers.

```
<HTML>
<HEAD>
<TITLE>A Universal Document</TITLE>
</HEAD>
<BODY>
<SCRIPT LANGUAGE="JavaScript">
// next line runs only on non-JavaScript browsers
<!--> <H1>Welcome to my Web site</H1>
// next lines appear only in JavaScript browsers
<!--
document.write("<H1>Welcome to my JavaScript-enhanced Web site</
H1>")
document.write("Last updated " + document.lastModified + ".")
//-->
</SCRIPT>
</BODY>
</HTML>
```

Listing 13-1: A comment trick to accommodate browsers of all kinds.

In the <SCRIPT> tag pair, the line that begins with the weird-looking comment construction <!--> is the interesting one. JavaScript ignores any line inside a <SCRIPT> tag that begins with the <!-- comment sequence, no matter what else follows it on that line. That beginning comment sequence is also the HTML beginning comment sequence. That same line finishes with the HTML end comment sequence (-->). Thus, when a non-JavaScript browser encounters this begin comment/end comment pair, it treats whatever comes after it as HTML to be rendered. JavaScript, on the other hand, ignores the trailing stuff on the line.

Below that starts the JavaScript code that only JavaScript-enabled browsers see. That's because all these lines are surrounded by the HTML begin comment/end comment pair, spread across as many lines of JavaScript as the page needs.

Anyone reading your source code who is not JavaScript-savvy will have a tough time figuring out what you're doing with all these comment tags, but this scheme allows you to interlace JavaScript and non-JavaScript HTML in the same document. Users see only material that you've deemed relevant for their browser level.

Even if you adopt this methodology, you should include some kind of message in your home page (perhaps displayed only to non-JavaScript browsers) that your site has more in store for people with JavaScript-enabled browsers (that's where the Dictator Model comes into play). One way to handle this is to add a footer-style section at the bottom of your home page that alerts all users to the JavaScript features of the page and site. This is where you would also have a link to your favorite JavaScript-enabled browser publisher's site for downloading of a new browser.

Go Crazy and Take It Slow

What I like most about the Sneak Attack method (whether or not you use the interlaced code scheme) is that it allows JavaScript fanatics to experiment and create wonderful pages for the *JavaScripterati*, while enticing the rest to join in and not completely excluding them from a site. Users with basic browsers can obtain useful information, whereas those with JavaScript-enabled browsers have an even better time at your site.

*C**hapter Fourteen*

One of the first questions that an experienced programmer asks about a programming environment concerns support for debugging code. Even the best coders in the world make mistakes when they draft their programs. Sometimes the mistakes are a mere slip of a finger on the keyboard; other times they are the result of not being careful with expression evaluation or object references. The cause of the mistake is not the issue: finding the mistake and getting help to fix it is.

In these pioneering days of JavaScript, there is little in the way of debugging support for scripters. Ideally, there would be a smart editor that we could use to write scripts. It would keep an eye on pairs of braces, parentheses, and quotes — alerting us when one of a pair is missing. As it stands now, however, we don't know that a problem exists with a script until we load the page or interact with the page in such a way that the faulty script fails.

Syntax versus Runtime Errors

As a page loads into a JavaScript-enabled browser, the browser attempts to create an object model out of the HTML and JavaScript code in the document. Some types of errors crop up at this point. These are mostly *syntax errors,* such as failing to include a closing brace around a function's statements. None of these errors have to do with values or object references, but are rather structural in nature.

Runtime errors involve failed connections between function calls and their functions, mismatched data types, and undeclared variables located on the wrong side of assignment operators. Such runtime errors can occur as the page loads if the script lines run immediately as the page loads. Runtime errors located in functions won't crop up until the functions are called — either as the page loads or in response to user action.

Because of the interpreted nature of JavaScript and the fact that we don't yet have syntax-checking tools, the distinction between syntax and runtime errors blurs. But as you work through whatever problem halts a page from loading or a script from running, you have to be aware of differences between true errors in language and your errors in logic or evaluation.

Error Messages

Netscape Navigator produces a large error dialog box whenever it detects even the slightest problem (Figure 14-1). At the top of the box is the URL of the document causing the problem and a line number. Below that is a (somewhat) plain-language description of the nature of the problem, followed by an extract of the code on which JavaScript is choking.

The line number provided in the error message is a valiant effort to help draw our attention to the problem line of code. All too often, however, the line number corresponds to nothing even remotely connected to the problem in the source document, whether you start counting lines from the top of the document or the top of the <SCRIPT> tag. Sometimes they line up, other times not. For the moment, I've given up using that line number as a pointer to anything.

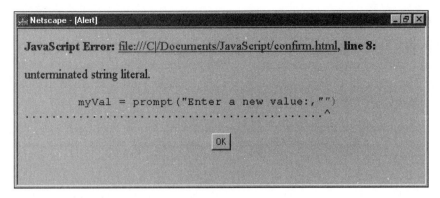

Figure 14-1: A typical error message window.

More revealing, at times — although not always accurate — is the code extract. For some syntax errors (such as missing halves of brace, parenthesis, and quote pairs), the extract is from the line of code truly affected by the problem. The extract won't help at all, unfortunately, on some missing items, such as a missing right brace in a function definition. At best, the error description "missing } after function body," lets you know that an imbalance exists in one of your function definitions. The blank line of code it shows you isn't of much help; and the line number could be off by several lines.

Because there are so many permutations of the potential errors you can make in scripts and the ways the JavaScript interpreter regards these errors, it is impossible to present hard-and-fast solutions to JavaScript error messages. What I will do, however, is list the most common error messages and relate the kinds of non-obvious problems that can trigger such messages.

"something is not defined"

This one is fairly easy. It usually means that you have a new variable name sitting in the position of a right-hand operand or a unary operand. This variable name has not been declared or assigned with any value prior to this erroneous statement. The word may also be meant to be a string, but you forgot to enclose it in quotes. Another possibility is that you misspelled the name of a previously declared variable. JavaScript rightly regards this item as a new, undeclared variable. Misspellings, you'll recall, include errors in upper- and lowercase in the very case-sensitive JavaScript world.

"something is not a function"

This error message can be one of the most frustrating, because in the script, it appears as though you have clearly defined a function by that name, and you're simply having an event handler or other running statement call that function. The first items to look for are as follows:

- The case of letters in the calling statement and function are identical.

- The object containing the event handler that calls this function has the same name (in the NAME= attribute) as the function.

This latter item is a no-no and confuses JavaScript into thinking that the function doesn't exist, even though the object name doesn't have parentheses appended to it and the function does.

I have also seen this error appear when other problems existed in the script above the function named in the error message. Whatever syntactical errors occurred in lines above that function made the browser ignore your valid-looking function definition. A missing brace, parenthesis, or quote half of a pair probably lurks somewhere in the lines above the good function.

"unterminated string literal"

In the code fragment displayed in the error window, the pointer usually appears at the first quote of a string it thinks is unterminated. If you simply forgot to close a string quote pair, the error most frequently appears when you try to concatenate strings or nest quoted strings. Despite the claim that you can nest alternating double and single quotes, I often have difficulties nesting beyond the second nested level (single quotes inside a double-quoted string). At different times I have gotten away with using a pair of \ " in-line quote symbols for a third layer deep. If that fails, I break up the string so that nesting goes no deeper than two layers. If necessary, I even back out the most nested string and assign it to a variable in the previous line — concatenating it into the more complex string in the next line. You can see an example of this in Chapter 20.

In the Windows versions of Netscape Navigator 2.0, you may also see this error if a string value is longer than 250 characters. But you can divide up such a string into smaller segments and concatenate strings later in the script with the plus (+) operator.

"missing } after function body"

This error usually is easy to recognize in a simple function definition because the closing brace is missing at the end of the function. But when the function includes additional nested items, such as if...else or for loop constructions, you begin dealing with multiple pairs of braces within the function. The JavaScript interpreter doesn't always determine exactly where the missing brace belongs and simply defaults to the end of the function. This is natural, I guess, because from a global perspective of the function, one or more of the right braces that would ripple down to the end of the function are usually missing. In any case, this error message means that a brace is probably missing somewhere in the function, although not necessarily at the end. Do an inventory count for left and right braces and see if there is a discrepancy in the counts. One of those nested constructions is probably missing a closing brace.

"something is not a numeric literal"

The variable name singled out in this error message is most likely a string value, a null value, or no value at all (the variable has been declared with the var statement, but not initialized with any value). The line of JavaScript that trips it up has an operator that demands a number. When in doubt about the data type of a variable destined for a math operation, use the parseInt() or parseFloat() functions to convert strings to numbers.

"something has no properties"

When a statement trips this error message, an object reference has usually gone awry. You have probably attempted to reference a property of a JavaScript object, but there is something wrong with the object reference. Most commonly, it has to do with the kinds of objects stored as arrays inside the browser (forms or links). If you are trying to retrieve the value property of a button named calcMe, for example, the following incorrect reference would trigger the "has no properties" error:

```
document.forms.calcMe.value
```

The error here would read "calcMe has no properties." What you've forgotten is that the forms property is an array and must be referenced as follows:

```
document.forms[0].calcMe.value
```

JavaScript has many of these kinds of references that include arrays (radio buttons in a radio object, options in a select object, and so on). Always double-check your object references when this error message appears.

"syntax error"

JavaScript is best at detecting true syntax errors and showing you the location of the problem. Even if the line counter is off, there is a good chance that the code fragment and pointer in the error dialog are accurate.

These aren't the only error messages you will encounter. Others are pretty smart (for example, when you use a single equal sign when you meant two in a conditional test of equality of two values). It's when the error message and your code don't seem to mesh that you have headaches.

Sniffing Out Problems

It doesn't take many error-tracking sessions to get you in the save-switch-reload mode quickly. Assuming that you know this routine, here are some techniques I use to find errors in my scripts when the error messages aren't being helpful in directing me to the problem.

Check the HTML tags

Even before looking into JavaScript code, I review the document carefully to make sure that all my HTML tags are written properly. That includes making sure that all tags have closing angle brackets and that all tag pairs have balanced opening and closing tags. Digging deeper, especially in tags near the beginning of scripts, I make sure that all tag attributes that must be enclosed in quotes have the quote pairs in place. A browser may be forgiving about sloppy HTML as far as layout goes, but the JavaScript interpreter isn't as accommodating. Finally, I ensure that the <SCRIPT> tag pairs are in place (they may be in multiple locations throughout my document) and that the LANGUAGE="JavaScript" attribute has both of its quotes.

Re-open the file

If I make changes to the document that I truly believe should fix a problem, but the same problem persists after a reload, I re-open the file via the File menu. Sometimes you run an error-filled script more than once and the browser's internals get a bit confused. Reloading does not clear the bad stuff away. Re-opening the file, however, clears the old one entirely from the browser's memory and loads the most recently fixed version of the source. If you have difficulties involving multiple frames and tables, you may even have to quit the browser and restart it to clear its cobwebs.

Find out what works

When an error message gives you no clue about the true location of a runtime problem, or you're faced with crashes at an unknown point, you need to find out what part of the script execution works properly. To narrow down the problem spot, insert an alert dialog box with a brief message you'll recognize (such as `alert("HERE")`). Start this at the beginning of any statements that execute and try the script again. Keep moving this line deeper into the script (perhaps into other functions called by outer statements) until the error or crash occurs. You now know where to look for problems.

Comment out statements

If the errors appear to be syntactical (as opposed to errors of evaluation), the error message may point to a code fragment many lines away from the problem. More often than not, the problem exists in a line somewhere above the one quoted in the error message. To find the offending line, begin commenting out lines one at a time (between reloading tests), starting with the line indicated in the error message. Keep doing this until the error message clears the area you're working on, pointing to some other problem below the original line (with the lines commented out, some value is likely to fail below). The most recent line you commented out is the one that has the beginning of your problem. Start looking there.

Checking expression evaluation

I've said many times throughout this book that one of the two common problems facing scripters is an expression that evaluates to something you don't expect. In a true debugger, we'd be able to single-step through script execution and watch the content of variables in a separate window. Because we don't have such a "luxury" in a JavaScript editor, we are left to our own devices for checking the values of variables during script execution.

The most important tool we use for this exploration is the alert dialog box. We are fortunate in that the alert dialog box shows us almost anything, even if it is not a string. Therefore, we can look at numbers and even complete objects.

Because most of the problems come within function definitions, it is best to start such explorations from the top of the function. Every time you assign an object property to a variable or invoke a string, math, or date method, insert a line below that line with an `alert()` method that shows the contents of the new variable value. Do this one statement at a time, save, switch, and reload. Study the value that appears in the alert to see if it is what you expect. If not, something is amiss in the previous line involving the expression(s) you used to achieve that value.

This is an excruciatingly tedious process for debugging a long function, but it is absolutely essential to track down where a bum object reference or expression evaluation is tripping up your script. When a value comes back as being <undefined> or null, more than likely the problem is an object reference that is incomplete (trying to access a frame without the `parent.frames[i]` reference), using the wrong name for an existing object (check case), or accessing a property or method that doesn't exist for that object.

Another tool to keep in your back pocket is the object property inspector. Using the special `for ... in` statement of JavaScript (Chapter 10), you can call the function in Listing 14-1 from anywhere within your scripts to view the values of all properties of an object. You may find, for instance, that your script inadvertently changes the property of an object when you aren't looking. Pass this function — both the actual object (as an unquoted name) and the name of the object (as a quoted string) — so the resulting alert dialog box explains what's what.

```
function showProps(obj,objName) {
    var result = ""
    for (var i in obj) {
        result += objName + "." + i + " = " + obj[i] + "\n"
    }
alert(result)
}
```

Listing 14-1: Property inspector function.

Navigator Crashes

Netscape Navigator 2.0, while seemingly reliable in its browser role, is not so stable when it comes to trying JavaScript statements that would normally be considered illegal. The browser isn't quite as robust as it will be in the future as far as protecting scripters from crashes when scripts attempt out-of-bounds tasks.

The seriousness of the crash depends partly on the internal error and the operating system. For instance, I've seen crashes on the Macintosh that range from just "unexpectedly quitting" Navigator (leaving everything else intact) to taking down the entire computer (necessitating a hard restart). Windows 95, on the other hand, protects the rest of the applications running when Navigator takes a dive.

Crashes unfortunately accrue to newcomers who mistakenly attempt to invoke document methods on an already-loaded document containing the script. Most of these methods — `document.close()`, `document.clear()`, `document.open()` — are intended for documents appearing in other frames or windows. JavaScript, especially in Navigator 2.0, takes offense and may "flatline" on you.

For more experienced scripters, the bulk of crashes in Navigator 2.0 come from attempting to communicate across windows and frames. This isn't illegal at all. But what often happens is that a statement tries to address an object no longer in the browser's memory. For example, if a variable contains a complete object reference to a second window's subobjects, that reference becomes invalid if another document is loaded into that second window. Attempting to use that variable as a reference will likely crash Navigator.

Another crash tends to occur in the realm of multi-frame documents. A script in a frameset document should refer to document objects in the frames only *after* all frames have been loaded (in response to the frameset's `onLoad=` event handler). For instance, trying to get the title of a document not yet loaded into a frame will likely crash Navigator.

The bottom line on most crashes comes back to object references. Not only must the references be in the correct syntax, but the objects must exist when the references are called in a script. Understanding the issues of loading documents — especially in multiple frames — is critical to avoiding these kinds of problems. If you experience crashes while developing a multi-frame environment, this is the first place to look for conflicts.

Preventing Problems

Because we don't have the crutches of a smart editor (which could tell us if we forgot to balance our braces), debugger, and variable watcher to lead us through pitfalls, it is up to us to do what we can to minimize bugs in the first place. I offer a number of suggestions that can help in this regard.

Getting structure right

Early problems in developing a page with scripts tend to be structural: knowing that your objects are displayed correctly on the page; making sure that your <SCRIPT> tags are complete; completing brace, parenthesis, and quoted pairs. I start writing my page by first getting down the HTML parts — including all form definitions . Because so much of a scripted page tends to rely on the placement and naming of interface elements, it's much easier to work with these items once you lay them out on the page. At that point, you can start filling in the JavaScript.

When you begin defining a function, repeat loop, or `if` construction, fill out the entire structure before entering any details. For example, when I define a function named `verifyData()`, I enter the entire structure for it:

```
function verifyData() {

}
```

I leave a blank line between the beginning of the function and the closing brace in anticipation of entering at least one line of code.

After I decide on a parameter to be passed and assign a variable to it, I may want to insert an `if` construction. Again, I fill in the basic structure:

```
function verifyData(form) {
    if (form.checkbox.checked) {

    }
}
```

This automatically pushes the closing brace of the function lower, which is what I want — putting it securely at the end of the function where it belongs. It also assures that I line up the closing brace of the `if` statement with that grouping. Further statements in the `if` construction push down the two closing braces.

If you don't like typing or don't trust yourself to maintain this kind of discipline when you're in a hurry to test an idea, you should prepare a separate document that has templates for the common constructions: <SCRIPT> tags, function, `if`, `if...else`, `for` loop, while loop, and conditional expression. Then if your editor and operating system support it, drag-and-drop the necessary segments into your working script.

Build incrementally

Without true debugging facilities for JavaScript, the worst tactic you can follow is to write tons of code before trying any of it. Error messages may point to so many lines away from the source of the problem that you'll never find the true source of difficulty. The save-switch-reload sequence is not painful like compiling code, so it is better to try your code every time you have written a complete thought — or even enough to test an intermediate result in an alert dialog box — to make sure that you're on the right track.

Test expression evaluation

Especially while you are learning the ins and outs of JavaScript, you may feel unsure about the results that a particular string, math, or date method yields on a value. The longer your scripted document gets, the more difficult it will be to test the evaluation of a statement. You're better off trying the expression in a more controlled, isolated environment, such as in a separate evaluation tester document you write with a couple text or textarea objects in it. Navigator users can use the internal JavaScript: location (Chapter 5) to test expressions. By doing this kind of testing in the browser, you save a great deal of time experimenting by going back and forth between the source document and the browser.

Build function workbenches

A similar situation exists for building and testing functions, especially generalizable ones. Rather than test a function inside a complex scripted document, drop it into a skeletal document that contains the minimum number of user interface elements you need to test the function. This task gets difficult when the function is closely tied to a lot of objects in the real document, but it works wonders for making you think about generalizing functions for possible use in the future. Display the output of the function in a text or textarea object or include it in an alert dialog box.

Testing Your Masterpiece

If your background strictly involves designing HTML pages, you probably think of testing as determining your users' ability to navigate successfully around your site. But a JavaScript-enhanced page — especially if the user enters input into fields — requires substantially more testing before you unleash it to the on-line masses.

A large part of good programming is anticipating what a user can do at any point and then being sure that your code covers that eventuality. With multi-frame windows, for example, you need to see how unexpected reloading of document affects the relationships between all the frames — especially if they depend on each other. Users will be able to resize their windows at any time (which causes a reload) or suspend document loading in the middle of a download from the server. How do these activities affect your scripting? Do they cause script errors based on your current script organization?

The minute you allow a user to type an entry into a form, you also invite the user to enter the wrong kind of information into that form. If your script expects only a numeric value from a field and the user (accidentally or intentionally) types a letter, is your script ready to handle that "bad" data? Or no data? Or a negative floating-point number?

Just because you, as author of the page, know the "proper" sequence to follow and the "right" kind of data to enter into forms, your users will not necessarily follow your instructions. In days gone by, such mistakes were relegated to "user error." Today, with an increasingly consumer-oriented World Wide Web audience, any such faults rest solely on the programmer — you.

If I sound as though I'm trying to scare you, I have succeeded. I was serious in the early chapters of this book when I said that writing JavaScript is programming. Users of your page are expecting the same polish and smooth operation (no script errors and certainly no crashes) from your site as from the most professional software publisher on the planet. Don't let them or yourself down. Test your pages extensively on as many Navigator hardware platforms as you can and with as wide an audience as possible before putting the pages on the server for all to see.

The Future of Tools

I am confident that JavaScript's popularity will spawn a cottage industry of authoring tools to bridge the gaps that exist at this early stage. Smart editors, function library managers, debuggers — they will all be in your scripting arsenal before too long. In the meantime, with a little ingenuity, you can get by.

Chapter Fifteen

Give users a field in which to enter data, and you can be sure that some users will enter the wrong kind of data. Often the "mistake" is accidental — a slip of the pinkie on the keyboard; other times, it's made intentionally to see just how robust your application is. Whether you solicit a user's entry for client-side scripting purposes or for input into a server-based CGI or database, you should use JavaScript on the client to handle validation of the user's entry. Even for a form connected to a CGI script, it is far more efficient from bandwidth, server load, and execution speed perspectives to let client-side JavaScript get the data straight before your server program deals with it.

Designing Filters

The job of writing data validation routines is essentially one of designing filters that weed out characters or entries that don't fit your programming scheme. Whenever your filter detects an incorrect entry, it should alert the user about the nature of the problem and let the user correct the entry.

Before you put any text or textarea object into your document that invites users to enter data, you must decide if there is any kind of entry that will disturb the execution of the rest of your scripts. For example, if your script must have a number from that field so it can perform calculations, you must filter out any entry that contains letters or punctuation — except for periods — if the program can accept floating-point numbers. Your task is to anticipate every possible entry users could make and let pass only those your scripts can use.

Not every entry field needs a data validation filter. For example, you may prompt a user for information stored as `document.cookie` or in a string database field on the server for retrieval later. If there is no further processing of that information, you may not have to worry about the specific contents of that field.

One other design consideration is to rethink the use of a field at all. If the range of choices for user entry is small (a dozen or fewer), it may make more sense to avoid the data entry problem altogether by turning that field into a select object. Your HTML attributes for the object assure that you control the kind of entry made to that object. As long as your script knows how to deal with each of the options defined for that object, you're in the clear.

Building a Library of Filter Functions

A number of basic data validation processes are used repeatedly in form-intensive HTML pages. Filters for integers only, numbers only, empty entries, alphabet letters only, and the like are put to use every day. If you maintain a library of generalizable functions for each of your data validation tasks, you can drop them into your scripts at a moment's notice and be assured that they'll work.

Making these functions generalizable requires careful choice of wording and logic so that they return Boolean values that make syntactical sense when they are called from elsewhere in your scripts. As you'll see later in this chapter when we build a larger framework around smaller functions, each function is usually called as part of an if...else conditional statement. Therefore, assign a name that fits logically as part of an "if" clause in plain language. For example, a function that checks whether an entry is empty might be named isEmpty(). The calling statement would be

```
if (isEmpty(value)) { …
```

From a plain-language perspective, the expectation is that the function returns true if the passed value is empty. With this design, the statements nested in the if construction handle the case in which the entry field is empty. We'll come back to this later when we start stacking multiple-function calls together in a larger validation routine.

To get you started with your library of validation functions, I provide a few in this chapter that you can both learn from and use as starting points for more specific filters of your own design. Some of these functions are put to use in the JavaScript application in Chapter 17.

isEmpty()

The first function, shown in Listing 15-1, checks to see if the incoming value is either empty or a null value. Adding a check for a null means that we can use this function for purposes other than just text object validation. For example, if another function defines three parameter variables but the calling function passes only two, the third variable is set to null. Should the script perform a data validation check on all parameters, the isEmpty() function responds that the null value is devoid of data.

```
// general purpose function to see if an input value has been
// entered at all
function isEmpty(inputStr) {
    if (inputStr == null || inputStr == "") {
        return true
    }
    return false
}
```

Listing 15-1: A function that sees if an entry is empty or null.

This function uses a Boolean Or operator (||) to test for the existence of a null value or an empty string in the value passed to the function. Because the name of the f unction implies a true response if the entry is empty, that is the value that goes back to the calling statement if either condition is true. Because a `return` statement halts further processing of a function, the `return false` statement lies outside of the `if` construction. If processing reaches this statement, it means that the `inputStr` value failed the test.

Should this seem like convoluted logic — return true when the value is empty — you can also define a function that returns the inverse values. You could name it `isNotEmpty()`. As it turns out, however, typical processing of an empty entry is better served when the test returns a true when it is empty — aiding the `if` construction that called the function in the first place.

isPosInteger()

The next function examines each character of the value to make sure that only the numbers from zero through nine with no punctuation or other symbols exist. The goal of the function in Listing 15-2 is to weed out any value that is not a positive integer.

```
// general purpose function to see if a suspected numeric input
// is a positive integer
function isPosInteger(inputVal) {
    inputStr = "" + inputVal
    for (var i = 0; i < inputStr.length; i++) {
        var oneChar = inputStr.charAt(i)
        if (oneChar < "0" || oneChar > "9") {
            return false
        }
    }
    return true
}
```

Listing 15-2: A function that tests for positive integers.

Notice that this function makes no assumption about the data type of the value passed as a parameter. If the value had come directly from a text object, it would already be a string, and the line that forces data conversion to a string would be unnecessary. But to generalize the function, the conversion is included to accommodate the possibility that it might be called from another statement that has a numeric value to check.

The function requires the input value be converted to a string because it performs a character-by-character analysis of the data. A `for` loop picks apart the value one character at a time. Rather than force the script to invoke the `string.charAt()` method twice for each time through the loop (inside the `if` condition), one statement assigns the results of the method to a variable which is then used twice in the `if` condition. It makes the `if` condition shorter and easier to read and is microscopically more efficient as well.

In the `if` condition, the ASCII value of each character is compared against the range of zero through nine. This is safer than comparing numeric values of the single characters because one of the characters could be non-numeric. You would encounter all kinds of other problems trying to convert that character to a number for numeric comparison. The ASCII value, on the other hand, is neutral about the meaning of a character: If the ASCII value is less than zero or greater than that of nine, the character is not valid for a true positive integer. The function bounces the call with a false reply. On the other hand, if the `for` loop completes its traversal of all characters in the value without a hitch, the function returns true.

isInteger()

The next possibility includes the entry of a negative integer value. Listing 15-3 shows that we must add an extra check for a leading negation sign.

```
// general purpose function to see if a suspected numeric input
// is a positive or negative integer
function isInteger(inputVal) {
    inputStr = "" + inputVal
    for (var i = 0; i < inputStr.length; i++) {
        var oneChar = inputStr.charAt(i)
        if (i == 0 && oneChar == "-") {
            continue
        }
        if (oneChar < "0" || oneChar > "9") {
            return false
        }
    }
    return true
}
```

Listing 15-3: Adding a check for a leading minus sign.

When a script can accept a negative integer, the filter must let the leading minus sign pass unscathed. We cannot just add the minus sign to the `if` condition of Listing 15-2 because we can accept that symbol only when it is in the first position of the value — anywhere else makes it an invalid number. To take care of the possibility, we add another if statement whose condition looks for a special combination: the first character of the string (as indexed by the loop counting variable) and the minus character. If both of these conditions are met, execution immediately loops back around to the update expression of the for loop (due to the continue statement) rather than carrying on the second if statement, which would obviously fail. By putting the i == 0 operation at the front of the condition, we assure that it will short-circuit the entire condition to false for all subsequent iterations through the loop.

isNumber()

The final numeric filter function in this series allows any integer or floating point number to pass, while filtering out all others (Listing 15-4). All that distinguishes an integer from a floating point number for data validation purposes is the decimal point.

```
// general purpose function to see if a suspected numeric input
// is a positive or negative number
function isNumber(inputVal) {
    oneDecimal = false
    inputStr = "" + inputVal
    for (var i = 0; i < inputStr.length; i++) {
        var oneChar = inputStr.charAt(i)
        if (i == 0 && oneChar == "-") {
            continue
        }
        if (oneChar == "." && !oneDecimal) {
            oneDecimal = true
            continue
        }
        if (oneChar < "0" || oneChar > "9") {
            return false
        }
    }
    return true
}
```

Listing 15-4: Testing for a decimal point.

Anticipating the worst, however, the function cannot just add a comparison for a decimal (actually for *not* a decimal) to the condition that compares ASCII values of each character. That would assume that no one would ever enter more than one decimal point into a text field. Sorry, but only one decimal point is allowed for this function (as well as for JavaScript math). Therefore, we add a Boolean flag variable (`oneDecimal`) to the function and a separate `if` condition that sets that flag to true when the first decimal point is encountered. Should another decimal point appear in the string, the final `if` statement has a crack at the character. Because the character falls outside the ASCII range of zero through nine, it fails the entire function.

If you want to accept only positive floating-point numbers, you can make a new version of this function, removing the statement that lets the leading minus sign through. Be aware that this function works only for values that are not represented in exponential notation.

Custom validation functions

The listings shown so far in this chapter should give you plenty of source material to use in writing customized validation functions for your applications. An example of such an application-specific variation (extracted from the application in Chapter 17) is shown in Listing 15-5.

```
// function to determine if value is in acceptable range
// for this application
function inRange(inputStr) {
    num = parseInt(inputStr)
    if (num < 1 || num > 586 && num < 596 || num > 599 && num <
700 || num > 728) {
        return false
    }
    return true
}
```

Listing 15-5: A custom validation function.

For this application, it is necessary to see if an entry is within multiple ranges of acceptable numbers. The value is converted to a number (via the `parseInt()` function) so that it could be numerically compared against maximum and minimum values of several ranges within the database. Following the logic of the previous validation functions, the `if` condition looked for values that were outside the acceptable range so it could alert the user and return a false value.

The `if` condition is quite a long sequence of operators. As you noticed in the list of operator precedence (Chapter 11), the Boolean And operator (`&&`) has precedence over the Boolean Or operator (`||`). Therefore, the And expressions evaluate first, followed by the Or expressions. Parentheses may help you better visualize what's going on in that monster condition:

```
if (num < 1 || (num > 586 && num < 596) ||
(num > 599 && num < 700) || num > 728)
```

In other words, we exclude four possible ranges from consideration:

- Values less than 1

- Values between 586 and 596

- Values between 599 and 700

- Values greater than 728

Any value for which any one of these tests is true yields a Boolean false from this function. Combining all these tests into a single condition statement eliminates the need to construct an otherwise complex series of nested if constructions.

Combining Validation Functions

When you design a page requesting a particular kind of text input from a user, you often need to call more than one data validation function to handle the entire job. For example, if you merely want to test for a positive integer entry, your validation should test for both the presence of any entry and the validation as an integer.

Once you know the kind of permissible data that your script will use after validation, it's time to plot the sequence of data validation. Because each page's validation task is different, I supply some guidelines to follow in this planning rather than prescribe a fixed route for all to take.

My preferred sequence is to start with examinations that require less work and increase the intensity of validation detective work with succeeding functions. I borrow this tactic from real life: When a lamp fails to turn on, I look for a pulled plug or a burnt-out light bulb before tearing the lamp's wiring apart to look for a short.

Using the data validation sequence from Chapter 17's data entry field (which must be a three-digit number within a specified range), I start with the test that requires the least amount of work: Is there an entry at all? Once my script is assured an entry of some kind exists, it next checks whether that entry is "all numbers as requested of the user." If so, the script compares the number against the ranges of numbers in the database.

To make this sequence work together efficiently, I created a master validation function consisting of nested if...else statements. Each if condition calls one of the generalized data validation functions. Listing 15-6 shows the master validation function.

```
// Master value validator routine
function isValid(inputStr) {
    if (isEmpty(inputStr)) {
        alert("Please enter a number into the field before
clicking the button.")
        return false
    } else {
        if (!isNumber(inputStr)) {
            alert("Please make sure entries are numbers only.")
            return false
        } else {
            if (!inRange(inputStr)) {
                alert("Sorry, the number you entered is not part of
our database.  Try another three-digit number.")
                return false
            }
        }
    }
    return true
}
```

Listing 15-6: Master validation function that calls a number of specific validation functions.

This function, in turn, is called by the function that controls most of the work in this application. All it wants to know is whether the entered number is valid. The details of validation are handed off to the isValid() function and its special-purpose validation testers.

I constructed the logic in Listing 15-6 so that if the input value fails to be valid, the isValid() function alerts the user of the problem and return false. That means I have to watch my trues and falses very carefully.

In the first validation test, being empty is a bad thing; thus, when the isEmpty() function returns true, the isValid() function returns false because an empty string is not a valid entry. In the second test, being a number is good; so the logic has to flip 180 degrees. The isValid() function returns false only if the isNumber() function returns false. But because isNumber() returns a true when the value is a number, I switch the condition to test for the *opposite* results of the isNumber() function by negating the function name (preceding the function with the Boolean Not operator

(!)). This operator works only with a value that evaluates to a Boolean expression — which the isNumber() function always does. The final test for being within the desired range works on the same basis as isNumber(), using the Boolean Not operator to turn the results of the inRange() function into the method that works best for this sequence.

Finally, if all validation tests fail to find bad or missing data, the entire isValid() function returns true. The statement that called this function can now proceed with processing, assured that the value entered by the user will work.

One additional point worth reinforcing, especially for newcomers, is that although all these functions seem to be passing around the same input string as a parameter, notice that any changes made to the value (such as converting it to a string or number) are kept private to each function. The original value in the calling function is never touched by these subfunctions — only copies of the original value. Therefore, even after the data validation takes place, the original value is in its original form, ready to go.

Date and Time Validation

You can scarcely open a bigger can of cultural worms than you do when you try to program around the various date and time formats in use around the world. If you have ever looked through the possible settings in your computer's operating system, you can begin to understand the difficulty of the issue.

Trying to write JavaScript that accommodates all of the world's date and time formats for validation would be an enormous, if not wasteful, challenge. My suggestion for querying a user for this kind of information is to either divide the components into individually validated fields (separate text objects for hours and minutes) or, for dates, to make entries select objects.

In the long run, I believe the answer will be a future Java applet that our scripts will call. The applet will display a clock and calendar on which the user clicks and drags control-panel-style widgets to select dates and times. The values from those settings will then be passed back to our scripts as a valid date object. In the meantime, divide and conquer.

Plan for Data Validation

I devoted an entire chapter to the subject of data validation because it represents the one area of error checking that JavaScript authors need to worry about. You want to prevent script errors at all cost. When your script will be acting on data entered by the user, you should use some kind of validation as your last line of defense against user-induced errors.

Chapter Sixteen

TABLES, FRAMES, AND

WINDOWS

In this chapter, I explain implementation issues surrounding tables, frames, and secondary windows. To get the most from this chapter — especially from the discussion about frames and windows — you should have a good understanding of the JavaScript object model for these objects as described in Chapter 7. You should also be familiar with the HTML tags for tables and frames. Information about these tags is available from the Netscape on-line library.

Scripting Tables

Working with HTML tables is a lot of fun, especially if, like me, you are not a born graphics designer. By adding a few tags to your page, your data can look more organized, professional, and appealing. Having this power under scripting control is even more exciting, because in response to previous user action or other variable info, such as the current date or time, a script can do things to the table as the table is being built.

You have two options in designing scripted tables for your pages. The design path you choose has a lot to do with whether you need to dynamically update some or all fields of a table (data inside <TD>...</TD> tags). To highlight the differences between the two styles, the following sections trace the implementation of a monthly calendar display in both *static* and *dynamic* forms in a single-frame window.

About the calendars

Because the emphasis here is about the way tables are scripted and displayed, I quickly pass over structural issues of the two calendar versions described in the following sections. They both implement calendar data the same way: as objects.

As you see in the next two listings, the calendars for display require the names of the months in my language (English) somewhere in the script so that they can be plugged into the calendar heading as needed. To make some of the other calendar calculations work (such as figuring out which day of the week is the first day of a given month in a given year), I define a method for my month objects. The method returns the JavaScript date object value for the day of the week of a month's first date. Virtually everything I do to implement the month objects is adapted from the custom objects discussion of Chapter 12.

One other issue important to Macintosh users of Netscape Navigator 2.0 is the JavaScript bug in the browser that causes most Date object methods to increase some values by one day. That is definitely the case here for determining the first day of each month. On the Macintosh version of Navigator 2.0, the calendars are off by one day. To adjust this, I could have implemented a special case that looks for the `navigator.userAgent` property, but it would also have to worry about the version number. A later version will surely fix this bug, so trapping all Mac Navigators isn't the right solution. Because this book listing will survive future versions of Netscape Navigator, I don't make any corrections for browser platforms or versions. The intent here is to display two ways to implement tables in an application whose context everyone should understand. This is not about implementing calendars.

Static tables

The issue of updating the contents of a table's fields is tied to the nature of an HTML document being loaded and fixed in the browser's memory. Recall that precious few properties of a document and its objects can be modified once the document is loaded. That is definitely the case for typical data points inside a table's <TD> tag pair. Once a document loads — even if part of the page has been written by JavaScript — none of its content (except for text and textarea field contents and a few limited form element properties) can be modified without a complete reload.

Listing 16-1 contains the static version of my monthly calendar. Scripted table assembly begins in the Body portion of the document. You can see the results in Figure 16-1.

```
<HTML>
<HEAD>
<TITLE>JavaScripted Static Table</TITLE>
<SCRIPT LANGUAGE="JavaScript">
<!-- start
// generic array constructor
function MakeArray(n){
    this.length = n
    return this
}
// function becomes a method for each month object
function getFirstDay(theYear){
    var firstDate = new Date(theYear,this.offset,1)
    return 1 + firstDate.getDay()
}
// month object constructor
function aMonth(name,length,offset) {
    this.name = name // used in calendar display
    this.length = length // used for knowing how many days to
display
    this.offset = offset // used as an index value
    this.getFirstDay = getFirstDay // method, defined above
}
// update February length when necessary
function getFebLength(theYear) {
    theYear = (theYear < 1900) ? theYear + 1900: theYear
    if ((theYear % 4 == 0 && theYear % 100 != 0) || theYear % 400
```

(continued)

```
== 0) {
      return 29
   }
   return 28
}
// create basic array
theMonths = new MakeArray(12)
// load array with one object for each month
theMonths[1] = new aMonth("January",31,0)
theMonths[2] = new aMonth("February",28,1)
theMonths[3] = new aMonth("March",31,2)
theMonths[4] = new aMonth("April",30,3)
theMonths[5] = new aMonth("May",31,4)
theMonths[6] = new aMonth("June",30,5)
theMonths[7] = new aMonth("July",31,6)
theMonths[8] = new aMonth("August",31,7)
theMonths[9] = new aMonth("September",30,8)
theMonths[10] = new aMonth("October",31,9)
theMonths[11] = new aMonth("November",30,10)
theMonths[12] = new aMonth("December",31,11)

// end -->
</SCRIPT>
</HEAD>

<BODY>
<H1>Month at a Glance (Static)</H1>
<HR>
<SCRIPT LANGUAGE="JavaScript">
<!-- start
// initialize some variables for later
var today = new Date()
var monthOffset = today.getMonth() + 1 // for index into our array
var thisMonth = theMonths[monthOffset].name // month full name
if (monthOffset == 2) {
    theMonths[2].length = getFebLength(today.getYear())
}
// which is the first day of this month?
var firstDay = theMonths[monthOffset].getFirstDay(today.getYear())
// total number of <TD>…</TD> tags needed in for loop below
var howMany = theMonths[monthOffset].length + firstDay
```

```
// start assembling HTML for table
var content = "<CENTER><TABLE BORDER>"
// month and year display at top of calendar
content += "<TR><TH COLSPAN=7>" + thisMonth + " " +
(today.getYear() + 1900) + "</TH></TR>"
// days of the week at head of each column
content += "<TR><TH>Sun</TH><TH>Mon</TH><TH>Tue</TH><TH>Wed</TH>"
content += "<TH>Thu</TH><TH>Fri</TH><TH>Sat</TH></TR>"
content += "<TR>"

// populate calendar
for (var i = 1; i < howMany; i++) {
    if (i < firstDay) {
        // 'empty' boxes prior to first day
        content += "<TD></TD>"
    } else {
        // enter date number
        content += "<TD>" + (i - firstDay + 1) + "</TD>"
    }
    // must start new row after each week
    if (i % 7 == 0 &&  i != howMany) {
        content += "</TR><TR>"
    }
}
content += "</TABLE></CENTER>"

// blast entire table's HTML to the document
document.write(content)
// end -->
</SCRIPT>
</BODY>
</HTML>
```

Listing 16-1: A static table generated by JavaScript.

In this page, a little bit of the HTML — the <H1> heading and <HR> divider —
is unscripted. The rest of the page consists entirely of the table definition, all of which
is constructed in JavaScript. Though you may want to interlace straight HTML and
scripted HTML within the table definition, a bug exists in Navigator 2.0 that makes
this hazardous. It's safest to define the entire table from the <TABLE> to </TABLE>
tags in JavaScript and post it to the page in one or more `document.write()` methods.

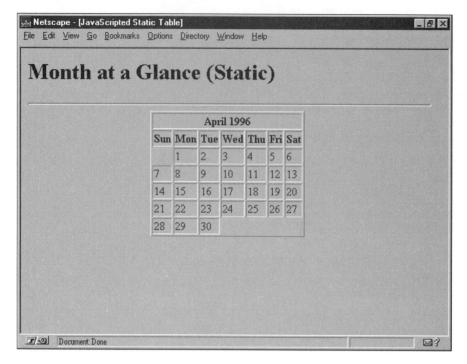

Figure 16-1: The static table calendar generated by Listing 16-1.

Most of the work for assembling the data points for the calendar occurs inside the for loop. Because not every month starts on a Sunday, the script determines the day of the week on which the current month starts. For all fields prior to that day, the for loop writes empty <TD></TD> tags as placeholders. Once the days of the month begin, the for loop writes the date number inside the <TD>...</TD> tags. The "boxes" in the calendar are not really objects — at least not objects that JavaScript can access. Therefore, whatever the script puts inside the tag pair is written to the page as flat HTML. Under script control like ours, however, the script can designate what goes into each data point — rather than writing fixed HTML for each month's calendar.

The important point to note in this example is that although the content of the page may change over time automatically (without having to redo any HTML for the next month), once the page is written, its contents cannot be changed. To bring a calendar like this even more to life, you can implement it as a dynamic table.

Dynamic tables

The only way to make data points of a table updatable is to turn those data points into text (or textarea) objects. The approach to this implementation is different because a combination of immediate and deferred scripting is going on here. Immediate scripting facilitates the building of the table framework, complete with fields for every modifiable location in the table. Deferred scripting allows users to make choices from other interface elements, causing a new set of variable data to appear in the table's fields.

Listing 16-2 turns the previous static calendar into a dynamic one by including controls that allow the user to select a month and year to display in the table. Compare the appearance of the dynamic version shown in Figure 16-2 against the static version in Figure 16-1.

```
<HTML>
<HEAD>
<TITLE>JavaScripted Dynamic Table</TITLE>
<SCRIPT LANGUAGE="JavaScript">
<!-- start
// generic array constructor
function MakeArray(n){
    this.length = n
    return this
}
// function becomes a method for each month object
function getFirstDay(theYear){
    var firstDate = new Date(theYear,this.offset,1)
    return firstDate.getDay()
}
// month object constructor
function aMonth(name,length,offset) {
    this.name = name // used in calendar display
    this.length = length // used for knowing how many days to
display
    this.offset = offset // used as an index value
    this.getFirstDay = getFirstDay // method, defined above
}
// update February length when necessary
function getFebLength(theYear) {
    theYear = (theYear < 1900) ? theYear + 1900: theYear
    if ((theYear % 4 == 0 && theYear % 100 != 0) || theYear % 400
```

(continued)

385

```
    == 0) {
         return 29
       }
     return 28
}
// create basic array
theMonths = new MakeArray(12)
// load array with one object for each month
theMonths[1] = new aMonth("January",31,0)
theMonths[2] = new aMonth("February",28,1)
theMonths[3] = new aMonth("March",31,2)
theMonths[4] = new aMonth("April",30,3)
theMonths[5] = new aMonth("May",31,4)
theMonths[6] = new aMonth("June",30,5)
theMonths[7] = new aMonth("July",31,6)
theMonths[8] = new aMonth("August",31,7)
theMonths[9] = new aMonth("September",30,8)
theMonths[10] = new aMonth("October",31,9)
theMonths[11] = new aMonth("November",30,10)
theMonths[12] = new aMonth("December",31,11)
// end -->
</SCRIPT>
</HEAD>

<BODY>
<H1>Month at a Glance (Dynamic)</H1>
<HR>
<SCRIPT LANGUAGE="JavaScript">
<!-- start
// initialize variable with HTML for each day's field
// all will have same name, so we can access via index value
// empty event handler prevents
// reverse-loading bug in some platforms
var oneField = "<INPUT TYPE='text' NAME='oneDay' SIZE=2
onFocus=''>"
// start assembling HTML for raw table
var content = "<FORM><CENTER><TABLE BORDER>"
// field for month and year display at top of calendar
content += "<TR><TH COLSPAN=7><INPUT TYPE='text'
NAME='oneMonth'></TH></TR>"
// days of the week at head of each column
```

```
content += "<TR><TH>Sun</TH><TH>Mon</TH><TH>Tue</TH><TH>Wed</TH>"
content += "<TH>Thu</TH><TH>Fri</TH><TH>Sat</TH></TR>"
content += "<TR>"

// layout 6 rows of fields for worst-case month
for (var i = 1; i < 43; i++) {
    content += "<TD>" + oneField + "</TD>"
    if (i % 7 == 0) {
        content += "</TR><TR>"
    }
}

content += "</TABLE>"
// blast empty table to the document
document.write(content)

// deferred function to fill fields of table
function populateFields(form) {
    // initialize variables for later from user selections
    var theMonth =
form.chooseMonth.options[form.chooseMonth.selectedIndex].text
    var theYear =
form.chooseYear.options[form.chooseYear.selectedIndex].text
    // initialize date-dependent variables
    var anchorDay = new Date(theYear-
1900,form.chooseMonth.selectedIndex,1)
    var monthOffset = anchorDay.getMonth() + 1
    var thisMonth = theMonths[monthOffset].name
    if (monthOffset == 2) {
        theMonths[2].length = getFebLength(anchorDay.getYear())
    }
    var firstDay =
theMonths[monthOffset].getFirstDay(anchorDay.getYear())
    var howMany = theMonths[monthOffset].length
    // set month and year in top field
    form.oneMonth.value = theMonth + " " + theYear
    // fill fields of table
    for (var i = 0; i < 42; i++) {
        if (i < firstDay || i >= (howMany + firstDay)) {
            // before and after actual dates, empty fields
```

(continued)

```
            // address fields by name and [index] number
            form.oneDay[i].value = ""
        } else {
            // enter date values
            form.oneDay[i].value = i - firstDay + 1
        }
    }
}
// end -->
</SCRIPT>
<SELECT NAME="chooseMonth">
<OPTION SELECTED>January<OPTION>February
<OPTION>March<OPTION>April<OPTION>May
<OPTION>June<OPTION>July<OPTION>August
<OPTION>September<OPTION>October<OPTION>November<OPTION>December
</SELECT>
<SELECT NAME="chooseYear">
<OPTION SELECTED>1995<OPTION>1996<OPTION>1997<OPTION>1998
</SELECT><P>
<INPUT TYPE="button" NAME="updater" VALUE="Update Calendar"
onClick="populateFields(this.form)">
</FORM>
</BODY>
</HTML>
```

Listing 16-2: A dynamic calendar table.

When you first load Listing 16-2, it creates an empty table. Even so, it may take a while to load, depending on the platform of your browser and speed of your computer's processor. This page creates a ton of text objects. An onLoad= event handler in the Body definition also could easily set the necessary items to load the current month.

From a cosmetic point of view, the dynamic calendar may not be as pleasing as the static one in Figure 16-1. Several factors contribute to this appearance.

From a structural point of view, it is essential to create a table that can accommodate any possible layout of days and dates that a calendar may require. That means a basic calendar consisting of six rows of fields. For many months, the last row will be completely empty. But because the table definition must be fixed when the page loads, this layout cannot change on the fly.

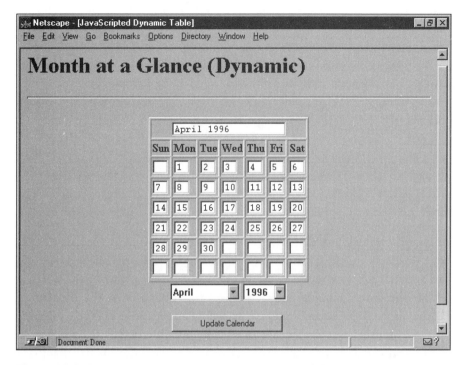

Figure 16-2: Dynamic calendar generated by Listing 16-2.

The more obvious cosmetic comparison comes from the font and alignment of data in text objects. You're stuck with what the browser presents in both categories. In the static version, you can define different font sizes and colors for various fields, if you want (such as coloring the entry for today's date). Not so in text objects.

What is a cosmetic disadvantage, however, is a boon to functionality and interactivity on this page. Instead of the user being stuck with an unchanging calendar month, this version includes pop-up menus from which the user can select a month and/or year of choice. Clicking the Update Calendar button refills the calendar fields with data from the selected month.

One more disadvantage to this dynamic table surfaces, however: All text objects are editable by the user. For many applications, this may not be a big deal. But if you are creating a table-based application that encourages users to enter values in some fields, be prepared (in other words, have event handlers in place) to either handle calculations based on changes to any field or alert users that the fields cannot be changed (and restore the correct value).

Hybrids

It will probably be the rare scripted table that is entirely dynamic. In fact, the one in Figure 16-2 is a hybrid of static and dynamic table definitions. The days of the week at the top of each column are hard-wired into the table as static elements. If your table design can accommodate both styles, implement your tables that way. The fewer the number of text objects defined for a page, the better the performance for rendering the page and the less confusion for the page's users. The application in Chapter 20 features several scripted hybrid tables.

Frames

Perhaps it is the new flexibility that frames offer to otherwise dull HTML pages that entices page designers to add frames to their sites. Frames certainly make sense in a number of applications, as you see in many examples earlier in this book. When a document in one frame contains interactive controls that modify the content of another frame on the fly, it makes a pretty compelling application. But working with frames in JavaScript trips up a lot of scripters. Although I addressed a number of these issues during the discussion of the frame object and elsewhere, it's time to bring these discussions together.

Creating frames

The task of defining frames in a document is the same whether you are using JavaScript or not. One HTML document, which the user never sees, defines the frameset for the entire browser window. Each frame must have a URL reference for a document to load into. For scripting purposes, it also is a good idea to assign a name to each frame with the NAME= attribute.

Referencing frames

How you employ a reference to a frame's document depends on where that frame is in relation to the frame that contains the document with the script. When a script refers to its own document's objects, the reference does not need to include a window object — although prepending the reference with self. is helpful for reading the script.

To get to another visible frame's object requires a complete reference that steps back out to the parent window — the framesetting window. Therefore, a script in a document located in FrameA refers to the title of the document in FrameB with the following reference:

```
parent.FrameB.document.title
```

If you omit the parent from the reference, JavaScript has no idea what you mean by FrameB. In other words, rather than making a lateral move across frames in the reference, you must help JavaScript back out to the parent and start its pathway to the desired frame object.

Top vs. parent

The window whose reference is synonymous with the top window is the window whose URL you see in the Location field of the browser. For a single-frame environment, the top window is the window you see; for a multiple-frame environment, the top window is the unseen window that contains the framesetting document governing the current display.

In a frameset relationship, the window containing the frameset definition is the parent of whatever frames are defined in that frameset. For this scenario — one parent and its direct descendants — the top and parent window are the same. You can use the references interchangeably. But if one of the descendant frames should, itself, be a framesetting document, a third generation is born. To frames of that third generation, the parent is the framesetting document in the second generation; the top window, however, is still the topmost, first-ever framesetting document of this family tree. The case of three or more generations of frames is pretty rare, but it may help you establish a convention for using parent and top in your object references. For example, if one frame wants to talk to another frame of the same parent, it is the "parentness" of the relationship that is important. There may be cases in which a completely different Web site loads your frameset into one of its frames, causing the top reference to fail miserably. Thus, using the parent reference is more appropriate than the top reference.

Inheritance vs. containment

Scripters who have experience in object-oriented programming environments probably expect frames to inherit properties, methods, functions, and variables defined in a parent object. That's *not* the case in JavaScript. You can, however, still access those parent items when you make a call to the item with a complete reference to the parent. For example, if you want to define a deferred function in the framesetting parent document that all frames can share, the scripts in the frames would refer to that function with this reference:

```
parent.myFunc()
```

You can pass arguments to such functions and expect returned values.

Some bugs linger in Navigator 2.0 that cause problems when accessing variables in a parent window from one of its children. If a document in one of the child frames unloads, a parent variable value dependent upon that frame may get scrambled or disappear. Using a temporary `document.cookie` for global variable values (such as in Chapter 20's application) may be a better solution.

Frame synchronization

A pesky problem for some scripters' plans is that it is dangerous — if not crash-prone in Navigator 2.0 — to include any immediate scripts in the framesetting document. Such scripts tend to rely on the presence of documents in the frames being created by this framesetting document. But if the frames have not yet been created and the documents loaded, the immediate scripts will likely crash and burn.

One way to guard against this is to trigger all such scripts from the frameset's `onLoad=` event handler. This handler won't trigger until all documents have successfully loaded into the child frames defined by the frameset. At the same time, be careful with `onLoad=` event handlers in the documents going into a frameset's frames. If one of those scripts relies on the presence of a document in another frame (one of its brothers or sisters), you are also doomed to eventual failure. Anything from a slow network or server to a slow modem can get in the way of other documents loading into frames in the ideal order.

One way to work around this is to create a string variable in the parent document that will act as a flag for successful loading of subsidiary frames (a Navigator 2.0 bug makes using a Boolean value risky). When a document loads into a frame, its `onLoad=` event handler can set that flag to a word of your choice indicating that it has loaded. The other frame's `onLoad=` event handler can wait (in a `while` loop) for the parent variable to turn to the successful loading value before proceeding with its processing.

Depending on other frames is a tricky business. Be sure to test your code thoroughly and handle issues such as a user's resizing the window in the middle of a multi-frame loading process. Resizing triggers a reload of the top window's document. This can have good or bad side effects on your code, depending on what your code is doing.

URLs for frames

Experienced scripters may be tempted to play around with some of the Navigator-specific internal URLs to fill the `SRC=` attribute of a `<FRAME>` definition. This is extremely hazardous unless you know precisely what you're doing. For instance, calling a JavaScript script defined elsewhere in the parent document (via a

SRC="javascript:myFunc()" attribute) does you no good if that function relies on objects of the frame you're defining: The function will try to run on a document that doesn't yet exist because it has not yet loaded. My advice: Load a real HTML document (even if it is a blank one) and then do your magic with an onLoad= event handler in the parent window's document.

Blank frames

It is often desirable to create a frame in a frameset but not put any document in there until the user has interacted with various controls or other user interface elements in other frames. Navigator has a somewhat empty document in one of its internal URLs (about:blank). But with Navigator 2.0 on the Macintosh, an Easter egg-style message appears in that window when it displays. This URL is also not guaranteed to be available on non-Netscape browsers. If you need a blank frame, create a blank HTML document for your server (Listing 16-3) and summon that document's URL in any SRC= or HREF= attribute for which you want a blank frame.

```
<HTML>
<HEAD><TITLE>Blank</TITLE></HEAD>
<BODY></BODY>
</HTML>
```

Listing 16-3: A blank document for blank frames.

Viewing frame source code

Studying other scripters' work is a major learning tool for JavaScript (or any programming language). You may have been frustrated, however, by the View Source menu option in the browser because it only shows source code for the framesetting document and not the code in the cool frames. But you can capture the frame code, provided it exists as an HTML document (or it was not generated entirely by JavaScript or a server CGI). Activate a frame by clicking anywhere on its background. Then choose Save Frame As from the File menu. Select the Source option in the Save dialog. Now you can look at the code in a text editor.

New Windows

Most of the intricacies about creating and defining new sub-windows via JavaScript are covered in the discussion about the window.open() method in Chapter 7. By now you should know that with Navigator 2.0, you cannot modify the window options of a window once it appears (including the primary browser window for your documents). At best, you can specify what options should appear in a new window and how big that window should be. But as to the location or layering of any window — that's out of the question for now.

What I'd like to elaborate on here is how to do further scripting from that sub-window. A valid question asked by more adventurous scripters is how to get a script in a sub-window to refer back to the window that created it.

By way of background, recall that when a script creates a new window with the window.open() method, there is no parent-child relationship established between the original and new window. The new window becomes is its own top and parent window. What you can do, however, is attach a reference to the original window as a new property of the new window's object. Listings 16-4 and 16-5 demonstrate how to accomplish this with a script in the main window and a separate document in the new window.

```
<HTML>
<HEAD>
<TITLE>Master of all Windows</TITLE>
<SCRIPT LANGUAGE="JavaScript">
function doNew() {
    myWind = window.open("1st16-
04.htm","","HEIGHT=200,WIDTH=400")
    // extra window.open() for Navigator 2.0 browsers with the bug
    myWind = window.open("1st16-
04.htm","","HEIGHT=200,WIDTH=400")
    myWind.creator = window
}
</SCRIPT>
</HEAD>
<BODY>
<FORM>
<INPUT TYPE="button" NAME="storage" VALUE="Make a Window"
onClick="doNew()">
</FORM>
</BODY>
</HTML>
```

Listing 16-4: Main window document that creates the new window and assigns it a new property.

```
<HTML>
<HEAD>
<TITLE>New Window on the Block</TITLE>
<BODY>
<FORM >
     <input type="button" value="Who's in the Main window?"
onClick="alert(self.creator.document.title)">
</FORM>
</BODY>
</HTML>
```

Listing 16-5: Document loaded from main window. Its button script summons the new property.

The document in Listing 16-4 has just one button: That button's sole task is to generate a new window of a specific size. Notice that after the window is generated, the doNew() function assigns a new property to the new window object (I use the property name creator, but you can use anything you like). Even though this script is in the main window's document, the object for the new window (represented by the myWind variable) is in the browser's memory for all objects currently open in the browser. By assigning the main window object to the creator property of the new window, that new window object now contains a complete reference to the main window.

In the new window, Listing 16-5 merely has one button and an event handler whose job is to display in an alert the title of the document in the main window. The reference to that information starts from within the new window (self) and its ad-hoc property (creator). This tells JavaScript to look at whatever window object that is (it happens to be the main window) and fetch the current document's title. Because the reference held by the creator property is to the main window (not the document that spawned the new window), you can change documents in the main window and (as long as the smaller window is still showing) use the button to fetch any valid property of current document in the main window.

You want to define this extra property only for HTML you create on the fly for a secondary window, or for documents that will only be opened by way of the main window and its property-setting statement. Fortunately, even if a window does not have a creator property, your script can still check to see if the property is null; if it is, then no link exists to another window, and your script should bypass any references to items in the creator's window.

Coming Up Next

In the remaining chapters, I practice what I've been preaching. Each chapter is devoted to a JavaScript-enhanced application aimed at demonstrating many of the techniques that you will probably want to include in your pages. The demonstration subject matter of these applications is inconsequential. The scripting techniques are what count. Descriptions within the chapters reveal some of the decision processes I went through in creating these pages, all of which can be seen on-line at my Web site (<http://www.dannyg.com/javascript/>). They are also on the CD-ROM accompanying this book. But sometimes it's a valuable exercise to see the performance of a site from a real on-line server rather than from a speedy hard disk.

$\mathcal{C}$hapter Seventeen

KEY CONCEPTS:

- Serverless database lookup

- Data entry validation

One of the first ideas that intrigued me about JavaScript was the notion

of delivering CGI-like functionality along with an HTML document. On

the Net, numerous small databases that currently require CGI scripting

and a back-end database engine to drive them. Of course, not everyone who has information to share has access to the server environment (or the expertise) to implement such a solution. JavaScript provides that power.

A Serverless Database

Before you get too carried away with the idea of letting JavaScript take the place of your SQL database, you need to recognize several limitations that prevent JavaScript from being a universal solution. First, any database you embed into an HTML document is read-only. Although you can script an interface and lookup routines for the user, there are no provisions for writing revised information back to the server, if that is your intention.

A second consideration is the size of the database. Unlike databases residing on servers, the entire database (or subset you define for inclusion into a single HTML document) must be downloaded to the user's browser before the user can work with the data. As a point of reference, think about image files. At 14.4 or 28.8 Kbps, how large an image file would you tolerate downloading? Whatever that limit may be (anywhere from 10 to 35K, depending on your patience) is what your database size limit should be. For many special-purpose collections, this is plenty of space, assuming one byte per character. Unlike what happens when he or she downloads an embedded image file, the user doesn't see special status bar messages about your database: To the browser, it's all part of the HTML coming in with the document.

The kind of data I'm talking about here is obviously text data. That's not to say you can't let your JavaScript-enhanced document act as a front end to data files of other types on your server. In fact, in Chapter 19, you can find an application that uses JavaScript tables in one document to assist locating and loading image files from the server on the fly.

The Database

As I was thinking about writing a demonstration of a serverless database, I encountered a small article in the *Wall Street Journal* that related information I had always suspected. The Social Security numbers assigned to virtually every U.S. citizen are partially coded to indicate the state in which you registered for your Social Security number. This information often reveals the state in which you were born. The first three digits of the nine-digit number comprise the code.

When the numbering system was first established, each state was assigned a block of three-digit numbers. Therefore, if the first three digits fall within a certain range, the Social Security Administration has you listed as being registered in the corresponding state or territory. I thought this would be an interesting demonstration for a couple of reasons.

First, the database is not that large, so it can be easily embedded into an HTML document without making the document too big to download even on slow Internet connections. Second, it offers some challenges to data entry validation, as you see in a moment.

Before young people from populous states write me that their numbers are not part of the database, let me emphasize that I am well aware that several states have been assigned number blocks not reflected in the database. This is only a demonstration of scripting techniques, not an official Social Security Administration page.

The Implementation Plan

All I started with was a printed table of data. I figured that the user interface for this application would probably be very plain: a text field in which the user could enter a three-digit number, a clickable button to initiate the search, and a text field to show the results of the lookup. Figure 17-1 shows the page. Pretty simple by any standards.

Given that user interface (I almost always start a design from the *interface* — how my page's users will experience the information presented on the page), I next had to plan the internals. I needed the equivalent of two tables: one for the numeric ranges, one for the state names. Because most of the numeric ranges are contiguous, I could get by with a table of the high number of each range. This meant that the script would have to trap elsewhere for the occasional numbers that fall outside of the table's ranges — the job of data validation.

Because the tables were so highly related to each other, I had the option of creating two separate arrays so that any given index value would correspond to both the numeric and state name entries in both tables. The other option was to create a two-dimensional array (Chapter 9) in which each array entry had data points for both the number and state name. For purposes of demonstration to first-time database builders, I decided to stay with two separate arrays. It is a little easier to visualize how the lookup process works with two separate arrays.

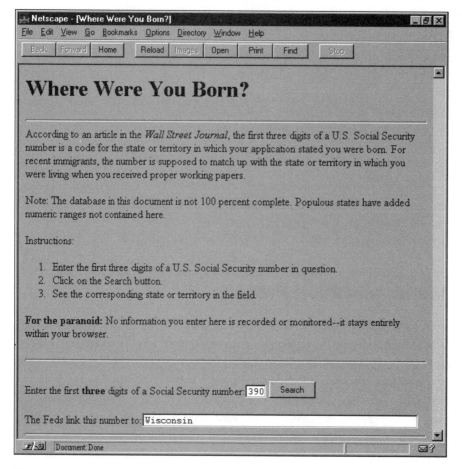

Figure 17-1: The Social Security number lookup page.

The Code

The HTML document starts normally through the definition of the document title.

```
<HTML>
<HEAD>
<TITLE>Where Were You Born?</TITLE>
```

Next comes a fairly large section of deferred function definitions within the Head. With all action taking place in response to a user's click of a button, all coding for creation of the arrays and lookup is located in the Head section.

```
<SCRIPT LANGUAGE="JavaScript">
<!-- hide this code from non-scriptable browsers
// generic object maker prepares an empty array of n items
function makeArray(n) {
    this.length = n
    for (var i=1; i <= n; i++)
        this[i] = null
        return this
}
```

Immediately after the starting `<SCRIPT>` tag comes the HTML comment beginning, so that most non-JavaScript-enabled browsers ignore all statements between the start and end comments (just before the `</SCRIPT>` tag). Failure to do this results in all code lines appearing in non-JavaScript browsers as regular HTML text.

Next comes the first function definition: the one that creates array objects. You will see in this application that I place utility function definitions close to the top of the script sections and put any action-oriented scripts (functions acting in response to event handlers) closer to the bottom of the script sections. My preference is to have all dependencies resolved before they are needed in a script. This carries over from the logic that dictates putting as many scripts in the Head as possible, so that even if the user (or network) should interrupt downloading of a page before every line of HTML reaches the browser, any user interface element relying on scripts will have those scripts loaded and ready to go. The order of functions in this example is not critical, because as long as they're all in the Head section, they are defined and loaded by the time the field and button appear at the bottom of the page. But once I develop a style, it's easier to stick with it — one less matter to worry about while scripting a complex application.

```
// create object listing all the top end of each numeric range
var ssn = new makeArray(57)
ssn[1] = 3
ssn[2] = 7
ssn[3] = 9
ssn[4] = 34
ssn[5] = 39
ssn[6] = 49
ssn[7] = 134
ssn[8] = 158
ssn[9] = 211
ssn[10] = 220
```

(continued)

```
ssn[11] = 222
ssn[12] = 231
ssn[13] = 236
ssn[14] = 246
ssn[15] = 251
ssn[16] = 260
ssn[17] = 267
ssn[18] = 302
ssn[19] = 317
ssn[20] = 361
ssn[21] = 386
ssn[22] = 399
ssn[23] = 407
ssn[24] = 415
ssn[25] = 424
ssn[26] = 428
ssn[27] = 432
ssn[28] = 439
ssn[29] = 448
ssn[30] = 467
ssn[31] = 477
ssn[32] = 485
ssn[33] = 500
ssn[34] = 502
ssn[35] = 504
ssn[36] = 508
ssn[37] = 515
ssn[38] = 517
ssn[39] = 519
ssn[40] = 520
ssn[41] = 524
ssn[42] = 525
ssn[43] = 527
ssn[44] = 529
ssn[45] = 530
ssn[46] = 539
ssn[47] = 544
ssn[48] = 573
ssn[49] = 574
ssn[50] = 576
ssn[51] = 579
```

```
ssn[52] = 580
ssn[53] = 584
ssn[54] = 585
ssn[55] = 586
ssn[56] = 599
ssn[57] = 728
```

After creating a blank array (named ssn) via the MakeArray() function, the script populates all 57 data points of the array. Because the MakeArray() function automatically assigns the zero entry of the array to a length property, we start loading data into entry number one. These data numbers correspond to the top end of each range in the 57-entry table. For example, any number greater than three but less than or equal to seven falls into the range of the second data entry of the array (ssn[2]).

```
// create object listing all the states/territories
var geo = new makeArray(57)
geo[1] = "New Hampshire"
geo[2] = "Maine"
geo[3] = "Vermont"
geo[4] = "Massachusetts"
geo[5] = "Rhode Island"
geo[6] = "Connecticut"
geo[7] = "New York"
geo[8] = "New Jersey"
geo[9] = "Pennsylvania"
geo[10] = "Maryland"
geo[11] = "Delaware"
geo[12] = "Virginia"
geo[13] = "West Virginia"
geo[14] = "North Carolina"
geo[15] = "South Carolina"
geo[16] = "Georgia"
geo[17] = "Florida"
geo[18] = "Ohio"
geo[19] = "Indiana"
geo[20] = "Illinois"
geo[21] = "Michigan"
geo[22] = "Wisconsin"
geo[23] = "Kentucky"
geo[24] = "Tennessee"
```

(continued)

```
geo[25] = "Alabama"
geo[26] = "Mississippi"
geo[27] = "Arkansas"
geo[28] = "Louisiana"
geo[29] = "Oklahoma"
geo[30] = "Texas"
geo[31] = "Minnesota"
geo[32] = "Iowa"
geo[33] = "Missouri"
geo[34] = "North Dakota"
geo[35] = "South Dakota"
geo[36] = "Nebraska"
geo[37] = "Kansas"
geo[38] = "Montana"
geo[39] = "Idaho"
geo[40] = "Wyoming"
geo[41] = "Colorado"
geo[42] = "New Mexico"
geo[43] = "Arizona"
geo[44] = "Utah"
geo[45] = "Nevada"
geo[46] = "Washington"
geo[47] = "Oregon"
geo[48] = "California"
geo[49] = "Alaska"
geo[50] = "Hawaii"
geo[51] = "District of Columbia"
geo[52] = "Virgin Islands"
geo[53] = "Puerto Rico"
geo[54] = "New Mexico"
geo[55] = "Guam, American Samoa, N. Mariana Isl., Philippines"
geo[56] = "Puerto Rico"
geo[57] = "Long-time or retired railroad workers"
```

We do the same for the array containing the states and territory names. Both of these array populators seem long but pale in comparison to what you would have to do with a database of many kilobytes. Unfortunately, JavaScript in Navigator 2.0 doesn't give you the power to load existing data files into arrays (that would be a cool feature); so any time you want to embed a database into an HTML document, you must go through this array-style assignment frenzy. If you at least can open a file containing the data in another window of your editor, you may be able to drag and drop the data between windows to avoid retyping all the data points.

```javascript
// JavaScript sees numbers with leading zeros as octal values, so
strip zeros
function stripZeros(inputStr) {
    var result = inputStr
    while (result.charAt(0) == "0") {
        result = result.substring(1,result.length)
    }
    return result
}
```

Now comes the beginning of the data validation functions. Under control of a master validation function, the stripZeros() function removes any leading zeros that the user may have entered. Notice that the instructions tell the user to enter the first three digits of a Social Security number. For 001 through 099, that means the numbers begin with one or two zeros. JavaScript, however, treats any numeric value starting with a zero as an octal value. Because we have to do some numeric comparisons for the search through the ssn[] array, the script must make sure that the entries (which are strings to begin with, coming as they do from text objects) can be converted to decimal numbers.

To strip any leading zeros, I use a while repeat loop. Here is a case in which a condition may exist prior to the loop — the value could lead with a zero — and I want the loop to deal with the data while that condition is true. Recall the discussion about how to decide between using a for or a while loop in Chapter 10. To me, this situation screams out for a while loop rather than a for loop. Within the loop, the value is treated as a string, using the charAt() method to test for the existence of a leading zero (at character index zero) and the substring() method to remove it from the result value (setting the result string to everything from character one to the end).

```javascript
// general purpose function to see if an input value has been
entered at all
function isEmpty(inputStr) {
    if (inputStr == null || inputStr == "") {
        return true
    }
    return false
}
```

(continued)

```
// general purpose function to see if a suspected numeric input
// is a positive integer
function isNumber(inputStr) {
    for (var i = 0; i < inputStr.length; i++) {
        var oneChar = inputStr.charAt(i)
        if (oneChar < "0" || oneChar > "9") {
            return false
        }
    }
    return true
}


// function to determine if value is in acceptable range for this
application
function inRange(inputStr) {
    num = parseInt(inputStr)
    if (num < 1 || (num > 586 && num < 596) || (num > 599 && num
< 700) || num > 728) {
        return false
    }
    return true
}
```

The next three functions are described in full in Chapter 15, which discusses data validation. In the last function, a copy of the input value is converted to an integer to allow the function to make necessary comparisons against the boundaries of acceptable ranges.

```
// Master value validator routine
function isValid(inputStr) {
    if (isEmpty(inputStr)) {
        alert("Please enter a number into the field before
clicking the button.")
        return false
    } else {
        if (!isNumber(inputStr)) {
            alert("Please make sure entries are numbers only.")
            return false
        } else {
            if (!inRange(inputStr)) {
                alert("Sorry, the number you entered is not part of
our database.  Try another three-digit number.")
```

```
                    return false
            }
        }
    }
    return true
}
```

The master validation controller function is also covered in depth in Chapter 15. This function is called by a statement that wants to know if it should proceed with the lookup process.

```
// Roll through ssn database to find index;
// apply index to geography database
function search(form) {
    var foundMatch = false
    var inputStr = stripZeros(form.entry.value)
    if (isValid(inputStr)) {
        inputValue = inputStr
        for (var i = 1; i <= ssn.length; i++) {
            if (inputValue <= ssn[i]) {
                foundMatch = true
                break
            }
        }
    }
    form.result.value = (foundMatch) ? geo[i] : ""
    form.entry.focus()
    form.entry.select()
}
// end code hiding -->
</SCRIPT>
</HEAD>
```

The search() function is the one called by the Search button's event handler. The handler passes along the entire form, which includes the button and both text objects.

To search the database, the script repetitively compares each succeeding entry of the ssn[] array against the value entered by the user. For this process to work, a little bit of preliminary work is needed. First comes an initialization of a variable, foundMatch, which comes into play later. Initially set to false, it will be set to true only if there is a successful match — information you need later to set the value of the result text object correctly for all possible conditions.

407

Next comes all the data preparation. After the entry is passed through the zero stripper, a copy is dispatched to the master validation controller, which, in turn, sends copies to each of its special-purpose minions. If the master validator detects a problem from the results of any of those minions, it returns false to the condition that wants to know if the input value is valid. Should the value not be valid, processing skips past the `for` loop and proceeds immediately to an important sequence of three statements.

The first is a conditional statement that relies on the value of the `foundMatch` variable that was initialized at the start of this function. If `foundMatch` is still false, that means that something was wrong with the entry and it could not be processed. To prevent any incorrect information from appearing in the result field, that field is set to an empty string if `foundMatch` is false. The next two statements set the focus and selection to the entry field.

On the other hand, if the entry is a valid number, the script finally gets to perform its lookup task. Looping through every entry of the `ssn[]` array starting with entry one and extending until the loop counter reaches the last item (based on the array's length property), the script compares the input value against each entry's value. If the number is less than or equal to a particular entry, the value of the loop counter (`i`) is frozen, the `foundMatch` variable is set to true, and execution breaks out of the `for` loop.

This time through the conditional expression, with `foundMatch` being true, the statement plugs the corresponding value of the `geo[]` array (using the frozen value of `i`) into the result field. Focus and selection are set to the entry field to make it easy to enter another value.

```
<BODY>
<H1>Where Were You Born?</H1>
<HR>

According to an article in the <CITE>Wall Street Journal</CITE>,
the first three digits of a U.S. Social Security number is a code
for the state or territory in which your application stated you
were born.  For recent immigrants, the number is supposed to match
up with the state or territory in which you were living when you
received proper working papers.<P>
Note: The database in this document is not 100 percent complete.
Populous states have added numeric ranges not contained here.<P>
Instructions:
<OL><LI>Enter the first three digits of a U.S. Social Security
number in question.</LI>
<LI>Click on the Search button.</LI>
<LI>See the corresponding state or territory in the field.</L1>
```

```
</OL>

<P><B>For the paranoid:</B> No information you enter here is
recorded or monitored—it stays entirely within your browser.<P>
<HR>
<FORM>
Enter the first <B>three</B> digits of a Social Security
number:<INPUT TYPE="text" NAME="entry" SIZE=3>
<INPUT TYPE="button" VALUE="Search" onClick="search(this.form)">
<P>
The Feds link this number to:<INPUT TYPE="text" NAME="result"
SIZE=50>
</BODY>
</HTML>
```

The balance of the code is the Body part of the document. The real action takes place within the Form definition. Each of the text objects is sized to fit the expected data. The button calls the search() function, passing its own form as a parameter.

Further Thoughts

If I were doing this type of application for production purposes, I would place the data in a two-dimensional array rather than in two separate arrays. To make that work requires one extra function and a different way of populating the data. Here is an example using the same variable names as the preceding listing:

```
// specify an array entry with two items
function dataRecord(ssn, geo) {
    this.ssn = ssn
    this.geo = geo
    return this
}

// initialize basic array
var numberState = new makeArray(57)

// populate main array with smaller arrays
numberState[0] = new dataRecord(3,"New Hampshire")
numberState[1] = new dataRecord(7,"Maine")
numberState[2] = new dataRecord(9,"Vermont")
```

The other changes (marked in boldface) occur in the search() function, which must address this data in a slightly different way than it did before:

```
function search(form) {
    var foundMatch = false
    var inputStr = stripZeros(form.entry.value)
    if (isValid(inputStr)) {
        inputValue = inputStr
        for (var i = 1; i <= numberState.length; i++) {
            if (inputValue <= numberState[i]).ssn {
                foundMatch = true
                break
            }
        }
    }
    form.result.value = (foundMatch) ? numberState[i].geo : ""
    form.entry.focus()
    form.entry.select()
}
```

All references to data are to the numberState[] array and its properties (either ssn or geo). With the data for each record arranged in a comma-delimited fashion, it may be easier to transfer data exported from an existing database to your script with less copying and pasting or dragging and dropping.

I truly believe that serverless databases offer a great opportunity to many creative JavaScripters.

Chapter _Eighteen_

APPLICATION: OUTLINE-STYLE

TABLE OF CONTENTS

KEY CONCEPTS:

- Multiple frames

- Clickable images

- Persistent data (cookie)

In your Web surfings, you may have encountered sites that implement

an expandable outline type of table of contents. I've long thought these

were great ideas, especially for sites with lots of information. An outline,

like the Windows Explorer or text-style Macintosh Finder windows, lets

411

the author present a large table of contents in a way that doesn't necessarily take up a ton of page space or bandwidth. From listings of top-level entries, a user can drill down to reveal only those items of interest.

No matter how much I like the idea, however, I dislike visiting these sites. A CGI program on the server responds to each click, chews on my selection, and then sends back a completely new screen, showing my choice expanded or collapsed. After working with outlines in the operating system and outliner programs on personal computers, the delays in this processing seem interminable. It occurred to me that implementing the outline interface as a client-side JavaScript would solve the delay problem and make outlines a more viable interface to a site's table of contents.

Design Challenges

The more I looked into implementing an outline, the more challenges I found ahead of me.

The first problem was that if I wanted users to click on little icons (widgets) representing the expanded and collapsed branches of the outline, JavaScript is not obvious about setting up an image for anything other than a link to another document. In other words, JavaScript in Navigator 2.0 does not turn an image into a clickable object with an event handler I could script. Surrounding an image with a link tag required the HREF= attribute, which would navigate away from the outline. The solution turns out to be a not-obvious URL you can use for the HREF= attribute: a call to a JavaScript function (described in Chapter 8). This also helped solve the next problem.

When a user clicks on an outline widget, the script must update the window or frame containing the outline to expand or collapse a portion of the outline. But we know that JavaScript does not allow dynamic updating of loaded windows or frames, no matter how the content is created (whether by HTML document or JavaScript). What the script needed was a way to represent the current state of the outline — a line-by-line rundown on whether a line was currently expanded or collapsed. If the script could save that state somewhere, the HREF= attribute could summon a JavaScript function whose sole job is to reload the current page without reopening it — with the history.go() method. Therefore, as a user clicked on a widget, the state of the outline created by that click would be generated in the script, saved, and then used to specify the expanded or collapsed state of each line as the page reloaded.

Just when I was congratulating myself on how clever I was, I realized that any attempt to save the state of the new outline in a variable was doomed: The reloading process restores variables to their natural state. I'd have to find another way to maintain the data.

The first method I used was to store the outline state (a string of 0s and 1s in which a 1 indicated that the item was expanded) in a text object. Text and textarea objects maintain their contents even through a document reload (but not a re-open). Although this was convenient, it was ugly because it meant that this field would have to be in the frame. One tactic was to make the frame a non-scrolling frame and stuff the field out of sight by pushing it to the far right with padding spaces inside a `<PRE>...</PRE>` tag. I posted an outliner with this implementation to my Web site initially, mostly to share the rest of my findings with the other JavaScript pioneers who were playing with the betas of Navigator 2.0.

As the betas became more stable, it was time to try Netscape's mechanism for storing persistent data on the client computer: the `document.cookie` property. Cookies are not unique to JavaScript. Any CGI can also store data, such as a user's login name and password for a site, in a cookie. The cookie did the trick. Information about the outline lasts in the cookie.txt file of any user's computer (or the MagicCookie file on the Mac) only as long as Navigator stays running. The next time the user visits the outline site, the cookie is rewritten for its temporary job.

Future versions of Netscape Navigator may allow users to turn off the cookie function for their client machines (some security issues surrounding the cookie feature have not been resolved as we go to press). If that becomes the case, you need to inform your users that the application requires cookies be turned on or to use alternate ways of storing persistent data (perhaps a frame of size 0 that contains a text field for the data). Watch the Netscape on-line library for future developments in this arena.

One last implementation detail that I wanted to overcome was the initial delay the first time a user clicked on one of the collapsed widgets in the outline. At that point, only one of three icon image files had been loaded and cached in the browser. Thus, a click on the collapsed icon meant that one or both of the other images would have to load, causing a brief delay until the images were cached. To prevent this delay, I worked the other two widget images into the heading of the outline document so that all widget images load and cache the first time the outline loads.

The Implementation Plan

I admit to approaching the outline technique without a specific goal in mind — not always the best way to go about it. In search of some logical and public domain data I could use as an example, I came upon the tables of information about food composition (grams of protein and fat, calories, and so on) published by the U.S. government. For this demonstration, I created one HTML document containing data for two hierarchical categories of foods: peas and pickles. At the beginning of each food category I assigned an anchor, to which the text entries of the outline point.

My design for this implementation calls for two frames set up as columns (see Figure 18-1). The narrower left column houses the outline interface. When the frameset loads, the wider right frame initially shows an introductory HTML document. Clicking on any of the links in the outline changes the view of the right-hand frame from the introductory document to the food data document. A link at the bottom of the food data document lets the user view the introductory document again in the same frame, if desired.

The Code

All the necessary files for this implementation of the outline are on the CD-ROM accompanying this book, so I will display here only the code for the framesetting document and the outline. If you look at this implementation on my Web site, the filenames may be different: For the sake of Windows 3.1 users of this book, all filenames on the CD-ROM have been converted to DOS versions.

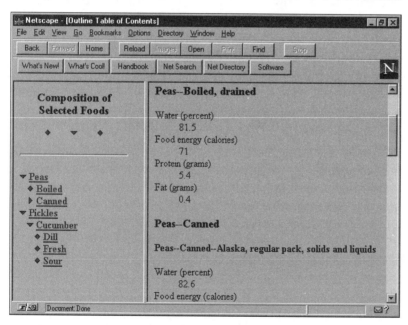

Figure 18-1: The outline in the left frame is dynamic and local.

Setting the frames

To establish the frames, the script creates a two-column format, assigning 35 percent of the page as a column to contain the outline.

```
<HTML>
<HEAD>
<TITLE>Outline Table of Contents</TITLE>
</HEAD>

<FRAMESET COLS="35%,65">

<NOFRAMES>
<H1>It's really cool...</H1>
<H2>...but only if you have Netscape Navigator 2.0</H2>
<HR>
<A HREF="index.html">Back to JavaScript Table of Contents</A>
</NOFRAMES>

    <FRAME NAME="Frame1" SRC="foodol.htm">
    <FRAME NAME="Frame2" SRC="olintro.htm">
</FRAMESET>
</HTML>
```

Because pages designed for multiple frames and JavaScript don't fare well in browsers incapable of displaying frames, it is always a good idea to include a <NOFRAMES> tag surrounding HTML to display for users of an old browser. You can substitute any link you like for the one shown here, which goes back to the main JavaScript page at my Web site.

The names I assign to the two frames aren't very original or clever, but they help me remember which is which. Because the nature of the contents of the second frame changes (either the introductory document or the data document), I couldn't think of a good name to reflect its purpose.

Outline code

Now we come to some lengthy code for the outline. Much of it deals with managing the binary representation of the current state of the outline. For each line of the completely exploded outline, the code designates a 0 for a line that has no nested items showing and a one for a line that has a nested item showing. This sequence of 0s and 1s (as one string) is the road map that the script follows when redrawing the outline. Cues from the 0 and 1 settings let the script know whether it should display a nested item (if there is one) or leave that item collapsed.

415

To help me visualize the inner workings of these scripts, I developed a convention that calls any item that has nested items beneath it a *mother*. Any nested item is that mother's *daughter*. A daughter can also be a mother if it has an item nested beneath it. You'll see how this plays out in the code shortly.

```
<HTML>
<HEAD>
<TITLE>Food Selection Outline</TITLE>
```

The food outline document starts out plainly enough, with the standard opening:

```
<SCRIPT LANGUAGE="JavaScript">
<!-- begin hiding

// **functions that establish objects and environment**
// basic array maker
function makeArray(n) {
    this.length = n
    return this
}
```

As a first utility function in the document's Head, I use a slightly different version of the canonical array maker. Rather than defining a bunch of empty entries, the function merely sets the length property. As explained in Chapter 9, a script can add entries to an array at any time after it has been created with the new keyword (below). If it weren't for JavaScript's requirement that an array's creation be funneled through one of these constructor functions, we could do without it altogether. It is required, however, and here it does the bare minimum.

```
// object constructor for each outline entry
// (see object-building calls, below)
function dbRecord(mother,display,URL,indent){
    this.mother = mother    // is this item a parent?
    this.display = display  // text to display
    this.URL = URL          // link tied to text
    this.indent = indent    // how deeply nested?
    return this
}
```

A more important constructor function builds each entry of the outline as an object with four properties. Therefore, for each outline item, our script (in the next batch of statements) creates a separate object (which will be one element of an array of objects).

Properties for each item include

- A Boolean value for whether the item is a mother (parent) object with one or more daughters nested beneath it.

- The string to display in the outline for the entry.

- The URL that the link created with the displayed text points to.

- An index value of how far (how many "tabs") the item is indented in the outline.

Every time the script draws the outline (below), it calls upon the properties of each object to get information about how it should be displayed.

```
// create object containing outline content and attributes
var db = new makeArray(10)
db[1] = new dbRecord(true,  "Peas",        "foods.htm#peas",0)
db[2] = new dbRecord(false, "Boiled",      "foods.htm#boiled",1)
db[3] = new dbRecord(true,  "Canned",      "foods.htm#canned",1)
db[4] = new dbRecord(false, "Alaska",      "foods.htm#alaska",2)
db[5] = new dbRecord(false, "Low-Sodium","foods.htm#losodium",2)
db[6] = new dbRecord(true,  "Pickles",     "foods.htm#pickles",0)
db[7] = new dbRecord(true,  "Cucumber",    "foods.htm#cucumber",1)
db[8] = new dbRecord(false, "Dill",        "foods.htm#dill",2)
db[9] = new dbRecord(false, "Fresh",       "foods.htm#fresh",2)
db[10] = new dbRecord(false,"Sour",        "foods.htm#sour",2)
```

After creating a new array, the script starts filling each entry with a new object representing each entry in the outline. If you were using this script as a model for your outline, this is where you would enter the data for its details. Properties passed as parameters to the dbRecord() constructor function essentially define the characteristics of the entire outline. The most deeply nested items of chains have their first properties set to false (i.e., they are not mothers), and the last parameters define how deeply nested the items are. In this example, all URLs point to the same document but to different anchor points within that document.

```
// ** functions that get and set persistent cookie data **
// set cookie data
function setCurrState(setting) {
    document.cookie = "currState=" + escape(setting)
}

// retrieve cookie data
```
(continued)

```
function getCurrState() {
    var label = "currState="
    var labelLen = label.length
    var cLen = document.cookie.length
    var i = 0
    while (i < cLen) {
        var j = i + labelLen
        if (document.cookie.substring(i,j) == label) {
            var cEnd = document.cookie.indexOf(";",j)
            if (cEnd ==   -1) {
                cEnd = document.cookie.length
            }
            return unescape(document.cookie.substring(j,cEnd))
        }
    }
    return ""
}
```

To preserve the binary digit string between redraws of the outline, this script must save that string to a place that won't be overwritten or emptied in the course of the document reload. The `document.cookie` fills that requirement nicely. Excerpting and adapting parts of Bill Dortch's cookie functions (Chapter 8), this script simplifies the writing of a cookie that disappears when the user next quits the browser.

Retrieving information from the cookie still requires a bit of parsing to be on the safe side. If other cookie writing were to come from the current server path, more than one cookie would be available to the current document. Parsing the entire cookie for just the portion that corresponds to the `currState=` labeled cookie assures that the script gets only the data previously saved to that label.

```
// **function that updates persistent storage of state**
// toggles an outline mother entry, storing new value in the
cookie
function toggle(n) {
    if (n != 0) {
        var newString = ""
        var currState = getCurrState() // of whole outline
        var expanded = currState.substring(n-1,n) // of clicked
item
        newString += currState.substring(0,n-1)
        newString += expanded ^ 1 // Bitwise XOR clicked item
```

```
        newString += currState.substring(n,currState.length)
        setCurrState(newString) // write new state back to cookie
    }
}
```

The `toggle()` function, which is pivotal in this outline scheme, receives as a parameter the index number of the array element that the user just clicked on. The purpose of this function is to grab a copy of the current outline state from the cookie, alter the binary representation of the clicked item, and feed the revised binary number back to the cookie (where it governs the display of the outline when the document reloads).

To make this happen, we must extract two pieces of information before any processing: the current state from the cookie and the current setting of the clicked item. The latter is saved in a variable named `expanded` because its 0 or 1 value represents the expanded state of that particular entry in the outline.

With those information morsels in hand, the script starts building the new binary string that gets written back to the cookie. The new string consists of three pieces: the front part of the existing string up to (but not including) the digit representing the clicked item, the changed entry, and the rest of the original string.

It is necessary to change the setting of the clicked item from a 0 to a 1 or vice versa. Although I could have implemented this a few different ways (e.g., a conditional expression or an `if...else` construction), I thought I'd exercise an operator that would otherwise get little use: the bitwise XOR operator (^). Because the values involved here are 0 and 1, performing an XOR operation with the value of one inverts the original value:

```
0 ^ 1 = 1
1 ^ 1 = 0
```

Okay, perhaps using an XOR operator is showing off. But the experience forced me to understand a JavaScript power that could come in handy in the future.

```
// **functions used in assembling updated outline**
// returns the proper GIF file name for each entry's control
function getGIF(n) {
    var mom = db[n].mother  // is entry a parent?
    var expanded = getCurrState().substring(n-1,n) // of clicked
item
    if (!mom) {
        return "daughter.gif"
    } else {
```

(continued)

```
if (expanded == 1) {
        return "exploded.gif"
    }
}
return "collapsd.gif"
}
```

At this point, the script starts defining functions to help the following script write the HTML for the new version of the outline. The getGIF() function determines which of the three widget image files needs to be specified for a particular entry in the outline. The script passes to it the index value to the array of entries created earlier in the script and calls this function once for each item in the outline as the script assembles the HTML.

The decision process for this function first tries to eliminate any item that ends a mother-daughter chain. Any item that is as deeply nested as it can be (i.e., it's not a mother) automatically gets the daughter.gif widget.

Now we're left with trying to figure out whether the item in the display should get an expanded or collapsed icon. The holder of this information is the cookie. Thus, the script extracts the binary setting for the entry under scrutiny. If the cookie shows that entry to be a 1, it means the item has nested items showing and it should get the exploded.gif image; otherwise, it should get the collapsd.gif image (note spelling to accommodate DOS filename restrictions).

```
// returns the proper status line text based on the icon style
function getGIFStatus(n) {
    var mom = db[n].mother  // is entry a parent
    var expanded = getCurrState().substring(n-1,n) // of rolled
item
    if (!mom) {
        return "No further items"
    } else {
        if (expanded == 1) {
            return "Click to collapse nested items"
        }
    }
    return "Click to expand nested items"
}
```

A similar excursion through each item determines what status message is assigned to the onMouseOver= event handler for each of the widget images. The decision tree is identical to that of the getGIF() function:

```
// returns padded spaces (in multiples of 3) for indenting
function pad(n) {
    var result = ""
    for (var i = 1; i <= n; i++) {
       result += "   "
    }
    return result
}
```

Making the indentations of nested items appear in HTML is best handled here by writing the entire outline as a preformatted segment (in `<PRE>...</PRE>` tags). Assisting in padding the spaces for indentation is the `pad()` function. It receives a value indicating how many "tabs" are required as a parameter and supplies the desired number of three-space empty strings accordingly.

```
// javascript: URL function for navigation from link reloads frame
function refreshMe() {
    history.go(0)
}
```

To force a redrawing of the outline so that it obeys the current settings of the `document.cookie`, you need to call the `go()` method of the history object, specifying an offset direction of 0. This means "Go to the current page."

```
// initialize 'current state' storage field
if (getCurrState() == "") {
    initState = ""
    for (i = 1; i <= db.length; i++) {
       initState += "0"
    }
    setCurrState(initState)
}
// end -->
</SCRIPT>
</HEAD>
```

The final task of the script running in the head is to initialize the cookie if it is empty. Using the length of the outline entry array as a counter, we build a string of 0s, with one 0 for each item in the outline. Each of those 0s in the parameter to the `setCurrState()` function corresponds to a collapsed setting for an entry in the outline. In other words, the first time the outline appears, all items are in the collapsed mode. If you modify the outline for your own use by creating your own db array of data, the initial state of the cookie will be set for you automatically based on the length you specify when creating the db array.

```
<BODY>
<SCRIPT LANGUAGE="JavaScript">
<!-- start
// build new outline based on the values of the cookie
// and data points in the outline data array.
// This fires each time the user clicks on a control,
// because the HREF for each one reloads the current document.
var prevIndentDisplayed = 0
var showMyDaughter = 0
document.write("<CENTER><H3>Composition of Selected Foods</H3>")
```

From here, the rest of the outline part of the page is created in JavaScript. After initializing a couple of variables for use later in the script, it writes out the centered headline for the outline frame. I chose an H3 level due to the scale of the outline's frame.

```
document.write("<PRE><IMG SRC='daughter.gif' HEIGHT=11 WIDTH=11
BORDER=0>    <IMG SRC='exploded.gif' HEIGHT=11 WIDTH=11 BORDER=0>
<IMG SRC='daughter.gif' HEIGHT=11 WIDTH=11 BORDER=0></PRE></
CENTER><HR>")
```

Still under control of the <CENTER> tag, the script displays a nice pattern using two of the widget images. They are in a <PRE>...</PRE> tag pair to allow a little horizontal padding of spaces between images. I chose to display these images here because they'll be cached in the browser the first time the outline displays. The third image, collapsd.gif, is automatically retrieved in the outline text that follows.

```
var newOutline = "<PRE><H4>"    // let padded spaces make indents
```

I define a new variable into which the script will accumulate the HTML for the outline. It begins with a <PRE> tag because the rest of the outline must accommodate space padding for indentations. It also sets all text in the outline to the same font as the <H4> header to match the weight of the widget icons.

```
// cycle through each entry in the outline array
for (var i = 1; i <= db.length; i++) {
    var theGIF = getGIF(i)                // get the image
    var theGIFStatus = getGIFStatus(i)    // get the status message
    var currIndent = db[i].indent         // get the indent level
```

```
var expanded = getCurrState().substring(i-1,i) // current state
// display entry only if it meets one of three criteria
if (currIndent == 0 || currIndent <=
prevIndentDisplayed || (showMyDaughter == 1
&& (currIndent - prevIndentDisplayed == 1))) {
    newOutline += pad(currIndent)
    newOutline += "<A HREF=\"javascript:refreshMe()\"
        onMouseOver=\"window.parent.status=\'" + theGIFStatus +
        "\';return true;\" onClick=\"toggle(" + i + ")\"><IMG
        SRC=\"" + theGIF + "\" HEIGHT=11 WIDTH=11 BORDER=0></A>"
    newOutline += " <A HREF=\"" + db[i].URL + "\" TARGET=\"Frame2\"
        onMouseOver=\"window.parent.status=\'View " +
        db[i].display
        + "...\';return true;\">" + db[i].display + "</A><BR>"
    prevIndentDisplayed = currIndent
    showMyDaughter = expanded
}
}
```

We're now at the real beef of this script: the part that assembles the HTML for the outline that displays as the document loads. In other words, it must read the current state data from the cookie and assemble widget images and text links according to the map of expanded and collapsed items in the cookie data. This happens within a for loop that cycles through every item in the database. Let's trace the logic of one entry.

First, we call upon two previously defined functions to grab the widget image URL and corresponding onMouseOver= message for the status bar. Two more variables contain the indent property for the item (that is, how many steps indented it is in the outline structure) and the current expanded state, based on the cookie's entry for that item.

Not every entry in the outline database is displayed. For instance, a nested item whose mother is collapsed won't need to be displayed. To find out if an entry should be displayed, the script performs a number of tests on some of its values. An item can be displayed if any of the following conditions are met:

- The item is a topmost item, with an indentation factor of zero.

- The item is at the same or smaller indentation level as the previous item displayed.

- The previous item was tagged as being expanded and the current item is indented from the previous item by one level.

Over the next few statements, the script pieces together the HTML for the outline entry, starting with however many three-space indentations are needed from the pad() function. Next comes the link that features the widget image. For each link

1. The HREF= attribute is the refreshMe() function.

2. The onMouseOver= event handler is set to adjust the status message to the previously retrieved message (notice the return true statement to make the setting take effect).

3. The onClick= event handler is set to call the toggle() function, passing the number of the item within the outline database. An onClick= event handler is carried out before the browser responds to the click of the link by navigating to the URL. Therefore, the toggle() function changes the setting of the cookie a fraction of a second before the browser refreshes the document (which relies on that new cookie setting).

4. The image is set to whatever was retrieved by the getGIF() function. It's important to specify the HEIGHT= and WIDTH= tags for the image, or Navigator 2.0 may not treat the status bar messages or toggle() function correctly until the outline reloads one time.

The script appends another link containing the text of the outline entry and its link to the same line of HTML as the widget link. In this HTML assembly process, numerous calls to properties of the db[] array fetch properties of the entry object for the URL and text to display (both in the page and in an onMouseOver= setting of the status bar). Notice, too, that the link sets the target of the link to the second frame.

Before we finish the loop, two variable values, prevIndentDisplayed and showMyDaughter, are updated with settings from the current traversal through the loop. These values influence the display of nested items for the next entry's journey through the loop.

```
newOutline += "</PRE>"
document.write(newOutline)

// end -->
</SCRIPT>

</BODY>
</HTML>
```

All that's left is to close up the preformatted tag and write the entire outline to the document. Standard tags finish the document definition.

Further Thoughts

Since my first posting of the outline to my Web site as an experimental page, I've heard from many scripters who have worked on variations of the theme. You can accomplish this kind of outline in many different ways. There have even been suggestions to the JavaScript wish list that an outline object be defined in the JavaScript vocabulary. Discussions about this idea tend to reveal that almost everyone who wants to implement an outline has different ideas about how it should be done. The beauty of creating your own outline in JavaScript is that you can make it behave the way you and your site need it.

This just in: An old bug in the Macintosh version of Netscape Navigator suddenly reappeared in release 2.01. See the food01.htm file on the CD-ROM for more information about this bug and the changes that you need to make to the code to accommodate it.

$\mathscr{C}$hapter Nineteen

Key Concepts:

- Multiple frames

- Tables

- CGI-like image assembly

Perhaps because some of the first examples of applying JavaScript

came from Netscape (while the language was still called LiveScript), the

notion of creating HTML-based calculators has run rampant. By the time

this book appears for the first time, there may well be a calculator for every kind of special-purpose calculation normally done by scientific calculators and personal computer programs — leaving only weather modeling calculations to the Crays of the world.

In the search for my calculator imprint on the JavaScript world, I looked around for something more graphical. Numbers, by themselves, are pretty boring; so any way the math could be enlivened was fine by me. Because I have been an electronics hobbyist since I was a kid, I recalled the color coding of electronic resistor components. The values of these gizmos aren't printed in plain numbers anywhere. You have to know the code and what the location of the colored bands means to arrive at the value of each one. I thought that this calculator would be fun to play with, even if you didn't know what a resistor is.

The Calculation

To give you an appreciation for the calculation that goes into determining a resistor's value, here is the way the system works. Three closely spaced bands determine the resistance value in ohms. The first (leftmost) band is the tens digit; the second (middle) band is the ones digit. Each color has a number from zero through nine assigned to it (black = 0, brown = 1, and so on). Therefore, if the first band is brown and the second band is black, the number you start off with is 10. The third band is a multiplier. Each color determines what power of ten the first digits are multiplied by. For example, the red color corresponds to a multiplier of 10^2. So $10 * 10^2$ equals 1000 ohms.

A fourth band, if present, indicates the tolerance of the component — how far, plus or minus, the resistance measurement can be due to variations in the manufacturing process. Gold means a tolerance of plus-or-minus 5 percent; silver is plus-or-minus 10 percent; and no band means a 20 percent tolerance. A pinch of extra space typically exists between the main group of three color bands and the one tolerance band.

User Interface Ideas

The quick-and-dirty, non-graphical approach was to use a single frame with four select objects defined as pop-up menus (one for each of the four color bands on a resistor), a button to trigger calculation, and a field to show the results. How dull.

It occurred to me that if I designed the art carefully, I could have JavaScript assemble an updated image of the resistor comprised of different slices of art: static images for the left and right ends of the resistor; and variable slivers of color bands for the middle. Rather than use the brute force method of creating an image for every possible combination of colors (3600 images total!), it would be far more efficient to have one image file for each color (12 plus one empty) and let JavaScript call them from the server, as needed, in the proper order. This kind of intelligence and user interaction would otherwise have to be handled with a CGI script on the server. But with this system, any dumb server can dish up the image files as called by the JavaScript script.

My final design called for a two-frame window (see Figure 19-1). In the top frame are the four pop-up menus and the button. Because the onChange= event handler doesn't work correctly with Windows versions of Netscape Navigator 2.0, I include a clickable button to trigger the calculation.

Figure 19-1: The Resistor Identifier with images inside a table border.

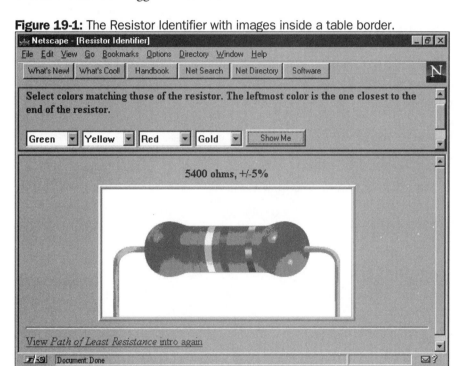

Scripts in the upper frame drive the display of the lower frame — actually writing via JavaScript all of the HTML that shows in the lower frame. To hold the art together on the page, a table border surrounds the images on the page, whereas the numeric value of the component appears as the title of the table.

The Code

Three HTML documents comprise the bulk of this application. One is a framesetter, which establishes the two frames in the browser window. Another document is what I call the Resistor Controls, because it contains the pop-up menus and scripts that control the meat of this application. The third document is an introductory HTML text document that explains what a resistor is and why you need a calculator to determine a component's value. The article is called *The Path of Least Resistance*. This last document, initially shown in the bottom frame when the page loads, goes away when the upper frame starts showing the resistor graphics. But that also means the graphics frame must have a link back to the introductory screen in case the user wants to read it again.

Although there are three documents (which are on the CD-ROM along with all the image files), we'll be looking closely only at one: Resistor Controls. It is the only one with JavaScript code in it.

```
<HTML>
<HEAD>
<TITLE>Resistor Controls</TITLE>
```

The document begins in the traditional way.

```
<SCRIPT LANGUAGE="JavaScript">
<!- - hide script from nonscriptable browsers
// generic object maker prepares an empty array of n items
function makeArray() {
     return this
}
```

As is my tendency in scripts that use arrays, I enter the array constructor function near the top of the Head. For this application, I've stripped the `makeArray()` constructor down to its barest minimum. Because none of the later scripts need to worry about the length of any of the arrays being created for this application, I don't even bother assigning an array property to represent the array's length. In fact, because of the way I need the index values of the array to line up with other objects whose index values start with zero, the zero entry of every array must be free and clear for my array data.

```
// create array listing all the multiplier values
var multiplier = new makeArray()
multiplier[0] = 0
multiplier[1] = 1
```

```
multiplier[2] = 2
multiplier[3] = 3
multiplier[4] = 4
multiplier[5] = 5
multiplier[6] = 6
multiplier[7] = 7
multiplier[8] = 8
multiplier[9] = 9
multiplier[10] = -1
multiplier[11] = -2
```

In calculating the resistance, the script needs to know the multiplier value for each color. If it weren't for the fact that the last two are actually negative multipliers (i.e., 10^{-1} and 10^{-2}), I could have used the index values without having to create this array. But the two out-of-sequence values at the end make it easier to work with an array rather than to try special-casing these instances in later calculations.

```
// create object listing all tolerance values
var tolerance = new makeArray()
tolerance[0] = "+/-5%"
tolerance[1] = "+/-10%"
tolerance[2] = "+/-20%"
```

Although the script doesn't do any calculations with the tolerance percentages, it needs to have the strings corresponding to each color to display in the pop-up menu. That's what the tolerance[] array is for.

```
// format large values into kilo and meg
function format(ohmage) {
    if (ohmage >= 10e6) {
        ohmage /= 10e5
        return "" + ohmage + " Mohms"
    } else {
        if (ohmage >= 10e3) {
            ohmage /= 10e2
            return "" + ohmage + " Kohms"
        } else {
            return "" + ohmage + " ohms"
        }
    }
}
```

Before the script displays the resistance value, it's important to format the numbers in values that are meaningful to those who know about these values. Just like measures of computer storage bytes, high quantities of ohms are preceded with "kilo" and "meg" prefixes, commonly abbreviated with the "K" and "M" letters. The format() function determines the order of magnitude of the final calculation (from another function below) and formats the results with the proper unit of measure.

```
// calculate resistance and tolerance values
function calcOhms(d1,d2,m,t) {
    var ohmage = (d1 * 10) + d2
    ohmage = eval("" + ohmage + "e" + multiplier[m])
    ohmage = format(ohmage)
    var tol = tolerance[t]
    return "" + ohmage + ", " + tol
}
```

The selections from the pop-up menus meet the calculation formulas of resistors in calcOhms(). Parameters arriving with this function are index values of the selected items in each of the four pop-up menus. Using the method I described earlier in discussing the way you can calculate the resistance from the colors, the first statement multiplies the pop-up value times ten to determine the tens digit and then adds the ones digit. From there, the value is multiplied by the exponent value of the selected multiplier value. Notice that the expression assembles the value first as a string to concatenate the exponent factor and then evaluates it to a number. That number is passed to the format() function for proper formatting (and setting of order of magnitude). In the meantime, the tolerance value is extracted from its array, and the combined string is returned to the calling statement, ready for display.

```
// utility function to extract the pathname to the current
document
function getPath(URL) {
    return URL.substring(0,(URL.lastIndexOf("/") + 1))
}
```

Before we get to the main driver behind all the action, we have one more utility function that helps in working with the URLs for the images, whether we're exploring these files locally or on a remote server. For best results, all URLs to files specified in JavaScript-assembled HTML should be absolute URLs. This extraction of the current base reference is applied to the names of individual files later to assure a proper reference.

```
// the main function that displays new colors and calculates
values
function showResistor(form) {
    var baseRef = getPath(parent.frames[1].document.location)
    var result = ""

    // get the colors and index values
    var firstDigit = form.firstSelect.selectedIndex
    var firstColor = form.firstSelect.options[firstDigit].text
    var secondDigit = form.secondSelect.selectedIndex
    var secondColor = form.secondSelect.options[secondDigit].text
    var multiplierDigit = form.multiplierSelect.selectedIndex
    var multiplierColor =
form.multiplierSelect.options[multiplierDigit].text
    var toleranceDigit = form.toleranceSelect.selectedIndex
    var toleranceColor =
form.toleranceSelect.options[toleranceDigit].text
```

The start of the main function of the resistor control begins by initializing a bunch of variable values. Of special importance are the values for the color names and the index values — all derived from the selectedIndex properties of each of the four pop-up menus. The script needs the color names to assign as image file names in a moment; the index values become calculation values.

```
// calculate the resistance
    var ohmage =
calcOhms(firstDigit,secondDigit,multiplierDigit,toleranceDigit)
```

Next we call the function that calculates the resistance value based on the selectedIndex values of the pop-up menus.

```
// assemble content for bottom frame
    result = "<HTML><BODY>"
    result +="<CENTER><TABLE BORDER=2><CAPTION ALIGN=top><B>" +
ohmage + "</B></CAPTION>"
    result +="<TD>"
    result +="<IMG SRC=" + baseRef + "resleft.gif WIDTH=127
                HEIGHT=182>" +
        "<IMG SRC=" + baseRef + firstColor + ".gif WIDTH=21
                HEIGHT=182>"+
```

(continued)

```
                  "<IMG SRC=" + baseRef + secondColor + ".gif WIDTH=21
                     HEIGHT=182>"+
                  "<IMG SRC=" + baseRef + multiplierColor + ".gif WIDTH=21
                     HEIGHT=182>"+
                  "<IMG SRC=" + baseRef + "spacer.gif WIDTH=17
                     HEIGHT=182>"+
                  "<IMG SRC=" + baseRef + toleranceColor + ".gif WIDTH=21
                     HEIGHT=182>"+
                  "<IMG SRC=" + baseRef + "resright.gif WIDTH=138
                     HEIGHT=182>"
        result += "</TD></TABLE></CENTER>"
        result += "<HR><A HREF=" + baseRef + "resintro.htm>View
<CITE>Path of Least Resistance</CITE> intro again</A>"
        result += "</BODY></HTML>"

        parent.frames[1].document.writeln(result)
        parent.frames[1].document.close()
}
// end script hiding — —>
</SCRIPT>
</HEAD>
```

Then begins the assembly of the HTML that becomes the lower frame. Everything here is defined in the Body portion of the scripted frame (although you could add a Head section and title, if you like).

All the data is part of a table. As a caption atop the table border, the script displays the results of the calculation as a string. After that, one table cell receives a sequence of image files, starting with the left end of the resistor. By specifying the image sizes, we speed up the rendering of the table and the images within the table. Below the table is a horizontal rule and a link that redisplays the resistor introduction document in the same lower frame.

To display the table and other data in the frame, we call the `document.writeln()` method and a `document.close()` method, the latter to close the layout stream opened by the `document.writeln()` method. Without the `document.close()` method, you might not see all images appear as they should. Both methods are directed to the document in the lower frame (`parent.frames[1]`).

Thus end the function definitions of the Head portion of this document. The balance of the document is about the Body of the upper frame, complete with definitions of the four pop-up menus.

```
<BODY>
<H4>Select colors matching those of the resistor.  The leftmost
color is the one closest to the end of the resistor.</H4>
<FORM>
<SELECT NAME="firstSelect"> //SIZE=4
     <OPTION SELECTED> Black
     <OPTION> Brown
     <OPTION> Red
     <OPTION> Orange
     <OPTION> Yellow
     <OPTION> Green
     <OPTION> Blue
     <OPTION> Violet
     <OPTION> Gray
     <OPTION> White
</SELECT>
<SELECT NAME="secondSelect">
     <OPTION SELECTED> Black
     <OPTION> Brown
     <OPTION> Red
     <OPTION> Orange
     <OPTION> Yellow
     <OPTION> Green
     <OPTION> Blue
     <OPTION> Violet
     <OPTION> Gray
     <OPTION> White
</SELECT>
<SELECT NAME="multiplierSelect">
     <OPTION SELECTED> Black
     <OPTION> Brown
     <OPTION> Red
     <OPTION> Orange
     <OPTION> Yellow
     <OPTION> Green
     <OPTION> Blue
     <OPTION> Violet
     <OPTION> Gray
     <OPTION> White
```

(continued)

435

```
(continued)
        <OPTION> Gold
        <OPTION> Silver
</SELECT>
<SELECT NAME="toleranceSelect">
        <OPTION SELECTED> Gold
        <OPTION> Silver
        <OPTION> None
</SELECT>
<INPUT TYPE="button" NAME="Calculate" VALUE="Show Me"
ALIGN="center" onClick="showResistor(this.form)">
</FORM>
</BODY>
</HTML>
```

This is all straight HTML stuff with the exception of the `onClick=` event handler of the button. It calls the `showResistor()` function, which does all the calculations and drawing into the lower frame.

Further Thoughts

The Macintosh version of Netscape Navigator renders the combination of pop-up menus and button in a less than esthetically pleasing manner. The pop-up menus don't have the expected down arrow icon, and the button doesn't align with the pop-ups. Because I elected not to do checking for Navigator platform or version, the common denominator of the calculation button necessary for Windows users is always shown. When Navigator lets the `onChange=` event handler of select objects to work correctly on all platforms, I'll do away with the button and let the pop-up button selections trigger the recalculation and display of the images.

At one point in the design process, I considered trying to align the pop-up menus with images of the resistor (or callout line images); but the differences in platform rendering of pop-up menus made that idea impractical.

You should notice from this exercise that I look for ways to blend JavaScript object data structures with my own data structures. For example, the select objects served multiple duties in these scripts. Not only did the text of each option point to an image file of the same name, but the index values of the same options were applied to the calculations. Things don't always work out that nicely, but whenever your scripts bring together user interface elements and data elements, look for algorithmic connections that you can leverage to create elegant, concise code.

$\mathcal{C}$hapter Twenty

KEY CONCEPTS:

- Multiple frames

- Multiple-document applications

- Multiple windows

- Persistent storage (cookies)

- Scripted image maps

- Tables

The list of key concepts for this chapter's application looks like the grand finale to a fireworks show. As JavaScript implementations go, it is, in some respects, over the top, yet not out of the question for presenting a practical interactive application on a Web site lacking control over the server.

Users of some Unix versions of Netscape Navigator 2.0 occasionally experience errors while running the JavaScript code described in this chapter. I provide this example as a snapshot of a work in progress because it demonstrates a number of individual techniques that are useful to many scripters. I will continue to experiment with this (and all the previous) applications on my Web site (http://www.dannyg.com), where you can see the latest revisions.

The Application

I wanted to implement a classic application often called a *decision support system*. My experience with the math involved here goes back to the first days of Microsoft Excel. More recently, I put the concepts to work for *MacUser* magazine in an application that assisted Macintosh shoppers in selecting the right model for their needs. Rather than design a program that had limited appeal (covering only one possible decision tree), I set out to make a completely user-customizable decision helper. All the user has to do is enter values into fields on a number of screens; the program performs the calculations to let the user know how the various choices rank.

Although I won't be delving too deeply into the math inside this application, it will be helpful for you to understand how a user approaches this program and what the results look like. The basic scenario is a user who is trying to evaluate how well a selection of choices measure up to the his or her expectations of performance. User input includes

- The name of the decision

- The names of up to five alternatives (people, products, ideas)

- The factors or features of concern to the user

- The importance of each of the factors to the user

- A user ranking of the performance of every alternative in each factor

What makes this kind of application useful is that it forces the user to rate and weigh a number of often-conflicting factors. By assigning hard numbers to these elements, the user leaves the difficult process of figuring out the weights of various factors to the computer.

Results come in the form of floating-point numbers between 0 and 100. As an extra touch, I've added a graphical charting component to the results display.

The Design

With so much user input necessary for this application, it was important to convey the illusion of simplicity. Rather than lump all text objects on a single scrolling page, I decided to break them up into five pages, each consisting of its own HTML document. As an added benefit, I could embed information from early screens into the HTML of later screens, rather than having to create all changeable items out of text objects. This "good idea" presented one opportunity and one rather large challenge.

The opportunity was to turn the interface for this application into something resembling a multimedia application using multiple frames. The largest frame would contain the forms the user fills out as well as the results page. Another frame would contain a navigation panel with arrows for moving forward and backward through the sequence of screens plus buttons for going back to a home page and getting information about the program. I also thought it a good idea to add a frame that provides instructions or suggestions for the users at each step. In the end, the design became a four-frame window, as shown in with the first entry screen in Figure 20-1.

Using a navigation bar also lets me demonstrate how to script a client-side image map — not an obvious task with Navigator 2.0.

On the challenge side of this design, it was necessary to find a way to maintain data globally as the user navigates from screen to screen. Every time one of the entry pages unloads, none of its text fields are available to a script. My first attack at this was to store the data as global variable data (mostly arrays) in the parent document that creates the frames. Because JavaScript allows you to reference any parent document's object, function, or variable (by preceding the reference with `parent.`), I thought this would be a snap. Unfortunately, Navigator 2.0 has a nasty bug that affects the storage of parent variables that depend on data coming from their children: if any child document unloads, the data gets jumbled.

My next hope was to use the `document.cookie` of the parent as the storage bin for the data. A major problem I faced was that this program needs to store a total of 41 individual data points, yet no more than 20 cookies can be allotted to a given URL pathname. But the cookie was the only solution for this application. For some of the data points (which are related in an array-like manner), I fashioned my own data structures so that one cookie could contain up to five related data points. That reduced my cookie demands to 17.

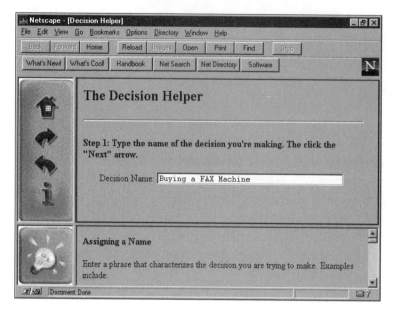

Figure 20-1: The Decision Helper window consists of four frames.

The Files

Before I get into the code, let me explain the file structure of this application. Table 20-1 gives a rundown of the files used in the Decision Helper.

Table 20-1
Files Comprising the Decision Helper Application

File	Description
dhLoad.htm	Framesetting parent document
dhNav.htm	Navigation bar document which contains some scripting
dhNav.gif	Image displayed in dhNav.htm
dhIcon.htm	Document for lower left corner frame
dhIcon.gif	Icon image for lower left frame
dh1.htm	First Decision Helper entry page
dh2.htm	Second Decision Helper entry page
dh3.htm	Third Decision Helper entry page
dh4.htm	Fourth Decision Helper entry page
dh5.htm	Results page
chart.gif	Tiny image file used to create bar charts in dh5.htm
dhHelp.htm	Sample data and instructions document for lower right frame
dhAbout.htm	Document that loads into a second window

There is a great deal of interdependence among these files. As you will see, assigning the names to some of these files was strategic for the implementation of the image map.

The Code

With so many JavaScript-enhanced HTML documents in this application, you can expect a lot of code. To best grasp what's going on here, first try to understand the structure and interplay of the documents, especially the way the entry pages rely on functions defined in the parent document. My goal in describing this is not to teach you how to implement this application, but rather how to apply the lessons I learned in building this application to the more complex ideas that may be aching to get out of your head and into JavaScript.

dhLoad.htm

Taking a top-down journey through the JavaScript and HTML of the Decision Helper, we start at the document that loads the frames. Unlike a typical framesetting document, however, this one contains JavaScript code in its Head section — code that many other documents rely on.

```
<HTML>
<HEAD>
<TITLE>Decision Helper</TITLE>
```

It is important to remember that in a multiple-frame environment, the title of the parent window's document is the name that appears in the window's title bar, no matter how many other documents are open inside its subframes.

```
<SCRIPT LANGUAGE="JavaScript">
<!-- start
function getCookieVal (offset) {
  var endstr = document.cookie.indexOf (";", offset)
  if (("" + endstr) == "" || endstr == -1)
    endstr = document.cookie.length
  return unescape(document.cookie.substring(offset, endstr))
}

function getCookie (name) {
  var arg = name + "=";
```

(continued)

```
  var alen = arg.length;
  var clen = document.cookie.length;
  var i = 0;
  while (i < clen) {
    var j = i + alen;
    if (document.cookie.substring(i, j) == arg)
      return getCookieVal (j);
    i = document.cookie.indexOf(" ", i) + 1;
    if (i == 0) break;
  }
  return null;
}


function setCookie (name, value) {
  document.cookie = name + "=" + escape (value) + ";"
}
```

Because this application relies on the document.cookie so heavily, these functions (slightly modified versions of Bill Dortch's Cookie Functions — Chapter 8) are located in the parent document. I simplified the cookie writing function because this application uses default settings for pathname and expiration.

```
function initializeCookies() {
    setCookie("decName","")
    setCookie("alt0","")
    setCookie("alt1","")
    setCookie("alt2","")
    setCookie("alt3","")
    setCookie("alt4","")
    setCookie("factor0","")
    setCookie("factor1","")
    setCookie("factor2","")
    setCookie("factor3","")
    setCookie("factor4","")
    setCookie("import","0")
    setCookie("perf0","")
    setCookie("perf1","")
    setCookie("perf2","")
    setCookie("perf3","")
    setCookie("perf4","")
}
```

When this application loads (or a user elects to start a new decision), it's important to grab the cookies we need and initialize them to basic values that the entry screens will use to fill entry fields when the user first visits them. All statements inside the `initializeCookies()` function call the `setCookie()` function, defined above. Parameters are the name of each cookie and the initial value — mostly empty strings. Before going on, study the cookie structure carefully. I'll be referring to it often in discussions of other documents in this application.

```
// JavaScript sees numbers with leading zeros as octal values, so
// strip zeros
function stripZeros(inputStr) {
    var result = inputStr
    while (result.substring(0,1) == "0") {
        result = result.substring(1,result.length)
    }
    return result
}


// general purpose function to see if a suspected numeric input
// is a positive integer
function isNumber(inputStr) {
    for (var i = 0; i < inputStr.length; i++) {
        var oneChar = charAt(i)
        if (oneChar < "0" || oneChar > "9") {
            return false
        }
    }
    return true
}


// function to determine if value is in acceptable range for this
// application
function inRange(inputStr) {
    num = parseInt(inputStr)
    if (num < 1 || num > 100) {
        return false
    }
    return true
}
```

These functions should look familiar to you. They were borrowed either wholesale or with minor modification from the data entry validation section of the Social Security number database lookup in Chapter 17. I'm glad I wrote these as generic functions, making them easy to incorporate into this script. Because many of the entry fields on two screens must be integers between 1 and 100, I brought the data validation functions to the parent document rather than duplicating them in each of the subdocuments.

```
// Master value validator routine
function isValid(inputStr) {
    if (inputStr != "" ) {
        inputStr = stripZeros(inputStr)
        if (!isNumber(inputStr)) {
            alert("Please make sure entries are numbers only.")
            return false
        } else {
            if (!inRange(inputStr)) {
                alert("Entries must be numbers between 1 and 100.
Try another value.")
                return false
            }
        }
    }
    return true
}
```

To control the individual data entry validation functions in the master controller, I again was able to borrow heavily from the application in Chapter 17.

```
function setDecisionName(str) {
    setCookie("decName",str)
}
function getDecisionName() {
    return getCookie("decName")
}
```

Each of the documents containing entry forms retrieves and stores information in the cookie. Because all cookie functions are located in the parent document, it simplifies coding in the subordinate documents to have functions in the parent document acting as interfaces to the primary cookie functions. For each category of data stored as cookies, the parent document has a pair of functions for getting and setting data. The calling statements pass only the data to be stored when saving information; the interface functions handle the rest, such as storing or retrieving the cookie with the correct name.

In the preceding pair of functions above, the decision name (from the first entry document) is passed back and forth between the cookie and the calling statement. Not only must the script store the data, but when the user returns to that screen later for any reason, the entry field must retrieve the previously entered data.

```
function setAlternative(i,str) {
    setCookie("alt" + i,str)
}
function getAlternative(i) {
    return getCookie("alt" + i)
}

function setFactor(i,str) {
    setCookie("factor" + i,str)
}
function getFactor(i) {
    return getCookie("factor" + i)
}

function setImportance(str) {
    setCookie("import",str)
}
function getImportance(i) {
    return getCookie("import")
}

function setPerformance(i,str) {
    setCookie("perf" + i,str)
}
function getPerformance(i) {
    return getCookie("perf" + i)
}
```

The balance of the storage and retrieval pairs do the same thing for their specific cookies. Some cookies are named according to index values (factor1, factor2, and so on), so their cookie-accessing functions require parameters for determining which of the cookies to access, based on the request from the calling statement. Many of the cookie retrieval functions are called to fill in data in tables of later screens during the user's trip down the decision path.

```
if (getDecisionName() == null) {
    initializeCookies()
}
// end -->
</SCRIPT>
</HEAD>
```

One sequence of code that runs when the parent document loads is the one that looks to see if there is a cookie structure set up. If there is none (the retrieval of a designated cookie returns a null value), the script initializes all cookies via the function described earlier.

```
<FRAMESET COLS="104,*">
    <FRAMESET ROWS="250,*">
        <FRAME NAME="navBar" SRC="dhNav.htm" SCROLLING=no>
        <FRAME NAME="icon" SRC="dhIcon.htm" SCROLLING=no>
    </FRAMESET>
    <FRAMESET ROWS="250,*">
        <FRAME NAME="entryForms" SRC="dh1.htm">
        <FRAME NAME="instructions" SRC="dhHelp.htm">
    </FRAMESET>
</FRAMESET>
</HTML>
```

The balance of the parent document defines the frameset for the browser window. It establishes some hard-wired pixel sizes for the navigation panel. This assures that the entire .gif file is visible whenever the frameset loads.

I learned an important lesson about scripting framesets along the way. I would make changes in the size of frames or other attributes in some of the documents opened in frames. Upon reloading, there would be no change. I found it necessary to reopen the frameset file from time to time. I also found it necessary to sometimes quit Navigator altogether and re-launch it for some changes to be visible. Therefore, if you seem to be making changes, but reloading the frameset doesn't make the changes appear, try re-opening or, as a last resort, quitting Navigator.

dhNav.htm

Because of its crucial role in controlling the activity around this program, we look into the navigation bar's document next. To accomplish the look and feel of a multimedia program, this document was designed as a client-side image map that has four regions scripted corresponding to the locations of the four buttons (see Figure 20-1). There is one function connected to each button (see the following example).

```
<HTML>
<HEAD>
<TITLE>Navigation Bar</TITLE>
<SCRIPT LANGUAGE="JavaScript">
<!-- start
function goHome() {
    alert("Navigate back to home page on a real site.")
}
```

The first function is linked to the Home button. For the listing here, we just present an alert dialog box replicating the action of navigating back to a real Web site's home page.

```
function goNext() {
    currLoc = parent.entryForms.document.title
    currOffset = parseInt(currLoc.charAt(2))
    if (currOffset <= 4) {
        ++currOffset
        parent.entryForms.location.href = "dh" + currOffset + ".htm"
        parent.instructions.location.hash = "help" + currOffset
    } else {
        alert("This is the last form.")
    }
}
```

Each of the arrow navigation buttons brings the user to the next or previous entry screen in the sequence. To facilitate this without building tables of document titles and names, I established a scheme for naming the documents so that a little algorithm determines which screen is currently in view and which screen is next (or previous) in the sequence.

The scheme involves ending the name of the HTML documents and titles with an index number ranging from one to five that represents their position in the series. To decide where to go next, the script first extracts the last character of the title of the document currently in the `entryForms` frame. As long as the offset number is no higher than the next-to-last document in the sequence, the script increments the index value by one and concatenates a new `location.href` for the frame. At the same time, the script advances the help document (lower right frame) to the anchor corresponding to the chosen entry screen by setting the `location.hash` property of that frame.

```
function goPrev() {
    currLoc = parent.entryForms.document.title
    currOffset = parseInt(currLoc.charAt(2))
    if (currOffset > 1) {
        --currOffset
        parent.entryForms.location.href = "dh" + currOffset + ".htm"
        parent.instructions.location.hash = "help" + currOffset
    } else {
        alert("This is the first form.")
    }
}
```

Similar action navigates to the previous screen of the sequence. This time, the index value is decremented by one, and there is a block when the current page is already the first in the sequence.

```
function goInfo() {
    var newWindow =
window.open("dhAbout.htm","","HEIGHT=275,WIDTH=400")
    newWindow =
window.open("dhAbout.htm","","HEIGHT=275,WIDTH=400")
}
// end -->
</SCRIPT>
</HEAD>
```

Clicking on the Info button displays a smaller window containing typical About-box data for the program (Figure 20-2). The script makes two calls to the `window.open()` method to work around a Navigator 2.0 bug for the Mac and Xwindow platforms. The same goes for leaving the second parameter blank.

```
<BODY>
<MAP NAME="navigation">
<AREA SHAPE="RECT" COORDS="23,22,70,67"
HREF="javascript:goHome()">
<AREA SHAPE="RECT" COORDS="25,80,66,116"
HREF="javascript:goNext()">
<AREA SHAPE="RECT" COORDS="24,125,67,161"
HREF="javascript:goPrev()">
<AREA SHAPE="RECT" COORDS="35,171,61,211"
HREF="javascript:goInfo()">
</MAP>
```

```
<IMG SRC="dhNav.gif" BORDER HEIGHT=240 WIDTH=96 ALIGN="left"
USEMAP="#navigation">
</BODY>
</HTML>
```

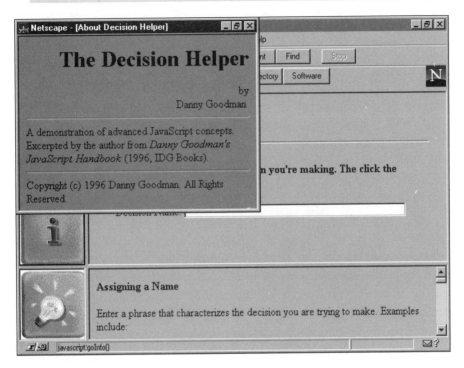

Figure 20-2: The About screen appears in a separate window.

In the Body of the document comes the part that allows us to script a client-side image map. Using tags to define client-side image maps, as we do here, differs from the method used in the Netscape technical note in only one regard: the content of the HREF= attribute for each <AREA> tag. Instead of pointing to an entirely new URL (the prescribed way), our attributes point to the JavaScript functions defined in the Head portion of this document. When a user clicks on the rectangle specified by an <AREA> tag, the browser invokes the function instead.

The only downside to this way of scripting image maps is that the status bar shows the contents of the HREF= attribute when the user rolls the mouse pointer atop any rectangle mapped for execution. In traditional image maps, the user sees a call to a server-based CGI script and the coordinates. Neither one is particularly friendly, but with Navigator 2.0, we cannot script the window.status property for an image map.

dh1.htm

Of the five documents that display in the main frame, dh1.htm is the simplest (Figure 20-1). It contains a single entry field, in which the user is invited to enter the name for the decision.

```
<HTML>
<HEAD>
<TITLE>DH1</TITLE>
<SCRIPT LANGUAGE="JavaScript">
<!-- start
function loadDecisionName() {
    var result = parent.getDecisionName()
    result = (result == null) ? "" : result
    document.forms[0].decName.value = result
}
// end -->
</SCRIPT>
</HEAD>
```

Only one function adorns the Head. It summons one of the cookie interface functions in the parent window. There is a test here in case there was a problem with initializing the cookies. Rather than show "null" in the field, the conditional expression substitutes an empty string.

```
<BODY
onLoad="loadDecisionName();document.forms[0].decName.focus()">
<H2>The Decision Helper</H2>
<HR>
<H4>Step 1: Type the name of the decision you're making. The click
the "Next" arrow.</H4>
<P><P>
```

After the document loads, it performs two tasks (in the onLoad= event handler). The first is to fill the field with the decision name stored in the cookie. This is important because users will want to come back to this screen to review what they entered previously. A second statement in the onLoad= event handler sets the focus of the entire browser window to the one text object. This is especially important in a multi-frame environment such as this design: When a user clicks on the navigation panel, that frame has the focus. To begin typing into the field, the user has to tab (repeatedly) or click to bring the focus to the field. By setting the focus in the script when the document loads, we save the user time and aggravation.

```
<CENTER>
<FORM>
Decision Name:
<INPUT TYPE="text" NAME="decName" SIZE="40"
onChange="parent.setDecisionName(this.value)">
</FORM>
</CENTER>
</BODY>
</HTML>
```

In the text field itself, an onChange= event handler saves the value of the field in the parent's cookie for the decision name. No special Save button or other instruction is necessary here because any navigation that the user does via the navigation bar automatically causes the text field to lose focus and triggers the onChange= event handler.

dh2.htm

For the second data entry screen (shown in Figure 20-3), five fields invite the user to enter descriptions of the alternatives under consideration. As with the decision name screen, the scripting for this page must both retrieve and save data in the fields.

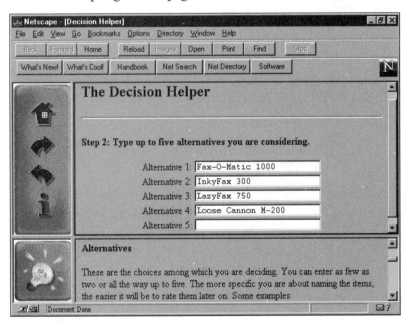

Figure 20-3: The second data entry screen.

```
<HTML>
<HEAD>
<TITLE>DH2</TITLE>
<SCRIPT LANGUAGE="JavaScript">
<!-- start
function loadAlternatives() {
    for (var i = 0; i < 5; i++) {
        var result = parent.getAlternative(i)
        result = (result == null) ? "" : result
        document.forms[0].alternative[i].value = result
    }
}
// end -->
</SCRIPT>
</HEAD>
```

In one function, the script retrieves the alternative cookies (there are a total of five) and stuffs them into their respective text fields (as long as their values are not null). This function script uses a `for` loop to cycle through all five items — something that many scripts yet to come in this application frequently do. Whenever a cookie is one of a set of five, the parent function has been written (above) to store or extract a single cookie, based on the index value. Text objects holding like data (defined below) are all assigned the same name, so that JavaScript lets us treat them as array objects — greatly simplifying the placement of values into those fields inside a `for` loop.

```
<BODY onLoad=
"loadAlternatives();document.forms[0].alternative[0].focus()">
<H2>The Decision Helper</H2>
<HR>
<H4>Step 2: Type up to five alternatives you are considering.</H4>
<P><P>
```

Once the document loads, its fields are filled by the function defined in the Head, and the first field is handed the focus to assist the user in entering data the first time.

```
<CENTER>
<FORM>
Alternative 1:
<INPUT TYPE="text" NAME="alternative" SIZE="25"
onChange="parent.setAlternative(0,this.value)"><BR>
Alternative 2:
```

```
<INPUT TYPE="text" NAME="alternative" SIZE="25"
onChange="parent.setAlternative(1,this.value)"><BR>
Alternative 3:
<INPUT TYPE="text" NAME="alternative" SIZE="25"
onChange="parent.setAlternative(2,this.value)"><BR>
Alternative 4:
<INPUT TYPE="text" NAME="alternative" SIZE="25"
onChange="parent.setAlternative(3,this.value)"><BR>
Alternative 5:
<INPUT TYPE="text" NAME="alternative" SIZE="25"
onChange="parent.setAlternative(4,this.value)"><BR>
</BODY>
</HTML>
```

Any change a user makes to a field is stored in the corresponding cookie. Each onChange= event handler passes its indexed value (relative to all like-named fields) plus the value entered by the user as parameters to the parent's cookie-saving function.

dh3.htm

With the third screen, the complexity increases a bit. Two factors contribute to this. One is that the limitation on the number of cookies available for a single URL pathname forces us to join together data into one cookie that might normally be distributed among five cookies. Second, with the number of text objects on the page (see Figure 20-4), it becomes more efficient (from the standpoint of tedious HTML writing) to let JavaScript deploy the fields. The fact that two sets of five related fields exist facilitates using for loops to lay out and populate them.

```
<HTML>
<HEAD>
<TITLE>DH3</TITLE>
<SCRIPT LANGUAGE="JavaScript">
<!-- start
function getFactor(i) {
    var result = parent.getFactor(i)
    if (result == null) {
        return ""
    }
    return result
}
```

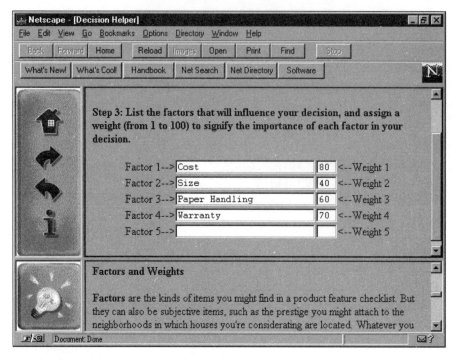

Figure 20-4: Screen for entering decision factors and their weights.

One initial function here is reminiscent of Head functions in previous entry screens. This one retrieves a single factor cookie from the set of five cookies.

```
function setImportance() {
    var oneRecord = ""
    for (var i = 0; i < 5; i++) {
        var dataPoint = document.forms[0].importance[i].value
        if (!parent.isValid(dataPoint)) {
            document.forms[0].importance[i].focus()
            document.forms[0].importance[i].select()
            return 0
        }
        oneRecord += dataPoint + "."
    }
    parent.setImportance(oneRecord)
    return 0
}
```

Values for the five possible weight entries are stored together in a single cookie. To make this work, I had to determine a data structure for the five "fields" of a single cookie "record." Because all entries are integers, I could choose any nonnumeric character other than the semicolon (which the browser uses as a delimiter between cookie entries). I arbitrarily selected the period.

The purpose of the setImportance() function is to assemble all five values from the five Weight entry fields (named "importance") into a period-delimited record that is ultimately sent to the cookie for safekeeping. Another of the many for loops in this application cycles through each of the fields, checking for validity and then appending the value with its trailing period to the variable (oneRecord) that holds the accumulated data. Once the loop finishes, the entire record is sent to the parent function for storage.

Although the function shows two return statements, the calling statement does not truly expect any values to be returned. Instead, I use the return statement inside the for loop as a way to break out of the for loop without any further execution whenever an invalid entry is found. Just prior to that, the script sets the focus and select to the field containing the invalid entry. JavaScript, however, is sensitive to the fact that a function with a return statement in one possible outcome doesn't have a return statement for other outcomes (an error message to this effect appears if you try the function without balanced returns). By putting a return statement at the end of the function, all other possibilities are covered to JavaScript's satisfaction.

```
function getImportance() {
    var oneRecord = parent.getImportance()
    if (oneRecord != null) {
        for (var i = 0; i < 5; i++) {
            var recLen = oneRecord.length
            var offset = oneRecord.indexOf(".")
            var dataPoint = (offset >= 0 ) ?
oneRecord.substring(0,offset) : ""
            document.forms[0].importance[i].value = dataPoint
            oneRecord = oneRecord.substring(offset+1,recLen)
        }
    }
}


// end -->
</SCRIPT>
</HEAD>
```

The inverse of storing the weight entries is retrieving them. Because the `parent.getImportance()` function returns the entire period-delimited record, this function must break apart the pieces and distribute them into their corresponding Weight fields. A combination of string methods determines the offset of the period and how far the data extraction should go into the complete record. Before the `for` loop repeats each time, it is shortened by one "field's" data. In other words, as the `for` loop executes, the copy of the cookie data returned to this function is pared down one entry at a time as each entry is stuffed into its text object for display.

```
<BODY onLoad="document.forms[0].factor[0].focus()">
<H2>The Decision Helper</H2>
<HR>
<H4>Step 3: List the factors that will influence your decision,
and assign a weight (from 1 to 100) to signify the importance of
each factor in your decision.</H4>
<P>
```

Upon loading the document, the only task necessary for the `onLoad=` event handler is to set the focus to the first entry field of the form.

```
<SCRIPT LANGUAGE="JavaScript">
<!-- start
var output = "<CENTER><FORM>"
for (i = 0; i < 5; i++) {
    output += "Factor " + (i+1) + "--><INPUT TYPE='text'
NAME='factor' SIZE='25' "
    var eHandler = " onChange=\'parent.setFactor(" + i +
",this.value)\'"
    output += eHandler + "VALUE=" + getFactor(i) + ">"

    output += "<INPUT TYPE='text' NAME='importance' SIZE='3' "
    eHandler = " onChange=\'setImportance()\'"
    output += eHandler + "VALUE=''>"

    output += "<--Weight " + (i+1) + "<BR>"
    document.write(output)
    output = ""
}
document.write("</FORM></CENTER>")
getImportance()
// end -->
```

```
</SCRIPT>
</BODY>
</HTML>
```

We script the contents of the form and its ten data entry fields in only a few lines of JavaScript code. Performed inside a `for` loop, the script assembles each line of the form, which consists of a label for the Factor (and its number), the factor input field, the importance input field, and the label for the Weight (and its number). Each line is written to the document with a `document.write()` method.

Each of the scripted text objects has an event handler. Notice that each event handler is first defined as a variable on a statement line just above its insertion into the string being assembled for the INPUT object definition. One reason for this is that the nested quote situation gets quite complex when you are doing this all in one massive assignment statement. Rather than mess with matching several pairs of deeply nested quotes, I found it easier to break out one portion (the event handler definition) as a variable value and then insert that preformatted expression into the concatenated string for the INPUT definition.

Notice how the different ways of storing the data in the cookies influences the ways existing cookie data is filled into the fields as the page draws itself. For the factors, which have one cookie per factor, the `VALUE=` attribute of the field is set with a specific indexed call to the parent factor cookie retriever one at a time. But for the importance values, which are stored together in the period-delimited chunk, a separate function call (`getImportance()`) executes after the fields are already drawn (with initial values of empty strings) and fills them all in a batch operation.

dh4.htm

Step 4 of the decision process (shown in Figure 20-5) is the most complex because of the sheer number of entry fields: 25 in all. Notice that this screen retrieves data from two of the previous screens and embeds the entries into the fixed parts of the table. It's all possible when you create those tables with JavaScript.

```
function setPerformance() {
    for (var i = 0; i < 5; i++) {
        var oneRecord = ""
        for (var j = 0; j < 5; j++) {
            var cellNum = j + (i * 5)
            var dataPoint =
document.forms[0].ranking[cellNum].value
```

(continued)

```
        if (!parent.isValid(dataPoint)) {
            document.forms[0].ranking[cellNum].focus()
            document.forms[0].ranking[cellNum].select()
            return 0
        }
        oneRecord += dataPoint + "."
    }
    parent.setPerformance(i,oneRecord)
}
return 0
}
```

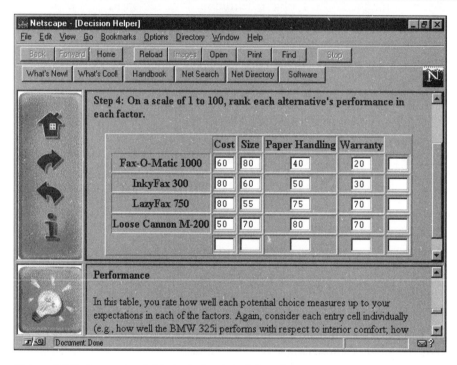

Figure 20-5: A massive table includes label data from earlier screen entries.

Functions for getting and setting performance data are complex because of the way I was forced to combine data into five "field" records. In other words, there is one parent cookie for each row of data cells in the table. To extract cell data for storage in the cookie, we use nested `for` loop constructions. The outer loop counts the rows of the table, while the inner loop (with the j counter variable) works its way across the columns for each row.

Because all cells are named identically, they are indexed with values from 0 to 24. Calculating the row (i * 5) plus the column number establishes the cell index value. After you check for validity, each cell's value is added to the row's accumulated data. Each row is then saved to its corresponding cookie. As in the code for dh3.htm, the return statement is used as a way to break out of the function if an entry is deemed invalid.

```
<HTML>
<HEAD>
<TITLE>DH4</TITLE>
<SCRIPT LANGUAGE="JavaScript">
<!-- start
function getPerformance() {
    var oneRecord = ""
    for (var i = 0; i < 5; i++) {
        oneRecord = parent.getPerformance(i)
        if (oneRecord == null) {
            continue
        }
        for (var j = 0; j < 5; j++) {
            var recLen = oneRecord.length
            var offset = oneRecord.indexOf(".")
            var dataPoint = oneRecord.substring(0,offset)
            var cellNum = j + (i * 5)
            document.forms[0].ranking[cellNum].value = dataPoint
            oneRecord = oneRecord.substring(offset+1,recLen)
        }
    }
}
// end -->
</SCRIPT>
</HEAD>
```

To retrieve the data and populate the cells for the entire table requires an examination of each of the five performance cookies, and for each cookie data, a parsing for each period-delimited entry. Once a given data point is in hand (one entry for a cell), it must go into the cell with the proper index.

```
<BODY onLoad="document.forms[0].ranking[0].focus()">
<H2>The Decision Helper</H2>
<HR>
<H4>Step 4: On a scale of 1 to 100, rank each alternative's
performance in each factor.</H4>
<P><P>
```

After the document is loaded, the onLoad= event handler brings focus to the first field of the table.

```
<SCRIPT LANGUAGE="JavaScript">
<!-- start
var output = "<CENTER><FORM NAME='perfRankings'><TABLE BORDER>"
output += "<TR><TD></TD><TD>"
for (i = 0; i < 5; i++) {
    var oneFactor = parent.getFactor(i)
    oneFactor = (oneFactor == null) ? "" : oneFactor
    output += "<TH>" + oneFactor + "</TH>"
}
output += "</TD>"
```

To lessen the repetitive HTML for all tables, we use JavaScript to assemble and write the data that defines the tables. In the first batch, the script uses yet another for loop to retrieve the factor entries from the parent cookie so that the words can be embedded into <TH> tags of the first row of the table. If every factor field is not filled in, the table cell is set to empty.

```
for (i = 0; i < 5; i++) {
    var oneAlt = parent.getAlternative(i)
    oneAlt = (oneAlt == null) ? "" : oneAlt
    output += "<TR><TD><TH>" + oneAlt + "</TH>"
    for (j = 0; j < 5; j++) {
        output += "<TD ALIGN=CENTER><INPUT TYPE='text' SIZE=3
NAME='ranking' VALUE='' onChange='setPerformance()'></TD>"
    }
    output += "</TR>"
    document.write(output)
    output = ""
}
document.write("</TABLE></FORM></CENTER>")
getPerformance()
// end -->
```

```
</SCRIPT>
</BODY>
</HTML>
```

Next comes the assembly of subsequent rows of the table. The first column displays the name of each alternative (within <TH> tags). The remaining columns are text objects, all with the same name and event handler. As each row of table definition is completed, it is written to the document. Once the table and form closing tags are also written, the `getPerformance()` function retrieves all cookie data for the fields and distributes it accordingly.

dh5.htm

From a math standpoint, dh5.htm's JavaScript gets pretty complicated. But because the complexity is attributed to the decision support calculations that turn the user's entries into results, I treat the calculation script shown here as a black box. You are free to examine the details, if you are so inclined.

Results appear in the form of a table (see Figure 20-6) with columns showing the numeric results and an optional graphical chart.

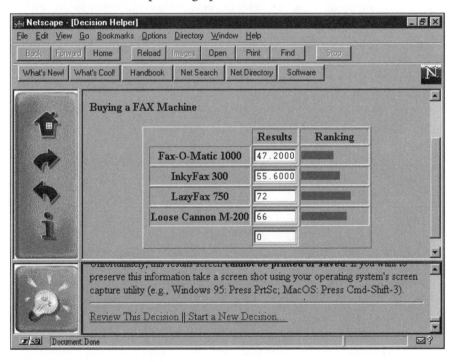

Figure 20-6: The results screen for a decision.

```
<HTML>
<HEAD>
<TITLE>DH5</TITLE>
<SCRIPT LANGUAGE="JavaScript">
<!-- start
function makeArray(n) {
    return this
}
var itemTotal = new makeArray()

function calculate() {
    var scratchpad = ""
    var importanceSum = 0
    var oneRecord = parent.getImportance()
    var weight = new makeArray(5)
    for (i = 0; i < 5; i++) {
        var recLen = oneRecord.length
        var offset = oneRecord.indexOf(".")
        scratchpad = oneRecord.substring(0,offset)
        importanceSum += (scratchpad == "" || scratchpad ==
"NAN(000)") ? 0 : parseInt(scratchpad)
        oneRecord = oneRecord.substring(offset+1,recLen)
    }
    oneRecord = parent.getImportance()
    for (i = 0; i < 5; i++) {
        recLen = oneRecord.length
        offset = oneRecord.indexOf(".")
        scratchpad = oneRecord.substring(0,offset)
        weight[i] = (scratchpad == "" || scratchpad == "NAN(000)")
? 0 : parseInt(scratchpad)/importanceSum * 100
        oneRecord = oneRecord.substring(offset+1,recLen)
    }
    for (i = 0; i < 5; i++) {
        oneRecord = parent.getPerformance(i)
        if (oneRecord == null) {
            continue
        }
        scratchpad = 0
        for (var j = 0; j < 5; j++) {
            var recLen = oneRecord.length
```

```
            var offset = oneRecord.indexOf(".")
            var dataPoint = oneRecord.substring(0,offset)
            scratchpad += (dataPoint != "" || dataPoint ==
"NAN(000)") ? parseInt(dataPoint) * weight[j] / 100 : 0
            oneRecord = oneRecord.substring(offset+1,recLen)
        }
        itemTotal[i] = scratchpad
    }
}
calculate()
// end -->
</SCRIPT>
</HEAD>
```

For our purposes, you only need to know a couple of things about the `calculate()` function. First, it calls all the numeric data stored in parent cookies to fulfill values in its formulas. Second, results are tabulated and placed into a five-entry indexed array called `itemTotal[i]`. This array is defined as a global variable, so its contents are available to scripts coming up in the Body portion of the document.

Constructing this function served up many reminders about keeping data types straight. Because the data stored in cookies was in the form of strings, when it came time to do some real math with those values, careful placement of the `parseInt()` function was essential to getting the math operators to work.

```
<BODY>
<H2>The Decision Helper</H2>
<HR>
<SCRIPT LANGUAGE="JavaScript">
<!-- start
document.write("<H4>" + parent.getDecisionName() + "</H4><P><P>")
var output = "<CENTER><FORM NAME='Results'><TABLE BORDER>"
output += "<TR><TD></TD><TD><TH>Results</TH><TH>Ranking</TH>"
output += "</TD>"
```

Because there is no user input in this screen, it is not necessary to set the focus with an `onLoad=` event handler here. But the results display relies heavily on stored and calculated values, so the table is constructed entirely out of JavaScript. That also means it can redisplay the decision name as part of the page.

```
for (var i = 0; i < 5; i++) {
    var oneAlt = parent.getAlternative(i)
    oneAlt = (oneAlt == null || oneAlt == "") ? "" : oneAlt
    itemTotal[i] = (oneAlt == "") ? 0 : itemTotal[i]
    output += "<TR><TD><TH>" + oneAlt + "</TH>"
    output += "<TD ALIGN=CENTER><INPUT TYPE='text' SIZE=7
NAME='ranking' VALUE=" + itemTotal[i] + "></TD>"
```

I need to break up the discussion of the for loop that produces the results because there are two distinct parts of this HTML assembly. The first, shown in the preceding example, assembles the first two cells of each row of the table. The first cell contains an embedded listing of the alternative name (in <TH> tags). To highlight the calculated values—and let the SIZE= attribute do the artificial job of truncating the floating-point number—the results are shown in text objects. For each row, the corresponding result in itemTotal[i] is inserted as the VALUE= attribute of the text object. The SIZE= attribute is set to 7, which allows the typical double-digit results, a decimal point, and four digits to the right of the decimal (an extra pixel shows on the Macintosh version, however).

```
    output += "<TD WIDTH=100>"
    chartWidth = Math.round(itemTotal[i])
    if (chartWidth > 0) {
        output += "<IMG SRC='chart.gif' HEIGHT=12 WIDTH=" +
chartWidth + ">"
    }
    output += "</TD></TR>"
    document.write(output)
    output = ""
}
document.write("</TABLE></FORM></CENTER>")
// end -->
</SCRIPT>
</BODY>
</HTML>
```

For extra pizzazz, a third column "draws" a bar chart within a 100-pixel wide cell. The bars are actually scalings of a one-pixel-wide .gif file (an orange line, 12 pixels tall). A single-color .gif image scales to fill whatever width is assigned in the WIDTH attribute. This is fast and far better than a more tedious method (tedious from the Web page author's point of view) of creating one hundred different .gif files, one for each possible width of the bar. I also could have used a one-pixel square .gif file, but the one-by-twelve pixel art was easier to work with in a graphics program.

dhHelp.htm

The only other code worth noting in this application is in the dhHelp.htm document, which appears in the lower right frame of the window. At the end of this document are two links that call separate JavaScript functions in this document's Head section. The Head functions are

```
<HEAD>
<TITLE>Decision Helper Help</TITLE>
<SCRIPT LANGUAGE="JavaScript">
<!--
function goFirst() {
    parent.entryForms.location = "dh1.htm"
    self.location.hash = "help1"
}
function restart() {
    if (confirm("Erase current decision and start a new one?")) {
        parent.initializeCookies()
        parent.entryForms.location = "dh1.htm"
        self.location.hash = "help1"
    }
}

// -->
</SCRIPT>
</HEAD>
```

One function merely returns the user to the beginning of the sequences for both the entry screens and the help screen. The second is a rare instance in which a confirm dialog box makes sense: It is about to erase all entered data. If the user says it's okay to go ahead, the parent window's function for initializing all cookies is called, and the navigation for both the entry and help screens goes back to the beginning.

```
<A HREF="javascript:goFirst()" onMouseOver="window.status='Go back
to beginning to review data...';return true"">Review This Decision
</A>||<A HREF="javascript:restart()"
onMouseOver="window.status='Erase current data and start
over...';return true"> Start a New Decision... </A>
```

The links at the bottom of the document (see Figure 20-6) are coded to trigger JavaScript functions (rather than navigate to URLs) and include `onMouseOver=` event handlers to provide more information about the link in the status bar.

Further Thoughts

If you've managed to follow through with this application's discussions, you'll agree that it is quite a JavaScript workout. But it proves that without a ton of code, even the first implementation of JavaScript in Navigator 2.0 provides enough functionality to add a great deal of interactivity and pseudo-intelligence to an otherwise flat HTML document.

As an alternate to cookies for data storage, I have also implemented a version that uses text objects defined in a frame defined with a 0 row height. This way further challenges synchronizing frames during reloading when a user resizes the browser window or navigates with the Back or Forward browser buttons.

I hope that the instruction in the earlier chapters and the sample applications in these recent chapters inspire you to create inventive applications of your own. JavaScript has the potential to add fun and value to the information and knowledge you share with the world or your colleagues via the World Wide Web. Take advantage of this outstanding opportunity.

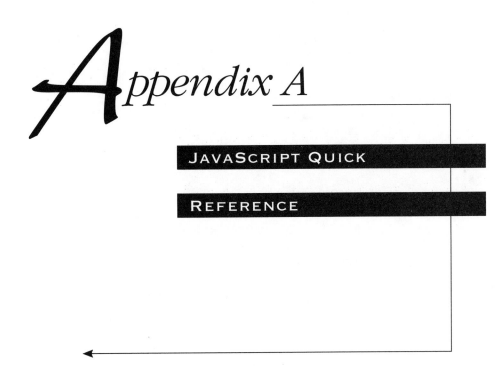

Appendix A

JavaScript Quick Reference

Window and Frame Objects

Creating

```
windowObject = window.open([parameters])

<BODY
    ...
    [onLoad="handlerTextOrFunction"]
    [onUnload="handlerTextOrFunction"]>
</BODY>
```

```
<FRAMESET>
    ROWS="ValueList"
    COLS="ValueList"
        onLoad="handlerTextOrFunction"]
        onUnload="handlerTextOrFunction"]>
    <FRAME SRC="locationOrURL" NAME="firstFrameName">
    ...
    <FRAME SRC="locationOrURL" NAME="lastFrameName">
</FRAMESET>
```

Properties

status	(string)
defaultStatus	(string)
frames	(array)
parent	(window object)
self	(window object)
top	(window object)
window	(window object)

Methods

alert(*message*)

confirm(*message*)

prompt(*message*, *defaultReply*)

open("*URL*", "*windowName*" [, "*windowFeatures*"])

close()

setTimeout("*expression*", *millisecondsDelay*)

clearTimeout(*timeoutIDnumber*)

Event Handlers

```
onLoad=

onUnload=
```

Location Object

Properties

href	(string)
hash	(string)
host	(string)
hostname	(string)
pathname	(string)
port	(string)
protocol	(string)
search	(string)

History Object

Property

length	(integer)

Methods

```
back()

forward()

go(relativeNumber | "URLOrTitleSubstring")
```

Document Object

Creating

```
<BODY
    [BACKGROUND="backgroundImageURL"]
    [BGCOLOR="#backgroundColor"]
    [TEXT="#foregroundColor"]
    [LINK="#unfollowedLinkColor"]
    [ALINK="#activatedLinkColor"]
    [VLINK="#followedLinkColor"]
    [onLoad="handlerTextOrFunction"]
    [onUnload="handlerTextOrFunction"]>
</BODY>
```

Properties

forms	(array)
location	(string)
title	(string)
alinkColor	(hexadecimal triplet or constant)
vlinkColor	(hexadecimal triplet or constant)
bgColor	(hexadecimal triplet or constant)
fgColor	(hexadecimal triplet or constant)
linkColor	(hexadecimal triplet or constant)
lastModified	(date string)
anchors	(array)
links	(array)
referrer	(string)
cookie	(string)

Methods

```
write("string")

writeln("string")

open(["mimeType"])

close()

clear()
```

Form Object

Creating

```
<FORM
    NAME="formName"
    [TARGET="windowName"]
    [ACTION="serverURL"]
    [METHOD=GET | POST]
    [ENCTYPE="MIMEType"]
    [onSubmit="handlerTextOrFunction"] >
</FORM>
```

Properties

elements	(array)
action	(URL)
method	(GET or POST)
target	(window name)
encoding	(MIME type)

Method

```
submit()
```

Event Handler

```
onSubmit=
```

Text, Textarea, and Password Objects

Creating

```
<FORM>
<INPUT
   TYPE="text"
   NAME="fieldName"
   [VALUE="contents"]
   [SIZE="characterCount"]
   [onBlur="handlerTextOrFunction"]
   [onChange="handlerTextOrFunction"]
   [onFocus="handlerTextOrFunction"]
   [onSelect="handlerTextOrFunction"]>
</FORM>

<FORM>
<TEXTAREA
   NAME="fieldName"
   ROWS="rowCount"
   COLS="columnCount"
   [onBlur="handlerTextOrFunction"]
   [onChange="handlerTextOrFunction"]
   [onFocus="handlerTextOrFunction"]
   [onSelect="handlerTextOrFunction"]>
   defaultText
</TEXTAREA>
</FORM>

<FORM>
<INPUT
   TYPE="password"
   NAME="fieldName"
   [VALUE="contents"]
   [SIZE="characterCount"]>
</FORM>
```

Properties

value	(string)
name	(string)
defaultValue	(string)

Methods

```
select()

focus()

blur()
```

Event Handlers

```
onChange=

onFocus=

onBlur=

onSelect=
```

Hidden Object

Creating

```
<FORM>
<INPUT
    TYPE="hidden"
    NAME="fieldName"
    [VALUE="contents"]>
</FORM>
```

Properties

value   (string)

name   (string)

defaultValue   (string)

Button, Submit, and Reset Objects

Creating

```
<FORM>
<INPUT
   TYPE="button" | "submit" | "reset"
   NAME="buttonName"
   VALUE="contents"
   [onClick="handlerTextOrFunction"] >
</FORM>
```

Properties

value   (string)

name   (string)

Method

click()

Event Handler

onClick=

Checkbox Object

Creating

```
<FORM>
<INPUT
    TYPE="checkbox"
    NAME="boxName"
    VALUE="buttonValue"
    [CHECKED]
    [onClick="handlerTextOrFunction"]>
    buttonText
</FORM>
```

Properties

checked   (Boolean)

name   (string)

value   (string)

defaultChecked   (Boolean)

Method

```
click()
```

Event Handler

```
onClick=
```

Radio Object

Creating

```
<FORM>
<INPUT
    TYPE="radio"
    NAME="buttonGroupName"
    VALUE="buttonValue"
    [CHECKED]
    [onClick="handlerTextOrFunction"]>
    buttonText
</FORM>
```

Properties

checked	(Boolean)
name	(string)
length	(integer)
value	(string)
defaultChecked	(Boolean)

Method

```
click()
```

Event Handler

```
onClick=
```

Select Object

Syntax

```
<FORM>
<SELECT
   NAME="listName"
   [SIZE="number"]
   [MULTIPLE]
   [onBlur="handlerTextOrFunction"]
   [onChange="handlerTextOrFunction"]
   [onFocus="handlerTextOrFunction"]>
   <OPTION [SELECTED] [VALUE="string"]>listItem
   [...<OPTION [VALUE="string"]>listItem]
</SELECT>
</FORM>
```

Properties

options[index]	(array)
selectedIndex	(integer)
options[index].text	(string)
options[index].value	(string)
options[index].selected	(Boolean)
length	(integer)
name	(string)
options[index].index	(integer)
options[index].defaultSelected	(Boolean)

Event Handler

```
onChange=
```

Link Object

Creating

```
<A HREF="locationOrURL"
    [NAME="anchorName"]
    [TARGET="windowName"]
    [onClick="handlerTextOrFunction"]
    [onMouseOver="handlerTextOrFunction"]>
    linkDisplayTextOrImage
</A>
```

Properties

```
links[index].target        (window name)

length                      (integer)
```

Event Handlers

```
onMouseOver=

onClick=
```

Anchor Object

Creating

```
<A NAME="anchorName">
    anchorDisplayTextOrImage
</A>
```

Navigator Object

Properties

appName	(string)
appVersion	(string)
appCodeName	(string)
userAgent	(string)

String Object

Property

length	(integer)

Methods

string.toLowerCase()

string.toUpperCase()

string.indexOf(*searchString* [, *startIndex*])

string.lastIndexOf(*searchString* [, *startIndex*])

string.charAt(*index*)

string.substring(*indexA*, *indexB*)

string.anchor("*anchorName*")

string.big()

string.blink()

string.bold()

string.fixed()

string.fontcolor(*colorValue*)

sting.fontsize(*integer1to7*)

string.italics()

string.link(*locationOrURL*)

string.small()

string.strike()

string.sub()

string.sup()

Math Object

Properties

Math.E

Math.LN2

Math.LN10

Math.LOG2E

Math.LOG10E

Math.PI

Math.SQRT1_2

Math.SQRT2

Methods

Math.abs(*val*)

Math.acos(*val*)

Math.asin(*val*)

Math.atan(*val*)

Math.ceil(*val*)

Math.cos(*val*)

Math.exp(*val*)

Math.floor(*val*)

Math.log(*val*)

Math.max(*val1*, *val2*)

Math.min(*val1*, *val2*)

Math.pow(*val1*, *val2*)

Math.random()

Math.round(*val*)

Math.sin(*val*)

Math.sqrt(*val*)

Math.tan(*val*)

Date Object

Methods

ateObj.getTime()	(0-...)
dateObj.getYear()	(70-...)
dateObj.getMonth()	(0-11)
dateObj.getDate()	(1-31)
dateObj.getDay()	(0-6)
dateObj.getHours()	(0-23)
dateObj.getMinutes()	(0-59)
dateObj.getSeconds()	(0-59)
dateObj.setTime(val)	(0-...)
dateObj.setYear(val)	(70-...)
dateObj.setMonth(val)	(0-11)
dateObj.setDate(val)	(1-31)
dateObj.setDay(val)	(0-6)
dateObj.setHours(val)	(0-23)
dateObj.setMinutes(val)	(0-59)
dateObj.setSeconds(val)	(0-59)
dateObj.getTimezoneOffset()	(0-...)
dateObj.toGMTString()	(string)
dateObj.toLocaleString()	(string)

```
Date.parse("dateString")

Date.UTC(date values)
```

Control Structures

```
if (condition) {
    statementsIfTrue
}

if (condition) {
    statementsIfTrue
} else {
    statementsIfFalse
}

variable = (condition) ? val1 : val2

for ( [initial expression]; [condition]; [update expression]) {
    statements
}

while (condition) {
    statements
}

for (var in object) {
    statements
}

with (object) {
    statements
}
```

Operators

Comparison

==	Equals
!=	Does not equal

>	Is greater than
>=	Is greater than or equal to
<	Is less than
<=	Is less than or equal to

Connubial

+	Plus
-	Minus
*	Multiply
/	Divide
%	Modulo
++	Increment
- -	Decrement
-val	Negation

Assignment

=	Equals
+=	Add by value
-=	Subtract by value
*=	Multiply by value
/=	Divide by value
%=	Modulo by value
<<=	Left shift by value
>>=	Right shift by value

>>>=	Zero fill by value
&=	Bitwise AND by value
^=	Bitwise OR by value
|=	Bitwise XOR by value

Boolean

&&	And
||	Or
!	Not

Bitwise

&	Bitwise And
|	Bitwise Or
^	Bitwise XOR
<<	Left Shift
>>	Right Shift
>>>	Zero Fill Right Shift

Functions

```
function functionName( [parameter1] … [, parameterN]) {
    statements
}
```

JavaScript Object Road Map

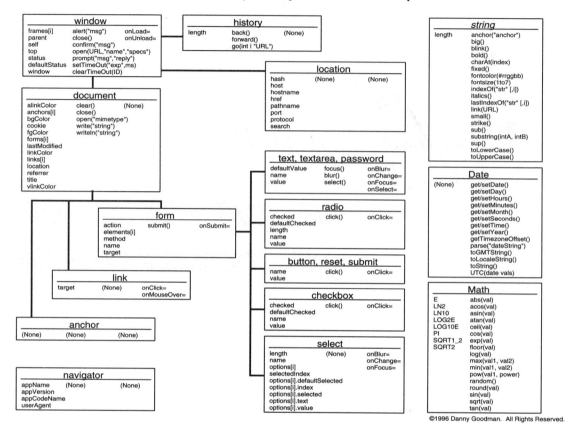

window

frames[i]	alert("msg")	onLoad=
parent	close()	onUnload=
self	confirm("msg")	
top	open(URL,"name","specs")	
status	prompt("msg","reply")	
defaultStatus	setTimeOut("exp",ms)	
window	clearTimeOut(ID)	

history

length	back()	(None)
	forward()	
	go(int l "URL")	

document

alinkColor	clear()	(None)
anchors[i]	close()	
bgColor	open("mimetype")	
cookie	write("string")	
fgColor	writeln("string")	
forms[i]		
lastModified		
linkColor		
links[i]		
location		
referrer		
title		
vlinkColor		

location

hash	(None)	(None)
host		
hostname		
href		
pathname		
port		
protocol		
search		

form

action	submit()	onSubmit=
elements[i]		
method		
name		
target		

link

target	(None)	onClick=
		onMouseOver=

anchor

(None)	(None)	(None)

navigator

appName	(None)	(None)
appVersion		
appCodeName		
userAgent		

text, textarea, password

defaultValue	focus()	onBlur=
name	blur()	onChange=
value	select()	onFocus=
		onSelect=

radio

checked	click()	onClick=
defaultChecked		
length		
name		
value		

button, reset, submit

name	click()	onClick=
value		

checkbox

checked	click()	onClick=
defaultChecked		
name		
value		

select

length	(None)	onBlur=
name		onChange=
options[i]		onFocus=
selectedIndex		
options[i].defaultSelected		
options[i].index		
options[i].selected		
options[i].text		
options[i].value		

string

length	anchor("anchor")
	big()
	blink()
	bold()
	charAt(index)
	fixed()
	fontcolor(#rrggbb)
	fontsize(1to7)
	indexOf("str" [,i])
	italics()
	lastIndexOf("str" [,i])
	link(URL)
	small()
	strike()
	sub()
	substring(intA, intB)
	sup()
	toLowerCase()
	toUpperCase()

Date

(None)	get/setDate()
	get/setDay()
	get/setHours()
	get/setMinutes()
	get/setMonth()
	get/setSeconds()
	get/setTime()
	get/setYear()
	getTimezoneOffset()
	parse("dateString")
	toGMTString()
	toLocaleString()
	toString()
	UTC(date vals)

Math

E	abs(val)
LN2	acos(val)
LN10	asin(val)
LOG2E	atan(val)
LOG10E	ceil(val)
PI	cos(val)
SQRT1_2	exp(val)
SQRT2	floor(val)
	log(val)
	max(val1, val2)
	min(val1, val2)
	pow(val1, power)
	random()
	round(val)
	sin(val)
	sqrt(val)
	tan(val)

©1996 Danny Goodman. All Rights Reserved.

$\mathcal{A}$ppendix B

JAVASCRIPT RESOURCES

ON THE INTERNET

Being an on-line technology, JavaScript has plenty of support on-line for scripters. Items recommended here were taken as a snapshot of the Net's offering in early 1996. Sites change. URLs change. Be prepared to hunt around for these items if the information provided here is out of date by the time you read this.

Newsgroups

There is a semi-secure newsgroup at Netscape for developers. I hesitate to list its URL because individuals not participating in Netscape's developer program may lose access to it at any instant. Another newsgroup, however, is open to the public. Use your news reader to access comp.lang.javascript. You can expect to get quick answers from a wide audience of experienced scripters here.

Listserv

A public JavaScript-oriented listserv is also available. To subscribe to it, send an e-mail message to

```
majordomo@obscure.org
```

In the body of the message, enter

```
subscribe javascript <your full name>
```

This listserv has a lot of traffic on it every day. You may prefer to start receiving the list as a digest. To subscribe that way, address the subscription request the same, but in the message body, enter the following:

```
subscribe javascript-digest <your full name>
```

Later you can change to individual messages, if you like.

World Wide Web

Web sources for JavaScript information are growing rapidly. Check Netscape's site (<http://home.netscape.com>) for the latest information about new releases and beta version documentation. You will also find a number of JavaScript pointers there.

The applications in Chapters 17 through 20 of this book are available on-line at my Web site (<http://www.dannyg.com>) and the IDG Books Web site (<http://idgbooks.com>). As I learn about new and interesting clearinghouses for JavaScript information on the Web, I will put pointers to them in my JavaScript pages. If you are experiencing difficulty with any of the scripts or discussions in this book, use the mail link on my site to ask me. But for general scripting questions, you will get a much faster response (sometimes from me) by going to the newsgroup or listserv.

*A*ppendix C

The accompanying cross-platform CD-ROM contains more than 130 HTML documents and explanations from the book, as well as free Web graphics, utilities, Netscape Navigator plug-ins, and save-disabled "tryout" versions of Web-related applications.

Files on this CD-ROM use both Windows and Macintosh environments. The CD-ROM does not have an installation program; instead, you access its contents by using your system's software. With Windows 95, access the software with My Computer or Windows Explorer; with Windows 3.x, use the File Manager. Mac users can access files using the Finder.

To run the JavaScripts on this CD-ROM, you simply need a JavaScript-enabled browser (such as Netscape Navigator). JavaScripts can be written with a simple text editor, word processor, or dedicated HTML editor.

Recommended System Requirements

The other CD-ROM software — including the clip media backgrounds, buttons, and textures, as well as the software demos — require a fairly robust system, depending upon which files you want to use.

For Windows 3.1, Windows 95 or Windows NT, you need a 486 or Pentium computer with 16MB of RAM, 20MB of hard disk space, at least a 640×480 256-color display, a Sound Blaster-compatible sound card, and a double-speed CD-ROM drive.

Macintosh users require System 7.0 or later; at least 8MB of RAM; a 68030, 68040, or PowerPC processor; and at least a 640×480, 256-color display.

Of course, you'll need a CD-ROM drive and plenty of hard disk space for either platform. Check the Readme files associated with the individual software for additional information.

Disc Contents

On this disc are the following:

JavaScript Listings for Macintosh and Windows text editors

These are complete HTML documents that serve as examples of most of the JavaScript vocabulary words in Part II of the book. The Macintosh and Windows Listings folders have many nested folders for specific chapters' listings. These files can be run with Netscape Navigator 2.0 or any other JavaScript-savvy browser.

Online JavaScript reference for Macintosh (Apple Guide format)

To install this help file, copy it (or an alias to it) to the same folder as the text editor(s) you use for writing JavaScript. If your text editor is open, close it, relaunch, and then choose `Danny Goodman's JavaScript Quick Reference` from the Help menu.

Online JavaScript reference for Windows (WinHelp format)

To install this help file, copy it to your hard disk. Run the help file by double-clicking on it in File Manager or Explorer.

JavaScript Object Road Map from Appendix A (Adobe Acrobat format)

If you like the road map illustration at the end of Appendix A, you can print it on a single sheet of paper with the help of the Adobe Acrobat Reader. You can access Adobe Acrobat Reader in GOODIES:ARTWORK:WEBTOOLS:MANUAL:folder. The file JSObjcts.pdf contains this illustration in PDF format. Before printing it, be sure to choose landscape orientation in the Page Setup dialog box of Acrobat Reader.

Macromedia Shockwave Plug-In for Netscape Navigator 2.0

Shockwave Plug-In is a plug-in for Netscape Navigator 2.0 which plays back Macromedia Director movies on the Word Wide Web. Install this player under Windows 95 by copying n32d40.exe to your Netscape plug-ins directory and then launching it. For Windows 3.1, use n16d40.exe.

.VoxWare ToolVox for the Web plug-in for Netscape Navigator 2.0 (Windows only)

This plug-in allows Web pages to stream audio and deliver up to 53:1 compression ratios. Install this player under Windows 95 by running wp32b029.exe. For Windows 3.1, run wp16b029.exe.

LiveUpdate Crescendo plug-in for Netscape Navigator 2.0

With Crescendo and Navigator running on your Macintosh or MPC sound card-equipped PC, you can enjoy background music as you surf the Web. Install this player under Windows 95 by copying midi32.exe to your Netscape plug-ins directory and then launching it. For Windows 3.1, use midi.exe. For the Macintosh, move the Crescendo! plug-in icon to the Netscape Navigator folder.

WebTools 1.1 Tryout from Artbeats

WebTools contains more than 40MB of buttons, bars, icons, and patterns from Artbeats and stat™ media. Macintosh installation: Click on the Start icon or access individual folders from the Finder. Windows installation: Run wt_ful.exe from the WEBTOOLS directory or access the sampler files directly.

Backgrounds from Texture Farm

This package offers superb photographic-quality background images in Kodak Photo CD format. Access from Adobe Photoshop or other Photo CD-savvy graphics application and adjust resolution.

Macromedia Director tryout

This is the premiere tool for creating interactive content for multimedia and the Web. Director files can be processed with Maxcromedia's Afterburner for playback over the Web using the Shockwave plug-in, included with this package. Macintosh installation: Click on the Director icon and follow instructions. Windows installation: Run DIRECTOR from the DIRCT40:EVALCOPY directory.

Adobe Photoshop 3.0 tryout

This is a save-disabled version of Adobe Photoshop 3.0 for Macintosh and Windows. Macintosh installation: Click on the Install Adobe Photoshop icon in the Install-Part1 folder and follow the instructions. Windows installation: Run SETUP from the Disk 1 folder.

Photoshop special effects filters demo from XAOS Tools (Mac only)

This package includes TypeCaster 1.1, Paint Alchemy 2, and Terrazzo. To install, double-click on the installer icons.

Kai's Power Tools 3 tryout from MetaTools

Award-winning special-effects filters for Adobe Photoshop. This package save-disabled versions of Kai's Power Tools 3 for Macintosh and Windows. Macintosh installation: Click on the Install 1 icon and follow the instructions. Windows installation: Run SETUP from the KPT demo directory.

Convolver tryout from MetaTools

This is an award-winning special effects and texture generator for Adobe Photoshop. Macintosh installation: Click on the Demo Version icon and follow instructions. Windows installation: Run SETUP from the Convolver directory.

Debabelizer Lite LE (Macintosh only)

This "lite" version of the award-winning Macintosh graphics translator will read and write BMP, GIF, PICT, and TIFF (Mac & IBM) files. To run it, click on the Debabelizer Lite LE icon.

Debabelizer Toolbox demo (Macintosh only)

This is a full demo of the premiere Macintosh graphics translator, which reads and writes 64 graphics formats. To install it, double-click on the Debabelizer 1.6.5 DEMO icon.

Check the Readme files on the CD-ROM for updated, detailed contents information.

Index

(continued)

(continued)

(continued)

IDG BOOKS WORLDWIDE, INC. END-USER LICENSE AGREEMENT

<u>Read This</u>. **You should carefully read these terms and conditions before opening the software packet(s) included with this book ("Book"). This is a license agreement ("Agreement") between you and IDG Books Worldwide, Inc. ("IDGB"). By opening the accompanying software packet(s), you acknowledge that you have read and accept the following terms and conditions. If you do not agree and do not want to be bound by such terms and conditions, promptly return the Book and the unopened software packet(s) to the place you obtained them for a full refund.**

1. **License Grant.** IDGB grants to you (either an individual or entity) a nonexclusive license to use one copy of the enclosed software program(s) (collectively, the "Software") solely for your own personal or business purposes on a single computer (whether a standard computer or a workstation component of a multi-user network). The Software is in use on a computer when it is loaded into temporary memory (i.e., RAM) or installed into permanent memory (e.g., hard disk, CD-ROM or other storage device). IDGB reserves all rights not expressly granted herein.

2. **Ownership.** IDGB is the owner of all right, title and interest, including copyright, in and to the compilation of the Software recorded on the disk(s)/CD-ROM. Copyright to the individual programs on the disk(s)/CD-ROM is owned by the author or other authorized copyright owner of each program. Ownership of the Software and all proprietary rights relating thereto remain with IDGB and its licensors.

3. **Restrictions On Use and Transfer.**

   (a) You may only (i) make one copy of the Software for backup or archival purposes, or (ii) transfer the Software to a single hard disk, provided that you keep the original for backup or archival purposes. You may not (i) rent or lease the Software, (ii) copy or reproduce the Software through a LAN or other network system or through any computer subscriber system or bulletin-board system, or (iii) modify, adapt, or create derivative works based on the Software.

   (b) You may not reverse engineer, decompile, or disassemble the Software. You may transfer the Software and user documentation on a permanent basis, provided that the transferee agrees to accept the terms and conditions of this Agreement and you retain no copies. If the Software is an update or has been updated, any transfer must include the most recent update and all prior versions.

4. **Restrictions on Use of Individual Programs.** You must follow the individual requirements and restrictions detailed for each individual program in Appendix C of this Book. These limitations are contained in the individual license agreements recorded on the disk(s)/CD-ROM. These restrictions include a requirement that after using the program for the period of time specified in its text, the user must pay a registration fee or discontinue use. By opening the Software packet(s), you will be agreeing to abide by the licenses and restrictions for these individual programs. None of the material on this disk(s) or listed in this Book may ever be distributed, in original or modified form, for commercial purposes.

5. **Limited Warranty.**

   (a) IDGB warrants that the Software and disk(s)/CD-ROM are free from defects in materials and workmanship under normal use for a period of sixty (60) days from the date of purchase of this Book. If IDGB receives notification within the warranty period of defects in materials or workmanship, IDGB will replace the defective disk(s)/CD-ROM.

   (b) **IDGB AND THE AUTHOR OF THE BOOK DISCLAIM ALL OTHER WARRANTIES, EXPRESS OR IMPLIED, INCLUDING WITHOUT LIMITATION IMPLIED WARRANTIES OF MERCHANTABILITY AND FITNESS FOR A PARTICULAR PURPOSE, WITH RESPECT TO THE SOFTWARE, THE PROGRAMS, THE SOURCE CODE CONTAINED THEREIN, AND/OR THE TECHNIQUES DESCRIBED IN THIS BOOK. IDGB DOES NOT WARRANT THAT THE FUNCTIONS CONTAINED IN THE SOFTWARE WILL MEET YOUR REQUIREMENTS OR THAT THE OPERATION OF THE SOFTWARE WILL BE ERROR FREE.**

   (c) This limited warranty gives you specific legal rights, and you may have other rights which vary from jurisdiction to jurisdiction.

6. Remedies.

(a) IDGB's entire liability and your exclusive remedy for defects in materials and workmanship shall be limited to replacement of the Software, which is returned to IDGB at the address set forth below with a copy of your receipt. This Limited Warranty is void if failure of the Software has resulted from accident, abuse, or misapplication. Any replacement Software will be warranted for the remainder of the original warranty period or thirty (30) days, whichever is longer.

(b) In no event shall IDGB or the author be liable for any damages whatsoever (including without limitation damages for loss of business profits, business interruption, loss of business information, or any other pecuniary loss) arising out of the use of or inability to use the Book or the Software, even if IDGB has been advised of the possibility of such damages.

(c) Because some jurisdictions do not allow the exclusion or limitation of liability for consequential or incidental damages, the above limitation or exclusion may not apply to you.

7. U.S. Government Restricted Rights. Use, duplication, or disclosure of the Software by the U.S. Government is subject to restrictions stated in paragraph (c) (1) (ii) of the Rights in Technical Data and Computer Software clause of DFARS 252.227-7013, and in subparagraphs (a) through (d) of the Commercial Computer—Restricted Rights clause at FAR 52.227-19, and in similar clauses in the NASA FAR supplement, when applicable.

8. General. This Agreement constitutes the entire understanding of the parties, and revokes and supersedes all prior agreements, oral or written, between them and may not be modified or amended except in a writing signed by both parties hereto which specifically refers to this Agreement. This Agreement shall take precedence over any other documents that may be in conflict herewith. If any one or more provisions contained in this Agreement are held by any court or tribunal to be invalid, illegal or otherwise unenforceable, each and every other provision shall remain in full force and effect.

Additional Software Notices

ARTBEATS® WEBTOOLS

The *Artbeats WebTools demo* included in this product is provided for your enjoyment from Artbeats quality product lines. It is only a small sampling of the large volume of design elements available on CD-ROM. They are licensed for YOUR use only, so we ask that you do not copy them for others. They may not be distributed as "clip art" products or any other product for sale that derives its value from the accompanying images whether in digital or print form. Artbeats develops and distributes libraries of quality backgrounds and textures for publishing, multimedia, and texture mapping. Other products include: *Marble & Granite 2, Leather & Fabric, Wood & Paper, Marble & Granite 1, Marbled Paper Textures*, and more.

Artbeats
Box 709
Myrtle Creek, OR 97457
541-863-4429; Fax: 541-863-4547
e-mail: artbeats@pioneer-net.efn.org; web: http://www.imagine-net.com/artbeatswebtools

stat™ media is a recognized pioneer in multimedia development whose Instant Buttons & Controls was the first third-party utility for speeding and easing the development of interactive multimedia. Version 2.0 is the current industry standard.

stat™ media
7077 East Shorecrest Drive
Anaheim Hills, CA 92807-4056
714-280-0038; Fax 714-748-0178
e-mail: gbirch@statmedia.com; web: http://www.statmedia.com

The art accompanying this file is original and exclusive to Artbeats. All rights reserved. ©1991–1996 ARTBEATS; © 1995 stat™ media.

MACROMEDIA SHOCKWAVE USERS: To obtain Macromedia Afterburner and additional information and demos for Shockwave, visit the Macromedia Web site at http://www.macromedia.com.

IDG BOOKS WORLDWIDE REGISTRATION CARD

RETURN THIS REGISTRATION CARD FOR FREE CATALOG

Title of this book: **Danny Goodman's JavaScript® Handbook**

My overall rating of this book: ❏ Very good [1] ❏ Good [2] ❏ Satisfactory [3] ❏ Fair [4] ❏ Poor [5]

How I first heard about this book:

❏ Found in bookstore; name: [6]

❏ Advertisement: [8]

❏ Word of mouth; heard about book from friend, co-worker, etc.: [10]

❏ Book review: [7]

❏ Catalog: [9]

❏ Other: [11]

What I liked most about this book:

What I would change, add, delete, etc., in future editions of this book:

Other comments:

Number of computer books I purchase in a year: ❏ 1 [12] ❏ 2-5 [13] ❏ 6-10 [14] ❏ More than 10 [15]

I would characterize my computer skills as: ❏ Beginner [16] ❏ Intermediate [17] ❏ Advanced [18] ❏ Professional [19]

I use ❏ DOS [20] ❏ Windows [21] ❏ OS/2 [22] ❏ Unix [23] ❏ Macintosh [24] ❏ Other: [25] _____
(please specify)

I would be interested in new books on the following subjects:
(please check all that apply, and use the spaces provided to identify specific software)

❏ Word processing: [26]

❏ Data bases: [28]

❏ File Utilities: [30]

❏ Networking: [32]

❏ Other: [34]

❏ Spreadsheets: [27]

❏ Desktop publishing: [29]

❏ Money management: [31]

❏ Programming languages: [33]

I use a PC at (please check all that apply): ❏ home [35] ❏ work [36] ❏ school [37] ❏ other: [38] _____

The disks I prefer to use are ❏ 5.25 [39] ❏ 3.5 [40] ❏ other: [41] _____

I have a CD ROM: ❏ yes [42] ❏ no [43]

I plan to buy or upgrade computer hardware this year: ❏ yes [44] ❏ no [45]

I plan to buy or upgrade computer software this year: ❏ yes [46] ❏ no [47]

Name: _____ Business title: [48] _____ Type of Business: [49] _____

Address (❏ home [50] ❏ work [51]/Company name: _____)

Street/Suite# _____

City [52]/State [53]/Zipcode [54]: _____ Country [55] _____

❏ **I liked this book!** You may quote me by name in future
IDG Books Worldwide promotional materials.

My daytime phone number is _____

IDG BOOKS

THE WORLD OF COMPUTER KNOWLEDGE

☐ YES!

Please keep me informed about IDG's World of Computer Knowledge.
Send me the latest IDG Books catalog.

COMPUTER
BOOK SERIES
FROM IDG

NO POSTAGE
NECESSARY
IF MAILED
IN THE
UNITED STATES

BUSINESS REPLY MAIL
FIRST CLASS MAIL   PERMIT NO. 2605   FOSTER CITY, CALIFORNIA

IDG Books Worldwide
919 E Hillsdale Blvd, STE 400
Foster City, CA 94404-9691